Contesting th
Empire, 1871-1918

Contesting the Past

The volumes in this series select some of the most controversial episodes in history and consider their divergent, even starkly incompatible representations. The aim is not merely to demonstrate that history is "argument without end," but to show that study even of contradictory conceptions can be fruitful: that the jettisoning of one thesis or presentation leaves behind something of value.

Published

Contesting the Crusades
Norman Housley

Contesting the German Empire 1871–1918
Matthew Jefferies

In preparation

European Renaissance
William Caferro

Reformations
C. Scott Dixon

The French Revolution
Paul Hanson

Vietnam
David Hess

Origins of the Second World War
Peter Jackson

The Enlightenment
Thomas Munck

Witch Hunts in the Early Modern World
Alison Rowlands

The Rise of Nazism
Chris Szejnmann

Contesting the German Empire, 1871–1918

Matthew Jefferies

Blackwell Publishing

© 2008 by Matthew Jefferies

BLACKWELL PUBLISHING
350 Main Street, Malden, MA 02148-5020, USA
9600 Garsington Road, Oxford OX4 2DQ, UK
550 Swanston Street, Carlton, Victoria 3053, Australia

The right of Matthew Jefferies to be identified as the Author of this Work has been asserted in accordance with the UK Copyright, Designs, and Patents Act 1988.

All rights reserved. No part of this publication may be reproduced, stored in a retrieval system, or transmitted, in any form or by any means, electronic, mechanical, photocopying, recording or otherwise, except as permitted by the UK Copyright, Designs, and Patents Act 1988, without the prior permission of the publisher.

Designations used by companies to distinguish their products are often claimed as trademarks. All brand names and product names used in this book are trade names, service marks, trademarks, or registered trademarks of their respective owners. The publisher is not associated with any product or vendor mentioned in this book.

This publication is designed to provide accurate and authoritative information in regard to the subject matter covered. It is sold on the understanding that the publisher is not engaged in rendering professional services. If professional advice or other expert assistance is required, the services of a competent professional should be sought.

First published 2008 by Blackwell Publishing Ltd

1   2008

Library of Congress Cataloging-in-Publication Data

Jefferies, Matthew.
  Contesting the German Empire, 1871–1918 / Matthew Jefferies.
    p. cm. – (Contesting the past)
  Includes bibliographical references and index.
  ISBN 978-1-4051-2996-1 (hardcover : alk. paper)
  ISBN 978-1-4051-2997-8 (pbk. : alk. paper)
  1. Germany–History–1871–1918.
  2. Germany–History–1871–1918–Historiography. I. Title.
  DD220.J44 2008
  943.08′4072–dc22
                                            2007017673

A catalogue record for this title is available from the British Library.

Set in 10/12.5pt Photina
by SPi Publisher Services, Pondicherry, India.
Printed and bound in Singapore
by Utopia Press Pte Ltd

The publisher's policy is to use permanent paper from mills that operate a sustainable forestry policy, and which has been manufactured from pulp processed using acid-free and elementary chlorine-free practices. Furthermore, the publisher ensures that the text paper and cover board used have met acceptable environmental accreditation standards.

For further information on
Blackwell Publishing, visit our website:
www.blackwellpublishing.com

Contents

Acknowledgments		vi
Introduction		1
1	The German Empire and its Historians	7
2	Great Men? Otto von Bismarck and Kaiser Wilhelm II	47
3	"Democracy in the Undemocratic State"?	90
4	"Familiar Features in an Unfamiliar Light"? Social and Cultural Perspectives	126
5	The *Kaiserreich* Transnational? Foreign Policy, Colonialism, and the First World War	164
6	Epilogue: Remembering Imperial Germany	193
Bibliography		203
Index		234

Acknowledgments

Much of this book was written during a sabbatical stay in Berlin, funded by grants from the Alexander von Humboldt Foundation and the European Science Foundation's project "Representations of the Past: The Writing of National Histories in Europe." I am indebted to both organizations, to Rüdiger vom Bruch of the Humboldt University for supporting my visit, and to Eike Eckert for the loan of his apartment. I must also thank the AHRC's Research Leave Scheme and the University of Manchester for providing me with a year free of teaching obligations. This book has benefited greatly from the careful reading and constructive criticisms of Stefan Berger, Geoff Eley, James Retallack, and Matthew Stibbe, together with the comments of Blackwell's anonymous reader. Finally I would like to express my gratitude to the following friends and colleagues: John Breuilly, Hartmut Pogge von Strandmann, John Röhl, Steve Parker, Henry Phillips, Kersti Börjars, Martin Durrell, Matthew and Victoria Philpotts, Amanda Mathews, Maxine Powell, Andrea Cross, Clare Farrow and Jenny Tully. Any mistakes or inaccuracies are, of course, my own.

Introduction

The more we know, the less we understand: that would seem to be the underlying message of many recent books on the German Empire. Anxious to avoid broad brushstrokes in black and white, contemporary specialists instead seek solace in infinite shades of grey, emphasizing the *Kaiserreich*'s ambiguities and ambivalences, complexities and contradictions. It is as if, James Retallack notes, "[t]he puzzles, paradoxes, and ironies of Wilhelmine Germany cannot be contained within the framework of 'either-or' questions."[1] Thus while the Empire has often been described as "Janus-faced" – after the Roman god of doors and gateways whose twin countenance faced backwards and forwards at the same time – even this schizophrenic characterization now appears insufficient. Geoff Eley, for example, has recently suggested that the historical reality is "more complex, more impermanent, and more fraught with internal inconsistencies and tensions than the Janus image would suggest."[2] This is, of course, no reason for regret: "Scholarly books should strive to present the past in all its complexity and above all in its proper context ... knowing that even our best efforts are but approximations of truth, invitations to controversy and revision," Fritz Stern once observed.[3] Even so, it would be understandable if confused students were to eschew the apparent equivocations of contemporary historiography in favor of the

---

1 J. Retallack, "Ideas into politics: Meanings of 'stasis' in Wilhelmine Germany," in G. Eley and J. Retallack, eds., *Wilhelminism and Its Legacies* (New York and Oxford, 2003), p. 248.
2 G. Eley and J. Retallack, "Introduction," in *Wilhelminism and Its Legacies*, p. 9.
3 F. Stern, "Comment on the place of historical controversy," in H. Lehmann, ed., *Historikerkontroversen* (Göttingen, 2000), pp. 180, 182.

comforting certainties of earlier accounts, or even to avoid the period altogether. There is, after all, no shortage of historical controversies in which the battle-lines appear more clearly and sharply drawn.

To do so, however, would be to miss out on an "extraordinary body of historical scholarship,"[4] whose quality and diversity stands comparison with that of any other episode in European history. This historiographical diversity is methodological and ideological as well as thematic, reflecting both the shifting enthusiasms of the historical profession and the violently changing circumstances in which historical research was conducted in Germany during the course of the twentieth century. Moreover, the volume and variety of work shows little sign of faltering, with dozens of important new studies appearing each year. It is perhaps surprising then that some of today's most widely-used historiographical surveys of the period are a quarter-century old.[5] With more recent titles, such as Retallack's *Germany in the Age of Kaiser Wilhelm II* or Roger Chickering's heavyweight *Historiographical Companion* also clocking up a decade of use, the need for an updated study is clear.[6] Whether this book proves a worthy heir only time will tell: like all historiographical surveys it runs the risk of instant obsolescence, but it does attempt to offer a clear snapshot of a complex and at times confusing scene.

Certainly, the sheer quantity of new scholarship on the *Kaiserreich* has made it increasingly difficult to force all the available information into a single satisfying synthesis. The *Contesting the Past* series, however, requires no such straitjacket of interpretation. This volume, like others in the series, instead aims to provide an accurate and accessible guide to recent debates, reflecting the main schools and approaches, while at the same time offering its own perspectives on the competing claims, and providing pointers to future developments. Its structure follows the general format of other titles in the series. Chapter 1 gives a historiographical overview, spanning more than a century of works on the Empire, from contemporary historians' views of Germany's "unification" in 1871 to the

---

4 R. Chickering, ed., "Preface," in *Imperial Germany. A Historiographical Companion* (Westport and London, 1996), p. vii.
5 Such as R. J. Evans, ed., "Introduction: Wilhelm II's Germany and the historians," in *Society and Politics in Wilhelmine Germany* (London, 1978); J. Retallack, "Social history with a vengeance? Some reactions to H.-U. Wehler's 'Das Deutsche Kaiserreich,'" *German Studies Review*, 7 (1984), pp. 423–50; R. Moeller, "The Kaiserreich recast? Continuity and change in modern German historiography," *Journal of Social History*, 17 (1984), pp. 655–83; and G. Eley, "Introduction," in *From Unification to Nazism. Reinterpreting the German Past* (Boston and London, 1986).
6 J. Retallack, *Germany in the Age of Kaiser Wilhelm II* (Basingstoke, 1996); R. Chickering, ed., *Imperial Germany*.

"reunification" of 1990, when political events once again had a significant impact on the historiography. The subsequent chapters each look at a particular area of debate, with Chapters 2 to 4 mirroring the course of historiographical fashion by moving from the top of imperial society down to its grassroots. Thus Chapter 2 looks at the controversial historical reputations of Bismarck and Kaiser Wilhelm II, and assesses the enduring value of the "personalist" approach; Chapter 3 examines the Empire's constitutional structures and political parties, often the focus of "structuralist" or "institutionalist" historians; while Chapter 4 considers a variety of "poststructuralist" approaches, as offered by the history of everyday life (*Alltagsgeschichte*), but also the perspectives of gender and cultural history. Chapter 5 turns to new directions in the area of foreign relations, colonialism, and war, assessing the impact of fresh enthusiasms such as post-colonial studies and transnational history. Finally, a short concluding section considers how the German Empire is remembered today, not only in the "memory studies" of professional historians, but among the wider public at large.

The book's architecture, in other words, represents an attempt to capture something of the remarkable pluralism that currently characterizes the historiography of Imperial Germany. As Chapter 4 makes clear, many of the most invigorating of recent impulses have come from beyond the previously established framework of debate: from "women's history and the study of gender; post-Foucauldian understandings of knowledge and disciplinary power; and the new cultural history."[7] Such developments should not be dismissed – as in one recent textbook – as a "bizarre" product of "scholarly adventurism and the desire to embroil [one's self] in new theories."[8] Yet it is vital too that older research should not be discarded simply because it predates the latest interpretative "turn" or, as Volker Berghahn puts it, "because we no longer bother to look at it."[9] This book attempts to give each approach a fair hearing, albeit one that is inevitably constrained by the limits of space and authorial competence. The intention is not to suggest that all approaches are equally valid or appropriate, but that each can make some kind of contribution. It is clear, however, that with such a wide range of approaches – based on different sets of assumptions and belonging to different scholarly traditions – one cannot easily form a comprehensive and harmonious whole. This might

---

7 G. Eley, ed., "Introduction 1," in *Society, Culture and the State in Germany, 1870–1930* (Ann Arbor, 1996), p. 16.
8 M. Seligmann and R. McLean, *Germany from Reich to Republic, 1871–1918* (Basingstoke, 2000), p. 1.
9 V. Berghahn, "The German Empire, 1871–1914. Reflections on the direction of recent research," *Central European History*, 35 (2002), p. 81.

not seem necessary or even desirable: Eley, for one, has expressed a preference for an open-ended "indeterminacy" rather than a forced "new synthesis," which he labels "a familiar hankering when historians sit down amid the fallout from successful critiques."[10] Even so, it is important to remember that while the variety of interpretative models can be taken as welcome evidence of the field's vitality, it can also suggest a worrying absence of consensus on the period's key questions. If it is true that "we can find in Wilhelmine Germany more or less what we go looking for,"[11] then it is only to be expected that some historians will warn of the dangers inherent in the current acceptance of ambiguity and polyvalence. Berghahn in particular has been vocal in expressing the fear that "in the midst of all the deconstruction, contingency, agency, and indeterminacy ... we have lost sight of the forest because we are so firmly focused on the trees."[12]

Despite such concerns, however, students and scholars alike continue to be drawn to the imperial era. As Berghahn – whose own research has moved some distance from the *Kaiserreich* – notes: "I confess that, like so many fellow historians, I continue to be fascinated by those decades before 1914."[13] Some, such as Joachim Radkau, find particularly compelling the extent to which the problems and pleasures of life in the Empire prefigure those of more recent German experience:

> Back then there was already a first "economic miracle," and countless people whose thoughts and actions entirely revolved around professional success and private happiness, unwilling to be disturbed by either Christian morality or national heroism. They loved above all a comfortable life, but differed from earlier Germans of the Biedermeier era because of their dynamic entrepreneurial mentality, their striving for increased consumption, their hunger for travel and often their sexual curiosity too.[14]

For others it is the striking modernity of the conflicts within Wilhelmine society, politics, and culture that provides the pull. Certainly, it is this aspect that has been at the forefront of many recent studies. As one 2006 call for conference papers put it: "the Empire was never as modern as it is today."[15]

---

10 G. Eley, ed., "Preface in *Society, Culture and the State in Germany*, p. vii.
11 J. Retallack, *Germany in the Age of Kaiser Wilhelm II*, p. 109.
12 V. Berghahn, "The German Empire, 1871–1914. Reflections," p. 77.
13 Ibid., p. 75.
14 J. Radkau, *Das Zeitalter der Nervosität. Deutschland zwischen Bismarck und Hitler* (Munich, 1998), p. 397.
15 S. O. Müller and C. Torp, "Das Deutsche Kaiserreich in der Kontroverse. Probleme und Perspektiven," call for papers, (Bielefeld, 2006).

Among the many reasons why the *Kaiserreich* remains so fascinating, however, three in particular stand out. First, there is the Empire's central role in the outbreak of the First World War; "*the* great seminal catastrophe of the twentieth century,"[16] which destroyed the Wilhelmine world and had such a profound effect on the course of European history. Whether or not Germany was solely, largely, or only partly to blame for the conflict, it was undoubtedly a central player in the events of July and August 1914. Second, of course, the Empire forms part of the pre-history of the Third Reich. It would be naïve to deny that much of the imperial era's fascination derives from its relationship to Hitler's Germany. Richard Evans's wish, expressed in 1978, that the German Empire should soon cease to act "as a battleground for rival theories of continuity and become instead a subject for historical research in its own right,"[17] may indeed have come true, but historians searching for the roots of National Socialism have continued to dig deep into imperial soil. Third, the Empire was the Germans' first successful attempt at forming something that resembled a nation-state. Its subsequent diminution, expansion, partition, and reunification helped to keep the "German question" alive for much of the twentieth century, for historians as well as policy makers. Indeed, it was only at the end of the millennium, with the growth of globalization and the rise of supranational bodies such as the European Union, that the continued centrality of such nation-states began to be questioned.

The process of rethinking and deconstructing the nation-state is far from over, but one early outcome has been the rise of transnational history, which first saw the light of day during the 1990s.[18] There is much to be said for its lofty vantage point, and its emergence has not left the *Kaiserreich* untouched. Indeed, it might one day be seen as the beginning of the end for national historiographies, and for the sort of comparative studies that were championed as an antidote to narratives of national exceptionalism, but which in practice often reinforced the nation-state paradigm. For the time being, however, it is likely that our preoccupation with national histories will continue. Not only is the infrastructure of historical research – archives, libraries, funding bodies, and professional associations – organized along national lines, but most historians continue to specialize on a specific national experience. Certainly, for the

---

16 G. F. Kennan, *The Decline of Bismarck's European Order* (Princeton, 1979), p. 3.
17 R. J. Evans, "Introduction: Wilhelm II's Germany and the historians," p. 32.
18 See J. Osterhammel, "Transkulturell vergleichende Geschichtswisssenschaft," in H.-G. Haupt and J. Kocka, eds., *Geschichte und Vergleich* (Frankfurt and New York, 1996), pp. 283–91; P. Clavin, "Defining Transnationalism," *Contemporary European History*, 14 (2005), pp. 421–39.

generations of historians whose works are discussed over the following pages, Germany's "shattered past" possessed a particular and special fascination of its own.[19] It is a fascination, moreover, which remains undiminished, even as the imperial epoch fades beyond the range of human memory.

---

19 The title of a recent collection of essays by K. Jarausch and M. Geyer: *Shattered Past. Reconstructing German Histories* (Princeton, 2002).

1
The German Empire and its Historians

Views of the Empire before 1960

The historiography of the German Empire is as old as the *Kaiserreich* itself. Indeed, one could argue that it is older still, since an extensive historical literature on the subject of Germany's territorial and political development pre-dated the founding of the Empire by several decades, and itself made a significant contribution to the formation of a German nation-state.[1] Of particular importance in this regard was the work of a small group of mid-nineteenth century liberal historians known as the Borussian or Prussian School, which began to develop the view that it was Prussia's historical mission to unite the German states – although without Austrian territory – under the political and military leadership of the Hohenzollern monarchy. Imbued with a belief in progress and a conviction that future developments could be discerned from careful study of the past, Borussian historians looked back through the decades to trace the rise of Prussia to its position of latent hegemony over the German lands. Initially their views were hotly contested, not least by Catholic historians, but the events of 1866–71 seemed to confirm the validity of their approach: "they enjoyed the celebrity that comes from being on the winning side," as Robert Southard puts it.[2]

---

1 For a detailed analysis of the issues raised in this chapter see S. Berger, *The Search for Normality. National Identity and Historical Consciousness in Germany since 1800* (Providence and Oxford, 1997); and G. G. Iggers, *The German Conception of History. The National Tradition of Historical Thought from Herder to the Present* (Middletown, 1968).
2 R. Southard, *Droysen and the Prussian School of History* (Lexington, 1995), p. 1.

The works of Johann Gustav Droysen (1808–86), whose *History of Prussian Politics*, published in 16 volumes between 1855 and 1886, first established the School, Max Duncker (1811–86), Heinrich von Sybel (1817–95), and Heinrich von Treitschke (1834–96) are the best-known examples of the Borussian approach. The founding of the German Empire represented the fulfillment of a long-cherished dream for these men, who were unable to prevent a strong streak of triumphalism from permeating the pages of their post-unification publications. Indeed for them, scholarship and partisanship were inseparable. Works such as Treitschke's *History of Germany in the Nineteenth Century* (1874–94), or Sybel's *Foundation of the German Empire* (1889–94), effectively became the official historiography of Imperial Germany and their influence continued to be felt well into the twentieth century. There was, of course, nothing peculiarly German about historians acting as nation-builders – it happened right across Europe in the nineteenth century, proceeding hand-in-hand with the discipline's professionalization[3] – but there were good reasons why historians in Germany should continue to identify so closely with their state long after 1871. For a start, German university professors were (and indeed still are) civil servants, so had "little incentive to bite the hand that fed them," as Stefan Berger puts it.[4] There was also the legacy of the early nineteenth-century German intellectual tradition that saw language and cultural identity as central to the *Volksgeist* or national spirit, and therefore placed philologists and historians in a privileged position, effectively guarding an ethnic Holy Grail. As a result, the historical profession – often tellingly referred to as a guild or fraternity (*Zunft*) – developed in Germany rather like a Masonic order, which not only closed ranks against outsiders but sought to speak with one voice when important "national" matters were at stake.

For a new generation of historians that emerged in the years around 1890, the Empire had already become part of everyday reality. Although no less patriotic than the Borussians, these historians attempted to distance themselves from their teachers. Self-consciously adopting the "scientific" method and "objective" approach of the famous Prussian historian Leopold von Ranke (1795–1886), the historians of the so-called Ranke Renaissance – above all Max Lenz (1850–1932) and Erich Marcks (1861–1938)[5] – upheld the traditions of German *Historismus*

---

3 See S. Berger, M. Donovan, and K. Passmore, eds., *Writing National Histories. Western Europe Since 1800* (London, 1999).
4 S. Berger, *The Search for Normality*, p. 8.
5 See H.-H. Krill, *Die Ranke-Renaissance. Max Lenz und Erich Marcks* (Berlin, 1962). In a recent biography Jens Nordalm has questioned whether Marcks should be regarded as a Neo-Rankean, although his arguments are not entirely convincing. See J. Nordalm, *Historismus und moderne Welt. Erich Marcks (1861–1938) in der deutschen Geschichtswissenschaft* (Berlin, 2003).

or "historism,"[6] which included, among other things, attempting to understand each historical period in its own terms, since all eras were (in Ranke's famous formulation) equally close or "immediate" to God. In practice this meant an inherent acceptance of the political status quo, an antipathy towards comparative history, and a rejection of efforts to judge historical individuals or institutions on the basis of external criteria. The Neo-Rankeans produced a host of narrative-based studies of the Reformation, the Prussian reform era of the early nineteenth century, and the diplomatic history of the major European states, with detailed attention paid to politics, philosophy, and religion, but with little consideration of social or economic forces. They also penned numerous biographies of "great men," such as Martin Luther, Frederick the Great, Napoleon, Kaiser Wilhelm I, and, of course, Otto von Bismarck.

In a 1901 essay on "Bismarck and Ranke," Lenz attempted to bring the values of his two seemingly very different heroes – the political man of action and the contemplative historian – into some kind of harmony, a synthesis of power (*Macht*) and spirit (*Geist*). The thing that linked the two men, Lenz argued, was their common belief in the primacy of a state's foreign policy.[7] Ranke's conviction that the internal structure of a state is conditioned by its external relations, and that history's first concern should, therefore, be foreign policy and the balance of power between states, was updated by Lenz and Marcks to include a global dimension. They, like the sociologist Max Weber (1864–1920) and many other middle-class contemporaries, believed that the founding of the *Kaiserreich* would come to mean little if it was not followed up by further expansion around the world. As a result, German historians in the 1900s saw themselves as "heralds of policy," helping to popularize and justify a host of nationalist and colonial causes, such as the Navy League and even – in the case of Dietrich Schäfer (1845–1929) – the militant demagogy of the Pan-German League.

Despite the social and political homogeneity of the German historians' guild, however, it would be incorrect to think of history in the Wilhelmine era as one-dimensional or devoid of debate. It is all too easy to forget that there were counter-narratives that viewed the "official" version of

---

6 The German term *Historismus*, which dates from around 1800, has been translated as both historism and historicism. The latter, however, has also been associated with a specific philosophical approach, identified by Karl Popper in *The Poverty of Historicism*, which attempted to predict the course of human history on the basis of past behavior, suggesting that history was developing towards a particular end according to predetermined laws. That is not what is suggested here. See S. Berger, "Historians and nation-building in Germany after reunification," *Past and Present*, 148 (1995), p. 188, n. 6.

7 H.-H. Krill, *Die Ranke-Renaissance*, p. 108.

German history with considerable skepticism. There were historians, for instance, who continued to uphold the historical identity of individual German states such as Bavaria and Saxony, or who clung to the idea of a "Greater Germany" (*Grossdeutschland*), rather than the Prussian-dominated "Little Germany" (*Kleindeutschland*) bequeathed by Bismarck. There was also a new school of economic history represented by Gustav Schmoller (1838–1917) and Otto Hintze (1861–1940), which led to an increasing interest in the "social question" at German universities. Certainly, Germany's leading historical journal, the *Historische Zeitschrift* (founded in 1859), was never short of argument. Particularly heated scholarly exchanges took place over the value of the ambitious psycho-cultural approach pioneered by Karl Lamprecht (1856–1915), whose *German History* of the 1890s was so different from either the Borussian or the Neo-Rankean schools that he became marginalized in German academia, though he was fêted in some of the Reich's regional historical associations and abroad.[8] Also on the margins, although no less vociferous, were Socialist and Catholic historians, with their own publications and debates. Within the historians' guild, however, it was the Neo-Rankeans who increasingly held the upper hand. Both Marcks and Lenz were often invited to address official gatherings, such as at the unveiling of Kaiser-Wilhelm monuments or the numerous anniversary dinners that littered the Wilhelmine social calendar. Despite their pretensions to objectivity, which only in fact extended as far as to establish the reliability of their sources, the Neo-Rankeans made no effort to disguise their own national liberal and anti-Catholic prejudices, and their contributions to such events offered little more than empty rhetoric and hollow pathos.

A characteristic feature of the Neo-Rankean approach, and of German historical writing in the 1900s in general, was the frequently-made suggestion that, whether for geographical, religious, or historical reasons, Germany's development and destiny differed from that of other European nations. The idea of a *Sonderweg* – a different or special historical path – took many different forms, but the tone was invariably positive. It was claimed that Germany's particular geopolitical situation (its *Mittellage*) demanded a strong state, with a large permanent army and an efficient civil service, standing above sectional interest and party politics. It was also argued that such a state was fully capable of generating reforms and innovations, as the Prussian reform era had demonstrated, and compared

---

8 See R. Chickering, "The Lamprecht controversy," in H. Lehmann, ed., *Historikerkontroversen*, pp. 15–30; also Chickering's *Karl Lamprecht. A German Academic Life, 1856–1915* (Atlantic Highlands, 1983).

favorably with the parliamentary factionalism and *laissez-faire* values of Victorian Britain, or the universalism of revolutionary France. This view, which was also to be found in more sophisticated form in the 1907 study *Cosmopolitanism and the Nation-State* by Friedrich Meinecke (1862–1954),[9] became exaggerated in the years around World War One, when the "deep" cultural values of German *Kultur* were frequently contrasted with the materialistic ethos of western *Zivilisation*, and academics like Werner Sombart (1863–1941) were moved to portray the conflict as a struggle between Anglo-Saxon materialism and German idealism, embodied by "merchants" and "heroes" respectively.[10] The significant contribution made by historians to Germany's war effort, whether in the form of petitions, pamphlets, or other kinds of propaganda, has been well documented.[11]

The establishment of the Weimar Republic ushered in a limited degree of liberalization of the German historical profession, with regard to both ideological and methodological approaches. Social Democrats, who like practicing Jews had effectively been barred from professorial chairs in the Empire, were now in theory able to pursue academic careers. Catholic historians, such as Franz Schnabel (1887–1966), could also look forward to better career prospects. Even so, the historical profession remained socially and politically elitist, in large part because of its patriarchal internal structures. The requirement to write a second dissertation (the *Habilitation*) before one stood a chance of being accepted into the ranks of the professoriate (the *Ordinarien*) was a particularly high hurdle for nonconformists to jump. The continued dominance of the Neo-Rankean approach meant that history in Germany – "the motherland of modern history" (Ernst Troeltsch) – was increasingly seen as old-fashioned and parochial by international standards. This perception was no doubt strengthened by the way in which German historians took it upon themselves to act as guardians of their nation's honor, playing a leading role in campaigns against the "unbearable yoke" of the Versailles Treaty, and in particular Article 231, the "war-guilt" clause.

---

9 F. Meinecke, *Cosmopolitanism and the National State* (Princeton, 1970); originally published in Germany as *Weltbürgertum und Nationalstaat. Studien zur Genesis des deutschen Nationalstaats* (Munich and Berlin, 1907).
10 W. Sombart, *Händler und Helden* (Munich and Leipzig, 1915). On Sombart see F. Lenger, *Werner Sombart, 1863–1941: Eine Biographie* (Munich, 1994).
11 See W. J. Mommsen, ed., *Kultur und Krieg: Die Rolle der Intellektuellen, Künstler und Schriftsteller im Ersten Weltkrieg* (Munich, 1996); J. Verhey, *The Spirit of 1914: Militarism, Myth and Mobilization in Germany* (Cambridge, 2000); M. Stibbe, *German Anglophobia and the Great War, 1914–1918* (Cambridge, 2001).

The conviction that Article 231 was unjust – that Germany had been no more culpable than the other great powers in 1914 – was virtually unanimous within the guild. Thus German historians had no qualms of conscience about receiving money from a secret government body, the Foreign Office's War Guilt Department (*Kriegsschuldreferat*), which was established in 1919 solely to contest Allied views on the origins of the war.[12] The department's twin-track propaganda campaign was impressive in scope: seemingly objective scholarly research was funded by a Coordinating Office for Research on the Causes of the War, which had its own monthly journal and which published the famous (but significantly incomplete) 40-volume document collection *The High Politics of the European Cabinets 1871–1914*;[13] at the same time (April 1921), a Working Committee of German Associations was set up to influence the views of the general public. Anything that could undermine the official view, such as an independent report written by the law professor Hermann Kantorowicz (1877–1940) on behalf of the Reichstag's War Guilt Committee, was suppressed: completed in 1927, the report was not published until 1967.[14]

Most German historians accepted the Weimar Republic either reluctantly (as in the case of Meinecke), or not at all.[15] Both Marcks and Lenz, whose pre-war national liberalism slid all too easily into national conservatism, condemned the Republic as a foreign imposition, alien to German historical traditions. In this the malign legacy of the "positive" *Sonderweg* idea was clear to see. The predominant view of the Empire remained unashamedly positive, even if historians were more critical in their assessments of the last Emperor. "Back to Bismarck!" was a call echoed by many in the guild. Dissenting voices, such as the left-liberal

---

12 See H. Herwig, "Clio deceived: Patriotic self-censorship in Germany after the war," in K. Wilson, ed., *Forging the Collective Memory: Government and International Historians through Two World Wars* (Providence and Oxford, 1996), pp. 87–127; A. Mombauer, *The Origins of the First World War. Controversies and Consensus* (London, 2002); U. Heinemann, *Die verdrängte Niederlage. Politische Öffentlichkeit und Kriegsschuldfrage in der Weimarer Republik* (Göttingen, 1983); W. Jäger, *Historische Forschung und politische Kultur in Deutschland. Die Debatte 1914–1980 über den Ausbruch des Ersten Weltkrieges* (Göttingen, 1984).
13 J. Lepsius, A. Mendelssohn-Bartholdy, and F. Thimme, eds., *Die große Politik der europäischen Kabinette von 1871–1914*, 40 vols. (Berlin, 1922–7).
14 H. Kantorowicz, *Gutachten zur Kriegsschuldfrage 1914. Aus dem Nachlaß herausgegeben und eingeleitet von Imanuel Geiss* (Frankfurt, 1967).
15 See B. Faulenbach, *Die Ideologie des deutschen Weges. Die Deutsche Geschichte in der Historiographie zwischen Kaiserreich und Nationalsozialismus* (Munich, 1980); also P. Schöttler, ed., *Geschichtsschreibung als Legitimationswissenschaft 1918–45* (Frankfurt, 1997). In English see R. Gerwarth, *Bismarck in Weimar. Germany's First Democracy and the Civil War of Memories, 1918–33* (Oxford, 2005).

Johannes Ziekursch (1876–1945), whose *Political History of the New German Empire* appeared in three volumes between 1925 and 1930,[16] and Eckart Kehr (1902–33), a student of Meinecke who wrote his doctoral thesis on *Battleship Building and Party Politics in Germany*,[17] were cold-shouldered. As one of the first historians to argue that an alliance of heavy industry and large landowners was a crucial and malign legacy of the Empire, Kehr would later become an important posthumous influence on a generation of German historians, but during his short lifetime he remained on the margins of the historical profession. More typical of attitudes was the conservative historian Adalbert Wahl (1871–1957), who described the Empire as "a highpoint in the history of humanity as a whole."[18]

Similar assessments continued to be published by Neo-Rankean historians after 1933, even if some swift footwork was needed to keep pace with the changing political circumstances. Hermann Oncken (1869–1945), a former student of Lenz who had been considered a political moderate in the 1920s, welcomed Hitler's first government as a "new concentration of German power," although he soon fell out with the regime. Gerhard Ritter (1888–1967), who would later be arrested because of his connections to the resistance, introduced his biography of Frederick the Great by linking the eighteenth-century Prussian king to Bismarck and the Führer.[19] Erich Marcks predictably took the same line with his old hero Bismarck. The *Kaiserreich* and Third Reich were thus "two stages in the same political development," according to Marcks.[20] The positive line of continuity "from Bismarck to Hitler" was also pursued by Otto Westphal (1891–1950) in his two-volume history *The Reich*, published in 1941.[21] Westphal, a council member of the Reich Institute for the History of the New Germany, made no secret of his wholehearted approval of Hitler's rule, but the extent to which the German historical profession as a whole responded to National Socialism has only recently become the subject of detailed scrutiny.

It was long claimed that the historical profession remained aloof from Nazism, and was largely successful in maintaining its commitment to

---

16 J. Ziekursch, *Politische Geschichte des neuen deutschen Kaiserreiches*, 3 vols. (Frankfurt, 1925–30).
17 E. Kehr, *Battleship Building and Party Politics in Germany 1894–1901* (Chicago and London, 1973), first published in Germany as *Schlachtflottenbau und Parteipolitik 1894–1901* (Berlin, 1930).
18 Quoted in E. Frie, *Das Deutsche Kaiserreich* (Darmstadt, 2004), p. 6.
19 G. Ritter, *Friedrich der Große. Ein historisches Profil* (Leipzig, 1936).
20 H.-H. Krill, *Die Ranke-Renaissance*, pp. 253–4.
21 O. Westphal, *Das Reich*, vol. 1 *Germanentum und Kaisertum*; vol. 2 *Aufgang und Vollendung* (Berlin, 1941).

objective scholarship throughout the Third Reich. This undoubtedly complacent view has been challenged by a host of studies since the 1990s,[22] but it remains far from easy to distinguish between National Socialist and national conservative elements in the historiography of the 1930s, or between "true believers" and "fellow travelers" within the guild. It is clear that generational factors were significant. For established university professors, 1933 did not necessarily represent a major watershed, since a nationalist, authoritarian, and anti-democratic outlook was already firmly in place by the time Hitler came to power. It had formed in the years around the First World War, hardened during the Weimar Republic, and only began to crumble after 1945. Thus a full-scale *Gleichschaltung* was not necessary, especially as potential dissidents – such as the liberal Catholic Franz Schnabel – could easily be forced into retirement. For a younger generation of aspiring academics, however, the new opportunities presented by the regime in areas such as ethnic history (*Volksgeschichte*),[23] or the so-called *Ostforschung* – the history of Eastern European territories to which Nazi Germany laid claim under the banner of *Lebensraum* – proved difficult to refuse.[24] The extent to which historians provided the justification for "ethnic cleansing," or even became "accessories to murder" through their involvement in Nazi research projects, remains a sensitive and controversial subject, as a dramatic debate at the 1998 German historians' conference in Frankfurt testified. The posthumous reputations of some of post-war West Germany's most respected historians – Theodor Schieder (1908–84), Werner Conze (1910–86), Karl Dietrich Erdmann (1910–90), Fritz Fischer (1908–99) and even Hans Rothfels (1891–1976), a Bismarck specialist of Jewish ancestry who was forced into exile by the Nazis in 1939 – have been tarnished as a result, and in some cases maybe "permanently contaminated" (Hans-Ulrich Wehler), although the dangers of a witch hunt are clear for all to see.[25]

---

22   See K. Schönwälder, *Historiker und Politik. Geschichtswissenschaft im Nationalsozialismus* (Frankfurt and New York, 1992); U. Wolf, *Litteris et Patriae. Das Janusgesicht der Historie* (Stuttgart, 1996); W. Schulze and O. G. Oexle, eds., *Deutsche Historiker im Nationalsozialismus* (Frankfurt, 1999); I. Haar, *Historiker im Nationalsozialismus. Die deutsche Geschichte und der "Volkstumskampf" im Osten* (Göttingen, 2000).
23   Despite its reactionary ideology *Volksgeschichte* could also be methodologically innovative, pre-empting some aspects of post-war social history. See W. Oberkrome, *Volksgeschichte. Methodische Innovation und völkische Ideologisierung in der deutschen Geschichtswissenschaft 1918–1945* (Göttingen, 1993).
24   See M. Burleigh, *Germany Turns Eastwards. A Study of "Ostforschung" in the Third Reich* (Cambridge, 1988).
25   V. Ullrich, "Späte Reue der Zunft. Endlich arbeiten die deutschen Historiker die braune Vergangenheit ihres Faches auf," *Die Zeit*, September 17, 1998; also S. F. Kellerhoff, "Pionieren der Sozialgeschichte droht Denkmalsturz. Werner Conze, Karl Dietrich Erdmann und Theodor Schieder unterstützten Hitlers Lebensraum-Ideologie," *Die Welt*, July 27, 1998.

The recent zeal for "outing" dead historians as Nazi sympathizers stands in stark contrast to the pattern of events in West Germany after 1945, when there was no concerted attempt to de-Nazify the guild. Only a handful of individuals who had been in the SS or involved in the most extreme kind of racial history lost their university positions after the war – Ernst Anrich, Günter Franz, Erwin Hölzle, Theodor Mayer – and even right-wing apologists such as Walther Hubatsch (1915–84) remained in employment. Certainly, there was a new mood of contrition and sobriety within the profession, best exemplified by Friedrich Meinecke's *The German Catastrophe* of 1946,[26] but even here there were signs of an inability to learn the lessons of the 1930s. Meinecke's attempts at self-criticism were genuine, but it evidently did not come easy for a man whose life was so entwined with the historical guild – he had attended Ranke's funeral in 1886 and edited the *Historische Zeitschrift* for nearly 40 years – to question all his earlier beliefs and assumptions. Indeed, it was not clear whether he saw the real "catastrophe" as being Hitler and the Holocaust, or Germany's defeat, degradation, and division. The men who formed the backbone of West Germany's historical profession after 1945 had all been born and educated in the Empire, and some had seen active service in World War One. They were certainly more critical of aspects of Germany's long-term development than the preceding generation, as the new editor of the *Historische Zeitschrift*, Ludwig Dehio (1888–1963), made clear in his quasi-metaphysical study of "balance of power or hegemony" (1948),[27] but most nevertheless tried to isolate the Third Reich as a "chance" event or "accident" of history, which could not have been predicted.[28] This traumatic episode had been caused, Gerhard Ritter argued, not by a deficit but by a surfeit of democracy, embodied in the rise of the vulgar masses, who were duped into supporting a demonic revolutionary from beyond the borders of the Empire. As for the *Kaiserreich*, their reading remained in essence conservative or national liberal, for all the criticisms of Germany's military leadership or the extremism of the Pan-German League. This was not surprising since, as Georg Iggers (born 1926) puts it: "[w]hat was left

---

26 F. Meinecke, *The German Catastrophe. Reflections and Recollections* (Cambridge, MA, 1950), first published in German as *Die deutsche Katastrophe* (Wiesbaden, 1946).
27 L. Dehio, *Gleichgewicht oder Hegemonie. Betrachtungen über ein Grundproblem der neueren Staatengeschichte* (Krefeld, 1948). In English see Dehio's *Germany and World Politics in the Twentieth Century* (London, 1960).
28 Meinecke uses the word *Zufall* ("chance" or "coincidence") in *Die deutsche Katastrophe*; others referred to Hitler as a *Betriebsunfall* (a "breakdown in the works" or "an industrial accident"). See J. Steinle, "Hitler als 'Betriebsunfall in der Geschichte.' Eine historische Metapher und ihre Hintergründe," *Geschichte in Wissenschaft und Unterricht*, 45 (1994), pp. 288–302.

in 1945 was essentially the profession of 1933 purged of its more liberal, critical elements."[29]

Methodological innovations were also conspicuous by their absence in the 1950s. It was as if German history, like British industry, was suffering from what Kenneth Barkin has referred to as the "ageing pioneer" syndrome.[30] Narrative history, with a particular emphasis on national politics and the state, remained the paradigm of historical scholarship, and all attempts to introduce analytical concepts from the social sciences were regarded with suspicion. The extent to which historians like Gerhard Ritter identified with the state was often betrayed by their choice of language: the German edition of Ritter's monumental *The Sword and the Sceptre*,[31] for instance, contains numerous expressions such as "our ambassador in London," while in one chapter there are no fewer than 25 references to the Entente powers as the "enemy" or our "opponents."[32] Although the likes of Lenz, Marcks, and Oncken were long dead, the leading figures in West German history still had strong personal links to the Neo-Rankeans: both Ritter and the Hamburg professor Egmont Zechlin (1896–1992), for instance, had studied under Oncken. It is ironic, therefore, that one of the few apparently progressive areas of German history in the "economic miracle" years – the structural approach to social history developed by Conze at Heidelberg, and to a lesser extent, Schieder in Cologne – should have been particularly badly affected by the revelations of the 1990s. Their innovative use of sociological models and quantifiable sources, such as demographic statistics, is now tainted by the knowledge that the same methods had earlier been used by Conze under the banner of *Volksgeschichte*, and specifically by Schieder in his "Poland Memorandum" of autumn 1939, with regard to the removal of the Jewish population (*Entjudung*) from Polish towns.[33] Since Conze and Schieder were academic father-figures to some of Germany's most prominent recent historians, including Martin Broszat, Wolfgang Mommsen, Lothar Gall and Hans-Ulrich Wehler, it is little wonder that the repercussions of the 1998 debate are still being felt today.

---

29 G. Iggers, ed., "Introduction," in *The Social History of Politics. Critical Perspectives in West German Historical Writing Since 1945* (Leamington Spa, 1985), p. 20.
30 Quoted by D. Blackbourn in *Populists and Patricians. Essays in Modern German History* (London, 1987), p. 25, n. 5.
31 G. Ritter, *The Sword and the Sceptre. The Problem of Militarism in Germany*, 4 vols. (Miami, 1969–73), first published in German as *Staatskunst und Kriegshandwerk. Das Problem des "Militarismus" in Deutschland* (Munich, 1954–68).
32 See I. Geiss, "Der Ausbruch des Ersten Weltkrieges," in *Studien über Geschichte und Geschichtswissenschaft* (Frankfurt, 1972), p. 12.
33 See G. Aly, *Macht-Geist-Wahl. Kontinuitäten deutschen Denkens* (Berlin, 1997).

Predictably, the harshest views of the Empire to be published between 1945 and 1960 came from outside of the West German historical establishment. Those forced into exile by the National Socialist regime led the way: Erich Eyck (1878–1964), a left-liberal lawyer and journalist who wrote a critical three-volume biography of Bismarck in Britain before and during World War Two;[34] the sociologist and intellectual historian Helmuth Plessner (1892–1985), who put forward his influential thesis of Germany as a "belated nation" as early as 1935, but did not receive a German university post (in sociology rather than history) until 1951;[35] and the historian Golo Mann (1909–94), who had followed his father – the novelist Thomas Mann – into exile in 1933, and was belatedly awarded a Chair at Stuttgart in 1960. His decision to return to Germany was not typical: of 134 exiled historians, only 21 returned to reside permanently in Germany.[36] By the standards of the 1950s guild, Golo Mann's view of German history was critical, even if his conviction that World War Two was forced upon Germany by "a lone villain" fitted neatly into West Germany's post-war consensus.[37] However, compared to the work of a new wave of German-American historians around 1960 it already seemed anachronistic. For men such as Hans Rosenberg (1904–88), Hans Kohn (1891–1971), George Mosse (1918–99), Fritz Stern (born 1926), and the US-born Leonard Krieger (1918–90), only one question really mattered: how could Nazism ever have happened?[38] In confronting this crucial conundrum history became "a work of diagnosis,"[39] in which there could be no recourse to a lone villain. Instead, the idea of the *Sonderweg* reappeared, though now the "political divergence of Germany from the West" (Leonard Krieger) took on a wholly negative guise. The *Sonderweg* would remain central to debates on the German

---

34 E. Eyck, *Bismarck. Leben und Werk* (Zurich, 1941–.4), published in English as *Bismarck and the German Empire* (London, 1950). Significantly, it was not published in Germany until 1963.
35 H. Plessner was given a Chair in Sociology at Göttingen in 1951. It was another eight years before his major work appeared in a German edition: *Die verspätete Nation. Über die politische Verführbarkeit bürgerlichen Geistes* (Stuttgart, 1959).
36 S. Berger, *The Search for Normality*, p. 40.
37 G. Mann, *Deutsche Geschichte des 19. und 20. Jahrhunderts* (Frankfurt, 1966), p. 811. First published in Germany in 1958; in English as *The History of Germany since 1789* (New York, 1968).
38 H. Rosenberg, *Bureaucracy, Aristocracy and Autocracy. The Prussian Experience 1660–1815* (Cambridge, MA, 1958); H. Kohn, *The Mind of Germany* (New York, 1960); G. L. Mosse, *The Crisis of German Ideology. Intellectual Origins of the Third Reich* (New York, 1964); F. Stern, *The Politics of Cultural Despair. A Study in the Rise of the German Ideology* (Berkeley, 1961); L. Krieger, *The German Idea of Freedom: History of a Political Tradition* (Chicago, 1957).
39 The phrase comes from W. Reddy, *Money and Liberty in Modern Europe. A Critique of Historical Understanding* (Cambridge, 1987), p. 14.

Empire for the next 30 years, before finally fading from view in the 1990s. For Rosenberg, who drew on earlier critiques from the likes of Friedrich Engels and Max Weber, Germany's "wrong turn" had socio-economic causes; Krieger, Kohn, Mosse, and Stern were more interested in its cultural or intellectual roots. A cruder version of the intellectual *Sonderweg* had featured in Anglo-American wartime propaganda, and in a host of English-language publications from the 1940s which sought to establish lines of continuity between Luther and Hitler, or locate a fatal flaw in the German national character (as in A. J. P. Taylor's widely-read polemic *The Course of German History*).[40] The work of historians such as Stern and Mosse displayed much greater subtlety than the populist pamphleteers, of course, but viewing German history from the teleological perspective of 1933 inevitably ran the risk of blurring or distorting their view of the Empire, as later critics were eager to point out. In the meantime, however, the exiles had succeeded in opening up new and profitable lines of enquiry, which would help to reinvigorate the study of modern German history, both in and outside the Federal Republic.

The Fischer Controversy

The story of the Fischer controversy has been told many times before, and often in considerable detail.[41] As the publication of Fritz Fischer's book *Griff nach der Weltmacht* (literally, the "grasp for world power")[42] occurred in the same year as the inauguration of President Kennedy and the building of the Berlin Wall (1961), it is now very much part of history

---

40 A. J. P. Taylor, *The Course of German History* (London, 1961 – first published 1945).
41 See J. A. Moses, *The Politics of Illusion. The Fischer Controversy in German Historiography* (London, 1975); I. Geiss, "Die Fischer-Kontroverse," in *Studien über Geschichte und Geschichtswissenschaft* (Frankfurt, 1972), pp. 108–98; A. Sywottek, "Die Fischer-Kontroverse. Ein Beitrag zur Entwicklung historisch-politischen Bewußtseins in der Bundesrepublik," in I. Geiss and B. J. Wendt, eds., *Deutschland und die Weltpolitik des 19. und 20. Jahrhunderts* (Düsseldorf, 1973), pp. 19–47; V. Berghahn, "Die Fischer Kontroverse – 15 Jahre danach," *Geschichte und Gesellschaft*, 6 (1980), pp. 403–19; H. Böhme, " 'Primat' und 'Paradigmata.' Zur Entwicklung einer bundesdeutschen Zeitgeschichtsschreibung am Beispiel des Ersten Weltkriegs," in H. Lehmann, ed., *Historikerkontroversen*; K. Jarausch, "Der nationale Tabubruch. Wissenschaft, Öffentlichkeit und Politik in der Fischer-Kontroverse," in M. Sabrow, R. Jessen, and K. Grosse Kracht, eds., *Zeitgeschichte als Streitgeschichte. Große Kontroversen seit 1945* (Munich, 2003); M. Stibbe, "The Fischer controversy over German war aims in the First World War and its reception by East German historians," *Historical Journal*, 46 (2003), pp. 649–68.
42 F. Fischer, *Griff nach der Weltmacht. Die Kriegszielpolitik des kaiserlichen Deutschland 1914–18* (Düsseldorf, 1961); edited version in English as *Germany's Aims in the First World War* (London, 1967).

itself. It may seem tempting, therefore, to overlook the controversy in favor of more recent debates, especially as Fischer himself died in 1999, aged 91. There are two reasons why this temptation should be resisted: first, because much of the research carried out on the *Kaiserreich* over the past five decades would have been unthinkable without it; and second because the battle-lines drawn up at the height of the controversy still scar the German historical landscape. In 2003 a young Potsdam historian with the unusual but highly appropriate name of Klaus Grosse Kracht (born 1969) published an essay which certainly caused a "big row" (*grosse Krach*) among German historians. The article, in a little-read journal of religious history, suggested that the young Fischer – who had himself studied theology – had been more actively engaged in National Socialism than was previously believed.[43]

Fischer, who was branded a radical, a Communist, even a traitor, by the German right in the 1960s, had never disguised the fact that he had joined the SA in 1933 and the Nazi Party itself four years later. What Kracht discovered, however, was that in the mid-1930s Fischer had also been close to the pro-Nazi "German Christians" and had signed a declaration by a number of theology professors in support of the Führer. He had also written a letter in March 1943 to Walter Frank (head of the Nazi Reich Institute for the History of the New Germany), thanking him for his "active support" in obtaining a chair at Hamburg University. In comparison with other recent historiographical earthquakes concerning post-war German historians and the Third Reich, it only measured about three on the Richter scale, and Kracht's implication that Fischer had been hypocritical – for demanding a more open and critical engagement with Germany's past, yet keeping his own past hidden – was unfounded. What was more significant, however, was the essay's reception. Not only were Kracht's findings reported most extensively in those conservative newspapers, such as *Die Welt* and the *Frankfurter Allgemeine Zeitung*,[44] which had been in the forefront of the campaign against Fischer in the early 1960s, but there were also curious links to the controversy's original protagonists. A former student of Egmont Zechlin for instance, the journalist and historian Volker Ullrich (born 1943), attacked Fischer in *Die Zeit*: "The famous historian, who was so impressively focused in taking

---

43 K. G. Kracht, "Fritz Fischer und der deutsche Protestantismus," *Zeitschrift für neuere Theologiegeschichte*, 10 (2003), pp. 224–52.
44 S. F. Kellerhoff, "Gewissermassen schizophren," *Die Welt*, January 17, 2004; J. H. Claussen, "Umgepoltes Denken – Erst völkisch, dann kritisch: Der Historiker Fritz Fischer," *Frankfurter Allgemeine Zeitung*, January 7, 2004. See also the *Frankfurter Allgemeine Zeitung* article of July 16, 2001, attacking Chancellor Gerhard Schröder for suggesting in a speech that Germany had "instigated" two world wars.

German war aims policies to task, was always so vague when it came to explaining his own career path," he wrote.[45] Even before the appearance of Kracht's essay, the right-wing historian Michael Stürmer (born 1938), had remarked in a retrospective interview: "When an assistant of the Reich Institute for the History of the New Germany [i.e., Fischer] claimed the moral high ground in attacking a man who had sat in the Gestapo's cells [i.e., Ritter], then something was wrong."[46] The zeal with which Fischer's opponents seized upon Kracht's modest revelations, and indeed the speed with which Fischer's erstwhile lieutenants leapt to his defence,[47] illustrates very clearly the passions aroused by the original controversy.

Fischer's "crime" in the 1960s was to challenge one of the longest-running taboos in German history. By suggesting that Germany was principally to blame for the outbreak of war in 1914 he shattered a consensus that had existed within the historians' guild since 1919: that the Treaty of Versailles had been an iniquitous example of "victor's justice." In the 1950s German historians had appeared to defuse the "war-guilt" question successfully. With little option but to accept the blame for World War Two on Hitler's posthumous behalf, the guild effectively managed to put the issue of World War One on a back-burner. In a spirit of post-war reconciliation, and with the need to integrate the Federal Republic of Germany into western institutions, there was even a joint statement issued by French and German historians, accepting that World War One had been a tragic product of the alliance system, for which no country could be held responsible. Lloyd George's famous phrase, that the great powers had "slithered over the brink into the boiling cauldron of war," became the formula around which consensus could be built. Of course, not everyone agreed – the American historian Bernadotte E. Schmitt and the Italian Luigi Albertini are famous examples[48] – but by the late 1950s the debate on the origins of the Great War appeared to have run its course.

In Germany such remarkable unanimity had only been possible because of the peculiar nature of the historians' guild, which had continued to resemble a highly-restrictive gentleman's club; an "old-boys-network" in which the members were expected to protect their own, and to close ranks

---

45 V. Ullrich, "Griff nach der Wahrheit. Der berühmte Historiker Fritz Fischer im Zwielicht," *Die Zeit*, January 15, 2004.
46 Interview with Stürmer in R. Hohls and K. Jarausch, eds., *Versäumte Fragen. Deutsche Historiker im Schatten des Nationalsozialismus* (Munich, 2000), p. 360.
47 See for instance H. Pogge von Strandmann, "Aus akutem Geldmangel in die Partei eingetreten," letter to *Frankfurter Allgemeine Zeitung*, February 4, 2004.
48 B. E. Schmitt, *The Coming of the War* (New York, 1930); L. Albertini, *The Origins of the War of 1914*, 3 vols. (Oxford, 1952–7).

under fire. Young historians who asked the wrong kind of questions could see their career expectations disappear in a plume of cigar smoke. Books which did not conform to the prevailing orthodoxies faced an uphill struggle to be published or – in the case of émigré historians like Hans Rosenberg or Francis Carsten (1911–98) – to be translated into German. That until the great expansion of higher education in the 1960s and 1970s there were only 15 universities (and around 170 professors of history) in the whole of West Germany also played a part. Fischer's great advantage was that he was an insider, both socially and politically, with the security of a Chair at Hamburg University. Methodologically too, Fischer worked very much within the Rankean tradition, focusing on "high" politics, the state and its foreign relations: *Griff nach der Weltmacht* was a 900-page opus based almost entirely on the scrutiny of original documents, and had the footnotes to prove it. By all accounts, its author did not set out with a particular thesis in mind, but simply followed the paper-trail through the German archives, which had only recently regained possession of key files confiscated by the Allies in 1945. Fischer and his research assistants – principally Imanuel Geiss (born 1931) and Helmut Böhme (born 1936) – were, however, extremely thorough, looking not only at diplomatic and foreign office records, but those of other Reich offices, the Prussian ministries, and other institutions too. Their first unexpected discovery in the Potsdam Central Archive of the GDR was the so-called "September Programme" of war aims prepared for Chancellor Bethmann Hollweg in 1914, which became the centerpiece of an essay for the *Historische Zeitschrift* in 1959,[49] but which did not yet trigger a full-scale confrontation within the guild.

The Fischer controversy, which broke out at the end of 1961, is generally considered a watershed in German historiography. Not everyone agrees: Gerhard A. Ritter (born 1929, and not to be confused with Fischer's opponent Gerhard Ritter), points to a number of influential studies in the 1950s and the breakthrough of social history in the second half of the 1960s, to indicate an evolutionary rather than a revolutionary process.[50] Others, such as Richard Evans, highlight the guild's break with its Rankean traditions in the second half of the 1960s as "the real

---

49 See F. Fischer, "Deutsche Kriegsziele, Revolutionierung und Separatfrieden im Osten, 1914–18," *Historische Zeitschrift*, 188 (1959), pp. 249–65. The document was actually first seen by Geiss before he joined Fischer in Hamburg, and had earlier been seen and ignored by Hans Herzfeld. Interview with Geiss in R. Hohls and K. Jarausch, eds., *Versäumte Fragen*, p. 222.
50 G. A. Ritter, *The New Social History in the Federal Republic of Germany* (London, 1991). Ritter's view is supported by W. Schulze, *Deutsche Geschichtswissenschaft nach 1945* (Munich, 1993), but contested by Berger, *The Search for Normality*, p. 63.

revolution in German historiography."[51] It is certainly true that while the controversy is often considered to have opened the way for new methodological approaches, this did not occur until around 1965–7, when major publications by Böhme, Rosenberg, and Ralf Dahrendorf all appeared.[52] Only the first and weakest chapter of *Griff nach der Weltmacht*, which looked at "German imperialism" and the development of war aims before 1914, suggested any kind of break with German historical traditions, and this was largely thanks to Böhme. It was not the Hamburg historian's methods, but the implications of his argument that were explosive. If, as the documents seemed to indicate, Germany had unleashed the First World War in a bid to secure hegemony over Europe and hence "world power" status, then the Second World War could no longer be put down to an evil dictator alone; if the aggressive foreign policy of the Third Reich represented a continuation of earlier German planning, then the guild's attempts to portray the Nazi era as fundamentally unconnected to the rest of German history would be fatally undermined. In the eyes of many German historians, who read Fischer's book with a mixture of anger and alarm, the threat it posed was not just scholarly. It was as if the very stability and integrity of the West German state was at stake. Thus the Fischer controversy became much more than an argument among historians: it became a political event, with parliamentary statements, newspaper editorials, television debates, and even an unpleasant whiff of "dirty tricks."[53] Unnecessary though much of this was, it was in large part due to the public nature of the controversy (together with the "Auschwitz trial" of 1963) that many younger Germans began to engage with their country's history for the first time. Indeed, Carl Schorske (born 1915) has written that the "shaping of Germany's future was almost as much at stake in the Fischer controversy as the truth about its past."[54] It was as if the wall of silence that had been built up since 1945, and which had undoubtedly played its part in stabilizing the early Federal Republic, had finally cracked. It would take the rest of the

---

51 R. J. Evans, "Wilhelm II's Germany and the historians," *Rethinking German History*, p. 33.
52 H. Böhme, *Deutschlands Weg zur Großmacht. Studien zum Verhältnis von Wirtschaft und Staat während der Reichsgründungszeit* (Cologne and Berlin, 1966); Hans Rosenberg, *Große Depression und Bismarckzeit* (Berlin, 1967); R. Dahrendorf, *Society and Politics in Germany* (New York, 1967), first published as *Gesellschaft und Demokratie in Deutschland* (Munich, 1965).
53 West German Foreign Office funding for Fischer's planned lecture tour of the US in 1964 was mysteriously withdrawn at the last minute, although the tour went ahead with American support.
54 C. Schorske, "An afterword," in H. Lehmann, ed., *Historikerkontroversen*, pp. 185–6.

decade – and particularly the student unrest of 1967–8 – before the wall crumbled, but Fischer had dealt an important blow.

Fischer's foremost opponents in the early 1960s, such as Ritter, Rothfels, Zechlin, and Hans Herzfeld (1892–1982), had all participated in the campaign against the "War-Guilt Lie" in the 1920s and continued to emphasize the essentially defensive nature of German policy in 1914.[55] Their objections were many and varied. The principal criticisms were aimed less at Fischer's catalogue of war aims documents – although he was accused of taking them too much at face value – than the "masochistic" or "self-flagellating" interpretation of Germany's role in July 1914, which covered only 50 pages and relied heavily on the work of Geiss. The part played by Bethmann Hollweg in the events of July 1914 became a particular focus of debate, as did Fischer's flat, functional prose style and "judgmental" tone. The latter was perceived to depart from the German historist tradition of seeking to understand the actions of individuals in their own terms through a process of sympathetic intuition, rather than assessing them against a set of transcendental norms. It is important to note that the hostility Fischer encountered did not just come from the "usual suspects." Independent spirits such as Ludwig Dehio, who had been an important influence on Fischer, and Golo Mann, also condemned *Griff nach der Weltmacht* as "fundamentally wrong." This undoubtedly represented the majority view in the guild at the time, even if the German-American historian Fritz Stern offered vocal backing to the underdog. The public nature of the controversy, however, ensured that Fischer soon gained a following of young historians eager to carry out further research on the Empire. Hartmut Pogge von Strandmann (born 1938), Bernd Jürgen Wendt (born 1934), Dirk Stegmann (born 1941), and in Britain, John Röhl (born 1939), were among those to identify with Fischer's cause. It is questionable whether there was ever a fully-fledged "Fischer School,"[56] but one of his later students, the left-wing publicist Bernd Schulte, has continued to fight Fischer's corner in a series of books, articles, and Internet essays.[57]

---

55 See G. Ritter, "Eine neue Kriegsschuldthese? Zu Fritz Fischers Buch 'Griff nach der Weltmacht,'" *Historische Zeitschrift*, 194 (1962), p. 668; G. Ritter, *Der Erste Weltkrieg. Studien zum deutschen Geschichtsbild* (Bonn, 1964).
56 Although his opponents often talked of a "Fischer School," one of his former students, Peter-Christian Witt, has denied it ever existed, pointing to Fischer's willingness to supervise students on a wide range of topics and with a great variety of scholarly approaches. P.-C. Witt, "Fritz Fischer," *Kasseler Universitätsreden*, 5 (Kassel, 1988), p. 16.
57 Most recently, B. F. Schulte, *Weltmacht durch die Hintertür. Deutsche Nationalgeschichte in der Dikussion*, vol. 2 (Hamburg, 2003).

By October 1964, when Fischer's theses were debated at the German historians' conference in Berlin, it was clear that the split was methodological as well as ideological, with a growing divide between those who continued to uphold "the primacy of foreign policy," and those, such as Wolfgang Mommsen (1930–2004), who wanted greater attention to be paid to the Empire's domestic power structures. It was in this context that the work of the young Weimar historian Eckart Kehr – who had suggested that domestic political considerations were behind the building of the Wilhelmine battle fleet – was "rediscovered." Kehr's provocative rewriting of Ranke's dictum, which now became "the primacy of domestic policy," summed up the new approach. The split was partly, but not wholly, along generational lines, since there were also younger historians such as Andreas Hillgruber (1925–90), who disputed the extent to which the Empire's foreign affairs were influenced by domestic factors. Hillgruber continued to emphasize the importance of Germany's international and geopolitical situation, or the "curse of geography" as he later put it.[58]

In *Griff nach der Weltmacht* the so-called "continuity question" had been downplayed by Fischer. The connections made between the Kaiser's and the Führer's war aims were more implicit than explicit. In the course of his subsequent publications, however, Fischer became more radical – although not always more convincing – in portraying a direct line of continuity between the *Kaiserreich* and the Third Reich. His second major book on the subject, *War of Illusions* (1969),[59] concentrated on the years between 1911 and 1914, and sought to tackle the questions raised but not fully answered by the first chapter of *Griff nach der Weltmacht*. It focused in particular on the "alliance of elite groups" which Fischer suggested was principally responsible for the continuity of policy between the two regimes. This time, an even wider range of documentary sources were consulted, including the records of political parties, economic pressure-groups, and industrial concerns. Unlike most of his contemporaries in the historians' guild, Fischer had developed an interest in social and economic history, fostered by his stays in Britain and the US during the 1950s, and by his reading of German émigré historians like Hans Rosenberg. The origins of World War One, Fischer suggested, could not be explained by reference to governments and diplomats alone, but required a much bigger picture than the statist Neo-Rankean model was able to provide. Belatedly, after a half century during which their guild

---

58   A. Hillgruber, *Die gescheiterte Großmacht. Eine Skizze des deutschen Reiches 1871–1945* (Düsseldorf, 1980).
59   F. Fischer, *Krieg der Illusionen. Die deutsche Politik von 1911 bis 1914* (Düsseldorf, 1969); in English as *War of Illusions* (London, 1974).

had "drifted into isolation,"[60] historians in Germany began to follow in the footsteps of their French, British, and US colleagues; expanding their focus from the state and its leaders to society as a whole. This so-called "paradigm shift"[61] should not be exaggerated, since many continued to uphold the "old" paradigm, but the late sixties certainly saw an increasing cross-fertilization between history and the social sciences. The new approach, variously labeled "historical social science," the "social history of politics," "critical history," or simply "Kehrite" (a neologism coined by Wolfgang Mommsen), eschewed great men and historic events, and focused instead on socio-economic structures. One of its most able practitioners, Jürgen Kocka, has referred to "social history" as the "magic password" of the late 1960s.[62] It was particularly useful for opening doors in Germany's new universities, such as Bochum and Bielefeld, where the atmosphere was very different from Tübingen and Heidelberg, and where many were willing to follow Fischer's lead in looking for specific lines of continuity in modern German history.

The Fischer controversy could not, and did not produce an outright "winner," but by the end of the decade Fischer's supporters clearly felt in possession of both the scholarly and the moral high ground. This is evident from the short book written in the early 1970s by the Australian historian John Moses, tracking the history of the controversy from a fiercely pro-Fischer standpoint.[63] Fischer's theses gained their author fame and respect abroad, and a fair few admirers at home, although Volker Berghahn (born 1938) warned in a 1980 essay that many German school textbooks were yet to incorporate Fischer's findings in their accounts of 1914.[64] It was also perhaps significant that despite honorary degrees from East Anglia, Sussex, Oxford, and a host of other foreign universities, Fischer was not recognized in a similar fashion in the Federal Republic until 1988. That it was the modern and modest University of Kassel which bestowed such an award on the octogenarian historian, rather than one of Germany's traditional seats of learning, spoke volumes for the bitterness with which many in the historians' guild continued to regard their most famous member.[65]

---

60   G. Iggers, "Introduction," in *The Social History of Politics*, p. 11.
61   The term was invented and popularized by the American physicist and historian of science Thomas Kuhn (1922–96).
62   Interview with Kocka in R. Hohls and K. Jarausch, eds., *Versäumte Fragen*, p. 388.
63   J. A. Moses, *The Politics of Illusion*.
64   V. Berghahn, "Die Fischer Kontroverse – 15 Jahre danach," *Geschichte und Gesellschaft*, 6 (1980), pp. 403–19.
65   P.-C. Witt, "Fritz Fischer," *Kasseler Universitätsreden*.

A "New Orthodoxy"?

The Fischer controversy and the negative *Sonderweg* thesis provided the dual impetus for a growing consensus that began to form among younger historians in the late 1960s. If the sociologist Ralf Dahrendorf (born 1929) had set the ball rolling with his *Society and Politics in Germany*, it was Hans-Ulrich Wehler (born 1931) who would become the most prominent representative of the new approach, along with Jürgen Kocka (born 1941) and Heinrich August Winkler (born 1938). Wehler had first come to prominence with a study of *Bismarck and Imperialism* in 1969, but his key text on Imperial Germany was to appear some four years later.[66] Wehler's *The German Empire 1871–1918* was very much a book of its time: written against the backdrop of the student unrest and political crises of the late 1960s, when its author was a lecturer in Cologne, it claimed to be a "problem-oriented historical structural analysis" and presented a deliberately provocative set of theses rather than the well-rounded narrative traditionally favored by Germany's master-historians. It disposed of the metaphysical literary vocabulary so beloved of the guild – "fate," "destiny," "tragedy," et cetera – which was a legacy of historism's roots in the Romantic era, and sought to replace it with the clear, rational language of enlightened scientific analysis. Admittedly, some of the new terminology – "social imperialism," "negative integration," "organized capitalism" – was equally problematic, a sub-scientific jargon that muddied rather than cleared the waters, but the discursive shift no doubt contributed to the book's daunting air of certainty.

At the heart of the approach adopted by Wehler and other critical historians was the conviction that the period from the 1860s to 1945 should be seen as a single historical epoch, during which Germany's development departed crucially from the route followed by the rest of the western world. By emphasizing Germany's *Sonderweg* these historians were not suggesting that the rise of Hitler was an inevitable product of Germany's course of development; or that factors like Germany's defeat in the First World War, the hyperinflation of 1923, or the Great Depression of the early 1930s were wholly insignificant. They did, however, seek to highlight long-term structural deficits that may have been more apparent in Germany than in other western nations, and so may have contributed to the catastrophic failure of democracy in 1933. Two weaknesses in

---

66 H.-U. Wehler, *Bismarck und der Imperialismus* (Cologne, 1969); H.-U. Wehler, *Das deutsche Kaiserreich* (Göttingen, 1973), in English as *The German Empire, 1871–1918* (Leamington Spa, 1985).

particular were highlighted: the nature of Bismarck's "blood and iron" unification, which led to a reliance on reform "from above," an exaggerated respect for armed force, and a general militarization of society; and second, the discrepancy between the Empire's rapid economic and social development on the one hand, and its resistance to political change on the other. The fateful combination of a modern economy and a backward state was seen as a product of the "failed" revolutions of 1848–9 and the weakness of the German bourgeoisie, which became "feudalized" and was therefore unable to dislodge the privileged representatives of the "pre-industrial elites" – principally the landed Junker aristocracy – from their position of political dominance in the government, bureaucracy, and army. This version of the *Sonderweg* thesis thus gained a new foundation in modernization theory, which had developed in the US in the 1950s.[67] "The price of Germany's exceptionalism," as William Reddy puts it, "was pathology; the exception that proved the rule. Where modernization and liberalism do not advance hand in hand, disaster follows."[68]

Wehler concurred with Fischer that the blame for Germany's misfortunes lay with an "alliance of elite groups," who not only led the Empire down the road to disaster, but would later "help Hitler into the saddle." The Empire, which was "pseudo-constitutional semi-absolutist" in character and not a proper constitutional monarchy as the guild had always claimed, was ruled by the "traditional oligarchies" from their stronghold in Prussia, first through the dictatorial figure of Otto von Bismarck, and later through an anonymous, authoritarian polycracy. The only way in which this anachronistic power structure could be preserved was by employing a series of cynical diversionary tactics, such as colonial policy ("social imperialism") and the fabrication of foreign crises, which helped to neutralize and deflect internal tensions outward. The formidable techniques of political and social control pioneered by Bismarck – an insidious mix of repression, indoctrination, manipulation, and compensatory sweeteners – continued to be employed long after the pilot had been dropped, in a desperate and doomed effort to defend the status quo against the irresistible "onslaught of new forces." Central to this interpretation of the Empire was the notion of *Sammlungspolitik*, a term first coined by the Prussian Finance Minister Johannes von Miquel in 1897 to denote a "rallying together" of conservative interests to defend the Empire from both its internal and external enemies. While Miquel had appeared to conceive of *Sammlungspolitik* merely as a short-term expedient, Wehler

---

67 See S. E. Berman, "Modernization in historical perspective. The case of Imperial Germany," *World Politics*, 53 (2000), pp. 431–62.
68 W. Reddy, *Money and Liberty in Modern Europe*, p. 14.

and other critical historians saw this "cartel of fear" as a cornerstone of the Empire's entire political edifice, erected in the so-called "second" or "internal" founding of the Reich in the late 1870s (when it was often referred to as the "alliance of iron and rye") and surviving with "remarkable continuity" right through to 1918 (or even, in the view of Stegmann, 1932).[69] In this they were following once more in the footsteps of Eckart Kehr, whose classic description of the 1890s *Sammlung* as a reactionary quid pro quo became an almost obligatory quote in books published on the Empire in the 1970s: "For industry the fleet, *Weltpolitik*, and expansion; for the agrarians, tariffs and the preservation of the Conservatives' social supremacy; and, as a consequence of this social and economic compromise, for the Center Party the political hegemony."[70]

West German history's turn to the social sciences in the late 1960s and 1970s was driven by a variety of factors. There was a greater willingness to embrace new approaches from abroad, manifest in the increasing number of English-language history books to be translated into German; a desire to reconnect with earlier progressive traditions in German historiography, exemplified by the rediscovery of Kehr and Rosenberg; and a rapid expansion of higher education in the Federal Republic which generated a huge increase in the number of younger academics.[71] Perhaps most important of all, however, was a change in the way West German historians perceived their own role in society. For more than a century, the historians' guild had seen itself primarily as a servant of the state. It had provided rulers and statesmen with "lessons" from history – to be used as models for future policy – and helped to engender a sense of national pride among the German people. In the aftermath of the Fischer controversy, many younger historians instead began to embrace a different kind of civic function: the Western historical tradition, which aspires to educate and instruct citizens to participate in the democratic control of their state. The proponents of historical social science believed in other words that they could assist in the political emancipation of the Germans from their authoritarian past, and create a new historical consciousness more suitable for a democratic republic.[72] As Georg Iggers puts it, a "belief in a liberal, social democracy" was "crucial to the critical 'social history of politics.'"[73]

---

69 D. Stegmann, *Die Erben Bismarcks. Parteien und Verbände in der Spätphase des Wilhelminischen Deutschlands: Sammlungspolitik 1897–1918* (Berlin, 1970).
70 E. Kehr, *Schlachtflottenbau und Parteipolitik* (Berlin, 1930), p. 205.
71 Between 1960 and 1975 the number of professorships and lectureships in Germany grew by 400 percent, and the number of assistants went up by 800 percent. See S. Berger, *The Search for Normality*, p. 64.
72 See J. A. Moses, *The Politics of Illusion*, pp. 67–8.
73 G. Iggers, "Introduction," *The Social History of Politics*, p. 27.

This political consensus, a shared faith in the *Sonderweg* (or "structural continuity") thesis, and a lively new journal – *Geschichte und Gesellschaft*, subtitled "A Journal for Historical Social Science," founded in 1975 – was just about all the critical historians had in common. They adopted a wide range of methodological and theoretical approaches – from the Frankfurt School, Marx (although in a strictly subordinate role), Habermas and particularly Max Weber – and were always a heterogeneous grouping. Even so, the fact that three of the leading practitioners, Wehler, Kocka, and Puhle, became professors at the University of Bielefeld, ensured that some began to talk of a Bielefeld School (or, more informally, the "Bielefelders").[74] One feature of this phase in the historiography of the German Empire was an impressive increase in the number of research-based monographs which started to appear. Works by Kocka, Hans-Jürgen Puhle (born 1940), Hartmut Kaelble (born 1940), and Hans-Peter Ullmann (born 1949), together with others by the former Fischer students Dirk Stegmann and Peter-Christian Witt (born 1943), were important in putting flesh on the bare bones of Wehler's structure, particularly with regard to the Empire's economy and society. By the mid-1970s, the University of Bielefeld was by no means the only stronghold of the "critical" historians, and such was their influence within the much-expanded guild that some began to suggest they had become a "new orthodoxy." That label is usually credited to the American historian James Sheehan (born 1937),[75] although Imanuel Geiss has suggested that it was actually Klaus Epstein who first coined the term,[76] and both Karlheinz Weissmann ("became to a very large degree the orthodoxy") and Gustav Seibt ("social history orthodoxy") used similar phrases as well.[77]

The extent to which the description was ever valid is highly questionable. Leading "Kehrites" were quick to dismiss suggestions that they were part of any kind of orthodoxy, and claimed the notion was largely an Anglo-Saxon misperception.[78] Certainly, the traditionalists within the guild did not simply disappear in the 1970s, and continued to present their critiques of both Fritz Fischer and historical social science in publications such as the *Historische Zeitschrift* and *Geschichte in Wissenschaft und Unterricht* (a journal for history teachers founded by Karl Dietrich

---

74 R. Fletcher, "Recent developments in West German historiography: The Bielefeld School and its critics," *German Studies Review*, 3 (1984), pp. 451–80.
75 Sheehan used it in a book review for the *Journal of Modern History*, 48 (1976), p. 567.
76 Interview with Geiss in R. Hohls and K. Jarausch, eds., *Versäumte Fragen*, p. 231.
77 Both quoted by S. Berger, *The Search for Normality*, p. 78.
78 See H.-J. Puhle, "Zur Legende von der Kehrschen Schule," *Geschichte und Gesellschaft*, 4 (1978), pp. 108–19.

Erdmann and which remained in conservative hands).[79] "The historist tradition," Stefan Berger argues, "was put on the defensive for a while, but it survived the challenge of historical social science largely intact."[80] The belated pluralization of approaches in German history in the 1970s, including the growth of women's history and *Alltagsgeschichte* (see Chapter 4) – which, as Berger points out, was only possible because "the first generation of critical historians had broken up the *juste milieu* of the national tradition"[81] – would seem to contradict the existence of any dominant orthodoxy. Yet others disagree. In 1972, Fischer's former lieutenant Imanuel Geiss had written: "precisely because of their experiences [at the hands of the guild] the new generation of historians … will hopefully never degenerate into an intolerant and anti-scientific orthodoxy of the kind that is only now finally leaving the stage."[82] By 1999, however, Geiss viewed the Bielefeld School as more "illiberal" than the "old orthodoxy," and even accused them of a "totalitarian disposition."[83] At the same time, Wolfram Fischer dubbed Wehler "Praeceptor Germaniae" [Germany's teacher], an ironic use of a title previously associated with the didactic nineteenth-century historian Heinrich von Treitschke.[84] A deep-seated resentment against Wehler and his supporters was also apparent at the aforementioned 1998 German historians' conference in Frankfurt, where the revelations surrounding Wehler's supervisor and mentor, Theodor Schieder, were used by some as a stick to beat his former pupil. "Does the new orthodoxy have brown [i.e., Nazi] roots?" asked one reviewer, while others could not resist a sense of *Schadenfreude* as the historian who had always been so vociferous in emphasizing his subject's moral and pedagogic responsibility, now found himself charged with failing to be "critical" when it came to his own mentor's dark past.[85]

Despite Geiss's claims to the contrary, the "new orthodoxy" was never as monolithic or as ruthless as the "old orthodoxy" of the pre-Fischer days. The expanded German higher education system of the 1970s was simply too big and heterogeneous for that, and there was no shortage of

---

79   See H.-G. Zmarzlik, "Das Kaiserreich in neuer Sicht," *Historische Zeitschrift*, 222 (1976), pp. 105–26; or K. Hildebrand, "Geschichte oder 'Gesellschaftsgeschichte'? Die Notwendigkeit einer politischen Geschichtsschreibung von den internationalen Beziehungen," *Historische Zeitschrift*, 223 (1976), pp. 328–57.
80   S. Berger, *The Search for Normality*, p. 79.
81   Ibid., p. 68.
82   I. Geiss, "Die Fischer-Kontroverse," in *Studien über Geschichte und Geschichtswissenschaft* (Frankfurt, 1972), p. 194.
83   Interview with Geiss in R. Hohls and K. Jarausch, eds., *Versäumte Fragen*, pp. 235–6.
84   Interview with W. Fischer in ibid., p. 115.
85   Ibid., p. 115. See also the review by P. Stelzel, "Hat die Neue Orthodoxie braune Wurzeln?," http://www.literaturkritik.de 11 (November 2001).

non-believers willing to challenge the dogmas of historical social science in print. That said, it is understandable how Wehler's brusque and combative manner could easily make enemies: the level of vituperation may have been lower than at the height of the Fischer controversy, but scholarly exchanges between German historians in the last third of the twentieth century remained notably more heated and more public than in the English-speaking world. One trenchant critic who nevertheless maintained reasonably good terms with Wehler was the Munich historian Thomas Nipperdey (1927–92), who was invited to set out his objections to Wehler's *Empire* in the first volume of *Geschichte und Gesellschaft*.[86] Nipperdey, a moderate traditionalist, accused Wehler of seeing history in black and white terms, rather than the more appropriate shades of grey; and of acting as both judge and jury over the German past. Evoking the best traditions of German historism, Nipperdey was particularly anxious that the imperial era should be assessed on its own merits, and not viewed simply as the pre-history of the Third Reich. He argued that there were many lines of continuity in German history: some of which ran from the Kaiser's to Hitler's Germany, but others to Weimar and the Federal Republic.[87] Nipperdey also bemoaned the absence of narrative and human personalities in Wehler's work, which affected its readability and risked alienating the general public. Above all, he suggested, it resulted in a lifeless, static picture which did not do justice to an evolving and shifting scene.

The "Anglo-Saxon" Challenge

A different kind of challenge to the alleged "new orthodoxy" began to emerge in the late 1970s from a group of young British historians led by Richard Evans (born 1947), David Blackbourn (born 1949) and Geoff Eley (born 1949). As Evans notes, these historians had no prior connection to Germany at all, other than growing up in the 1950s amidst the still pervasive presence of the Second World War. If the initial impetus had been "to find out why the Germans had fought the war, and why Hitler had come to power,"[88] the belated arrival in Britain of the Fischer

---

86 T. Nipperdey, "Wehlers 'Kaiserreich.' Eine kritische Auseinandersetzung," *Geschichte und Gesellschaft*, 1 (1975), pp. 539–60, later reprinted in T. Nipperdey, *Gesellschaft – Kultur – Theorie* (Göttingen, 1976).
87 T. Nipperdey, "1933 und die Kontinuität der deutschen Geschichte," *Historische Zeitschrift*, 227 (1978), pp. 86–111.
88 R. J. Evans, "Introduction," in *Rethinking German History* (London, 1987), pp. 2–3.

controversy – *Griff nach der Weltmacht* appeared in an English translation in 1967 and two years later Fischer himself came to give a series of lectures – ensured that many who commenced postgraduate studies in German history around 1970 did so on the *Kaiserreich* rather than the Third Reich. Evans, Blackbourn, and Eley all proceeded to write well-respected research monographs of their own,[89] but it was two collaborative ventures which made the biggest impact: first, a collection of essays edited by Evans entitled *Society and Politics in Wilhelmine Germany* (1978) and then Blackbourn and Eley's *Mythen deutscher Geschichtsschreibung* (1980) which was republished in expanded form as *The Peculiarities of German History* (1984).[90] Until these two volumes, the notoriously insular guild had generally ignored British studies of German history, unless they could be instrumentalized for propaganda purposes (as in the campaign against the Versailles Treaty) or used to lend weight to a particular professor's pet thesis. There were some exceptions to the rule, of course, but the effects of two world wars cast a long shadow over both the content and reception of work by British historians on Germany. Even Evans, whose book on the German feminist movement was well received on both sides of the Atlantic, ruefully recalls that it received just one short review in a West Germany historical journal, and only then because the reviewer happened to be working on the same topic.[91] Such complacent disinterest would change, however, with the publication of *Society and Politics in Wilhelmine Germany*, and especially *The Peculiarities of German History*, which attracted considerable attention in the German media and would later be acknowledged as an important historiographical landmark.

Both books confronted Wehler's view of the Empire head-on. Together they highlighted one of the key paradoxes (and weaknesses) of the "new orthodoxy." For all its much-vaunted internationalism and social scientific approach, it had continued very much in the national traditions of the historical guild, focusing on high politics and the state, to the virtual exclusion of the Empire's non-Prussian territories and vast swathes of German society. The "old" and the "new" orthodoxy had fought on "the same battleground," as Evans put it.[92] One of the key premises of

---

89 R. J. Evans, *The Feminist Movement in Germany, 1894–1933* (London, 1976); D. Blackbourn, *Class, Religion and Local Politics in Wilhelmine Germany: The Centre Party in Württemberg before 1914* (London, 1980); G. Eley, *Reshaping the German Right: Radical Nationalism and Political Change After Bismarck* (New Haven and London, 1980).
90 R. J. Evans, ed., *Society and Politics in Wilhelmine Germany* (London, 1978); D. Blackbourn and G. Eley, *Mythen deutscher Geschichtsschreibung* (Frankfurt, 1980); in English as *The Peculiarities of German History* (Oxford, 1984).
91 R. J. Evans, "Introduction," in *Rethinking German History*, p. 5.
92 R. J. Evans, "Wilhelm II's Germany and the historians," in *Rethinking German History*, p. 45.

Society and Politics in Wilhelmine Germany was, therefore, to open up new perspectives on the *Kaiserreich*, to ensure that the voices of women, peasants, unemployed workers, and other groups on the margins – geographical as well as social – could finally be heard: "When the history of Wilhelmine Germany is approached from below, familiar features appear in an unfamiliar light," Evans observed.[93] While not all his contributors could be said to have followed this agenda, Evans backed up his claim with a formidable series of edited volumes published during the course of the 1980s. The other main aim of the 1978 collection was, in Evans words, "to rehabilitate Wilhelmine society as an object of study in its own right, and not to treat it as merely as a prelude to the Nazi era": an aspiration which echoed Nipperdey's earlier critique of the "new orthodoxy," and would become a mantra for many young researchers on the Empire in years to come.[94]

The challenge posed by *The Peculiarities of German History*, however, was even more fundamental. The premise of this avowedly historiographical book was, in Blackbourn's allusive phrase, that "all national histories are peculiar, but some appear to be more peculiar than others."[95] By contesting the whole notion of German exceptionalism, the book called into question not only the "new orthodoxy's reading of the *Kaiserreich*, but of modern German history as a whole." Blackbourn and Eley's attack came not from the right, as most of Wehler's German critics had done, but from the Neo-Marxist left. They argued that the *Sonderweg* constructed by historians in the 1960s and 1970s was not based on any kind of genuine comparative history, but on an idealized vision of Anglo-American development. The very notion of a "special path" implied there was a "normal path" against which Germany should be measured, which they found both methodologically and empirically problematic. The "new orthodoxy" had relied too heavily on a misguided and romantic notion of what a successful bourgeois revolution should look like, and so had failed to see how far the Empire actually met the needs of middle-class Germans. In bemoaning the absence of a "heroic" conquest of power in the manner of 1789, the proponents of the *Sonderweg* had overlooked the fact that the bourgeoisie usually became the leading class in nineteenth-century Europe in a gradual or "silent" manner, through the "capitalist economic system and in civil society, in the sphere of property relations, the rule of law, associational life, certain dominant values."[96] Hence there

---

93   Ibid., p. 46.
94   Ibid., p. 50.
95   D. Blackbourn, in D. Blackbourn and G. Eley, *The Peculiarities of German History*, p. 286.
96   D. Blackbourn, "The discreet charm of the bourgeoisie," in *Populists and Patricians*, p. 76.

was no reason why a bourgeois revolution should have to require the establishment of parliamentary government along Westminster lines before it could be regarded as "successful" or "complete." Moreover, terms such as "feudal" or "pre-industrial" were inappropriate in the context of the Imperial German elites, since even the notorious Junkers – "those all-purpose villains of modern German history"[97] – were capitalist farmers, engaged in a free market and with free mobility of labor. If anything, therefore, it was a case of "embourgoisement" rather than "feudalization." The German experience was, Blackbourn and Eley concluded, merely a "heightened version" of what happened elsewhere.

Blackbourn, Eley, and Evans did not, of course, agree on every aspect of the Empire, but one common theme linking all their work in the 1980s was the conviction that ordinary people – even peasants – must be viewed as active subjects, and not merely as passive objects of German history. This was perhaps most clearly apparent in their contributions to the debate on the nature of political mobilization in the Wilhelmine era. Where Wehler and the "new orthodoxy" stressed the importance of demagogic manipulation "from above," the British historians saw a significant degree of autonomous self-mobilization "from below." A good case in point is Eley's work on the Navy League, an organization previously regarded as a prime example of manipulative social imperialism. In Eley's reading the League was also, in part, an expression of a new kind of radical nationalism which was developing at grassroots level from the 1890s onwards.[98] Such findings had important implications for one of the central theses of the "Kehrites," the so-called *Sammlungspolitik*. As we have seen, Wehler, Stegmann, and others emphasized the stability and longevity of this conservative pact, which they claimed was sustained by a host of manipulative techniques. The British historians now offered an alternative picture: of fragile, *ad hoc* arrangements, shifting uncertainly as Germany's leaders struggled to "harness forces that could not be fully controlled."[99]

For all their ideological and methodological differences, certain similarities seemed to exist between the young British historians' critique of the Bielefeld School and the earlier attack by Nipperdey. In fact, at this time the Munich historian was still reluctant to relinquish the *Sonderweg* model and remained unconvinced by what he termed Eley's "somewhat crude personal Marxism."[100] Even so, the robustness of Blackbourn and

---

97 D. Blackbourn, "The politics of demagogy," in *Populists and Patricians*, p. 221.
98 See G. Eley, *Reshaping the German Right*.
99 D. Blackbourn, "The politics of demagogy," p. 219.
100 See T.Nipperdey in Kolloquien des Instituts für Zeitgeschichte, *Deutscher Sonderweg – Mythos oder Realität* (Munich, 1982), p. 17.

Eley's challenge to the "new orthodoxy" was sufficient to guarantee a positive reception from some of German history's most conservative figures, ever eager to "normalize" their country's past. No doubt embarrassed by this unwelcome support, Blackbourn and Eley made strenuous efforts to acknowledge the valuable contribution of historical social science, but this could not prevent a fierce and personal counter-attack from the Bielefelders.[101] Once passions had cooled, however, commentators began to suggest that the gulf was not actually as wide as it first appeared. Georg Iggers, for instance, noted of Blackbourn and Eley: "They, too, focus on the interrelation of society and politics; they too see continuities in German history even if these are more complex than those seen by the critical school; and they, too, are critical historians who write history from political and social commitment."[102] Meanwhile Volker Berghahn questioned whether "the often bitter polemics had not obscured the fact that the two sides in the debate were merely looking at the same problem from opposite angles."[103] Certainly, while important differences remained, the mid- to late-1980s did witness a thaw in relations between the Bielefeld School and its British critics. This was symbolized in the establishment of several large-scale research projects to investigate on a comparative basis the history of the bourgeoisie (or, more accurately, the *Bürgertum*), and to test the rival claims of the "feudalization" and "embourgeoisement" theses.[104] The fact that one of the research projects was based in Bielefeld, at the very heart of the "new orthodoxy," is testament not only to the impact Blackbourn and Eley's work made on the German historians' guild, but also to Wehler and Kocka's willingness to review some of their most basic assumptions. A rash of subsequent publications came up with conflicting conclusions but offered little support

---

101 See, for example, H.-U. Wehler, "'Deutscher Sonderweg' oder allegemeine Probleme des westlichen Kapitalismus? Zur Kritik an einigen 'Mythen deutscher Geschichtsschreibung,'" *Merkur*, 35 (1981), pp. 477–87; G. Eley, "Antwort an Hans-Ulrich Wehler," *Merkur*, 35 (1981), pp. 757–9; H.-U. Wehler, "Rückantwort an Geoff Eley," *Merkur*, 35 (1981), p. 760; H.-J. Puhle, "Deutscher Sonderweg: Kontroverse um eine vermeintliche Legende," *Journal für Geschichte*, 3 (1981), pp. 44–5.
102 G. Iggers, "Introduction," in *The Social History of Politics*, p. 45.
103 V. Berghahn, "Introduction to the second edition," *Germany and the Approach of War in 1914*, p. 7.
104 The first of these projects, initiated by Werner Conze, predated the Blackbourn and Eley controversy. The second was established at Bielefeld in 1986, with the aim of examining the "Social history of the bourgeoisie: Germany in international comparison." A third project, run by Lothar Gall from Frankfurt, examined the *Bürgertum* in some 14 German cities between 1780 and 1870. Issues raised by this research are discussed in D. Blackbourn and R. J. Evans, eds., *The German Bourgeoisie* (London, 1989) and by J. Breuilly in "The elusive class: Some critical remarks on the historiography of the bourgeoisie," *Archiv für Sozialgeschichte*, 38 (1998), pp. 133–8.

for the "feudalization" thesis, which all but disappeared from accounts of the Empire in the 1990s.

One reason for the Bielefelders' initial hostility to Blackbourn and Eley's work was no doubt the suspicion that their emphasis on the pluralism and modernity of Wilhelmine Germany, and their frequent references to zoos, theaters, and concert halls, had apologist undertones; that the pre-Fischer guild's elegiac evocation of the "good old days" could once again be ushered in through the back door. This was certainly not their intention. Both Blackbourn and Eley have written extensively on the "dark sides" of the Empire, but they reject the idea of a simple linear progression from the *Kaiserreich* to the Third Reich. Continuities, they argue, should be located not in the discrepancy between economic modernity and socio-political backwardness, but in the pathology of bourgeois modernity itself. It cannot be denied, however, that in the wake of *The Peculiarities of German History* a number of English-language historians produced studies with a rather more "optimistic" view of the Empire than had been the norm in post-Fischer West Germany. A good case in point was a misguided essay collection entitled *Another Germany*, edited by Jack Dukes and Joachim Remak, which consciously sought to reverse the "trap built into all recorded history – the disproportionate survival of the negative," and not surprisingly ended up with what most considered to be an unduly positive picture.[105]

Before we leave the Anglo-Saxon challenge to the "new orthodoxy," it is important to note that it did not just come "from below." While Richard Evans found widespread sympathy for his conviction that "social history belongs in the centre of German history,"[106] his British colleague John Röhl faced an altogether stiffer task in attempting to revive interest in monarchical history and biography at a time when both seemed to have become hopelessly outdated (see Chapter 2). In its own way, however, Röhl's prodigious output on Kaiser Wilhelm II, along with biographies by the Americans Thomas Kohut and Lamar Cecil,[107] posed as serious a threat to the "new orthodoxy" as Evans, Blackbourn, or Eley. The last emperor had become a virtual non-person in Wehler's *Empire*, meriting just seven references in the original German edition, but Röhl challenged

---

105 J. R. Dukes and J. Remak, eds., *Another Germany. A Reconsideration of the Imperial Era* (Boulder and London, 1988). The quote is originally from Barbara Tuchman.
106 R. J. Evans, "Introduction," in *Rethinking German History*, p. l.
107 L. Cecil, *Wilhelm II., vol. 1. Prince and Emperor, 1859–1900* (Chapel Hill and London, 1989); L. Cecil, *Wilhelm II. vol. 2. Emperor and Exile, 1900–1941* (Chapel Hill and London, 1996); T. Kohut, *Wilhelm II and the Germans. A Study in Leadership* (Oxford and New York, 1991).

this view with several lively collections of essays and the start of a mammoth three-volume biography.[108] His approach was predictably condemned by the Bielefelders as "personalist" and, therefore, inherently conservative and historist, while his British colleague Evans was no more sympathetic: "This is history as the butler saw it. But does the keyhole really afford the best perspective on the past?"[109] Röhl, however, fiercely denied the charge of "personalism" and argued with some justification that his focus on the royal court did not preclude consideration of either structures or historical theory.

The East German View

Today it is all too easy to forget that until the dramatic events of 1989–90, a separate historical tradition, with its own particular perspective on the German Empire, had evolved in the territory of the German Democratic Republic. The East German view of the *Kaiserreich* is often overlooked, or dismissed as worthless, since its prime function was to provide political legitimation for the Communist state. Yet no historian works in an ideology-free zone, and every political system seeks legitimation. In this regard there were interesting parallels between the Marxist-Leninist historiography of the GDR and the equally didactic "historical social science" in the Federal Republic. The similarities were not purely functional: both endorsed the primacy of domestic politics; both were severely critical of the bourgeoisie for failing to fulfill its "historical mission"; and, as Evans observed in the late 1970s, both shared an aesthetic similarity too. "Historical monographs in West Germany have come more and more to resemble a kind of social-democratic mirror-image of their East German counterparts," he wrote, "with empirical material being sandwiched between two slices of theoretical discussion – and, as often as not, effectively unrelated to either of them."[110] Of course, there was also much that divided GDR historians from the "new orthodoxy": the latter's use of "modernization" theory; the "feudalization" concept; above all, the

---

108 J. C. G. Röhl and N. Sombart, eds., *Kaiser Wilhelm II - New Interpretations* (Cambridge, 1982); J. C. G. Röhl, ed., *Der Ort Kaiser Wilhelms II. in der deutschen Geschichte* (Munich, 1991); J. C. G. Röhl, *The Kaiser and his Court. Wilhelm II and the Government of Germany* (Cambridge, 1994); J. C. G. Röhl, *Young Wilhelm. The Kaiser's Early Life 1859–1888* (Cambridge, 1998); J. C. G. Röhl, *Wilhelm II. The Kaiser's Personal Monarchy 1888–1900* (Cambridge, 2004).
109 In a 1983 review of Röhl and Sombart, eds., *Kaiser Wilhelm II - New Interpretations*. See R. J. Evans, "From Hitler to Bismarck," in *Rethinking German History*, p. 59.
110 R. J. Evans, "Wilhelm II's Germany and the historians," p. 35.

conviction that the real inadequacy of the Empire lay in "the inherent flaws of the exploitative, class-divided capitalist system, which neither social integration nor any parliament could have remedied."[111]

History was the most generously funded of all the humanities in the GDR, but this support came at a high price: it was expected to justify and legitimate a system of "real existing socialism" which paid only lip-service to the principles of academic freedom and critical scholarship. Karl Marx and Friedrich Engels, the spiritual fathers of the GDR, had seen history as part of a developmental process, inextricably linked to the present and the future, and subject to recurring and ascertainable laws. If, as they believed, the shape of the future could be "read" by the study of past developments, then it followed that the future was a necessary concern for the historian as well. In practice this meant that GDR historians would not only be expected to research the past, but also to play an active role in building the Workers' and Peasants' State. A distinctive GDR history first began to emerge around 1951, when an earlier Communist view which had developed in the years of Nazi tyranny and saw German history as one long tale of authoritarian "misery" – another version of the negative *Sonderweg*[112] – was rejected in favor of a new and more positive reading, which portrayed the GDR as the "lawful" heir of a proud democratic-revolutionary tradition. From this perspective the Empire was viewed as a "crucial social advance," which for all its faults (monopoly capitalism, imperialism, and militarism) had given the growing working class new opportunities to organize on a national scale.[113]

East Germany's progressive heritage, stretching back to the Peasants' Revolt of the sixteenth century, was sketched out in a 1951 textbook entitled *The Development of Germany and the German Labor Movement until the Fall of Fascism*,[114] which effectively placed the history of the labor movement at the centre of German national history (echoing the efforts of the Borussian School to give Prussia similar pride of place a century

---

111 A. Dorpalen, *German History in Marxist Perspective. The East German Approach* (Detroit, 1985), p. 238.
112 The so-called *Misere* approach was associated with the Hungarian Marxist theorist Georg Lukács and the German historian Alexander Abusch. See A. Fischer and G. Heydemann, "Weg und Wandel der Geschichtswissenschaft und des Geschichtsverständnisses in der SBZ/DDR seit 1945," in A. Fischer and G. Heydemann, eds., *Geschichtswissenschaft in der DDR*, vol. 1 (Berlin, 1988), pp. 3–30.
113 H. Wolter, *Bismarcks Außenpolitik 1871–81. Außenpolitische Grundlinien von der Reichsgründung bis zum Dreikaiserbündnis* (East Berlin, 1983), p. 5
114 *Die Entwicklung Deutschlands und der deutscher Arbeiterbewegung bis zum Sturz des Faschismus* (East Berlin, 1951).

earlier).[115] The book was prepared by a team of historians under the leadership of Kurt Hager (1912–98), head of the propaganda department of the Socialist Unity Party's Central Committee, and a powerful influence on GDR history throughout the lifetime of the republic. At the first statewide meeting of East German historians in 1952, Hager called on all those present to learn the lessons of Marx and Engels, and to adopt "historical materialism" as their method.[116] Historians should recognize, in other words, that history was driven not by ideas or individuals (the unscientific "idealist" conception of history which prevailed in the West), but by the development and ownership of modes of production. Only by studying these changes, which were subject to universally valid laws, could history become truly scientific. It was immediately clear, however, that there were embarrassing gaps in the existing Marxist-Leninist scholarship, in terms of both historical periods and social classes. Many of these gaps would remain untouched by GDR historians until the 1980s, since, at the Party's behest, historians' efforts were to be focused on a few selected highlights of German history: principally the Reformation and Peasants' Revolt; the Revolutions of 1848–9; and the rise of the working class. Historical research institutes were established at the German Academy of Sciences in East Berlin and at the Universities of East Berlin, Halle, and Leipzig, and a rational division of labor was agreed, with each institute focusing on a different "strategic area." Ominously, "scientific cadres" – political appointees with a special training in Marxism-Leninism – were also appointed to each institute, to ensure the historians did not deviate from their designated tasks, though it was not until 1964, when a special department to coordinate all historical research was established at the Academy of Sciences, that centralized control was finally secured.[117] The last remaining regular contacts between East and West German historians were broken off at around the same time.

It is difficult to pass judgment on the achievements of GDR history in this period, given the high degree of political control and the absence of a free scholarly culture. Most assessments of GDR historiography do, however, acknowledge that valuable empirical work was carried out in a number of areas, such as "revolutions, social history and everyday life."[118] Writing in the mid-1980s, the American Georg Iggers – by no

---

115 S. Berger, "National paradigm and legitimacy: Uses of academic history writing in the 1960s," in P. Major and J. Osmond, eds., *The Workers' and Peasants' State. Communism and Society in East Germany under Ulbricht 1945–71* (Manchester, 2002), p. 252.
116 A. Dorpalen, *German History in Marxist Perspective*, p. 49.
117 Ibid., p. 51.
118 K. H. Pohl, "Einleitung: Geschichtswissenschaft in der DDR," in K. H. Pohl, ed., *Historiker in der DDR* (Göttingen, 1997), p. 17.

means an apologist for East Germany – referred to the "great contributions of DDR historical studies" in the area of social and economic history, particularly with regard to the impact of industrialization.[119] Works such as the eight-volume *History of the German Labor Movement* or Jürgen Kuczynski's monumental *History of the Condition of Workers under Capitalism* were certainly impressive in scope, and were recognized in the West as the product of serious research.[120] Other GDR ventures to receive praise were *Germany and the First World War*, a three-volume collection which appeared in 1968, and a monumental compendium on the history of German political parties, edited by Dieter Fricke and published on both sides of the wall.[121]

The very narrow parameters for historical research set in 1951 remained largely unchanged until the early 1970s, when the onset of the era of détente, together with changes at the top of the East German state – most notably the replacement of Walter Ulbricht by Erich Honecker in 1971 – ushered in a limited but significant opening up of GDR history. While non-conformists struggled to find a niche in areas such as church history, which enjoyed a partial autonomy, an expanded definition of the GDR's "heritage" (*Erbe*)[122] broadened the range of acceptable topics open to "mainstream" East German historians: Luther, Frederick the Great, Bismarck, and the history of Prussia more generally, all became the subject of research in the late 1970s and particularly the 1980s. This shift from a selective to a more integral approach had a number of causes. The GDR's desire "to back-project their own statehood onto the historical identity of the part of Germany they occupied, so that Luther or Frederick the Great ... appeared retrospectively East German" was a factor,[123] as was Erich Honecker's personal interest in Prussian history,[124] but it must

---

119   G. Iggers, "Foreword," in A. Dorpalen, *German History in Marxist Perspective*, p. 17.
120   Institut für Marxismus-Leninismus beim ZK der SED, *Geschichte der deutschen Arbeiterbewegung*, 8 vols. (East Berlin, 1966); J. Kuczynski, *Die Geschichte der Lage der Arbeiter unter dem Kapitalismus*, 38 vols. (East Berlin, 1961–72).
121   F. Klein et al., *Deutschland im Ersten Weltkrieg*, 3 vols. (East Berlin, 1968–9); D. Fricke, ed., *Lexikon zur Parteiengeschichte 1789–1945: Die bürgerlichen und kleinbürgerlichen Parteien und Verbande in Deutschland* (Leipzig and Cologne, 1983–6).
122   A distinction was made in GDR historiography between East Germany's broad "heritage" and its more narrowly-defined historical "tradition." The latter, based on the history of the working class, was of course valued more highly. See U. Neuhäußer-Wespy, "Erbe und Tradition in der DDR. Zum gewandelten Geschichtsbild der SED," in A. Fischer and G. Heydemann, eds., *Geschichtswissenschaft in der DDR*, vol. 1, pp. 129–54.
123   R. J. Evans, "German history – past, present and future," in G. Martel, ed., *Modern Germany Reconsidered*, pp. 238–9.
124   See J. Petzold, "Politischer Auftrag und wissenschaftliche Verantwortung von Historikern in der DDR," in K. H. Pohl, ed., *Historiker in der DDR*, p. 100.

primarily be seen as a consequence of East Germany's political ambitions. It was hoped that references to the national heritage could help to legitimize the concept of a separate "socialist German nation."[125] History in the GDR had possessed a strong "national(ist) orientation" since the early 1950s,[126] but the more pronounced emphasis on its Prussian heritage in the 1980s now led to the curious situation that Marxist East German historians were often less critical of the *Kaiserreich* than their colleagues in the "bourgeois" West.

GDR research into Prussian history was centered in Berlin, while the Karl-Marx-University in Leipzig continued its established focus on labor and world history. Historians in both institutes, however, appear to have had increasing difficulty in fitting their empirical findings into a Marxist-Leninist framework. For some time, East German history books had been quietly turning orthodox Marxist theory on its head by paying far greater attention to developments in the "superstructure" (such as politics), than to the changing modes of production at the economic "base."[127] The most acclaimed products of East German history in the Honecker era, such as Hartmut Zwahr's work on the formation of the Leipzig working class,[128] or the two-volume biography of Bismarck by Ernst Engelberg (see Chapter 2), appeared impressive precisely because these authors were able to loosen the constraints of the ideological straitjacket more than most. In their very different ways, however, both Zwahr (born 1936) and Engelberg (born 1909) remained exceptions to the rule. When regular meetings between East and West German scholars were tentatively revived in the early 1980s, the inability of GDR historians to back up their theoretical positions with empirical research (or vice-versa) was recognized on both sides. Indeed, as Martin Sabrow notes, this recognition led to anxious discussions in the Central Institute for History at the Academy of Sciences, and an internal acknowledgement that GDR history was falling short of international standards.[129]

After reunification in 1990 there were heated and often bitter exchanges over the extent to which East German historians had been forced

---

125 A. Blänsdorf, "Die deutsche Geschichte in der Sicht der DDR," *Geschichte in Wissenschaft und Unterricht*, 39 (1988), p. 274.
126 S. Berger, "National paradigm and legitimacy," p. 256.
127 See A. Dorpalen, *German History in Marxist Perspective*, p. 27.
128 H. Zwahr, *Zur Konstituierung des Proletariats als Klasse. Strukturuntersuchung über das Leipziger Proletariat während der industriellen Revolution* (Berlin, 1978).
129 M. Sabrow, "Der Streit um die Verständigung. Die deutsch-deutschen Zeithistorikergespräche in den achtziger Jahren," in A. Bauerkämper, M. Sabrow, and B. Stöver, eds., *Doppelte Zeitgeschichte. Deutsch-deutsche Beziehungen 1945–90* (Bonn, 1998), p. 129.

to conform, or had timidly adapted to circumstances through self-censorship. Fierce verbal attacks on former GDR historians – very few of whom were able to retain their university posts – came principally from two quarters: young dissidents, such as Armin Mitter and Stefan Wolle, who had been excluded from jobs in the GDR; and the grandees of the West German historical guild, who were determined not to "turn a blind eye" as their scholarly fathers had done after 1945. One of the latter, Hans-Ulrich Wehler, declared in 1991 that for decades the "overwhelming majority of GDR historians" had "prostituted themselves as the intellectual lackeys of a late Stalinist party," and had therefore lost all credibility.[130] It was a sweeping judgment, but one that was very much in keeping with the Borussian mood of triumphalism which swept through western Germany in the aftermath of reunification.

The End of the *Sonderweg?*

Although the enlarged Federal Republic of the 1990s possessed neither the borders nor the institutions of Bismarck's Empire, there was a palpable sense among German historians, on the moderate left as well as the conservative right, that some kind of normality had been restored; that Germany's "long road to the West" had finally reached its destination.[131] This was apparent not only in the desire to consign GDR historiography to the scrapheap, but also in an upsurge of interest in Germany's first unification and its subsequent history. It had become fashionable in the 1970s and 1980s to think of the Federal Republic as a "post-national" state – to argue that the Germans were better off divided, since that was the way they had lived for the most of their history – but such arguments disappeared with almost unseemly haste in the 1990s. Whether one sees this as part of a deeply disturbing attempt to sanitize and "renationalize" German identity, as Stefan Berger does, or agrees with Heinrich August Winkler that it marked a welcome return to European normality, the consequences for the historiography of the *Kaiserreich* have been largely positive. One by one, the major historians of the post-Fischer era stepped forward to offer their considered reflections on the Empire and its history: Nipperdey, Mommsen, Ullmann, Wehler, and

---

130 Quoted by W. Bramke, "Freiräume und Grenzen eines Historikers im DDR-System," in K. H. Pohl, ed., *Historiker in der DDR*, p. 29.
131 The title chosen by Heinrich A. Winkler for his two-volume history of modern Germany was *Der lange Weg nach Westen*, vol. 1. *1806–1933* and vol. II. *1933–1990* (Munich, 2000).

Winkler among them.[132] Some of these authors sought to address an audience far beyond the scholarly community, and as the public rediscovered its interest in accessible works of history, new publishing opportunities arose for younger and less prominent historians too.[133] Of course, the *Geschichtswelle*, or history boom, of the 1990s was by no means only a German phenomenon. In the English-speaking world, where history was "flavor of the month," readers could choose from a wider selection of titles on Imperial Germany than ever before.[134] Inevitably this substantial corpus of post-reunification scholarship provides much of the raw material for the following chapters, although the reflective nature of many of these studies means they are stronger on past historiographical battles than on current debates.

Since the merits of individual titles cannot be discussed here, a few general observations on the post-1990 historiography must suffice. The most obvious common characteristic has been the move away from the *Sonderweg* paradigm. Blackbourn and Eley's contribution has been previously mentioned, but it is important to recognize that the Britons were not solely responsible for this development. It was already apparent in the early 1980s that many German historians considered this central plank of the "new orthodoxy" to be conceptually flawed,[135] and it was further undermined by the results of the comparative *Bürgertum* research of the

---

132 T. Nipperdey, *Deutsche Geschichte, 1866–1918*, vol. 1. *Arbeitswelt und Bürgergeist* (Munich, 1990); T. Nipperdey, *Deutsche Geschichte, 1866–1918*, vol. 2. *Machtstaat vor der Demokratie* (Munich, 1992); W. J. Mommsen, *Das Ringen um den nationalen Staat: Die Gründung und der innere Ausbau des Deutschen Reiches unter Otto von Bismarck 1850 bis 1890* (Berlin, 1993); W. J. Mommsen, *Bürgerstolz und Weltmachtstreben: Deutschland unter Wilhelm II 1890–1918* (Berlin, 1995); H.-P. Ullmann, *Das deutsche Kaiserreich 1871–1918* (Frankfurt, 1995); H.-U. Wehler, *Deutsche Gesellschaftsgeschichte*, vol. 3. *Von der "Deutschen Doppelrevolution" bis zum Beginn des Ersten Weltkriegs, 1849–1914* (Munich, 1995).
133 See works such as D. Hertz-Eichenrode, *Deutsche Geschichte 1871–1890. Das Kaiserreich in der Ära Bismarck* (Stuttgart, 1992); D. Hertz-Eichenrode, *Deutsche Geschichte 1890–1918. Das Kaiserreich in der wilhelminischen Zeit* (Stuttgart, 1996); W. Loth, *Das Kaiserreich. Obrigkeitsstaat und politische Mobilisierung* (Munich, 1996); V. Ullrich, *Die nervöse Großmacht. Aufstieg und Untergang des deutschen Kaiserreichs* (Frankfurt,1997); E. Frie, *Das Deutsche Kaiserreich* (Darmstadt, 2004).
134 J. Retallack, *Germany in the Age of Kaiser Wilhelm II*; V. Berghahn, *Imperial Germany 1871–1914: Economy, Society, Culture and Politics* (Providence and Oxford, 1994); W. J. Mommsen, *Imperial Germany 1867–1918: Politics, Culture and Society in an Authoritarian State* (London, 1995 – first published in Germany in 1990); D. Blackbourn, *The Fontana History of Germany, 1780–1918. The Long Nineteenth Century* (London, 1997); M. Seligmann and R. McLean, *Germany from Reich to Republic 1871–1918* (Basingstoke, 2000); E. Feuchtwanger, *Imperial Germany 1850–1918* (London, 2001).
135 Institut für Zeitgeschichte, *Deutscher Sonderweg. Mythos oder Realität?*; J. Kocka, "Der 'deutsche Sonderweg' in der Diskussion," *German Studies Review*, 5 (1982), pp. 365–79; H. Grebing, ed., *Der deutsche Sonderweg in Europa 1806–1945. Eine Kritik* (Stuttgart, 1986).

late 1980s. If the majority at that time still favored its retention, it was for political and pedagogic rather than scholarly reasons. The idea that the course of German history had gone badly awry had been central to the establishment and the legitimation of the Federal Republic after 1945, and remained an important part of West Germany's political identity: "If you eliminate the *Sonderweg* thesis then you break the backbone of Germany's political consciousness since 1945," Kurt Sontheimer argued in 1982.[136] The fear that such a step would play into the hands of ultra conservatives, who wish to deny the existence of problematic continuities in Germany's history and seek to relativize their nation's historical guilt, was still a concern for Berger in the mid-1990s.[137] By then, however, it was clear that its supporters had conceded so much ground that the concept (as originally conceived) was no longer viable. Although one should be wary of pronouncing the *Sonderweg* dead and buried – it is unlikely to ever fully disappear – few were still propagating an unrevised version of Germany's "special path" at the century's end.[138]

In a 1998 essay with the revealing title "After the End of the *Sonderweg*," Jürgen Kocka accepted that the "pre-modern" and "feudal" characteristics of the Empire had been exaggerated, and acknowledged that the word *Sonderweg* was itself unhelpful.[139] Those, like Kocka, who nevertheless wished to retain at least some sense of German specificity, were forced to redefine their terms: Karl Dietrich Bracher spoke of Germany's "special consciousness"; Helga Grebing of "distinctive difficulties"; and Wehler – in his ambitious structural history of German society or *Gesellschaftsgeschichte* – replaced the notion of a "special path" with Germany's "special conditions."[140] More recently, Hartwin Spenkuch has argued that although the central argument of the *Sonderweg* thesis does not fit the Empire as a whole, it can still be applied to Prussia.[141] Whether any of these modifications to the *Sonderweg* represents a substantial improvement is open to doubt; more significant is the fact that by making concessions and seeking common ground, the historians of the Bielefeld School helped to defuse an issue that had earlier provoked polemical excesses on both

---

136 K. Sontheimer in *Deutscher Sonderweg. Mythos oder Realität?* p. 32.
137 S. Berger, *The Search for Normality*, pp. 117–18.
138 The left-wing political scientist Reinhard Kühnl was one. See his *Deutschland seit der Französischen Revolution. Untersuchungen zum deutschen Sonderweg* (Heilbronn, 1996).
139 J. Kocka, "Nach dem Ende des Sonderwegs. Zur Tragfähigkeit eines Konzepts," in A. Bauerkämper, M. Sabrow, and B. Stöver, eds., *Doppelte Zeitgeschichte*.
140 K. D. Bracher, in *Deutscher Sonderweg. Mythos oder Realität?* p. 46; H. Grebing, *Der deutsche Sonderweg in Europa*, p. 199; H.-U. Wehler, *Deutsche Gesellschaftsgeschichte*, vol. 3.
141 H. Spenkuch, "Vergleichsweise besonders? Politisches System und Strukturen Preußens als Kern des 'Deutschen Sonderwegs,'" *Geschichte und Gesellschaft*, 29 (2003), pp. 262–93.

sides. The extent of the consensus should not be exaggerated – as a further sharp exchange of views between Wehler and Eley in the mid-1990s made clear[142] – but a real convergence of positions was nevertheless apparent. Not only did the words *Sonderweg* and "feudalization" disappear, but there was a less judgmental tone and a greater sensitivity to the era's numerous ambiguities. There was general agreement that the Empire underwent some dramatic changes during its 47 year existence, not just economically and socially, but politically too. Many of these changes were caused by "factors of a non-intentional nature," rather than the conscious decisions of Germany's elites.[143] On the other hand, it also became widely accepted that although the German experience may only have been an "intensified version of the norm," the unprecedented simultaneity (or "tragic contemporaneity" to use Nipperdey's phrase) of three of the modern world's most fundamental challenges – the national question, the constitutional question, and the social question – did present the Empire with a particularly formidable set of problems.

It was, of course, no coincidence that the fading of the *Sonderweg* paradigm occurred in the 1990s. Its decline was in part a consequence of the "normalization" of German affairs brought about by reunification, but the *Sonderweg* was also a classic example of the kind of "metanarrative" that has met with increasing historiographical skepticism in the post-modern era. This is borne out by the fact that no other master narrative has emerged to take its place. Instead, as Kenneth Ledford notes, "[t]he focus of historical research has ... tended to shift from sweeping interpretation and master narrative to the inner workings of institutions, the social construction and cultural meaning(s) of categories such as religion, class, and gender, and to a tolerance of ambiguity."[144] The danger inherent in this otherwise positive development is clear: a sheer mass of detail, freed from the restraints of an overarching story, could end up obscuring rather than clarifying the bigger picture. If a "diffuse Pointillism" comes to replace the structured synthesis, Wehler recently argued, the historical profession risks failure in its duty to interpret and explain the past.[145] Ledford's quote hints at another significant trend in the historiography too: the range of methodological approaches being adopted by historians of the German Empire is

---

142 See Wehler's review article in *Central European History*, 29 (1996), pp. 541–72, and Eley's reply in *Central European History*, 31 (1998), pp. 197–227.
143 C. Lorenz, "Beyond good and evil?," *Journal of Contemporary History*, 30 (1995), p. 756.
144 K. Ledford, "Comparing comparisons: Disciplines and the *Sonderweg*," *Central European History*, 36 (2003), p. 372.
145 H.-U. Wehler, *Historisches Denken am Ende des 20. Jahrhunderts* (Göttingen, 2001), p. 102.

wider than ever before. Indeed, historians today are more likely to disagree on conceptual and methodological issues than on the character of the Empire itself. While historiographical diversity is to be welcomed, if historians cannot agree on the correct questions to ask they will be in no position to complain when others – journalists, film-makers, or Internet activists – take on that role instead. In this sense at least, Wehler's concern seems justified.

Finally, it has been suggested that the post-1990 historiography is noticeably more positive about the Empire than that of the 1970s and 1980s.[146] Although there is an element of truth in this assertion, it is also misleading. With the exception of the area of foreign policy – where there has undoubtedly been some attempt to revive "pre-Fischer" positions – the 1990s produced no significant study of the Empire which genuinely merits the label "apologist." What is undoubtedly the case, however, is that the "reunification" of 1990 has made the *Kaiserreich* seem less like a historical aberration and more like a precursor to today's Germany. For some this is a cause for concern; for others a source of pride, yet it is nevertheless striking how all recent historians have sought to provide a balanced picture of this fascinating era, in which one can find examples of light and shadow in remarkably equal measure.

---

146 See S. Berger, *The Search for Normality*, p. 112.

2
Great Men? Otto von Bismarck and Kaiser Wilhelm II

In 1983 Richard Evans boldly asserted that "the biographical approach in its present form has reached the limits of its usefulness."[1] Since then, however, historical biography appears to have undergone a spectacular renaissance, with works on modern German history, such as Ian Kershaw's *Hitler* or Ulrich Herbert's *Best*,[2] leading the way. Popular with the reading public, biographies are frequently to be found at the top of both the history sales charts and the critics' picks of the year, while television producers seem more than ever in thrall to Ralph Waldo Emerson's dictum that "there is properly no history, only biography." The two principal figures in the history of the German Empire, Otto von Bismarck and Kaiser Wilhelm II, have both been the focus of increased scholarly attention in recent years, while many of the era's leading politicians, generals, and industrialists have found their biographers too. With this in mind, it might appear as if Evans's confident prognosis was spectacularly wrong, once again proving that historians should stick to the past rather than attempting to predict the future. In fact, his reference to biography "in its present form" was a significant caveat, because Kershaw and Herbert can be said to have created a genuinely new kind of biography, approaching their respective subjects with the skeptical eye of the structuralist historian, and instinctively looking "to downplay

---

1 R. J. Evans, "From Hitler to Bismarck," in *Rethinking German History*, p. 89.
2 I. Kershaw, *Hitler*, 2 vols. (London, 1998–2000); U. Herbert, *Best. Biographische Studien über Radikalismus, Weltanschauung und Vernunft 1903–1989* (Bonn, 1996).

rather than to exaggerate" the part played by the individual in complex historical processes.[3] Of course, biographers have always attempted to provide historical context, but Kershaw and Herbert do more than this, integrating the story of a single life into a structural history of German society more successfully than many would have thought possible. Since such works remain the exception rather than the rule, however, they do not necessarily invalidate the general thrust of Evans's argument. In other words, just because Kershaw's *Hitler* might provide fresh insights into the nature of National Socialism, one cannot assume that each new biography of Bismarck will have a similar effect for the German Empire. Evans's skepticism, therefore, about "the adequacy of an approach which is based on the assumption that a nation's fate is determined by a single individual, or even a small group of individuals," remains valid, whatever television or Hollywood might think.[4]

Certainly, the sort of history that personalizes complex developments, or reduces causality to the actions and intentions of a small ensemble of historical actors is viewed with suspicion by most of today's historians. Few would now agree with the Scottish historian Thomas Carlyle (1795–1881) that "history, the history of what man has accomplished in this world, is at bottom the History of the Great Men who have worked here."[5] Not only is "the whole notion of historical greatness ... in the last resort futile,"[6] but an excessive concentration on individual intentions inevitably obscures the complex web of pre-conditions underpinning all historical actions. As Karl Marx recognized some 150 years ago, "Men make their own history, but they do not make it just as they please; they do not make it under circumstances chosen by themselves, but under circumstances directly encountered, given and transmitted from the past."[7] Even so, the "great man" school of history has undoubtedly left its mark on the study of the German Empire, and its legacies are hard to avoid. Carlyle (himself a well-known Germanophile and biographer of Frederick the Great) had many admirers on the Continent, but historians like Treitschke, Lenz, or Marcks scarcely needed any encouragement to focus on "heroes, hero-worship, and the heroic in history." Indeed, it was the centrality of biography to the German historist tradition which made it so suspect to historians of the "new orthodoxy," for whom few charges were more damning than that of "personalism."

---

3 I. Kershaw, *Hitler*, vol.1, *1889–1936 Hubris*, p. xii.
4 R. J. Evans, "From Hitler to Bismarck," pp. 55–6.
5 T. Carlyle, *On Heroes, Hero-worship and the Heroic in History* (London, 1872).
6 I. Kershaw, *Hitler*, vol.1, p. xiv.
7 K. Marx, *The Eighteenth Brumaire of Louis Bonaparte* (Moscow, 1977), p. 10.

One only has to read a few pages of one the pre-1945 hagiographies of Bismarck – which, as David Blackbourn observes, performed much the same function as Bismarck towers and monuments[8] – to understand why historical biography is still regarded as an inherently conservative or apologist genre by many in the German historical guild today. Although the very earliest literature on the *Reichsgründer* (founder of the Empire) was dominated by critical essays from political opponents,[9] the first biographies – in Germany at least – were written by dedicated disciples. Both Lenz and Marcks contributed biographical studies that fell into this category,[10] but the apogee of Bismarck panegyric was probably Arnold Oskar Meyer's ultra-nationalist *Bismarck. The Man and the Statesman*,[11] which was completed in the summer of 1943 and was described by its author as "my contribution to national service during the war."[12] Meyer (1872–1944), did not live to see his book in print, but in an epilogue Wilhelm Schüssler suggested that his work would survive as a "monument to the way in which a German, an austere northerner, a Lutheran, a hot-blooded patriot and a researcher passed judgment."[13] Thankfully it did not, despite a West German reprint in 1949.

For historians wary of the "great man" tradition, the founding of the German Empire undoubtedly presents real problems. Back in 1978 the American Gordon Craig (1913–2005) opened his major study of *Germany 1866–1945* with a question: "Is it a mistake to begin with Bismarck?"[14] Eighteen years later Wilfried Loth (born 1948) had no such concerns: "Every history of the Empire must begin with Bismarck," he wrote.[15] Thomas Nipperdey was even more emphatic. Volume 2 of his *German History 1866–1918* opens with a Biblical fanfare: "In the Beginning there was Bismarck."[16] Conscious of the reaction this line was likely to provoke,

---

8   D. Blackbourn, "Bismarck: the sorcerer's apprentice," in *Populists and Patricians*, p. 33.
9   Such as the liberal politician Ludwig Bamberger's *Monsieur de Bismarck* (Paris, 1868).
10 M. Lenz, *Geschichte Bismarcks* (Leipzig, 1902); E. Marcks, *Bismarck* (Stuttgart and Berlin, 1909). The latter, which stops in 1848, was intended to be volume 1 of the authorized Bismarck biography but Marcks was unable to finish the job. His *Otto von Bismarck. Ein Lebensbild* (Stuttgart and Berlin, 1915) is a succinct treatment of Bismarck's career as a whole.
11 A. O. Meyer, *Bismarck. Der Mensch und der Staatsmann* (Stuttgart, 1949, first published 1944).
12 Quoted in A. J. P. Taylor, *Bismarck. The Man and the Statesman* (Harmondsworth, 1995, first published 1955), p. 272.
13 Quoted in H. Hallmann, ed., *Revision des Bismarckbildes. Die Diskussion der deutschen Fachhistoriker 1945–55* (Darmstadt, 1972), p. XVI.
14 G. Craig, *Germany 1866–1945* (Oxford, 1978), p. 1.
15 W. Loth, *Das Kaiserreich. Obrigkeitsstaat und politische Mobilisierung*, p. 23.
16 T. Nipperdey, *Deutsche Geschichte 1866–1918*, vol. 2, *Machtstaat vor der Demokratie*, p. 11.

Nipperdey went to unusual lengths to justify his choice of words.[17] The *Reichsgründung*, he argued, "had many causes, and stands in a mesh of structural conditions and anonymous processes ... but it cannot be disputed: Bismarck determined this founding of the German Reich; it was he who recognized, and also steered, the currents of the age which bore him on. Without him, everything would have been different."[18] For all the unfashionability of the "great man" approach, each of the major studies of the German Empire to be published since 1990 can be said to accept Bismarck's central role in the narrative. The index to Volker Ullrich's popular synthesis *The Nervous Great Power* is indicative: "Bismarck, Otto Fürst von, 20 ff., 24, 26–40, 45–123," and so on[19] Even the arch-structuralist Wehler gives Bismarck pride of place in his most recent account of the Empire, referring to him as "the most successful professional politician in nineteenth-century Europe," "a political power *sui generis*," and "one of the great masters of the German language in the nineteenth century."[20] Indeed, as one reviewer observed, Bismarck "hovers like a giant" over Wehler's 1,500 pages, with a more central role than in the equivalent volume of Nipperdey's history.[21]

Wehler, it should be stressed, never resorts to the kind of emotive language employed by Klaus Hildebrand (born 1941), whose description of Bismarck's achievement recalls star-struck eulogies to the "blacksmith of German unity" from a century ago: "Finally it was Bismarck, who in a specific situation let the glowing fire burst into flames, and presented the Germans with the longed-for warmth of a nation-state, without starting a destructive conflagration and without harming them through direct exposure to the heat of the necessary battles."[22] The East German Marxist Ernst Engelberg, although more balanced in his overall judgment of Bismarck's career, was no less fulsome when praising his intellectual gifts: "No one had more courage than him when it came to rethinking or thinking anew ... no one came close to the precision of his powers of observation and creative imagination."[23] Bismarck's latest British biographers are also convinced of his pivotal role in the decade of unification.

---

17 Not only did this phrase suggest an unmistakably "personalist" approach, it also repeated a stylistic device Nipperdey had used before: his *Deutsche Geschichte 1800–1866. Bürgerwelt und starker Staat* (Munich, 1983) starts: "In the Beginning there was Napoleon."
18 T. Nipperdey, *Deutsche Geschichte 1866–1918*, vol. 2, p. 11.
19 V. Ullrich, *Die nervöse Großmacht 1871–1918*, p. 706.
20 H.-U. Wehler, *Deutsche Gesellschaftsgeschichte*, vol. 3, pp. 264, 334, and 266 respectively.
21 J. Breuilly, "Auf dem Weg zur deutschen Gesellschaft? Der dritte Band von Wehlers 'Gesellschaftsgeschichte,'" *Geschichte und Gesellschaft*, 24 (1998), p. 154.
22 K. Hildebrand, *Das vergangene Reich*, p. 853.
23 E. Engelberg, *Bismarck. Urpreuße und Reichsgründer* (Berlin, 1985), p. 451.

Edgar Feuchtwanger speaks of his "almost superhuman dexterity" and "dazzling virtuosity" in converting former opponents into devoted followers, while Katharine Lerman (born 1954) suggests "it is impossible to argue that things would have turned out much the same if Bismarck had not been at the helm or that his personality did not make a significant difference."[24] Despite all this, however, the degree to which an individual can really be considered the "founder" of an Empire remains a moot point, and it provides an appropriate starting point for our consideration of the *Kaiserreich*'s recent historiography. The chapter will also examine two other important aspects of the Bismarckian era before switching its attention to the man perceived as the Iron Chancellor's antipode, Kaiser Wilhelm II.

To What Extent Was Bismarck the "Founder" of the German Empire?

Nipperdey notwithstanding, the history of the first German nation-state does not begin with Bismarck, and its eventual establishment was not an achievement of the Prussian minister-president alone. As Geoff Eley rightly stresses:

> [t]he creation of a united Germany was placed on the political agenda by organized radical and liberal agitation between the 1830s and 1860s. The process of proposing the category of the German nation and of organizing public life into a new political community of citizens owed little to the initiative of the Prussian government. In fact, the real work of constituting the German nation had to be conducted in *opposition* to the existing sovereign authorities by civil initiative and voluntary association.[25]

When Bismarck was appointed minister-president of Prussia in 1862, at a time of liberal revival and constitutional crisis, he undoubtedly responded to the challenge in an innovative way, effectively placing himself at the head of what he referred to as "the revolutionary party" (becoming, in A. J. P. Taylor's memorable phrase "half country-squire, half-revolutionary").[26] Yet although the man dubbed the "white revolutionary" is sometimes

---

24 E. Feuchtwanger, *Imperial Germany 1850–1918*, p. 34; E. Feuchtwanger, *Bismarck* (London and New York, 2002), p. 258; K. A. Lerman, *Bismarck* (London, 2004), p. x.
25 G. Eley, "Bismarckian Germany," in G. Martel, ed., *Modern Germany Reconsidered*, pp. 19–20.
26 A .J. P. Taylor, *Bismarck. The Man and the Statesman*, p. 176.

compared to the sorcerer's apprentice, who conjured up spirits he could not control, Bismarck's agenda had more prosaic origins than the spirit world.[27] It was Germany's much-maligned liberals who provided Bismarck with most of his cues, not least by correctly locating their own failure in 1848 in an excess of idealism (*Idealpolitik*) and a lack of power-political realism (*Realpolitik*). Indeed, the concept of *Realpolitik* itself, which came to be seen as the very essence of cynical Bismarckian politics, was in fact a term coined by a disenchanted liberal journalist, August Ludwig von Rochau in 1853.[28] One could, therefore, argue, as Michael Stürmer does, that Bismarck only succeeded because he "produced the policies that liberal Germany desired."[29] Certainly, "liberal Germany" made a distinctive contribution to the founding of the German Empire, and the once common argument that 1866-7 represented some kind of betrayal of liberal principles – the selling out of freedom for the sake of national unity – is seldom seen nowadays. As Michael Hughes makes clear, "to the majority of German Liberals the second was an essential precondition of the first."[30]

No one would dispute that as Prussian minister-president in the 1860s Bismarck had a crucial influence on the course of events, but there are important ways in which the historian can challenge or qualify the "great man" mythology. For a start, Bismarck himself was acutely aware of the limits to which men – great or otherwise – can shape history. One of his favorite Latin proverbs was "one cannot make a wave, only ride it,"[31] and many of his most famous quotes point to the insignificance or powerlessness of the individual: "clinging to history's coat tails," "steering the tides of time," "riding the forces of history," and so on. Second, one must remember the highly vulnerable nature of Bismarck's position: as a servant of the crown, he could have been removed from office at any moment. He had no party or institutional powerbase to back him up, and (despite the impression conveyed by Wehler's *The German Empire*) even at the height of his powers he was never a dictator with complete freedom of action. That he survived in power for so long was a testament

---

27 The description of Bismarck as a "white revolutionary" was originally used by the liberal politician Ludwig Bamberger in 1868, before the US diplomat and politician Henry Kissinger adopted it as the title of a 1968 essay. It is nowadays particularly associated with the historian Lothar Gall, who made it the central theme of his acclaimed biography (first published in Germany in 1980): *Bismarck. The White Revolutionary*, 2 vols. (London, 1986).
28 A. L. von Rochau, *Grundsätze der Realpolitik, angewendet auf die staatlichen Zustände Deutschlands* (1853). Ironically von Rochau was one of Bismarck's most vocal critics at the time.
29 Quoted by G. Eley, "Bismarckian Germany," p. 20.
30 M. Hughes, *Nationalism and Society. Germany 1800-1945* (London, 1988), p. 132.
31 E. Feuchtwanger, *Bismarck*, p. 4.

to his political skill, his careful planning for different contingencies, but above all his luck. A man with the temperament of a gambler, Bismarck made the most of his decade-long winning streak. Indeed, it could be said that he lived off it for the rest of his life.

Third, the degree to which he was able to create the external crises and opportunities faced by Prussia in the decade before the *Reichsgründung* should not be exaggerated. Few now believe he possessed any kind of timetable or master-plan for unification. This view was advanced by much of the pre-1945 literature, but it was never based on firm evidence, relying heavily on prophetic remarks Bismarck was supposed to have made in 1862 to Disraeli, the British Leader of the Opposition, at a dinner-party in London.[32] Even if the "master-plan" thesis is dismissed, there is still a tendency within the historiography to portray Bismarck as a sovereign master of events, dictating both their tempo and direction. Ultimately this is no more convincing than the willfully contrary view of A. J. P. Taylor (1906–90) who saw him purely as an opportunist, making policy on a day-to-day basis. In reality, Bismarck's statesmanship is perhaps best characterized by what Otto Pflanze termed the "strategy of alternatives":[33] the keeping open of a variety of courses, which Gall suggests "became his tactical byword and one he employed with ever-increasing skill."[34] Wily strategist though he was, however, he did not possess demonic powers and could not dictate the actions of other states. To take one obvious example, for all his cynicism and trickery, he could not force France to declare war on Prussia in 1870.[35]

Fourth, it should not be forgotten that the "Little German" Empire of 1871 was only one of several potential outcomes considered by Bismarck in the 1860s. Contrary to the view put forward in his predictably self-justifying memoirs and accepted uncritically by his first biographers, Bismarck did not follow a consistent path towards this single goal.[36]

---

32 Bismarck allegedly suggested that once in charge he would reform the army, find a pretext for war with Austria, destroy the German Confederation and unite Germany under Prussian leadership. However since the story only turned up many years later, in the memoirs of a Saxon diplomat, it must be regarded with skepticism, especially as there are no corroborating accounts.
33 See O. Pflanze, *Bismarck and the Development of Germany*, vol. 1, *The Period of Unification, 1815–1871* (Princeton, 1963).
34 L. Gall, Bismarck. *The White Revolutionary*, vol. 1, p. 208.
35 For the latest research on this episode see D. Wetzel, *A Duel of Giants. Bismarck, Napoleon III, and the Origins of the Franco-Prussian War* (Madison, 2001); and J. Wawro, *The Franco-Prussian War: The German Conquest of France in 1870–1871* (Cambridge, 2003).
36 Originally published as O. von Bismarck, *Erinnerungen und Gedanke* (1898), then republished in an edition by Horst Kohl as *Otto von Bismarck. Gedanken und Erinnerungen*, 2 vols. (Stuttgart, 1898), Bismarck's memoirs became one of the greatest publishing successes of the

Michael Hughes (1942–93) took this argument further than most: "It was never Bismarck's wish or intention to unify Germany in the way he did in 1871," he contended, "[h]e was pushed into it by forces beyond his control inside and outside Germany."[37] Before 1866 Bismarck appears to have given serious thought to a peaceful division of the German states into separate Prussian and Austrian spheres of influence, probably along the line of the River Main (even if such a "dualist" solution is unlikely to have satisfied him for very long). Similarly, after 1866, he did not consider a union between the North German Confederation and the southern German states as either imminent or necessarily desirable. Certainly, there was no inevitability about the extension of German unity south of the Main, a step he famously referred to in 1869 as "a fruit not ripe for plucking."[38]

Finally, and perhaps most importantly, one must also acknowledge that things could have turned out very differently. Bismarck's fame and reputation were built on the back of Prussia's military victories against Denmark (1864), Austria and the south German states (1866), and France (1870–1).[39] Clear-cut though these triumphs might appear in retrospect, they were precarious undertakings which could easily have cost Bismarck his job, if not his life. "However straightforward Bismarck's unification policy might have appeared to later nationalist historians," Wehler observes, "at [the Battle of] Königgrätz it stood on a knife's edge."[40] Prussia's eventual victory over the forces of Austria and Saxony was only secured because of developments for which Bismarck was not responsible and did not fully understand: the expansion of the railway network; new weapons technology; higher levels of literacy; and improved telegraphic communications. The long-term shift in Prussia's favor brought about by these changes "did not make Prussian victory inevitable," John Breuilly (born 1946) points out, "it merely made it probable whereas just five years earlier it would have been improbable."[41]

---

nineteenth century, selling over 300,000 copies in the first few days of December 1898 alone. The first English edition followed shortly afterwards: *Bismarck, the Man and the Statesman, Being the Reflections and Reminiscences of Otto Prince von Bismarck*, 2 vols. (London, 1899).

37 M. Hughes, *Nationalism and Society*, p. 102.

38 In a letter to Werther, 26 February 1869, quoted in K. A. Lerman, *Bismarck*, p. 144 and elsewhere.

39 It was only in hindsight, of course, that these collectively became known as the "Wars of German Unification." See W. Carr, *The Origins of the Wars of German Unification* (London, 1991).

40 H.-U. Wehler, *Deutsche Gesellschaftsgeschichte*, vol. 3, p. 295.

41 J. Breuilly, *The Formation of the First German Nation-State, 1800–1871* (Basingstoke, 1996), p. 82.

Historians wary of the problematic nature of Bismarck-based narratives can adopt a number of alternative explanatory strategies. One is to emphasize the economic dimension to the *Reichsgründung*: to argue that Germany was united less by "blood and iron" than by "coal and iron" in John Maynard Keynes' famous phrase, or that "nationalism is generated among a people by the growing awareness of its economic backwardness and by the desire for a modern economy," as Robert Berdahl argued.[42] Since Prussia (or at least some of it) was at the forefront of German economic development, this approach is generally no less Prussocentric than Bismarck-based accounts. From the middle of the century onwards there was undoubtedly growing pressure from entrepreneurs, chambers of commerce, and organizations like the Congress of German Economists for more integration between the German states. "Up to 1848 German nationalism had been mainly an ideological force," Feuchtwanger notes, "it now paired with the economic self-interest of Germany's most dynamic class to demand a greater unity."[43] In general, however, Feuchtwanger plays down the importance of economics in the story of German unification. Those who take it more seriously usually owe allegiance to the Marxist tradition – Marx saw political unification as an inexorable consequence of the dynamics of capitalist expansion[44] – or belong to the German school of historical social science. The most important work in the latter category was Helmut Böhme's *Germany's Path to Great Power Status* (1966), which focused on the economic dimension of the struggle for supremacy between Austria and Prussia, and greatly downplayed Bismarck's role. Indeed, Böhme argued explicitly that the founding of the German Empire "can no longer be written as part of Otto von Bismarck's biography."[45]

In Böhme's view, Austria's military defeat at Königgrätz was ultimately less significant than its renewed failure a year earlier to join the German *Zollverein*; the key institution in economic narratives of German unification. This Prussian-dominated customs union, founded in 1834, abolished internal tariff barriers between member states and established trade treaties with external territories (including Austria). It was built up in stages, but by the early 1850s its borders already foreshadowed those of the later German Empire.[46] It increased inter-dependence among

---

42 R. Berdahl, "New thoughts on German nationalism," *American Historical Review*, 77 (1972), p. 72.
43 E. Feuchtwanger, *Imperial Germany 1850–1918*, p. 6.
44 A. Dorpalen, *German History in Marxist Perspective*, pp. 218–19.
45 H. Böhme, ed., *Die Reichsgründung* (Munich, 1967), p. 8.
46 The founder members were Prussia, Bavaria, Saxony, and Württemberg, together with a number of smaller states. Baden and Nassau joined in 1835, followed by Frankfurt (1836),

its members, and was used by Prussia to exert political pressure on the smaller German states, but its members fought on opposite sides in 1866 and the extent to which it made some kind of political unification more likely is still disputed by historians.[47] Although there are those who consider it a vital step towards a German nation-state, others dismiss its contribution as minimal, citing Ernst Renan's famous quip "a custom's union is not a fatherland."[48] Most take a middle position, often drawing a parallel with the contemporary European integration process to show that the path from economic union to political union is neither straight nor smooth. Heinrich August Winkler, for instance, suggests "in the area of trade policy the German Customs Union anticipated the Little German solution, without making it inevitable,"[49] and Hans-Peter Ullmann agrees: "The most one can say is that economic processes fostered the founding of the Empire, and made other possible solutions to the national question, such as the Greater Germany with Austria, less probable."[50]

Another of the principal ways in which historians can subvert the "great man" narrative is to emphasize the role of the national movement in German unification. The nineteenth century is, of course, often characterized as the "age of nationalism," and by the 1860s it was sufficiently strong in the German states "to make the pursuit of any overtly anti-national policy difficult, if not impossible."[51] There was not, however, anything resembling a nationalist mass movement. It remained a predominantly Protestant, urban, male and middle-class cause, and its principal organization, the National Association (1859) never had more than 25,000 members.[52] Beyond this there were a host of ostensibly non-political organizations which formed a broader popular basis for the national movement – gymnastics clubs, choral societies, riflemen's clubs,

---

Brunswick (1841), Hanover (1851), Oldenburg (1852), Schleswig-Holstein (1866), Mecklenburg and Lübeck (1868), Alsace-Lorraine (1871). The hanseatic ports of Hamburg and Bremen did not join until 1888.

47 For a succinct discussion of the historiography of the *Zollverein* see H. Kiesewetter, "Economic preconditions for Germany's nation-building in the nineteenth century," in H. Schulze, ed., *Nation-Building in Central Europe* (Leamington Spa, 1987), pp. 81–105.

48 See R. Dumke, "Der deutsche Zollverein als Modell ökonomischer Integration," in H. Berding, ed., *Wirtschaftliche und politische Integration in Europa im 19. und 20. Jahrhundert* (Göttingen, 1984), pp. 72–101.

49 H. A. Winkler, *Der lange Weg nach Westen*, vol. 1, p. 215.

50 H.-P. Ullmann, *Das Deutsche Kaiserreich 1871–1918*, p. 15.

51 J. Breuilly, *Austria, Prussia and Germany, 1806–1871* (Harlow, 2002), p. 8.

52 In fact, the National Association did not aspire to be a mass movement and charged a high membership subscription which restricted working-class membership. See S. Na'aman, *Der deutsche Nationalverein. Die politische Konstituierung des deutschen Bürgertums 1859–1867* (Düsseldorf, 1987).

and the like – and national feelings were also expressed at cultural festivals and anniversary celebrations, such as those commemorating the "national poet" Friedrich Schiller in 1859.[53] Yet much of this sentiment was vague and, just as it had been in the revolutions of 1848–9, remained divided between supporters of the Little German and Greater German solutions. It is hardly surprising, therefore, that most of today's historians play down the role of nationalism in the founding of the Empire. They argue that it was more a consequence than a cause of unification, pointing to the development of both an official nationalism from above, and more aggressive forms of grassroots nationalism from below, as products of the imperial era itself.[54]

However, to see the *Reichsgründung* solely as a feat of Prussian arms would be to overlook two important "national" aspects of the 1871 settlement. While it is correct to argue that the "creation of the Second Reich is first of all a political phenomenon ... not the consequence of inescapable geographical or economic facts,"[55] it is also the case that Bismarck's "revolution from above" was only possible because of the cultural, economic, and political formation of the nation in the years before 1871. Of course, Bismarck was no nationalist,[56] and his primary aim was to extend Prussian power, but his decisions "were informed by a sense of the importance of nationality in modern German politics."[57] Second, and more specifically, it is important to recognize the extent to which the *Reichsgründung* was dependent on Bismarck's informal alliance with Little German national liberalism, facilitated by the famous Indemnity Bill of September 1866. This tactical agreement with his former enemies has been described as an act of "political genius" and Bismarck's "real political feat."[58] Nowhere was the liberal contribution to unification more apparent than in the raft of legislation enacted in the North German Confederation between 1867 and 1870. As Eley puts it, "Germany was re-made during the 1860s and 1870s, both territorially-constitutionally and socially-culturally, and it was re-made along the lines German liberals had broadly envisaged."[59] Certainly, the introduction of more than 80

---

53 See D. Düding, "The nineteenth-century German nationalist movement as a movement of societies," in H. Schulze, ed., *Nation-Building in Central Europe*, pp. 19–49.
54 See M. Hughes, *Nationalism and Society*, p. 101. Hughes argues that "nationalism played a marginal role" in the process of founding the Reich.
55 E. Feuchtwanger, *Imperial Germany 1850–1918*, p. xvi.
56 For a discussion of this issue see O. Pflanze, "Bismarck and German nationalism," *American Historical Review*, (1955), pp. 548–66. After 1871, and particularly after 1890, Bismarck tried to style himself as a German nationalist, but his efforts were hardly convincing.
57 J. Breuilly, *The Formation of the First German Nation-State*, p. 113.
58 Ibid., p. 83; H.-U. Wehler, *Deutsche Gesellschaftsgeschichte*, vol. 3, p. 282.
59 G. Eley, "Bismarckian Germany," p. 26.

new laws had a genuinely liberalizing and mobilizing effect, ushering a period of rapid modernization in northern Germany which did not go unnoticed in the south. Without this compromise with national liberalism, which was particularly important in generating popular enthusiasm in the build-up to war with France, Bismarck's prospects would have been bleak. An act of "naked Prussian self-interest would only have experienced a short-lived triumph," Wehler suggests.[60] It also meant that after 1871 Bismarck "was as much the prisoner of the liberals as they were the followers he manipulated."[61] The establishment of the first German nation-state thus had "two faces" (Dieter Langewiesche), even if it is invariably just a single mustachioed countenance which stares out from the cover of books on the Empire.

A further way in which historians seek to qualify and contextualize the "great man" narrative is to internationalize the events of 1866–71. The so-called "German question" has always been an international issue, or to put it another way, the "balance of power in Germany has historically been an integral part of the balance of power in Europe."[62] This was apparent in 1815, 1848, 1945, and again in 1989–90. Things were no different in 1866–71, when it could be argued that the founding of the Empire only became possible because of a unique window of opportunity in European affairs. It would probably not have happened without a fortunate combination of factors: the unification of Italy, which acted as a model for many liberal nationalists in the German states; the new balance of power created by Russia's defeat in the Crimean War, which led to a temporary turning-away from Europe and a break with its former ally Austria; Britain's preoccupation with domestic and imperial issues, which meant it regarded change in Central Europe with "sympathetic disinterest"; and finally, France's increasingly desperate search for foreign policy successes under its weakening Emperor Napoleon III. One recent historian to place great emphasis on this international context is Volker Ullrich:

> Generations of historians have attributed the completion of German unity to the towering political genius of Bismarck. In fact, it was decisively facilitated by an unusual international set of circumstances: that "trough in the waves of great-power politics" (Ludwig Dehio) following the Crimean War of 1854–6, which largely removed great-power pressure from Central Europe.[63]

---

60 H.-U. Wehler, *Deutsche Gesellschaftsgeschichte*, vol. 3, p. 282.
61 E. Feuchtwanger, *Imperial Germany 1850–1918*, p. xviii.
62 J. Breuilly, *The Formation of the First German Nation-State*, p. 106. See also W. E. Mosse, *The European Powers and the German Question, 1848–1871* (Cambridge, 1958).
63 V. Ullrich, *Die nervöse Großmacht*, p. 26.

So where does this leave Bismarck's contribution to the founding of the German Empire? One of his most respected biographers, the American Otto Pflanze, has no doubts: "Bismarck did succeed in 'making history.' His own career shows that he was overly pessimistic about the impact of individual personality upon the historical process."[64] Of course, having devoted half a lifetime to writing a three-volume biography of the great man, Pflanze was unlikely to conclude otherwise, but historians more skeptical of the role of individuals in history still acknowledge Bismarck's ability to "utilize decisively the favorable conditions of the moment" (Imanuel Geiss).[65] Wehler, for instance, argues that "he came much more fully to terms with the industrial revolution than has been realised by those historians who would like to brand him as an old-fashioned cabinet politician,"[66] and Breuilly highlights another characteristic feature of nineteenth-century Europe which Bismarck seemed instinctively to understand: that "[u]nder modern political conditions there are powerful pressures pushing states towards some kind of identification with their subjects. This is linked to the greater participation of people in affairs of government; with the transformation of subjects into citizens."[67] Bismarck saw, in other words, that in an age of territoriality and nation-state formation, only Prussia could be the basis of a "single sovereign and territorial state in which German nationality dominated."[68]

This is not to argue that the Little German solution was the only show in town. It remains a common failing of many widely-read accounts of German history that insufficient attention is paid to other potential outcomes.[69] Even if one discounts as implausible the kind of 1848-style liberal unification from below championed by Erich Eyck in his critical Bismarck biography of the 1940s,[70] one can still identify four possible alternatives to the "greater Prussia" which emerged from the events of 1866–71: a reformed German Confederation; a dualist division of the German states into separate Austrian and Prussian spheres of influence; a so-called *Trias* solution, with the southern German states forming a third bloc between the two major powers (as advocated by the Saxon statesman Friedrich Ferdinand von Beust); or some kind of decentralized Central

---

64 O. Pflanze, "Bismarck's Realpolitik," in J. J. Sheehan, ed., *Imperial Germany*, p. 172.
65 Quoted in S. Berger, *The Search for Normality*, p. 116.
66 H.-U. Wehler, "Bismarck's imperialism, 1862–1890," in J. J. Sheehan, ed., *Imperial Germany*, p. 190.
67 J. Breuilly, *The Formation of the First German Nation-State*, p. 106.
68 Ibid., p. 103.
69 One work to stress the openness of the German question is J. J. Sheehan's *German History 1770–1866* (Oxford, 1989).
70 E. Eyck, *Bismarck and the German Empire* (London, 1950).

European federation incorporating the non-German Habsburg territories as well. As we have seen, Borussian historians and their Neo-Rankean successors considered the Prussian route to be pre-ordained by history, and most subsequent historians have tended to agree. As Breuilly observes, it remains much easier to criticize the Borussian view than to replace it.[71] The leading German historian of the 1950s and 1960s, Gerhard Ritter, dismissed as "wishful thinking" the arguments of those who claimed that Prussian and Austria could have stayed as they were, or formed a loose Central European federation. Such thinking, articulated by Bismarck's contemporary antagonist Constantin Frantz (1817–91),[72] and subsequently by Catholic historians such as the liberal Franz Schnabel and the conservative Heinrich von Srbik (1878–1951),[73] "assumes that there would have been some kind of possibility for the Germans to remain artificially detached from the great movement of nationalism in the nineteenth century," Ritter contended.[74] In his view the die had already been cast in the first half of the century, long before Bismarck took up the reins. Nevertheless, the arguments of Schnabel and von Srbik enjoyed something of a renaissance after 1945. With the creation of separate West and East German states, Bismarck's Empire began to appear as an exceptional interlude in an otherwise long history of division; and in the light of two murderous world wars the modest virtues of the Holy Roman Empire or the German Confederation seemed worthy of rediscovery. As Stefan Berger puts it: "[t]he delegitimation of the Bismarckian nation-state went hand-in-hand with the search for alternatives. Some historians began to argue that the Holy Roman Empire or the German Federation had been more appropriate than a unified nation-state which was almost certain to upset the balance of power in Europe over and over again."[75]

With Germany once again reunited, the most recent German-language studies of the Empire's foundation have largely lost sight of such concerns. The events of 1989–90 seemed to confirm the validity of the Little German solution; to show that even after 40 years of division, most Germans still considered a single nation-state their natural home. Thus while criticisms may be leveled at the means of achieving the *Reichsgründung* ("blood and

---

71 J. Breuilly, *The Formation of the First German Nation-State*, p. 6.
72 Frantz put forward the idea in his *Untersuchungen über das Europäische Gleichgewicht* (1859) of a voluntary central European union – consisting of the German states, Holland, Sweden, and Denmark, and guaranteed by British support – as a way of reining in the political ambitions of France and Russia.
73 See H. von Srbik, "Die Bismarck-Kontroverse," in H. Hallmann, ed., *Revision des Bismarckbildes*, p. 201.
74 G. Ritter, "Geschichte als Bildungsmacht" (1946), in ibid, p. 8.
75 S. Berger, *The Search for Normality*, p. 61.

iron") or at the shortcomings of the imperial constitution, the historical validity of the Little German solution – the rise of Prussia and the fall of Austria – is often taken for granted. In fact it has been largely left to English-language historians to remind readers that this was not necessarily the case; and to point out that from an Austrian (or, indeed, Bavarian Catholic) perspective, the so-called "unification" of 1871 appeared more like a partition or division.[76]

Was There a "Second Founding of the Empire" in the Late 1870s?

For the best part of a decade those liberals who had chosen to co-operate with Bismarck had little reason to rue their decision. From the establishment of the North German Confederation in 1867 to the end of the so-called "Delbrück era" in 1876, they were directly involved in shaping Germany's new political arrangements. Liberal majorities in the imperial Reichstag, often comprising left liberal Progressives as well as National Liberals and Free Conservatives, passed a series of classical state-building measures (including new commercial and criminal legal codes, a high court, a unified currency, and a central bank) and extended earlier reforms introduced in the North German Confederation to the south German states. Much of this was co-ordinated by Rudolf Delbrück, the head of the Reich Chancellor's office, who was effectively Bismarck's deputy in the early years of the Empire. Although the liberals' still had a major goal to achieve – the introduction of full parliamentary government with ministerial responsibility – the new political structures (see Chapter 3) seemed to provide a workable basis for future reform. From their perspective, it was a case of the glass being half-full rather than half-empty. In the second half of the 1870s, however, the outlook for liberalism was to grow darker, as the Empire underwent what George Windell described as "a constitutional crisis more fateful if less dramatic than the famous Prussian constitutional conflict of the 1860s."[77] Indeed some historians argue that this crisis led to a fundamental re-founding of the Reich in a more conservative guise. They believe, in other words, that the "external" foundation of the Empire at Versailles in 1871 was followed by a second "internal" foundation less than a decade later.

---

76 See M. Hughes, *Nationalism and Society*, ch. 5.
77 G. Windell, "The Bismarckian Empire as a Federal State, 1866–1880," *Central European History*, 2 (1969), p. 302.

Historians had long been aware of the significant set of changes that occurred in the late 1870s. The Grand Duke of Baden had recognized an imminent "change of system" (*Systemwechsel*) as early as April 1878, and contemporary opponents of Bismarck were soon using the phrase "internal founding of the Empire." It featured too in the work of Weimar revisionists like Ziekursch and Kehr. Yet it was only really in the 1960s that this "conservative turn" came to be regarded as a caesura every bit as significant as 1871. Two historians, Hans Rosenberg and Helmut Böhme, were particularly important in advancing this view, which became a cornerstone of the "new orthodoxy" and of the *Sonderweg* thesis. The importance Böhme attached to it is evident in the following quote: "With the year 1879 Prusso-Germany's 'own' way, in contrast to both western democracy and Russian autocracy, was finally secured; as was the position of the Prussian aristocracy in the army, higher bureaucracy and diplomatic corps. Only now was the Prussian hegemony in Germany established conclusively, and only now were the contours of the 'Reich' clearly defined."[78] It was at this juncture, Böhme argued, that the fateful alliance (*Sammlung*) between agrarian Junkers and heavy industrialists was forged, which was to prove such an obstacle to future political reform. Consequently, Winkler chose it as one of the *Turning Points in German History*, emphasizing in particular the moral and political fall of German liberalism, and Wolfgang Mommsen termed it "the great domestic political watershed."[79] As with other aspects of the "new orthodoxy," however, the notion of a second *Reichsgründung* came under intense scrutiny in the last decades of the twentieth century. The major studies of the 1990s are thus more cautious in their judgments, even though some still see it as an important juncture in modern German history. Before we consider the arguments on both sides, however, it will be necessary to outline briefly the principal changes that were implemented in the late 1870s and, first, the context in which they occurred.

In one of his typically pithy sentences, A. J. P. Taylor remarked that "[a]ll revolutionaries become conservative once they are in power, and Bismarck had always longed for tranquility even when he was a revolutionary."[80] Yet having established the Empire, the role of consolidator did not come easily to Bismarck, whose multiplicity of offices and pivotal role

---

78 H. Böhme, *Deutschlands Weg zur Großmacht*, p. 420.
79 H. A. Winkler, "1866 und 1878: Der Machtverzicht des Bürgertums," in C. Stern and H. A. Winkler, eds., *Wendepunkte deutscher Geschichte, 1848–1975* (Frankfurt, 1979), pp. 37–60; W. J. Mommsen, "The German Empire as a system of skirted decisions," in *Imperial Germany 1867–1918*, p. 16.
80 A. J. P. Taylor, *Bismarck. The Man and the Statesman*, p. 194.

meant there was never much prospect of tranquility. Not only did he have to work within the double bind of separate Prussian and imperial constitutions, controlling two separate though connected executives, but he needed to do so while simultaneously retaining the faith of the Prussian monarchy, obtaining parliamentary majorities, and respecting federal sensitivities. He was, as Lerman observes, in serious danger of becoming "a prisoner of the institutional system he had devised."[81] It was perhaps not entirely surprising, therefore, that Bismarck's first years as Imperial Chancellor were marked by bouts of poor health, self-pity, and depression, together with prolonged absences from Berlin. When, in May 1875, he offered to stand down, it was probably not just a tactical move, even if the resignation letter became one of his standard methods of crisis management in years thereafter.

The Reichstag arithmetic of the early 1870s meant Bismarck was forced to govern with liberal majorities, but he was soon on the lookout for ways of reducing what he saw as a dangerous dependence; partly for ideological reasons, but more importantly to increase his own room for maneuver. In a classic 1958 essay Pflanze argued that in the early years of the Empire, Bismarck had been more worried about keeping the particularist tendencies of the individual states in check, than by vaulting liberal ambitions. By the late 1870s this had changed. There no longer seemed any danger of the Reich disintegrating, since the 25 member states had accepted the new political arrangements with remarkably little dissent, but the 1874 Reichstag election results suggested a growing threat from left liberal Progressives. The army budget, which had caused the Prussian constitutional crisis of the early 1860s, had resurfaced as a bone of contention between crown and parliament. Indeed, liberal demands for constitutional reform more generally, particularly from parliamentarians like Eduard Lasker, were beginning to test the Chancellor's patience. It now suited Bismarck, Pflanze suggested, to attempt to redress the balance of power at the cost of liberals in the Reichstag.[82] The first victim was the faithful Delbrück, who had run the Reich administration during the Chancellor's frequent absences from Berlin, and in so doing had become a potential rival. The fact that he had a close working relationship with liberal leaders merely sealed his fate, although he did manage to resign before he was sacked. Delbrück's departure in 1876 did not, however, remove Bismarck's concerns about his personal job security. The eventual succession of Crown Prince Friedrich Wilhelm, who with his English wife Vicky was regarded as more liberal in outlook than Kaiser Wilhelm I, loomed

---

81 K. A. Lerman, *Bismarck*, p. 160.
82 O. Pflanze, "Bismarcks Realpolitik," pp. 155–79.

large in Bismarck's calculations. Fear of a future Westminster-style "Gladstone ministry," and a new era of liberal reform, was one of the main factors which lay behind the conservative turn of the late 1870s.

Another was Bismarck's recognition that the *Kulturkampf* – the divisive struggle between the Prussian state and the Roman Catholic Church, which had been unleashed with liberal support in the early 1870s – had proved counter-productive. Bismarck had originally seen the *Kulturkampf* as a convenient way of appeasing the liberals without giving in to their demands for constitutional reform. It had also reflected Bismarck's personal prejudices, as well as his paranoid fear that the Empire might be undermined from within by Poles, Alsatians, or Bavarians. Yet far from weakening the cohesion of Catholic Germany, the *Kulturkampf* strengthened it, and gave it a formidable political voice in the form of the Center Party, which commanded nearly a quarter of all Reichstag seats. Although in the short term Center leaders like Ludwig Windthorst – one of the Chancellor's most vocal parliamentary critics – were unlikely to become allies, Bismarck recognized that the Reichstag votes of the Center could become a useful potential alternative to those of the liberals.

Two other factors behind the shift to the right in the late 1870s were financial in character. Since 1873 the German Empire, like most of Europe, had been suffering from the effects of an economic downturn. Although with the benefit of hindsight it is clear that contemporaries were wrong to think of it as a "Great Depression," the problems were sufficient in the eyes of many Germans to discredit the principles of economic liberalism, along with its most prominent representatives. Falling wages and rising social tensions manifest in the growth of both socialism and anti-Semitism, led to increasingly vocal calls for protectionist measures from the leaders of heavy industry and subsequently from agricultural producers too. Newly-founded pressure groups began to develop innovative forms of agitation, which quickly made their mark on ministers and officials. At the same time, the Reich government was facing a particular financial problem of its own. It was supposed to be funded from the income of the *Zollverein*, from customs duties and indirect taxes. While it had a constitutional right to levy direct taxes, Bismarck preferred direct taxation to remain the prerogative of the individual states, which each paid an annual contribution (*Matrikularbeitrag*) towards the costs of running what was initially a very small imperial administration. By the end of the 1870s, however, it had become apparent that these means were insufficient to cover the rapidly growing expenditure of the Reich government, whose annual deficits were rising with each passing year. It did not escape Bismarck's attention that the introduction of protective tariffs on a range of goods would have the double benefit of shielding some domestic producers – although not, of course, consumers – while at the same time bringing in much needed revenue to the imperial coffers.

It was in this context that, during the course of 1878–9, the fateful cluster of measures dubbed the "second founding of the Empire" was introduced. The first, in October 1878, was a repressive Anti-Socialist Law, banning all "social democratic, socialist, or communist" activity short of standing for election. It was passed at the second time of asking in the wake of two assassination attempts on Kaiser Wilhelm I (for which Social Democrats were blameless). The law not only identified a new "enemy within," but also damaged the liberal movement, which was split over whether or not to accept what was clearly an illiberal measure. Indeed, some historians see the liberals rather than the socialists as the law's true target. Second, following Bismarck's "Christmas Letter" to the Bundesrat in December 1878 in which he acknowledged the benefits of protectionism, free trade was replaced by tariffs on grain and iron in July 1879. The tariffs themselves were set at a comparatively low level, which has led some commentators to suggest their motivation was more political than fiscal, but they could and would be increased in later years (1885, 1887, 1902), and their symbolic impact belied their modest scale. The liberal era, for which free trade was such a powerful emblem, appeared to have passed and the beneficiaries of protectionism would henceforth fight tooth and nail to retain their privileges. Third, following the death of Pope Pius IX in February 1878, tentative signs of an end to the *Kulturkampf* became apparent. Bismarck quickly entered direct negotiations with his successor Pope Leo XIII, whose conciliatory approach contrasted with the still hostile stance of the Center party. Although it would be the mid-1880s before any anti-Catholic legislation was removed from the statute books, a slow thaw in Bismarck's relations with political Catholicism could begin. In July 1879 the Prussian Minister for Education and Ecclesiastical Affairs, Adalbert Falk – a hero for many liberals because of his prominent role in the attack on Catholicism – was replaced by the conservative Robert von Puttkamer. It was Puttkamer who, as Minister of the Interior from 1881, allegedly oversaw a "purge" of liberal sympathizers in the higher civil service, which henceforth became an even greater bastion of aristocratic privilege. Finally, to ensure the safe passage of his bills through the Reichstag – newly composed following a snap election in the summer of 1878 – Bismarck increasingly found his majorities not in the liberal constellation of the early 1870s but from an alignment consisting of Conservatives, Free Conservatives and a much weakened National Liberal Party, which was shorn of its right wing in 1879, and then its left wing in 1880.

It is striking to observe how far the debate about the "second founding of the Reich" has remained focused on the figure of Bismarck and his intentions. For all the "new orthodoxy's" criticisms of personalist and historist approaches, the practitioners of historical social science were not able to replace the "great man" altogether. In fact, as Eley notes, "the turn to economic and social history has done very little to dislodge Bismarck from his role as the directive genius of German history between 1862 and 1890."[83] Of course, where Bismarck was formerly cast as the hero of German history, in the 1960s and 1970s he became the villain. The hagiographic Bismarck myth of the Wilhelmine era was replaced by what Andreas Biefang refers to as "the negative Bismarck myth":[84] the "Daemon of the Germans,"[85] whose formidable abilities were used to trick the liberals, manipulate the masses and set German history on course for the tragedies of the twentieth century. Indeed, by placing particular emphasis on Bismarck's "Germanization" and anti-Polish re-settlement policies in the eastern marches, together with his occasional anti-Jewish remarks, Wehler's *The German Empire* consciously constructed links between Bismarck and a later German chancellor. It is in accounts of the alleged re-founding of the Reich that this negative Bismarck myth can be seen most clearly. The unholy alliance put together by the Chancellor in 1878–9 – "a coalition of Junker landowners, industrial barons, the now purified conservative bureaucracy and the military" – is blamed for forestalling "the democratic aspirations of Germans for at least a generation."[86]

It is an argument that certainly has its merits, not least in what Kenneth Barkin refers to as its "enormous explanatory power": its ability to account for the vulnerability not only of the Empire but also of the Weimar Republic; and to illuminate lines of continuity with the Third Reich as well.[87] Few would dispute that the position of German liberalism, and the National Liberals in particular, was severely weakened after the events of the late 1870s. Regardless of whether the primary purpose of the tariff legislation was fiscal or political, the Empire's embrace of protectionist policies did have an enduring long-term impact. And, although the extent should not be exaggerated, the cumulative effect of the changes

---

83 G. Eley, "Bismarckian Germany," p. 6.
84 A. Biefang, *"Der Reichsgründer?" Bismarck, die nationale Verfassungsbewegung und die Entstehung des Deutschen Kaiserreichs* (Friedrichsruh, 1999), p. 6.
85 The title of a recent book by Johannes Willms, *Bismarck. Dämon der Deutschen. Anmerkungen zu einer Legende* (Munich, 1997).
86 K. Barkin, "1878–1879. The second founding of the Reich," *German Studies Review*, 10 (1987), p. 221.
87 Ibid., p. 224.

was to shift the balance of German politics rightwards. This was certainly the perception of contemporary observers. Nevertheless, most recent accounts are skeptical about the notion of a second founding of the Empire. This is largely because detailed research into each of the crucial episodes in 1878–9 suggests that Bismarck was not operating to a plan, or at least not to a master-plan for the re-founding of the Empire. As with the first *Reichsgründung*, the decisions of the late 1870s gain their coherence only retrospectively. At the time, the Chancellor was as much reacting to events as shaping them, and probably had only two consistent aims: to strengthen his own position above the parties; and to find a stable Reichstag majority somewhat further to the right (ideally with the National Liberals, but without their troublesome left wing). Beyond this, as Lerman notes, "it was not always obvious even to Bismarck himself where he was heading."[88] The liberal Lasker observed in his memoirs that Bismarck in 1877–8 seemed like a man waiting for something to turn up; something "that would enable him, by stirring up popular passions, to recover the initiative."[89] In his view, it was only the attempts on the life of the Kaiser in May and June 1878 which gave Bismarck a purpose and spurred him into action.

Of recent accounts, Winkler alone continues to uphold the notion of a conservative re-founding of the Empire without reservation.[90] At the other end of the spectrum are those who dismiss the second *Reichsgründung* almost out of hand, such as the late Andreas Hillgruber: "the two decades from 1871 to 1890 form a single continuous epoch," he argued.[91] Wehler, whose earlier works helped popularize the Böhme thesis, has distanced himself from what he now refers to as an "over-emphasized judgment."[92] He has also conceded ground to his critics on the issue of *Sammlungspolitik*, acknowledging that "due to insuperable internal conflicts" the relationship between industrialists and agrarians should not be thought of as "monolithic": "rather it remained a tense alliance, at times disturbed by serious antagonisms." In characteristically acerbic fashion, however, Wehler remarks that for all the clashes and conflicts within the "alliance of iron and rye," it was not simply "an artificial construct of the imagination of misguided historians."[93] Lothar Gall (born 1936) agrees that the shift from a reformist to a reactionary policy was a significant one.

---

88 K. A. Lerman, *Bismarck*, p. 162.
89 Quoted in E. Feuchtwanger, *Imperial Germany*, p. 75.
90 H. A. Winkler, *Der lange Weg nach Westen*, vol. 1, p. 245.
91 A. Hillgruber, *Otto von Bismarck: Gründer der europäischen Großmacht Deutsches Reich* (Göttingen, 1978), p. 72.
92 H.-U. Wehler, *Deutsche Gesellschaftsgeschichte*, vol. 3, p. 934.
93 Ibid., p. 935.

Henceforth Bismarck was no longer the "white revolutionary," but a Metternich-style conservative, battling vainly against the tides of time. Unlike Wehler, however, Gall emphasizes the weakness of the new arrangements, which led not to order and stability but to chaos and a general loss of direction.[94] Others see 1878–9 as a significant caesura for a completely different reason: not because of what changed, but what did not change. The clearest expression of this view comes from the Marxist Engelberg, who argues that "historical and political progress" demanded change in the late 1870s, but found its path was blocked.[95] Feuchtwanger agrees: "The change of course in 1879 was not so much a refoundation of the Reich as a reinforcement of the existing liberal deficit," he suggests.[96]

The majority of English-language historians acknowledge the important contribution of both Rosenberg's and Böhme's work, but are unconvinced by the "new orthodox" interpretation. Margaret Anderson, for instance, remarks wryly that it is all "a rather weighty historical burden for a tariff policy ... to bear."[97] In an essay co-written with Barkin, she also questions whether there was ever actually a "Puttkamer Purge," and highlights "the degree to which we perceive the German Empire, even today, through nineteenth-century liberal eyes."[98] Just because Germany's liberals saw the move away from free trade and the ending of the *Kulturkampf* as a triumph of reaction, does not mean we should make their viewpoint our own. In fact, all the major European countries apart from Britain responded to the economic downturn by adopting defensive measures: Russia, Italy, France, and Austria-Hungary each raised tariff barriers between 1876 and 1881. There was, moreover, no inherent reason why the shift to protectionism should have become a barrier to further political reform. After all, the nation with the highest tariffs in the nineteenth century was the USA, suggesting "that free trade and democracy were not universally intertwined."[99] Bismarck and the National Liberals, moreover, continued to co-operate after 1879, just as the Chancellor had often

---

94 L. Gall, *Bismarck. The White Revolutionary*, vol. 2, pp. 134–5.
95 E. Engelberg, *Bismarck*, vol. 2, *Das Reich in der Mitte*, p. 319.
96 E. Feuchtwanger, *Bismarck*, p. 260.
97 M. L. Anderson, *Windthorst. A Political Biography* (Oxford, 1981), p. 236.
98 M. L. Anderson and K. Barkin, "The myth of the Puttkamer purge and the reality of the Kulturkampf," *Journal of Modern History*, 54 (1982), p. 673. Although they were able to find "purge victims" in previous and later decades, they could not locate a single official (apart from government ministers) who was purged for his political views in the 1880s (p. 656).
99 K. Barkin, "1878–1879. The second founding of the Reich," p. 230. The key issue, Barkin suggests (p. 226) "is why Germany maintained high protection after prosperity returned in the mid-1890s, not why it was introduced in the first place."

worked with conservatives in the years before the turn. To divide the Bismarckian era into the "liberal" 1870s and the "conservative" 1880s, would, therefore, strike most historians today as simplistic, even though some authors still follow this schema in their chapter headings.[100] If the domestic political history of the Empire has to be divided in two, many would argue that the watershed is better located in the 1890s, than in 1878–9.

How Do Historians Characterize Bismarck's Rule?

By the end of the twentieth century the Iron Chancellor had been the subject of some 7,000 publications, including over 50 scholarly biographies.[101] The centenary of his death in 1998 triggered a new wave of academic conferences, magazine features, and, of course, yet more biographies. Anyone endeavoring to read just a fraction of these works will be struck by a depressing degree of repetition, for there is remarkably little dispute about any major aspect of Bismarck's life story. Tellingly, even Engelberg's East German biography of the 1980s was largely indistinguishable in its narrative from its West German counterparts.[102] The well-worn pattern of this familiar story is, moreover, unlikely to be challenged by the discovery of new sources of information: all the richest seams have been fully exploited and less promising ones abandoned. The latter included some half-hearted attempts at introducing the methods of "psychohistory" to the study of Bismarck – analyzing, for instance, the psychological basis of Bismarck's health problems, or his relationship with his bourgeois mother (bad) and his Junker father (good) – but short of raising the dead it is hard to see how this approach could contribute very much.[103] Engelberg's loving exploration of the Bismarck family tree, tracing it right back to late medieval times, was a similarly questionable exercise.[104] Fortunately, the debate surrounding Bismarck's politics and

---

100 E. Feuchtwanger, *Imperial Germany*, and D. Hertz-Eichenrode, *Deutsche Geschichte 1871–1890. Das Kaiserreich in der Ära Bismarck*, are two recent examples.
101 K. Urbach, "Between saviour and villain. 100 years of Bismarck biographies," *Historical Journal*, 41 (1998), p. 1142.
102 E. Engelberg, *Bismarck. Urpreuße und Reichsgründer* (Berlin, 1985); E. Engelberg, *Bismarck: Das Reich in der Mitte Europas* (Berlin, 1990). The first volume was published simultaneously on both sides of the Wall, and the West German media celebrated it as an important political as well as historiographical event. The reception within the historians' guild, however, was less positive.
103 See O. Pflanze, *Bismarck and the Development of Germany*, 3 vols. (Princeton, 1963–90).
104 See the opening chapters of E. Engelberg, *Bismarck. Urpreuße und Reichsgründer*.

the character of his long period in office has been a good deal livelier and more productive. Did Bismarck have a "system?" If so, can it be described as "Bonapartist?" Was he a man of his time, or rather a late-flowering example of an eighteenth-century "cabinet politician?" Does his leadership fall into the category of "charismatic" rule? Such questions go beyond his life and work as an individual; they are inextricably linked to the course of German history as a whole, and in this sense David Blackbourn is surely right to describe Bismarck as "a touchstone of attitudes among historians towards the German past."[105] Yet he also has a contemporary resonance. For anyone interested in political processes and the exercise of power, this cynical, empirical, and egotistical statesman, who knew a thing or two about media manipulation and "spin," remains an object of considerable fascination.

As we have seen, historical judgments of Bismarck cover the full spectrum from hero to villain. There is general agreement, however, that he was a more impressive and successful figure on the international stage than in the domestic arena. As Dorpalen put it, "[t]here is almost unanimous agreement today that the man whose proudest achievement was the establishment of a powerful German state, greatly weakened his own creation by the shortcomings of his internal policies."[106] Although there have certainly been attempts to revise an unduly positive view of his foreign policy, it would take a breathtakingly bold act of revisionism to suggest that, in the long term, Bismarck's domestic policies were anything other than a failure. However, it was not simply the case that Bismarck took one less seriously than the other. While he endorsed the maxim of foreign policy's primacy, and his training lay almost exclusively in that field, he also spent the best part of three decades attempting to shape Prussia and Germany's internal affairs, and remained unwilling to hand over formal responsibility to a subordinate.[107] Any verdict on Bismarck's rule must, therefore, take both areas into consideration, particularly as they were linked in a number of ways (not only in the obvious case of colonial policy, but also for instance in the issue of tariffs – which seriously affected the Empire's relations with Russia – or in the Chancellor's consistent hostility to "revolutionary" movements at home and abroad). Indeed, many historians argue that his foreign and domestic policies were essentially two sides of the same coin: "the consolidation and defense

---

105 D. Blackbourn, "Bismarck: the sorcerer's apprentice," in *Populists and Patricians*, p. 33.
106 A. Dorpalen, "The German historians and Bismarck," *Review of Politics*, XV (1953), p. 61.
107 For a few months in 1873 Bismarck gave up the post of Prussian minister-president to his friend Albrecht von Roon, but soon realized the experiment was not working.

of what had already been achieved, internally and externally," as Hillgruber put it.[108]

Two aspects of Bismarck's foreign policy have attracted particular historiographical interest: his use of alliances and his attitude to the colonial question. With regard to the former, historians rightly acknowledge Bismarck's sober appraisal of the international situation in the aftermath of 1871: that even without further expansion the Empire's "semi-hegemonic" position in the center of the continent was a potentially precarious one; and that this "unfinished" nation-state, whose creation had undoubtedly upset the balance of power in Europe, would have to consider itself complete (or "satiated," as Bismarck put it), if it was not to face the nightmare scenario of three of the five great powers forming a hostile alliance against it (Bismarck's *cauchemar des coalitions*). Many accounts still emphasize the clarity and consistency of the Chancellor's general objectives, pointing to documents such as the memorandum he dictated to his son at Bad Kissingen in June 1877, in which he stated that the aim of the Empire's foreign policy should be to achieve "an overall political situation in which all the great powers except France have need of us, and are as far as possible kept from forming coalitions against us by their relations with one another"; while simultaneously attempting to deflect great-power conflicts to the periphery of Europe (such as the Balkans) or beyond, in order to ease pressure on the Empire at its center.[109] Yet there are obvious dangers in taking Bismarck's words at face value, and the complex reality of German foreign policy in the 1880s often stood in stark contrast to the deceptive simplicity of such statements. Certainly, by the time of Bismarck's forced departure in 1890, the web of treaties and agreements – which constituted what is sometimes rather grandly referred to as Bismarck's "system" – was so intricate that he was famously compared to a juggler keeping five glass balls in the air at the same time.

Whether Bismarck's juggling act was a towering diplomatic achievement, tragically fritted away by his successors; an improvised set of stop-gaps, which owed more to desperation than cool calculation; or was simply too clever for its own good, since some of the secret treaty commitments appeared to contradict each other, is a matter on which historians continue to disagree. Taking their cue from Gall, the majority of contemporary historians characterize Bismarck's attempts to preserve the status quo as an increasingly complicated "system of expedients" rather than any kind of grand design. Instead of highlighting the "systematic"

---

108 A. Hillgruber, *Otto von Bismarck*, p. 71.
109 K. A. Lerman, *Bismarck*, p. 211.

aspects of the post-1879 order, they stress its makeshift nature, and suggest that Bismarck's later policies, both at home and abroad, often amounted to little more than crisis management. Wilfried Loth is typical: after 1879, he suggests, "Bismarck achieved only defensive victories in the sense of a temporary entrenchment of the status quo, and as time passed he lost all credibility."[110] There are, however, exceptions to this picture. Among recent English-language accounts, Seligmann and McLean's *From Reich to Republic* offers a strikingly positive (and rather old-fashioned) assessment of Bismarck's "dextrous diplomatic strategy," highlighting five basic objectives which they suggest he followed throughout his period in office: to ensure Germany's semi-dominant position over the continent through consolidation rather than further expansion; to maintain the isolation of France; to safeguard Austria-Hungary's future as a great power; to maintain cordial relations with Russia; and to avoid becoming isolated. Dividing Bismarckian foreign policy into three stages – consolidation (1871–8); alliance-building (1879–85); and stop-gaps (1885–90) – they acknowledge that the system "began to show signs of strain" in the latter phase, but nevertheless concur with A. J. P. Taylor that the Iron Chancellor's "greatest achievement" was to give his country, and the European continent, peace for 40 years.[111] Lerman's *Bismarck* is more skeptical: "Bismarck's control of German foreign policy and his multidimensional grasp of the complexities of international relations once attracted much admiration from diplomatic historians," she writes, but recent scholarly criticism of his "crisis management without real prospects" (Konrad Canis) has stripped away much of the mystique. Moreover, "[i]n seeking to ensnare the powers of Europe in a series of peacetime alliances, Bismarck, perhaps unwittingly, contributed to the long slide towards the First World War."[112]

Although by the 1880s Bismarck had become an admired and respected, if not fully trusted, figure across Europe (particularly after his skilful handling of the Congress of Berlin in 1878), he was subject to growing criticism of his foreign policy from within Germany itself. It came from informed insiders, such as the Foreign Office mandarin Friedrich von Holstein, and from wider public opinion. The latter, manifest in the rise of radical nationalist and colonialist agitation, was becoming an increasingly important element in European politics, and threatened to undermine not only Bismarck's fragile web of alliances, but also the integrity of Germany's principal ally, Austria-Hungary. Feuchtwanger contrasts the

---

110 W. Loth, *Das Kaiserreich*, p. 67.
111 M. Seligmann and R. McLean, *Germany from Reich to Republic*, pp. 39–40.
112 K. A. Lerman, *Bismarck*, pp. 220–1.

growing clamor for imperial acquisitions and territorial expansion with Bismarck's more traditional approach, which he describes as "a product of cabinet diplomacy in the style of Metternich."[113] The view that Bismarck's foreign policy resembled the kind of diplomacy that had flourished in the age of absolutism was the orthodox view among West German historians until the late 1960s, but it is less common today. In the 1950s, despite their many disagreements on other aspects of German history, the Protestant conservative Gerhard Ritter and the liberal Catholic Franz Schnabel agreed that Bismarck was a statesman whose intellectual roots lay in the eighteenth century, a "delayed Richelieu," whose model was Frederick the Great, and whose guiding principle was *raison d'état*.[114] The historians who advanced this view were motivated primarily by their desire to separate the "born statesman" Bismarck from the "archdilettante" Hitler (Ritter). To this end, they portrayed Bismarck as a man who stood aloof from the spirit of his age, an elitist who "appeared more modern than he was in reality,"[115] an "antediluvian" (Gustav Adolf Rein) who not only hated the telephone and electric light, but also had no real understanding of mass movements such as nationalism or socialism. A variation on this theme was played by Hans Rothfels, who argued that Bismarck understood such "irrational" populist causes only too well, and, therefore, recognized the serious dangers inherent in them. Either way, the conclusion was the same: that he should be spared any association with the twentieth-century tyrant. After all, Bismarck was a master of moderation, whose essential category was the state rather than the *Volk* or nation, and whose wars were like duels, fought honorably and without recourse to base emotions. Indeed, those searching for the roots of the twentieth-century's aggressive hyper-nationalism would be more likely to find them amongst Bismarck's erstwhile opponents in the Frankfurt Parliament of 1848–9 than in the Iron Chancellor himself.

Despite its fall from favor, this conservative picture of Bismarck as a "man out of season" re-appears from time to time. Johannes Willms' 1997 study *The Daemon of the Germans* is one recent example: "Bismarck was, and is, persistently attested with a modernity of political thought," he writes, yet "[s]uch an interpretation has absolutely no foundation. Bismarck's political thought was ... anything but modern."[116] Most contemporary historians reject this line of argument, however, and

---

113 E. Feuchtwanger, *Bismarck*, p. 233.
114 G. Ritter, "Europa und die deutsche Frage," extract in H. Hallmann, ed., *Revision des Bismarckbildes*, p. 81.
115 H. Holborn, "Bismarck's Realpolitik," in L. Gall, ed., *Das Bismarck-Problem in der Geschichtsschreibung nach 1945* (Cologne, 1971), p. 239.
116 J. Willms, *Bismarck. Dämon der Deutschen*, p. 62.

agree with the former American diplomat and politician Henry Kissinger that Bismarck's mixture of realism, empiricism, cynicism, and Darwinism "represented a new age."[117] "His views reflected the revolt of the nineteenth century against the seventeenth and eighteenth centuries," as Pflanze put it.[118] While his objective – to preserve the Prussian military monarchy in a rapidly changing world – may indeed have been conservative and anachronistic, the means he used to achieve it were certainly not: "Unlike the great practitioners of cabinet diplomacy ... he did not limit the forces which he exploited to the government of states. He included also the revolutionary social and political movements of modern times."[119] Engelberg is another to emphasize the modern dimensions to Bismarck's persona, highlighting the way in which he was able to look beyond the narrow horizons of his class to accept revolution (albeit from above) as a valid political weapon. What kind of eighteenth-century cabinet politician, he suggests, could have deposed four princes – one king, one elector, and two dukes – as Bismarck did in 1866, without any regard for legitimacy or the established order of things?[120] Instead, Engelberg characterizes Bismarck's rule as a form of "Bonapartism," "even if Bonapartist terror-elections along the infamous lines of Napoleon III's France were impossible" in the German Empire.[121]

As a GDR historian (and an ideological hardliner in the 1950s and 1960s), it was hardly surprising that Engelberg should turn to a concept developed by Karl Marx to define Bismarck's rule. First coined by Marx in his 1852 essay *The Eighteenth Brumaire of Louis Bonaparte*, and thereafter applied to Bismarck by such disparate characters as the arch-conservative Ludwig von Gerlach and Marx's comrade Friedrich Engels, the term "Bonapartism" was re-activated in the West by Wehler and Böhme in the late 1960s. In his study of *Bismarck and Imperialism*, Wehler used it to denote a particular kind of accommodation between the bourgeoisie, nobility, and military, to defend "a traditional, unstable social and political structure which found itself threatened by strong forces of social and political change." This stabilization was to be achieved by "undisguised repression as well as limited concessions" (such as social welfare legislation), and involved "diverting attention away from constitutional policy towards economic policy, away from the question of emancipation at home towards compensatory successes abroad."[122] It also involved the

---

117   H. Kissinger, "Der weiße Revolutionär," in L. Gall, ed, *Das Bismarck-Problem*, p. 413.
118   O. Pflanze, "Bismarck's Realpolitik," p. 161.
119   O. Pflanze, "Bismarck and German nationalism," p. 554.
120   E. Engelberg, *Bismarck und die Revolution von oben* (Brunswick, 1987), p. 18.
121   Ibid., p. 18.
122   H.-U. Wehler, "Bismarck's imperialism, 1862–1890," p. 183.

use of plebiscitary techniques to appeal directly to the people, over the heads of troublesome politicians (as demonstrated by Bismarck's introduction of universal male suffrage for Reichstag elections, in an effort to circumvent the liberals). "Rarely has a new conventional wisdom become so quickly established" as Wehler's view of Bismarck, Allan Mitchell suggested, but it was not long before the Bonapartism thesis itself came under fire in both German and Anglo-American historical journals.[123] Ironically, East German commentators were among Wehler's fiercest critics, as a consequence of his unorthodox use of Marxist terminology,[124] but Western historians such as Mitchell ("a morass of illogic") and Gall were scarcely less dismissive.

Gall argued that although there may have been superficial similarities between Napoleon III's France and Bismarck's Germany, they were not consciously engineered, or utilized, by the Chancellor. Indeed, they could not have been, given the completely different constellation of forces which prevailed in the German Empire, with its formidable conservative bastions in the monarchy, army, and civil service. Unlike Louis Napoleon, Bismarck did not come to power through a *coup d'état* and never resorted to an actual referendum. He could not have hoped to enjoy the same degree of political freedom and room for maneuver as the French Emperor.[125] Bruce Waller, another biographer of Bismarck, agrees: "[t]he word 'Bonapartism' is not really helpful in assessing Bismarck's style of government. His mixture of old and new ideas on domestic and foreign policy was unique … He was also not simply a leftover from cabinet diplomacy, or the opposite, a characteristic figure of his age."[126] Even so, similarities between Bismarck and Napoleon III's techniques of rule undoubtedly existed, and the German Chancellor was by no means ignorant of developments in post-1851 France (where he had briefly served as Prussian Ambassador in 1862). When Bismarck introduced his old age pension legislation to the Reichstag in the 1880s, he openly admitted that he had been influenced by the example of Napoleon III's social insurance policies.[127] There was thus "at the very least a Bonapartist strain in Bismarck's policies," as Blackbourn puts it,

---

123 See A. Mitchell, "Bonapartism as a model for Bismarckian politics," and the replies from O. Pflanze, C. Fohlen, and M. Stürmer, *Journal of Modern History*, 49 (1977), pp. 181–209.
124 Wehler's analysis did not treat imperialism as a specific phase of capitalist development (i.e. the Marxist-Leninist view), but rather as a political technique to divert attention from domestic difficulties. See A. Dorpalen, *German History in Marxist Perspective*, p. 256.
125 L. Gall, *Bismarck. Der weiße Revolutionär*, p. 569.
126 B. Waller, *Bismarck*, p. 40.
127 See M. Seligmann and R. McLean, *Germany from Reich to Republic*, p. 36.

"and the motif of a deliberately dramatized politics is certainly not just a construct of later historians."[128] Yet it was for the most part a matter of style rather than substance, and to apply the concept to Bismarck's rule more generally is problematic, given the very obvious social, economic, and constitutional differences between the German and French Empires.

At the heart of the debate over Bismarck's Bonapartism was the puzzling question of why a hitherto vocal critic of colonial adventures should embark on the construction of a German colonial empire in 1884, especially as there seemed to be compelling reasons why Germany should refrain from colonial entanglements. Wehler argued that in fact there was no sudden change in Bismarck's thinking, but "a remarkable continuity of both the ideas and the methods of free-trade commercial expansionism" (i.e., "informal empire" along British lines), dating right back to the 1860s. "There were however some motives, which, contrary to his previous experience and hopes, induced Bismarck for some time to involve the state in the governance of Protectorates."[129] For Wehler, these motives were predominantly socio-economic in character. As a "pragmatic expansionist," Bismarck may have anticipated genuine economic benefits from colonies in Africa such as German South-West Africa, Togo, Cameroon (all 1884), and German East Africa (1885); or from Kaiser-Wilhelm-Land and the Bismarck Archipelago in the Pacific (both 1885), but more importantly their acquisition offered a diversionary escape from the adverse effects of industrialization and recession, and a short-term boost for pro-government candidates in the 1884 Reichstag election campaign. The parallel with Napoleon III's use of colonial engagements was clear, lending weight to Wehler's notion of Bismarck as a Bonapartist. However, not all historians agree that foreign policy objectives or considerations of national prestige "were only incidental" in Bismarck's brush with colonialism. Hillgruber, for instance, acknowledged the domestic considerations, but argued Bismarck's prime motivation was external: to seek an accommodation with France, in order to take advantage of Britain's difficulties in Afghanistan, Egypt, and the Sudan.[130] Feuchtwanger also favors a foreign policy explanation, but suggests Bismarck's "immediate aim was to distract French attention from Alsace-Lorraine and put Britain under pressure to tie herself more positively to Germany."[131] A further possibility is put forward by Seligmann and McLean: that Bismarck's concern over the imminent monarchical

---

128 D. Blackbourn, "Politics as theatre," in *Populists and Patricians*, pp. 249–50.
129 H.-U. Wehler, "Bismarck's imperialism, 1862–1890," p. 185.
130 A. Hillgruber, *Otto von Bismarck*, p. 78.
131 E. Feuchtwanger, *Imperial Germany*, p. 91.

succession in Germany led him to seek ways in which to drive a wedge between the anglophile Crown Prince Friedrich Wilhelm (the future Kaiser Friedrich III) and Great Britain. By developing colonies in Africa, Bismarck "had a ready-made mechanism for generating Anglo-German diplomatic incidents whenever he wished,"[132]

At around the same time that Wehler was advancing the notion of Bismarck as a Bonapartist, his contemporary Michael Stürmer began to reactivate a subtly different alternative: the idea of Bismarck as a "Caesarist."[133] This term, which was frequently used by nineteenth-century German historians to describe the rule of Cromwell and both Napoleons as well as Bismarck, was dismissed by Marx as a "superficial analogy," with little practical value because of the huge differences between ancient and modern societies.[134] Yet it did have the important advantage of not being specifically related to another contemporary statesman, and many of Bismarck's classically-educated liberal opponents were certainly conscious of parallels between their own age and Roman times, when emperors side-stepped troublesome political elites by appealing directly to the masses, and plebeians were appeased by a diet of "bread and circuses." Gall notes that rhetorical allusions to the governance of the Roman Empire became a "veritable topos" of German political life in the early 1880s.[135] At that time, the terms Caesarist and Bonapartist were often used synonymously, and this practice is continued by some historians today, although it should be noted that neither term has enjoyed great favor in recent years. It is telling than both Wehler and Stürmer have sought to move beyond the Bonapartist-Caesarist model. Indeed, even in the early 1970s, Stürmer was anxious not to push the Caesarist line too far, pointing out that "Caesarism never superseded legitimate monarchy or the Junker interest, and remained basically one means among others used by a conservative statesman."[136]

One further category to be employed by historians attempting to characterize Bismarck's exercise of power is the concept of "charismatic rule."

---

132   M. Seligmann and R. McLean, *Germany from Reich to Republic*, p. 49.
133   See M. Stürmer, "Bismarck in perspective," *Central European History*, 4 (1971), pp. 291–331; also his *Regierung und Reichstag im Bismarckstaat 1871–1880: Cäsarismus oder Parlamentarismus?* (Düsseldorf, 1974).
134   Quoted by H. Gollwitzer, "Der Cäsarismus Napoleons III im Widerhall der öffentlichen Meinung Deutschlands," *Historische Zeitschrift*, 173 (1952), p. 68.
135   L. Gall, *Bismarck. The White Revolutionary*, vol. 2, p. 130. See, for example, Ludwig Bamberger's speech in the Reichstag debate on Bismarck's accident insurance bill in 1881, when he compared Bismarck's Germany "to the Roman Republic in its decline," quoted by Gall, p. 131; or the 1880 letter from Rudolf Haym to the historian Treitschke, quoted by M. Stürmer, "Bismarck in perspective," p. 306.
136   M.Stürmer, "Bismarck in perspective," p. 329.

It was Wehler, formerly the standard-bearer of the Bonapartist paradigm, who in volume 3 of his *Gesellschaftsgeschichte* turned to this concept first developed by Max Weber in the final years of the nineteenth century. Weber suggested that charismatic rule applied where legitimation was drawn not from tradition (as in the case of monarchy), or from legality and an electorate (as in modern democracy), but from the belief that a ruler possessed extraordinary personal abilities or powers. This specific Weberian meaning of "charisma" is, therefore, rather different from the established current usage: Bismarck, a balding, rather corpulent man with a monotonous high-pitched voice and an alarming tendency to break down in tears, did not possess what nowadays passes for charisma. Nor can it be said that Wehler's paradigm shift met with critical acclaim either, even if many reviewers were quick to commend his willingness to rethink his earlier position. It was perhaps unfortunate that Wehler's magnum opus was quickly followed by the first volume of Kershaw's *Hitler*, in which the British historian also turned to Weber in an attempt to categorize the nature of the Führer's rule. Most found Kershaw's candidate a more likely choice, since Bismarck – unlike Hitler, or indeed Mussolini or Lenin – had no party of devoted followers, and remained an appointee of the crown, who could be disposed of at any time. When that time came, in the spring of 1890, there was little sense of shock and even fewer tears.[137] As Stürmer puts it, "Bismarck's dismissal met with widespread indifference, even a feeling of relief. Very rarely was the Kaiser to find himself so much in tune with public opinion as when he telegraphed his illusive 'The course remains the same. Full steam ahead!'"[138]

Although Bismarck's departure may have been overdue, Wilhelm II's eager acceptance of the *Reichsgründer*'s resignation in only the second year of his reign was to have fatal consequences for the Kaiser's later historical reputation, at least according to Nicolaus Sombart (born 1923). Henceforth, "[t]he standard by which critics measured the Kaiser, explicitly or implicitly, was Bismarck." As the ex-chancellor's reputation grew beyond all bounds, particularly after his death in 1898, so the Kaiser's image declined in equal proportion.[139] Indeed, Sombart suggests, Bismarck and Wilhelm henceforth became polar opposites in the historiography of the Empire: the "great man," who had forged it in

---

137 It should be noted, however, that following his dismissal Bismarck did indeed build up a substantial popular following, as the pilgrimages to his estate at Friedrichsruh in the 1890s testified. See M. Hank, *Kanzler ohne Amt: Fürst Bismarck nach seiner Entlassung 1890–98* (Munich, 1980).
138 Ibid., p. 310.
139 N. Sombart, *Wilhelm II. Sündenbock und Herr der Mitte* (Berlin, 1996), p. 22.

iron and blood; and the "stupid boy,"[140] who brought it down in an orgy of self-indulgent and incompetent neo-absolutism. These two men became the "positive and negative poles" around which the whole "myth" of German history since 1871 was constructed: a myth that exonerated Bismarck for all the negative consequences of unification, and instead placed full responsibility for the Empire's failings on the shoulders of the Kaiser.

How Useful are "Psychohistorical" Approaches in Explaining the Reign of Wilhelm II?

With a humiliating physical disability, recurring suggestions of mental instability, and an ambiguous national and sexual identity – not to mention a difficult relationship with his mother – the last Kaiser certainly appears a suitable case for psychohistorical treatment. Accordingly, all Wilhelm II's biographers since Emil Ludwig in the 1920s have at least made reference to his troubled psychological state,[141] even if some ultimately resist the temptation to don their white coats.[142] For Ludwig (1881–1948), it was Wilhelm's need to compensate for his withered left arm that took center-stage; for others it was the lack of affection he received from his cruelly disappointed and hence ultra-critical parents; or the desire to "win back" his neglectful father from his mother's dominant influence. Yet historians of Imperial Germany are generally cautious of such attempts to use psychology or medicine to explain the nature of the Kaiser's 30-year reign. Psychohistory – which emerged in the US in the late 1950s and 1960s with the ambitious aim of making Freudian psychoanalysis central to historical investigation – has fallen from favor since its heyday in the 1970s, when publications such as *The Journal of Psychohistory* (1973) and *The Psychohistory Review* (1976) were first founded.[143] Its proponents have been accused of "reductionism, irresponsible overstatement, and historical misunderstanding,"[144] of "emphasizing

---

140 Bismarck's own characterization of Wilhelm II, quoted by E. Feuchtwanger, *Bismarck*, p. 262.
141 E. Ludwig, *Wilhelm der Zweite* (Berlin, 1925). Ludwig was a prolific and best-selling biographer, but not a professional historian.
142 Lamar Cecil's *Wilhelm II. Prince and Emperor, 1859–1900* is a good example of biography which eschews psychohistorical speculation.
143 For a critique of psychohistory see J. Barzun, *Clio and the Doctors: Psycho-History, Quanto-History, and History* (Chicago, 1974).
144 R. Waite, review of C. Strozier and D. Offer, eds., *The Leader: Psychohistorical Essays*, in *The American Historical Review*, 91 (1986), p. 355.

unconscious motive rather than conscious purpose," of assuming that "all people are the same regardless of time and place," and of "failing to account for the social determinants of psychological attitudes and individual actions."[145] Our consideration of the literature on the Empire's second "great man," therefore, begins with a brief assessment of the contribution of psychohistory to our understanding of Wilhelm II, before moving on to the much-debated question of the Kaiser's "personal rule."

As Christopher Clark (born 1960) observes, attempts at a medical diagnosis of Wilhelm's condition have "tended to follow contemporary trends in popular science: 'nervous debility' in the 1890s; dynastic degeneracy in the early Republican era; Freudian paradigms in the 1920s and periodically thereafter; 'repressed homosexuality' from the 1970s; neurology in the 1980s; and, in the gene-obsessed *fin de siècle* of the twentieth century, 'the gene of George III.'"[146] The dangers of medicalizing Wilhelm II, whether through psychohistory or what Clark refers to as "retrospective neuroscience," are clear. For a start, the evidence is largely circumstantial and often contradictory. Second, a preoccupation with psychological or neurological factors can obscure the actual rational basis for apparently illogical actions, as well as removing all sense of historical context. If, moreover, medical information is not used in a responsible manner – to shed light on significant decisions, for instance – history risks becoming little more than an upmarket form of gossip, in which intimate details about an individual's private life are exposed purely for their own sake (Evans's "history as the butler saw it"). Some of the literature on Wilhelm's sexuality comes close dangerously to this category, even if Isabel Hull puts forward a spirited case to justify her in-depth study of the Kaiser's relationships with the homoerotically-charged "Liebenberg Circle."[147]

Furthermore there are specific problems with the psychoanalytic approach. Even if one accepts the validity of psychoanalysis as a diagnostic method (which many do not), Wilhelm will never be able to take his place on the psychiatrist's couch, and efforts to analyze him posthumously are bound to be highly speculative. In any case, to attempt a diagnosis without the necessary clinical training and experience inevitably smacks of dilettantism. One historian more qualified than most to speculate on Wilhelm's state of mind is the American Thomas Kohut (born 1951), grandson of a prominent Viennese psychoanalyst and himself a graduate

---

145 T. Kohut, "Psychohistory as history," in *The American Historical Review*, 91 (1986), pp. 336, 338.
146 C. Clark, *Kaiser Wilhelm II* (Harlow, 2000), p. 21.
147 I. Hull, *The Entourage of Kaiser Wilhelm II, 1888–1918* (Cambridge, 1982).

of the Cincinnati Psychoanalytical Institute. Although critical of much psychohistory which he dismisses as "pathography," Kohut is convinced that the past's psychological dimension "remains a historical subject of decisive importance."[148] In his study of *Wilhelm II and the Germans* Kohut applies his favored approach – a form of psychoanalytic theory known as "self psychology" – to the Kaiser. Unlike many earlier writers, Kohut argues that Wilhelm's physical handicap was not the issue. Indeed, mastering his disability was the "greatest developmental accomplishment, perhaps the greatest single achievement of his life."[149] The real problem lay in his relationship with his parents: "Wilhelm wanted a strong and domineering father and a tender and compassionate mother. Instead, his father was compassionate and his mother was domineering."[150] As a consequence of his parents' lack of empathy, Wilhelm failed to develop healthy self-esteem, becoming a "narcissistically disturbed" man with a childlike craving for people to "mirror" him and affirm his sense of self-worth.[151] According to Kohut, this helps to explain Wilhelm's "driven self display" as the peripatetic *Reisekaiser*, and also the alleged psychological congruence between the Kaiser and his subjects, famously highlighted by contemporaries such as Friedrich Naumann and Walther Rathenau. The Kaiser became widely recognized as the symbol and mouthpiece of the *Kaiserreich* precisely because he shared its tensions and contradictions, in a way that a more consistent ruler would have found impossible.

Much of Kohut's analysis rings true, although the heavy emphasis on Wilhelm's upbringing is not wholly convincing since another of Wilhelm's recent biographers, the British historian John Röhl, suggests that by nineteenth-century standards Wilhelm's parents were warm and affectionate. Röhl's own emphasis lies on heredity (notably the genetically inherited blood disease porphyria, which was probably responsible for the "madness" of King George III of England and spread through the royal houses of Europe) and organic damage, such as the "minimal cerebral dysfunction" which Wilhelm may have suffered as a result of oxygen deprivation during a traumatic breech-birth. He examines the medical evidence, both from the birth itself and from the subsequent horrific attempts to "cure" the infant Willy, in almost forensic detail.[152]

---

148   T. Kohut, "Psychohistory as history," p. 352.
149   T. Kohut, *Wilhelm II and the Germans. A Study in Leadership* (New York, 1991), p. 44.
150   Ibid., p. 78.
151   Ibid., p. 9.
152   See J. Röhl, *Young Wilhelm. The Kaiser's Early Life 1859–1888*.

The gargantuan scale of Röhl's three-volume portrait of the Kaiser makes it one of the defining landmarks of recent scholarship on German history, even if it also confirms the veracity of Emerson's observation that "great geniuses have the shortest biographies." Its length is swollen by extensive quotations from contemporaries, which certainly add to the documentary value of the enterprise, but should not be taken too much at face value since, as Kohut points out, Wilhelm was a "transference figure," on to whom people projected their diverse hopes and aspirations.[153]

While biographers are frequently accused of falling into the trap of empathizing too closely with their subjects, this is most definitely not a charge that can be leveled at the Sussex historian. As one reviewer observed, "Röhl milks the sheer awfulness with deadpan relish."[154] Indeed, for the aforementioned Sombart, the flaw in Röhl's magnum opus lies in precisely the opposite direction: "The reason? He does not love the Kaiser."[155] Sombart's own idiosyncratic study of Wilhelm, subtitled *Scapegoat and Lord of the Center*, is undoubtedly a much less substantial piece of scholarship than Röhl's, but it does offer an interesting take on psychohistory. Sombart acknowledges that one cannot solve the "riddle" of Wilhelm II with "individual-psychological explanatory models" alone. In his view, monarchs have their own psychology, far removed from the mundane world of their bourgeois subjects. To understand Wilhelm, he suggests, one must enter the "sacred-magical sphere" of kingship: the ceremonies, rituals, and symbolic acts which were so central to Wilhelm's own perception of his role, but which modern man has lost the capacity to comprehend. Much of this territory was explored more soberly by another German, Elisabeth Fehrenbach, in the 1960s,[156] but Sombart is correct to acknowledge Wilhelm's achievement in giving his position some kind of substance and meaning. He is surely wrong, however, to see the long, slow decline in Wilhelm's reputation as an inevitable consequence of his "assassination" of the Empire's founder. Given the genuinely high hopes aroused by the young Emperor's accession, and the relief with which many people greeted Bismarck's departure, Wilhelm started with considerable credit in the bank. That this was so quickly expended was due more to his manifold shortcomings as a ruler than the overly sympathetic Sombart would have us believe. The last emperor did become something of a scapegoat after 1918, when it suited the Germans to blame the "degenerate" on the throne, but the

---

153 T. Kohut, review of Röhl, *Young Wilhelm*, *Central European History*, 29 (1996), p. 137.
154 D. Blackbourn, "How wicked and horrid," *London Review of Books*, 15 July 1999, p. 20.
155 N. Sombart, *Wilhelm II. Sündenbock und Herr der Mitte*, p. 7.
156 E. Fehrenbach, *Wandlungen des deutschen Kaisergedankens, 1871–1918* (Munich, 1969).

catalogue of blunders laid at Wilhelm's doors was not just down to malicious myth-making.

It would be fair to say that Sombart's efforts to rehabilitate the Kaiser's reputation have not been well received. Blackbourn, for instance, dismissed one of his essays as "a baffling mixture of aperçu and cliché, insight and silliness, invigoratingly energetic thought and deadly rebarbative prose."[157] Yet he does at least deserve recognition for being one of the few twentieth-century German writers to take Wilhelm II seriously. Until recently, the German historical guild studiously ignored the last Kaiser, who was so obviously not a "great man" in the mould of Bismarck or Frederick the Great.[158] This neglect left the field open to journalists, publicists, and English-language historians who, as we have seen, have been at the forefront of work on Wilhelm II for the past three decades. There are many, of course, who would argue that all of this is essentially irrelevant: that to focus on any single individual is bound to distort our view of German society as a whole. Certainly, if one believes that Wilhelm II was merely a "shadow emperor," a largely insignificant element in Germany's polycratic leadership in the 1890s and 1900s, then there is indeed little point in subjecting his medical and psychological history to such detailed scrutiny. However, if one believes as Röhl does, that Wilhelm II was a "powerful and pernicious ruler," a kind of "missing link" between Bismarck and Hitler,[159] then his personal character assumes a much greater importance, especially if one concurs with Jonathan Steinberg that the Kaiser was "one of those strange figures in history whose personalities have had more effect on the course of affairs than their deeds."[160] While it is quite possible to accept the importance of individual personality in history without necessarily endorsing the psychohistorical approach, one's ultimate judgment on the value of such work is likely to depend on how seriously one takes the notion of Wilhelm's "personal rule." It is to this issue that we now must turn.

---

157 D. Blackbourn, "The Kaiser and his entourage," in *Populists and Patricians*, p. 48.
158 The only notable exception was W. J. Mommsen. However, since the start of the new millennium, a new, younger generation of German academics has begun to focus on neglected aspects of Wilhelm's reign. See T. H.Benner, *Die Strahlen der Krone. Die religiöse Dimension des Kaisertums unter Wilhelm II. vor dem Hintergrund der Orientreise 1898* (Marburg, 2001); S. Samerski, ed., *Wilhelm II. und die Religion. Facetten einer Persönlichkeit und ihres Umfelds* (Berlin, 2001); L. Reinermann, *Der Kaiser in England. Wilhelm II. und sein Bild in der britischen Öffentlichkeit* (Paderborn, 2001); and H. Afflerbach, ed., *Wilhelm II. als Oberster Kriegsherr im Ersten Weltkrieg. Quellen aus der militärischen Umgebung des Kaisers 1914–1918* (Munich, 2004).
159 Phrases taken by John Röhl's preface to *Wilhelm II. The Kaiser's Personal Monarchy, 1888–1900* (Cambridge, 2004), p. xiii.
160 J. Steinberg, quoted by T. Kohut, *Wilhelm II and the Germans*, pp. 3–4.

To What Extent Did Wilhelm II Succeed in Establishing "Personal Rule"?

An excessive emphasis on individuals risks obscuring the many continuities that existed between Bismarckian and Wilhelmine Germany. With these in mind, the events of 1890 should perhaps not really be described as a "transformation of German political life,"[161] although the majority of recent accounts do accept that Wilhelm's arrival on the throne made a significant difference. Indeed, Wolfgang Mommsen describes his impact as "devastating,"[162] while Seligmann and McLean go as far as to state: "Most of the disasters which befell Germany after 1888 can be attributed to the actions of Wilhelm II." They give two reasons: first, "Wilhelm's determination to reaffirm the semi-absolutist character of the Prussian monarchy by re-establishing the practice whereby the monarch ruled personally; [and] second, the fact that the new Kaiser's unstable personality made him peculiarly unsuited to fill the role of absolute ruler."[163] The phrase "personal rule" (or *persönliches Regiment*) is, however, problematic and comes with a host of excess baggage. As Clark points out, it "meant different things to different people and has never acquired an agreed or stable meaning, a fact that has muddled the scholarly dispute over its applicability."[164] It was famously used by the royal favorite and future chancellor Bernhard von Bülow in a letter of 1896 ("With me, personal rule – in the good sense – would really begin"), but also by some of the Kaiser's fiercest contemporary critics (such as the journalist Maximilian Harden, who wrote in 1902: "The Kaiser is his own Reich Chancellor. All the important political decisions of the past twelve years have been made by him").[165] It resurfaced in the title of a 1948 book on the Wilhelmine era by Erich Eyck, and has been a feature of the historiographical debate virtually ever since.[166]

Eyck's thesis, which took the Kaiser's absolutist aspirations at face value, met with a skeptical reception. The legalistically-minded conservatives

---

161 T. Kohut, *Wilhelm II and the Germans*, p. 128.
162 W. J. Mommsen, "Kaiser Wilhelm II and German Politics," *Journal of Contemporary History*, 25 (1990), p. 289.
163 M. Seligmann and R. McLean, *Germany from Reich to Republic*, p. 61.
164 C. Clark, *Kaiser Wilhelm II*, p. vii. For the history of the term see I. V. Hull, "Persönliches Regiment," in J. C. G. Röhl, ed., *Der Ort Kaiser Wilhelms II in der deutschen Geschichte* (Munich, 1991), pp. 3–23.
165 Both quoted by J. C. G. Röhl, *The Kaiser and his Court. Wilhelm II and the Government of Germany* (Cambridge, 1994), pp. 120–1.
166 E. Eyck, *Das persönliche Regiment Wilhelms II. Politische Geschichte des Deutschen Kaiserreiches von 1890 bis 1914* (Zurich, 1948).

who dominated the guild in the 1950s were quick to highlight Wilhelm's apparent adherence to the Prussian and Imperial constitutions, as well as the shortcomings in his character which would have limited his effectiveness as an absolute ruler.[167] After the historiographical earthquakes of the 1960s, the "new orthodoxy" was equally dismissive, with Wehler and other members of the Bielefeld School employing Hans Delbrück's contemporary characterization of Wilhelm as a "shadow emperor." In Wehler's *German Empire* Wilhelm was "a weak figure atop a clay pedestal," and his *Gesellschaftsgeschichte* continues to portray the Kaiser in a peripheral role.[168] However, Eyck's thesis – or a refined version of it – found an important supporter in John Röhl, who made his mark with a 1967 study of German high politics after Bismarck's fall.[169] Röhl's book drew heavily on newly discovered or previously neglected primary sources, such as the voluminous papers of the Kaiser's friend and confidante Philipp Eulenburg, which the British historian later published in edited form. Since then, Röhl and Wehler have appeared as the leaders of two opposing factions, although in fact they share rather more than one might imagine: both belong to the post-Fischer generation and possess a strong antipathy towards the apologist efforts of the "old orthodoxy"; both pursue an unashamedly "top down" approach; and both take a pessimistic view of the prospects for reform in a system of constitutional monarchy where "the main emphasis was placed on the noun and not the adjective."[170]

The clearest statement of Röhl's position comes in a series of essays published over a three-decade period and collected in the volume *The Kaiser and his Court*. These valuable essays focus less on Wilhelm himself than "on the structural foundations on which his so-called 'personal rule' was first erected and then sustained."[171] As his quotation marks imply, Röhl has always been conscious of the term's troublesome and potentially misleading nature: "Wilhelm II might have dreamed of establishing absolute rule for himself, but it remained no more than a dream. Even his severest critics did not believe that he ever practised such a form of rule."[172] Instead, Röhl prefers the more neutral concept of the "kingship mechanism," first developed by the sociologist Norbert Elias (1897–1990)

---

167 See E. R. Huber, "Das persönliche Regiment Wilhelms II," *Zeitschrift für Religion und Geistesgeschichte*, 3 (1951), pp. 134–48; F. Hartung, "Das persönliche Regiment Kaiser Wilhelms II," *Sitzungsberichte der deutschen Akademie der Wissenschaften zu Berlin* (Berlin, 1952).
168 H.-U. Wehler, *The German Empire*, p. 64.
169 J. C. G. Röhl, *Germany without Bismarck. The crisis of government in the Second Reich, 1890–1900* (London, 1967).
170 H.-U. Wehler, *The German Empire*, p. 54.
171 J. C. G. Röhl, *The Kaiser and his Court*, p. 1.
172 Ibid., p. 3.

to refer to the pattern of relationships and mentalities created by the interplay of a monarch, his officials, and the royal court. According to Röhl, the Kaiser's formidable powers of patronage and appointment led to a system of flattery and favor, in which the "whole government of the Reich and Prussia, all the higher civil service, indeed in the last analysis the entire *classe politique* of Wilhelmine Germany, were suffused with the desire to win or retain the favour of the 'All-Highest Person.' "[173] It is not enough, therefore, just to locate particular pieces of legislation that were produced on Wilhelm's initiative: one must consider those measures that were blocked by officials fearful of losing "All-highest confidence" ("negative personal rule"); and also the malign contribution of his entourage, "which was selected purely on the basis of the monarch's inclinations" and can be said to have represented "the institutionalisation of the Kaiser's personality."[174] A system constructed on the flimsy basis of regal favor, in which lines of communication and decision-making bypassed the nominally responsible government, and in which the heads of the military and naval cabinets could gain access to the emperor more easily than his chancellor, resulted in a state of affairs not altogether different from Wehler's "polycratic, but uncoordinated authoritarianism."[175] Far from undermining his case, however, Röhl sees this as clear evidence of the "kingship mechanism" in action.

He is also quick to emphasize that the Kaiser's involvement in Wilhelmine politics was not constant and consistent, but fell into five distinct stages. Thus the dismissal of Bismarck (1888–90) was followed by a phase of direct personal interventions, which one might term "improvised personal rule" (1890–7); once the Kaiser's chosen men were in place, a decade-long phase of "institutionalized personal rule" could begin, in which active personal involvement became less necessary (1897–1908); a third phase commenced with Wilhelm on the defensive following the traumatic crises of 1907–8 (the Eulenburg scandal and the *Daily Telegraph* Affair),[176] and lasted up to the outbreak of war in 1914; it was only during the conflict itself that Wilhelm finally became a "shadow emperor."[177] Most historiographical discussion has revolved around the second phase, which began with a series of ministerial changes in the

---

173   Ibid., pp. 123–4.
174   Ibid., *The Kaiser and his Court*, p. 117.
175   H.-U. Wehler, *The German Empire*, p. 62.
176   On the scandals that dogged Wilhelm II's reign see M. Kohlrausch, *Der Monarch im Skandal: Die Logik der Massenmedien und die Transformation der wilhelminischen Monarchie* (Berlin, 2005).
177   J. C. G. Röhl, *The Kaiser and his Court*, pp. 116–17.

summer of 1897. According to Röhl, Kaiser Wilhelm was "in complete control of the Executive in Berlin" for the next three years, acting as "his own chancellor" until Bülow's appointment in 1900.[178] Thereafter, Röhl suggests, "the less the Kaiser felt obliged to intervene, the better the system was working."[179]

While there can be no doubt that Wilhelm and his advisors did meet with some success in their efforts to increase his personal involvement in government, Röhl's specific interpretations have been frequently challenged, and not only by the Bielefelders. In a dismissive review of one of Röhl's books, Evans opted for sarcasm: "Far from being the moving cog at the center of the German governmental machine, Wilhelm II was usually a spanner in the works."[180] A more measured critique came from Eley, who nevertheless noted: "In domestic politics the crucial governing axis for the years 1897–1900 was that of Miquel and Arthur von Posadowsky ... while Miquel was careful not to lose the Kaiser's ear, 'personal rule' was certainly not the organizing priority of his politics."[181] Wilhelm's personal policy enthusiasms of the late 1890s – repressive legislation against the labor movement, naval expansion, and the Prussian Canal Bill – were not matched by similar initiatives after 1900: "Towards the major political questions of the period," Eley suggests, "the Kaiser could not have been more indifferent."[182] James Retallack (born 1955) agrees, noting "all too often we are told nothing concrete about the policies that were actually implemented by Wilhelm's capriciously chosen men."[183] Clark believes it is possible "to discern in the emperor's domestic political initiatives a consistent – if ill-thought-through and poorly articulated – objective, namely to integrate and enlarge the politically 'neutral' middle ground in German politics and culture and to set his monarchy squarely within it," but adds that he was "unable, despite many energetic interventions, to realise this programme in any meaningful way, or even consistently to impose his will on the executive."[184]

Meanwhile, Lerman's acclaimed study of the slippery and sycophantic Bülow has shown that he was too self-centered to have ever been a mere

---

178   J. C. G. Röhl, *Germany without Bismarck*, pp. 278–9.
179   J. C. G. Röhl, "Introduction," in J. Röhl and N. Sombart, eds., *Kaiser Wilhelm II. New Interpretations*, p. 15.
180   R. J. Evans, "From Hitler to Bismarck," in *Rethinking German History*, p. 63.
181   G. Eley, "The view from the throne: The personal rule of Kaiser Wilhelm II," *Historical Journal*, 28 (1985), p. 479.
182   Ibid., p. 481.
183   J. Retallack, "Wilhelmine Germany," in G. Martel, ed., *Modern Germany Reconsidered*, p. 42.
184   C. Clark, *Kaiser Wilhelm II*, pp. 59, 259.

"tool" of the Kaiser, even though he was never under any illusions about the ultimate source of his authority.[185] It is clear that Bülow, who was extremely adept at "managing" his sovereign, did not simply respond to direct orders from above. Indeed, some historians argue that Wilhelm's periodic involvement in governmental affairs owed more to the fluctuating influence of his friends and advisors than any coherent strategy of his own. Thus it peaked in the 1890s, when the influence of Eulenburg was at its height (and Wilhelm "was virtually a cipher for Eulenburg's pet schemes")[186] but declined markedly thereafter. An extreme version of this thesis was presented by Ekkehard-Teja Wilke in the 1970s, who argued that Wilhelm was essentially the captive of manipulative power-brokers with their own personal agendas.[187] Few historians found Wilke's book convincing, but many regard the Kaiser's impulsiveness (he quickly gained the sobriquet "Wilhelm the Sudden"), his inconsistency, and indiscipline as serious impediments to his chances of ever becoming a monarch who would "rule as well as reign." As Feuchtwanger puts it, "the only limit to the personal regime was his own ignorance, inconsistency and lack of a coherent plan."[188] His restless hunger for travel, which meant that he was absent from Berlin for more than six months each year, also hindered his prospects.

It is unfortunate that the term "personal rule" has become so well established, since it misleads and provokes in roughly equal measure. Clearly the Kaiser was no dictator, nor was he the coordinator of policy for any sustained period, yet to govern the Empire against the Kaiser's wishes was – in the long run at least – simply not possible. Wilhelm II was the single most powerful person in the Empire, and much more than an occasional fly in the ointment. His influence was greater in the 1890s than it was in the 1900s, but his gradual marginalization in domestic politics was to some extent counterbalanced by his determined retention of the *Kommandogewalt* – his extra-parliamentary "power of command" over the army – which Mommsen terms "the last bastion of royal influence against the onslaught of democracy."[189] Moreover, although there is general agreement that Wilhelm's powers diminished further after 1914, his interventions could still be decisive. Holger Afflerbach has recently argued that there were three ways in which the Kaiser continued to play a

---

185 K. A. Lerman, *The Chancellor as Courtier. Bernhard von Bülow and the Governance of Germany, 1900–1909* (Cambridge, 1990).
186 G. Eley, "The view from the throne," p. 482.
187 E.-T. P. W. Wilke, *Political Decadence in Imperial Germany* (Urbana and London, 1976).
188 E. Feuchtwanger, *Imperial Germany*, p. 126.
189 W. J. Mommsen, "Kaiser Wilhelm II and German politics," p. 305.

significant role in wartime: as an "umpire" called upon to resolve internal disputes; as the man who continued to control the lever of personnel policy (at least until 1916); and as someone who still possessed a veto on all important decisions.[190] This view is supported by Hull, who notes: "Kaiser Wilhelm was in fact far more active in setting broad wartime policy than it first seems. The view of the passive, indecisive Kaiser was the product of wartime political polemics."[191]

John Röhl undoubtedly deserves great credit for reminding us of the "monarchocentric" nature of the German Empire. He has never suggested – as Mommsen implied in the title of one of his last publications[192] – that the Kaiser should bear personal responsibility for all the German Empire's misfortunes. That would indeed be simplistic, given the complexities of the state and society over which Wilhelm ruled. There were, as we shall see in Chapter 3, significant limits to the Kaiser's authority. He was only one factor in a complex political system, in which the parties, pressure groups, and mass media all played an increasing part, but he was a vital factor nevertheless. It is for this reason that purely structural approaches are likely to be every bit as flawed as wholly personal ones. Ultimately, a combination of the two will be required if historians are to find convincing answers to their many important questions regarding Wilhelm II and the governance of Germany.

---

190 H. Afflerbach, "Wilhelm II as Supreme Warlord in the First World War," in A. Mombauer and W. Deist, eds., *The Kaiser. New Research on Wilhelm II's Role in Imperial Germany* (Cambridge, 2003), pp. 195–216.
191 I. V. Hull, "Military culture, Wilhelm II and the end of the monarchy in the First World War," in A. Mombauer and W. Deist, eds., *The Kaiser*, p. 237.
192 W. J. Mommsen, *War der Kaiser an allem schuld? Wilhelm II. und die preußisch-deutschen Machteliten* (Munich, 2002).

3
"Democracy in the Undemocratic State"?

Democracy in the Undemocratic State was the title given by a Canadian historian, Brett Fairbairn (born 1959), to a 1997 study of two Wilhelmine election campaigns.[1] The phrase captures the essential paradox of the Empire's political life: the co-existence of an authoritarian, undemocratic government, appointed by the Kaiser, with a lively parliamentary assembly and comparatively free elections. This paradox only begins to make sense if one acknowledges that the Empire was the result of a compromise – albeit an unequal one – between the forces of conservatism and liberal nationalism. The most convincing accounts of its institutions and structures are those that recognize this dual heritage; which accept, in the words of Wolfgang Mommsen, that while "the Empire owed its existence to a 'revolution from above' rather than to a voluntary act on the part of the people, in the course of time its citizens came to perceive it as the embodiment of the German nation state."[2] As with all compromises, it fully satisfied no one, and in many ways the Empire remained an "unfinished nation state."[3] Certainly, both Bismarck and the liberals soon had reasons for regret, but their difficult relationship was nevertheless

---

1 B. Fairbairn, *Democracy in the Undemocratic State. The Reichstag Elections of 1898 and 1903* (Toronto, 1997).
2 W. J. Mommsen, *Imperial Germany 1867–1918*, p. vii.
3 The phrase was used as early as 1871 by Edmund Jörg, and more recently by Theodor Schieder in *Das deutsche Kaiserreich von 1871 als Nationalstaat* (Göttingen, 1992, first published 1961).

"more than a marriage of convenience" (Theodor Schieder). For all its weaknesses and contradictions, the Empire developed a presence and legitimacy which was sufficiently robust to survive more than four decades of political turbulence, and four years of ruinous warfare, before finally succumbing only in the wake of a catastrophic military defeat. This chapter focuses on the many debates that surround the constitution, government, and political life of Imperial Germany. How, and by whom, was the Empire governed? Was there a "silent" or creeping parliamentarization before 1914, or was Germany locked in a fatal political stalemate during the final peacetime years? What do recent works on the electoral history of the *Kaiserreich* contribute to our understanding of the period as a whole?

How, and By Whom, Was the Empire Governed?

If the founding of the Empire had been the work of Bismarck alone, acting solely in the interests of Prussia's ruling elite, then its constitution would undoubtedly have been different from the one finally approved by the Reichstag on April 16, 1871. The delicate balance of powers enshrined in this short document of 78 articles, which was first drafted in 1866–7 for the North German Confederation but later amended on several occasions, certainly reflected Bismarck's personal priorities and concerns – to uphold the monarchical principle, prevent parliamentary rule, and ensure Prussian hegemony – but it was not just a Machiavellian desire to divide and rule, or a cynical attempt to camouflage the true nature of Prussia's dominance, which gave the constitution its particular character.[4] The constitution, which took the form of a voluntary treaty between sovereign states, was the product of a specific social and political context, in which liberal constitutionalism and Germany's federal traditions were powerful forces that could not be easily ignored. Indeed, many Prussian conservatives recognized this by giving the new arrangements a cool reception: one even wrote that they were being "forced to drink the liberal cup to the dregs."[5] One must be wary, therefore, of attempts to portray the constitution simply as a piece of political subterfuge,

---

4 For the precise wording of the constitution see E. M. Hucko, ed., *The Democratic Tradition. Four German Constitutions* (Leamington Spa, 1980), pp. 121–45. Specific discussions of the constitution in English include H. W. Koch, *A Constitutional History of Germany in the Nineteenth and Twentieth Centuries* (London and New York, 1984); and M. John, "Constitution, administration, and the law," in R. Chickering, ed., *Imperial Germany*, pp. 185–214.
5 Moritz von Blanckenburg, quoted by James Retallack in *Notables of the Right. The Conservative Party and Political Mobilization in Germany, 1876–1918* (London, 1988), p. 14.

a masterful Bismarckian sleight of hand to obscure a *de facto* Prussian military takeover. A. J. P Taylor's account in *The Course of German History* is one example;[6] Wehler's characterization of the *Kaiserreich* as a "Bonapartist dictatorship based on plebiscitary support and operating within the framework of a semi-absolutist, pseudo-constitutional military monarchy" is another.[7] As Mommsen notes of the latter, such "one-dimensional interpretations" from the early years of historical social science tended to airbrush out the liberal contribution to the Empire; ignoring, for instance, the "impressive number of far-reaching changes that the Reichstag made to legislation during Bismarck's years in power, ranging from measures affecting the constitution itself to the social insurance laws."[8]

Yet Mommsen's characterization of the Empire as "a semi-constitutional system with supplementary party-political features" is itself problematic, not least because of his claim that it was "immobile and inflexible" and "incapable of undergoing evolutionary change."[9] Actually, during the five decades of its existence, the Empire underwent considerable evolutionary change. As Michael John suggests, "[t]he rapidity with which the empire's legislative competence was extended ... was a reminder that the 1871 constitution was by no means static and inflexible."[10] John cites the Empire's leading constitutional lawyer, Paul Laband, who estimated that while ten formal constitutional changes had occurred by 1907 (none of which were of major significance), there were many more informal changes through political practice. The "open-ended" and "plastic" nature of the Empire's constitution, with its "peculiar indeterminacy," its "fluid character," and "its capacity to change hands unexpectedly" has often been highlighted by historians,[11] as has an 1851 quote by its architect, who likened a constitution to "an empty vessel whose contents are determined by those in power."[12] David Blackbourn concludes: "The complex and contradictory nature of Bismarck's handiwork, far from suggesting some kind of historical straitjacket which confined the form of the Imperial polity, should alert us rather to its plasticity."[13]

---

6   A. J. P. Taylor, *The Course of German History*, pp. 127–55.
7   H.-U. Wehler, *The German Empire*, p. 60.
8   W. J. Mommsen, "The German Empire as a system of skirted decisions," in *Imperial Germany 1867–1918*, p. 5.
9   Ibid., p. 5; W. J. Mommsen, "The latent crisis of the Wilhelmine Empire," in *Imperial Germany 1867–1918*, p. 143.
10 M. John, "Constitution, administration, and the law," p. 189.
11 The first two adjectives come from D. Blackbourn, "Politics as theatre," in *Populists and Patricians*, p. 253; the other descriptions from Christopher Clark, *Kaiser Wilhelm II*, p. 258.
12 Quoted by B. Waller, *Bismarck*, p. 37.
13 D. Blackbourn, "The discreet charm of the bourgeoisie," in *The Peculiarities of German History*, p. 276.

Historians have long disputed the constitution's other attributes, although most agree that it produced "one of the most complex political systems ever devised."[14] Lothar Gall argued that its strength was a "freedom from theory, system and dogma,"[15] while Otto Pflanze praised the way in which Bismarck found a place "for all the important political forces of the country: the German nation, the various political parties, the Hohenzollern crown, the Prussian government, and the dynasties and governments of the lesser states." He argued, moreover, that "the constitution created the possibility of an equilibrium among these various forces, the controlling position of which ... Bismarck himself occupied."[16] H. W. Koch believed that the constitution was undoubtedly "a very imperfect instrument," but stressed it was by no means "doomed from the start."[17] However, many other historians – particularly those identified with the "new orthodoxy" – have followed Max Weber in taking a more pessimistic view.[18] Michael Stürmer dubbed it a "constitution without a future," Volker Berghahn a "quasi-autocracy," and Hans-Ulrich Wehler a "pseudo-constitution."[19] It has also been labeled a "hotch-potch" (A. J. P. Taylor), a *monstrum* (Wolfgang Sauer) and an "unnatural growth" (John Röhl), which ultimately left the Empire "ungovernable" (Fritz Stern).

A more sober term, much favored by German legal historians, is "dualistic." This refers not to the co-existence of the Prussian and imperial administrations, but to the clear separation of powers (in both Prussia and the Reich) between the non-elected executive and the elected legislature. Much of the specialist debate has focused on whether Germany's dualistic system should be regarded as a distinctive state form in its own right (a view traditionally associated with Otto Hintze, and subsequently Ernst Rudolf Huber) or merely as a transitional stage on the road to parliamentary rule (the view of Ernst-Wolfgang Böckenförde).[20] Writing in 1934, another of Germany's most prominent and controversial legal theorists, the neo-conservative Carl Schmitt (1888–1985),

---

14 K. A. Lerman, *The Chancellor as Courtier*, p. 41.
15 Quoted by W. J. Mommsen, "A delaying compromise: The Imperial constitution of 1871," in *Imperial Germany 1867–1918*, p. 23.
16 O. Pflanze, "Bismarck's Realpolitik," in J. J. Sheehan, ed., *Imperial Germany*, p. 168.
17 H. W. Koch, *A Constitutional History of Germany*, p. 123.
18 W. J. Mommsen, "A delaying compromise," p. 23.
19 M. Stürmer, *Regierung und Reichstag im Bismarckstaat, 1871–1880: Cäsarismus oder Parlamentarismus* (Düsseldorf, 1974), p. 16; V. Berghahn, *Modern Germany. Society, Economy and Politics in the Twentieth Century* (Cambridge, 1987), p. 22; for Wehler quote see note 7.
20 See M. John, "Constitution, administration, and the law," pp. 191–2.

characterized the Second Empire as a system of "skirted decisions."[21] Although his critique of the *Kaiserreich* was severely tainted by his obvious admiration for the newly-established Third Reich, Schmitt's phrase remains one of the most useful ways of viewing the imperial system, and was later employed by Mommsen as the title of an influential essay.[22] Among the questions left unanswered by the constitution were such central issues as the relationship between the imperial and Prussian governments and the relative status of the various Reich institutions. In practice, as a result of these and other "skirted decisions," the Empire had the potential to evolve in quite different directions. If one compares the written constitution with its unwritten counterpart – generally a more reliable guide to political reality – one can indeed identify a number of significant changes. These are perhaps best traced by looking briefly at each of the Empire's major institutions in turn.

In 1871 it appeared as if the Bundesrat – the Federal Council comprising 58 appointed representatives of the German princes and free cities, including 17 from the Kingdom of Prussia – was to become the Empire's most important institution and true seat of power. It was the certainly the Empire's most unusual institution. In the absence of a constitutional court, it was to adjudicate in constitutional conflicts and disputes between the 25 member states, which each retained their own governments and parliaments. More importantly, the Bundesrat was also intended to perform a series of executive functions, and its committees were effectively to function as imperial ministries. Bismarck, who was sensitive to federal concerns, even made a point of avoiding the term "imperial government," referring instead to the will of the "confederated governments" (*verbündeten Regierungen*). Historians are agreed, however, that this quickly became a constitutional fiction. The Bundesrat, which met in secret, did theoretically play an important part in the legislative process, and could block any proposals for constitutional change if 14 or more of its delegates were instructed to do so, but it did not become the Reich government and was seldom central to decision making. Although historians see it as a significant obstacle to reform (not least because Prussia's block vote represented an effective veto on change), its day-to-day role was limited, and its importance declined further after Bismarck's departure. In fact, the governments of the federal states frequently complained they knew less about imperial policy than the Reichstag.[23] This was particularly apparent in

---

21 C. Schmitt, ed., "Staatsgefüge und Zusammenbruch des zweiten Reiches," in *Der Deutsche Staat der Gegenwart*, vol. 6 (Hamburg, 1934), p. 25.
22 W. J. Mommsen, "The German Empire as a system of skirted decisions," pp. 1–19.
23 See K. A. Lerman, *The Chancellor as Courtier*, p. 253.

July 1914, where the Bundesrat discussed only routine matters, and representatives of the state governments had to rely on Berlin gossip for news of the developing international crisis.

When the Iron Chancellor's successors spoke of the "imperial executive" (*Reichsleitung*), they were referring not to the Bundesrat but to the real government of the Empire, in the shape of the chancellor and his state secretaries. As the only imperial minister, the chancellor was appointed by the Kaiser and acted as the agent of the Bundesrat, which he chaired. Liberals succeeded in making the chancellor formally "accountable" (under the so-called "Bennigsen Law" of 1867), but this did not mean he was "responsible" to the Reichstag. In other words, though he could be asked to defend his actions in parliament, his position was not dependent on a Reichstag majority and he could not be forced out by a vote of no-confidence. As the first chancellor, Bismarck was initially assisted only by a small private office, and relied on the Prussian ministries to service the Bundesrat and provide support in drafting legislation. This untidy administrative overlap was to some extent justified by the fact that Bismarck simultaneously occupied the roles of Prussian minister-president and foreign minister: a combination of functions that was not specified in the constitution, but which Bismarck and most of his successors found essential. Despite tentative indications of change under Bülow in the 1900s – particularly in the era of the short-lived "Bülow Bloc" (1907–9) – the imperial chancellor remained ultimately answerable to the Kaiser alone, as Bethmann Hollweg's survival after a parliamentary vote of no-confidence in 1913 made clear.

Beyond the chancellor, other imperial ministries were not envisaged in the 1871 constitution, yet as the demands on the *Reichsleitung* grew, a series of Reich offices were created – including foreign affairs, justice, the interior, the treasury, the navy, and finally in 1907, colonial affairs – each of which was overseen by a state secretary. The state secretaries were not ministers, and there was no imperial cabinet: instead, they answered individually to the chancellor and were expected to correspond only through him. Even so, this bureaucratic expansion further complicated the tangled relationship between the Reich and Prussian administrations. The emergence of an imperial executive above and beyond the Bundesrat proved possible because of Article 17, which Michael John describes as a "Trojan horse" within the constitution.[24] While some liberal contemporaries entertained hopes of the *Reichsleitung* evolving into a British-style

---

24 The article stipulated that imperial legislation and ordinances required the counter-signature of the chancellor, who thereby undertook responsibility for these measures. See M. John, "Constitution, administration, and the law," p. 189.

cabinet government, individually and collectively responsible to parliament, others stoutly defended the idea of government by "non-partisan" officials as a Germanic alternative to the vagaries of party rule. As things stood, politicians were expressly forbidden from becoming state secretaries without first relinquishing their Reichstag seats, and imperial post-holders were instead generally selected from the same narrow social elite as their Prussian ministerial counterparts. They were, as Mommsen puts it, "closely bound to the throne through the oath of office, tradition and recruitment."[25] Civil service careers, at least in the higher echelons, were out of the question for socialists, and were difficult for left liberals, Jews, and even Catholics.[26] However, although there was still an overrepresentation of Prussian nobles in the imperial administration in 1914, there were also clear signs that the Reich interest was becoming stronger and the Prussian interest weaker.[27] Indeed, some have suggested that the Prusso–German relationship was effectively reversed during the lifetime of the Empire: Bismarck had intended Prussia to rule the Reich, but in the later Wilhelmine years it was the Reich that came to rule Prussia. In other words, whereas Bismarck had liaised with the governments of the major states in the Bundesrat before attempting to introduce a new bill, which had probably been prepared in a Prussian ministry, Bülow was more likely to consult with the leaders of the pro-government Reichstag parties before introducing a bill prepared in one of the imperial offices. A linguistic hint of this shift was apparent in the way the *Reichsleitung* was increasingly referred to as the imperial government (*Reichsregierung*). It could also be observed in Wilhelm II's own perception of his role as an imperial monarch, in contrast to his grandfather who had remained first and foremost the King of Prussia.

Indeed the constitution's "fluidity" was nowhere more apparent than in the contrasting roles played by Germany's three emperors. In theory each enjoyed the same powers. According to the constitution, the Kaiser was responsible for foreign policy; for declaring war (subject to the approval of the Bundesrat); for appointing and dismissing the chancellor, and for all other key personnel issues in the Prussian and Reich civil service. Under Article 24 he could also open and close the Reichstag at the time of his choosing, provided that dissolution was accompanied by a date for new elections. If necessary he could enforce closure by armed force, through

---

25 W. Mommsen, "A delaying compromise," p. 38.
26 See J. C. G. Röhl, "Higher civil servants in Wilhelmine Germany," in *The Kaiser and His Court*, pp. 131–49.
27 E. Feuchtwanger, *Imperial Germany*, p. 105. According to Feuchtwanger, the Reich bureaucracy numbered some 500 men by the end of the 1870s, and by 1914 it was about 2,000-strong.

his supreme power of command over the army and navy. The fact that a *coup d'état* or *Staatsstreich* never occurred does not diminish the seriousness of the threat, which was real enough before 1900 even if it became a "taboo" (Thomas Kühne) thereafter.[28] Finally, the Kaiser possessed further prerogatives as King of Prussia, including the sole right to initiate legislation through "his" Ministry of State. In practice, of course, the first Kaiser was largely content to take a backseat, allowing Bismarck to wield effective though not unlimited power. After the short interlude of Friedrich III's 99-day reign, the accession of Wilhelm II saw the same constitution now become the potential basis of "personal rule." In so doing, Wilhelm II was effectively attempting to take the constitution at its word – to turn Bismarck's fiction into reality – even if he boasted that he did not know the constitution and had never read it.[29] It was perhaps fitting, therefore, that in the aftermath of the *Daily Telegraph* Affair – a domestic crisis that blew up in the autumn of 1908 after the Kaiser's indiscreet comments on Anglo-German relations were allowed to appear in a British newspaper – it was again on constitutional grounds that Wilhelm II found himself increasingly sidelined from domestic politics, the "kingship mechanism" notwithstanding. He even had to issue a humiliating statement, agreeing to "respect his constitutional obligations." As Christopher Clark astutely observes, it was as if "[t]he peculiar indeterminacy of the German constitution permitted the concentration of power in the hands of the sovereign, but also facilitated its dissipation."[30]

The prominent role played by courtiers and royal favorites in Wilhelm II's Germany – men such as General Waldersee and Philipp Eulenburg – was itself a consequence of the constitution, at least according to Blackbourn. The "constitution of the Reich required a high level of activity in the interstices of the formal system," he notes. "The legacy of constitutional dualism ... encouraged intense, behind-the-scenes consultations and short-term agreements, in which politics often became a matter of brokering."[31] Also located in the "interstices of the formal system" were the Kaiser's three private secret cabinets – for civil, military, and naval affairs – which were intended to perform an advisory role, but were viewed by some insiders as a kind of shadow government, with better access to the emperor than the chancellor himself. The power of such

---

28 See M. Stürmer, "Staatsstreichgedanken im Bismarckreich," *Historische Zeitschrift*, 209 (1969), pp. 566–615; H. Pogge von Strandmann, "Staatsstreichpläne, Alldeutsche und Bethmann Hollweg," in I. Geiss and H. Pogge von Strandmann, eds., *Die Erforderlichkeit des Unmöglichen* (Frankfurt, 1965), pp. 296–317.
29 T. Schieder, *Das deutsche Kaiserreich von 1871 als Nationalstaat*, p. 92.
30 C. Clark, *Kaiser Wilhelm II*, p. 258.
31 D. Blackbourn, "Politics as theatre," in *Populists and Patricians*, p. 254.

extra-constitutional institutions is one of the reasons why Hans-Peter Ullmann describes the Empire as, among other things, "a military state" (*Militärstaat*),[32] in which the army was a quasi-autonomous force, an "institutional legacy of absolutism within an otherwise constitutional *Rechtsstaat*."[33] The infamous Zabern Affair of 1913 – when a German lieutenant's insult to the population of an Alsatian town triggered a crisis in which the army appeared able to act outside the law – provides powerful evidence for this view.[34] Indeed, the army has been referred to as the "neuralgic point" (Michael John) of the whole Prusso–German constitutional system, because there was no Secretary of State for War in the Reich administration; no single institution with responsibility for military planning; and no clear chain of command between the Military Cabinet, the Prussian War Ministry, and the army's General Staff (though all were ultimately answerable to the Prussian King). Military spending was a source of recurrent conflict too, because the constitution had deliberately fudged the issue of army funding. As Clark points out, of the four occasions on which the Reichstag was dissolved prematurely – in 1878, 1887, 1893, and 1906 – "three occurred for reasons related to the control of military expenditure."[35]

The Reichstag was elected by universal (male), equal, secret, and direct suffrage, with a minimum voting age of 25. Only active soldiers, convicted criminals, asylum residents, and recipients of poor-relief were barred from the ballot box. Elections were held in 397 single-member constituencies whose boundaries were not redrawn during the lifetime of the Empire.[36] The successful candidate had to achieve more than half of the vote. If this did not occur, a second "run-off" election was held some ten days later between the two leading candidates (by the 1890s around a half of all contests required a second ballot). The unusually progressive Reichstag franchise, which was much more inclusive than German liberals had desired, confounded contemporaries when it was first introduced for elections to the North German Confederation's parliament in 1867. At the time it was arguably the most generous franchise in Europe – only the Greeks and the French enjoyed universal manhood suffrage sooner – though it is important to remember that it existed alongside much more

---

32 H.-P. Ullmann, *Das Deutsche Kaiserreich 1871–1918*, p. 37.
33 C. Clark, *Kaiser Wilhelm II*, p. 116.
34 See D. Schoenbaum, *Zabern 1913: Consensus Politics in Imperial Germany* (London, 1982).
35 C. Clark, *Kaiser Wilhelm II*, p. 67.
36 There were originally 382 constituencies but this was increased in 1874 following the enfranchisement of the *Reichsland* Alsace-Lorraine. The failure to change constituency boundaries in line with demographic change greatly favored parties with rural strongholds and handicapped parties with a more urban base.

restrictive and unequal suffrages in local government and for elections to state parliaments. In Prussian Landtag elections, for example, a public and indirect form of voting was used, and this together with the infamous taxed-based "three-class" franchise ensured that the lower house remained in the hands of conservative forces right up to 1918, despite mounting pressure for change. Similarly, "reform" of Saxony's state electoral law in 1896 amounted to nothing more than a shameless manipulation of the franchise in a calculated attempt to stem the rise of Social Democracy.[37]

Bismarck's motives for the introduction of universal manhood suffrage in Reichstag elections have been examined in some depth. It is generally agreed that he wished to outflank the liberals – who had proved stubborn opponents during the Prussian constitutional conflict of the early- to mid-1860s – by appealing directly to the conservative instincts of the peasantry. While some see Bismarck's flirtation with the "revolutionary" franchise as a typically opportunistic gamble, others suggest that Bismarck's interest in democratic elections was far from a sudden whim. According to Peter Steinbach (born 1948), for instance, Bismarck had become convinced as early as the 1850s that elections need not have a destabilizing effect; and this view had hardened during a short diplomatic posting to Napoleon III's Paris in 1862, when he saw how a monarchical government could turn the universal franchise and parliamentary institutions to its own advantage.[38] Either way, Bismarck's attempt "to overthrow parliamentarism with parliamentarism"[39] was an innovation he quickly came to regret. As Fairbairn observes, "[t]he suffrage Bismarck created with unliberal intentions became within a generation the most potent vehicle of political participation in Germany. The Reichstag suffrage was the single most important precondition, or engine, for the growth of participation before the turn of the century."[40] It was not long before parliament was dominated by parties critical of Bismarck and his program. In 1881, for instance, less than one-third of the Reichstag's elected members belonged to parties wholly supportive of the government. As Jonathan Sperber (born 1952) points out, this illustrates

---

37 See J. Retallack, "'What is to be done?' The red specter, franchise questions, and the crisis of German hegemony in Saxony, 1896–1909," *Central European History*, 23 (1990). On the other hand, reforms led to more inclusive state elections in the south German states of Baden (1904), Württemberg (1905), and Bavaria (1906).
38 P. Steinbach, "Reichstag elections in the Kaiserreich: The prospects for electoral research in the interdisciplinary context," in L. E. Jones and J. Retallack, eds., *Elections, Mass Politics, and Social Change in Modern Germany* (Cambridge, 1992), p. 133.
39 K. A. Lerman, *Bismarck*, p. 129.
40 B. Fairbairn, "Political mobilization," in R. Chickering, ed., *Imperial Germany*, p. 306.

very well "the difference between the government and constitution of Imperial Germany and that of a parliamentary regime ... the prime minister of a parliamentary government would have had to resign after such a defeat ... Bismarck was under no such obligations."[41]

Despite this, historians now agree that the importance of the Reichstag, its committees, and of the political parties represented in it, all grew markedly during the lifetime of the Empire.[42] This was partly as a result of an increased workload and a vastly increased budget, as the imperial role expanded into areas such as social welfare and naval ship-building legislation, but it was also because of a growing self-confidence and assertiveness among the Reichstag's members themselves. Parliamentary arithmetic became an increasingly important factor in the calculations of Germany's leaders, and despite the constitutional limitations placed on the Reichstag it did become the focus of national political life. Certainly, it was more than just a "fig-leaf for absolutism," as the Wilhelmine socialist Karl Liebknecht once dismissively put it. As we shall see, however, this does not necessarily mean that the *Kaiserreich* was on the road to parliamentary government by 1914. Although the Reichstag increasingly sought to influence the government's legislative program, and private meetings between the chancellor and party leaders became more commonplace, its main constitutional weapon remained essentially negative: to block or amend the executive's legislative or budgetary proposals.[43] The defeat of the government's Sedition Bill (*Umsturzvorlage*) of 1894–5 or the Hard Labor Bill (*Zuchthausvorlage*) of 1899 demonstrated that the Reichstag was more than a pseudo-parliamentary "talking shop," but the executive's power to dissolve parliament and call for new elections always gave Bismarck and his successors important leverage over the politicians. Denied the chance to form governments, the Reichstag parties – which were not recognized by the constitution – were left with an unenviable choice: to co-operate with the executive in the uncertain hope of exercising some modest influence, or to enjoy the luxury of permanent opposition. It was a system that threatened to turn parties into lobby groups for narrow sectional interests, and to nurture what Blackbourn terms "an irresponsible politics of posture."[44] It was also a

---

41 J. Sperber, *The Kaiser's Voters. Electors and Elections in Imperial Germany* (Cambridge, 1997), pp. 189–90.
42 This applies even to H.-U. Wehler, see vol. 3 of his *Gesellschaftsgeschichte*, p. 1038.
43 The largest area of expenditure by far, however, was the army budget, which Bismarck ensured was not discussed on an annual basis. The Reichstag did finally acquire the right to negotiate it in 1874, but only once every seven years (the so-called *Septennat*). This was reduced to a five-year cycle in 1893. The naval budget was agreed annually.
44 D. Blackbourn, "Politics as theatre," in *Populists and Patricians*, p. 257.

system that encouraged political leaders to make generous promises, yet provided no mechanism for those promises to be redeemed.[45] While it is a myth that the Reichstag could not initiate legislation of its own – it could in certain circumstances under Article 23 of the constitution – its bills could not become law without the support of the Bundesrat. Moreover, such key areas as foreign policy and the army remained under the royal prerogative and were, therefore, largely shielded from parliamentary influence.

"Who rules?," the exasperated question posed by the Austrian Foreign Minister Count Berchtold when confronted by contradictory telegrams from the German chancellor and from the chief of the German General Staff in July 1914, may have been relatively easy to answer for the Bismarckian Empire, but it was clearly a more challenging proposition for the period after 1890. Bismarck's dominance of German high politics for the best part of three decades is undisputed, and it was hardly surprising that no one proved able to fill his shoes. In Wilhelm II's case, of course, it was not for want of trying. His constitutional and extra-constitutional prerogatives, together with the corrupting influence of the "kingship mechanism," gave him huge potential power, even if he possessed neither the temperament nor the tenacity to put it to effective use. As for Bismarck's successors as chancellor – "the well meaning Caprivi, the senile Hohenlohe, the pliant Bülow and the grey bureaucrat Bethmann Hollweg"[46] – they had the thankless task of trying to make the Bismarckian system work in a time of rapid social, economic, and political change. "Only a genius or a man driven by ambition and lust for power can covet this post" was Bethmann's weary assessment of his unenviable role.[47] Was the British iconoclast A. J. P. Taylor therefore correct in his famous historiographical response to Berchtold's question: "What a joke! No one ruled in Berlin"?[48]

"The problem with words such as 'rule' and 'authority,'" Katharine Lerman notes, "is that they do not appear to allow scope for pressures from below, or for constraints on those who occupy high positions, and that they thus suggest a straightforward pyramidal organisation of power which few if any would embrace."[49] As a historian who never allowed the facts get in the way of a memorable one-liner, such concerns may not have bothered Taylor, but his punning response should not

---

45 D. Blackbourn, "The politics of demagogy," in *Populists and Patricians*, p. 234.
46 R. J. Evans, ed., *Society and Politics in Wilhelmine Germany*, p. 17.
47 K. A. Lerman, *The Chancellor as Courtier*, p. 44.
48 A. J. P. Taylor, *The Course of German History*, p. 187.
49 K. A. Lerman, *The Chancellor as Courtier*, p. 6.

simply be dismissed as an attempt to achieve a cheap laugh. After all, Hans-Ulrich Wehler – a very different kind of historian – has written in similarly damning terms about the "polycratic chaos" within the Empire's "inert" and "ossified" political system.[50] In fact, while consensus is notoriously elusive among historians, there would be little dissent today from the notion that power in the Empire was dispersed and polycratic. The term "chaos," by contrast, is unhelpful in a scholarly context: subjective and imprecise, it also lends an inadvertently comic undertone, suggesting slapstick capers in the corridors of power (as in this observation by Taylor: "The events of 1906 to 1909 reduced the Bismarckian constitution to chaos ... 'full steam ahead' no doubt, but no one even attempting to hold the wheel or set a course").[51] More seriously, few would nowadays accept Taylor or Wehler's portrait of a system in stasis. As Peter Brandt puts it, "[e]ven if tendencies towards inertia were again getting stronger in the immediate pre-war period there can be no question of stagnation in political developments."[52] On the contrary, the whole post-1890 period has come to be seen as a time "of far-reaching political change, in which the entire structure of the public domain was re-ordered."[53] As a result, generalizations about the Empire based on a simple division into Bismarckian and Wilhelmine eras have given way to more differentiated perspectives, which distinguish between various phases within the Wilhelmine era itself, and which can better reflect the continually shifting nature of power-relationships, both between individuals and institutions.

A key to understanding this shift in perspective is provided by James Retallack: "Historians," he wrote, "must sometimes choose whether to analyse politics as a system or a process."[54] So far in this chapter we have largely followed the former approach, viewing the Empire through its constitution. On this basis, one could reasonably conclude that Wilhelmine Germany was ruled by an oligarchy of some 20 to 50 men: the Kaiser and the chiefs of his three private cabinets; the chancellor and his eight state secretaries in the Reich administration; the chief of the Reich Chancellery; the eight ministers in the Prussian administration; and so on. This list represents one answer to Berchtold's question, but it is not the only answer. For, if we examine Wilhelmine politics as a process, a more complex and dynamic picture emerges. This is not the "still-life of an

---

50 H.-U. Wehler, *The German Empire*, pp. 64–5.
51 A. J. P. Taylor, *The Course of German History*, p. 181.
52 P. Brandt, "War das Deutsche Kaiserreich reformierbar? Parteien, politisches System und Gesellschaftsordnung vor 1914," in K. Rudolph and C. Wickert, eds., *Geschichte als Möglichkeit. Über die Chancen von Demokratie* (Essen, 1995), p. 209.
53 G. Eley, *Reshaping the German Right*, p. 15.
54 J. Retallack, *Germany in the Age of Kaiser Wilhelm II*, p. 46.

authoritarian regime,"[55] but something more reminiscent of an early abstract by Kandinsky or Malevich: an image of flux and movement, in which colorful forces were engaged in transformative struggles. It also means looking at what might be termed the "bigger picture," because some of the most significant changes were occurring not at the highest echelons of politics, but at the grassroots. As Peter Steinbach puts it:

> It is now clear that the shaping of political life under Bismarck and Wilhelm II was not determined solely by caucus leaders in the Reichstag, by the press in Berlin, or by a circle of top officials in the government. Rather, the political culture was shaped to a large extent by the resonance of political arguments at lower political levels and among a national electorate.[56]

"Silent Parliamentarization" or Political Stalemate?

In a 2003 article, the political scientist Marcus Kreuzer (born 1964) suggested that historians of Imperial Germany's political development fall into three main historiographical camps, which he rather crudely labeled "optimists," "pessimists," and "skeptics." In the first group he placed a number of predominantly German political scientists and historians, past and present, such as Manfred Rauh, Thomas Nipperdey, Werner Frauendienst, Ernst-Wolfgang Böckenförde, Christoph Schönberger, and David Schoenbaum, who "subscribe to an evolutionary conception of political development in which continuous political reforms incrementally transformed Germany's political system." The second category was dominated by doyens of the "new orthodoxy," including Wehler, Winkler, and Berghahn, who present "a static view of Germany's political development." Sandwiched between these two camps, Kreuzer suggested, are skeptics like Gerhard A. Ritter and David Blackbourn, "who acknowledge Germany's gradual transformation but judge it to be too feeble and too offset by counter-developments, ultimately to lead to full regime change."[57] While Kreuzer was no doubt correct to assert that studies of the Empire tend to accentuate either the positive or negative aspects of its political development, his simplistic categorizations obscure the subtleties and nuances contained in the best work on this subject. That the majority of current historians belong in the "skeptical" camp is apparent in historians' rejection of both the darkly pessimistic vision of Wehler's *Kaiserreich*

---

55 Ibid., p. 3.
56 P. Steinbach, "Reichstag elections in the Kaiserreich," p. 144.
57 M. Kreuzer, "Parliamentarization and the question of German exceptionalism: 1867–1918," *Central European History*, 36 (2003), pp. 329–30.

and its unduly optimistic counterpart, Manfred Rauh's thesis of "silent parliamentarization," as well as in the demise of the once-mighty *Sonderweg* paradigm (see Chapter 1).[58]

Rauh (born 1942), a conservative political scientist, published the first of his two books on the Empire in 1973, the same year as Wehler's *Kaiserreich*.[59] Despite their very different outlooks, Rauh and Wehler shared a number of common traits: a polemical and provocative sense of certainty; a marked tendency to overstate and exaggerate; and a discursive tone that seemed harsh even by German standards. Rauh's argument, which was presented more cautiously and convincingly in his first book than in his second, was based on the shifting relationship between the Bundesrat and the Reichstag. He suggested that the rise in power of the latter signaled a slow and steady, if unheralded, transition towards parliamentary rule. This was based on a step-by-step learning process, which proceeded irrespective of the fact that most of those involved were expressly opposed to it. The lack of enthusiasm for parliamentary rule among the Empire's political parties has always been cited as one of the main obstacles to parliamentarization, so this formed an important plank in Rauh's argument.[60] By focusing almost exclusively on the Reichstag and Bundesrat, however, Rauh overlooked other bases of power in the Empire – most notably the civil service and army – which were not subject to parliamentarization, even in small increments. Significantly, Rauh was never able to build an equivalent of the "Bielefeld School," but he was not an altogether lone voice. He had both antecedents, like Werner Frauendienst (1901–66), and contemporary kindred spirits, such as Gustav Schmidt and Dieter Grosser.[61] More weighty backing came from Ernst-Wolfgang Böckenförde (born 1930) and Thomas Nipperdey, who

---

58 Of the post-1990 synthetic works and textbooks on the Empire (see Chapter 1) only Nipperdey's can really be characterized as "optimistic." Berghahn, Winkler, Wehler, and Mommsen have all made concessions but clearly remain in the "pessimist" camp. The books by Ullrich, Loth, Retallack, Blackbourn, Feuchtwanger, Seligmann, and McLean, and even Ullmann, on the other hand, can all be regarded as belonging to the "skeptical" category.

59 M. Rauh, *Föderalismus und Parlamentarismus im Wilhelminischen Reich* (Düsseldorf, 1973); M. Rauh, *Die Parlamentarisierung des Deutschen Reiches* (Düsseldorf, 1977). The first book, based on Rauh's doctoral dissertation, only goes up to 1909. The second book takes the story on to 1918.

60 See D. Langewiesche, "Das Deutsche Kaiserreich – Bemerkungen zur Diskussion über Parlamentarisierung und Demokratisierung Deutschlands," *Archiv für Sozialgeschichte*, 19 (1979), p. 638.

61 See W. Frauendienst, "Demokratisierung des deutschen Konstitutionalismus in der Zeit Wilhelms II," *Zeitschrift für die gesamte Staatswissenschaft*, 113 (1957); G. Schmidt, "Deutschland am Vorabend des Ersten Weltkriegs," in M. Stürmer, ed., *Das kaiserliche Deutschland. Politik und Gesellschaft 1871–1914* (Düsseldorf, 1970); D. Grosser, *Vom monarchischen Konstitutionalismus zur parlamentarischen Demokratie* (The Hague, 1970).

enthusiastically adopted Rauh's notion that the Empire was standing "on the threshold of a parliamentary system" at the outbreak of war in 1914.[62]

The debate sparked by Rauh in the 1970s soon burnt itself out, not least because the study of political institutions fell out of historiographical fashion. Thus, despite the best efforts of Germany's Commission for the History of Parliamentarism and Political Parties, which continued to publish important monographs and essay collections under the leadership of Gerhard A. Ritter, it was not until the turn of the century that the parliamentarization debate was reignited.[63] The revival of interest, which was manifest in important essays by Thomas Kühne, Christoph Schönberger, and Mark Hewitson, together with the aforementioned article by Marcus Kreuzer, was partly inspired by a wave of publications on the Empire's elections, which hit the bookshelves in the mid-1990s and will be discussed below. Kreuzer's article, as well as offering a useful survey of the literature, contributed to the debate in its own right. Firmly on the side of the optimists, the American political scientist attempted to place German political developments in five key areas – "government formation, [the] Reichstag's legislative powers, [the] role of the Bundesrat, legislative norms, and developmental sequencing"[64] – in a comparative context. Echoing an earlier argument by Blackbourn and Eley, Kreuzer criticized all three historiographical camps for using the Westminster model as the yardstick to measure the progress of parliamentarization in Germany, when the "political institutions and experience of Britain simply are too singular" to be employed as a benchmark.[65] In particular, he suggested that historians have been wrong in making British-style parliamentary control over government formation "the central condition for parliamentarization," when this "varies a great deal, even among fully parliamentarized political systems."[66] He argued, moreover, that the Reichstag did have "growing control" over the government – albeit "in a negative fashion" – through its willingness to censure the chancellor or his state secretaries,[67] and through its increasing ability to set the legislative

---

62 The title of a section in M. Rauh, *Die Parlamentarisierung des Deutschen Reiches*, pp. 147–288.
63 See T. Kühne, "Parlamentarismusgeschichte in Deutschland: Probleme, Erträge und Perspektiven einer Gesamtdarstellung," *Geschichte und Gesellschaft*, 24 (1998), pp. 323–38. Since its establishment in 1951, the Commission has published over 130 volumes on different aspects of German parliamentary history.
64 M. Kreuzer, "Parliamentarization and the question of German exceptionalism," p. 335.
65 Ibid., p. 334.
66 Ibid., p. 335.
67 The Reichstag's power of censure was not part of the original constitution but began to evolve in parliamentary practice after 1890. The censure mechanism, which became

agenda. Indeed, Kreuzer concluded, when compared to other legislatures the powers of the Reichstag were actually quite impressive, standing broadly on a par with equivalent bodies in Belgium, the Netherlands, Switzerland, and the Scandinavian countries, and even with today's US Congress and European Parliament.[68]

Kreuzer's systematic comparison of different European and North American legislatures across time was praised for demonstrating "the potential of universalizing social science approaches to disputed historical questions,"[69] even if a number of his more eyebrow-raising assertions appeared to be based on very limited or inaccurate information. As Kreuzer himself conceded, "we know surprisingly little about the Reichstag's internal workings and even less about the Bundesrat," not to mention the largely unseen "power relations between the Reichstag, Bundesrat, and Reichsregierung."[70] Precisely this deficit was addressed by Christoph Schönberger (born 1966) in a 2001 essay.[71] Although labeled an "optimist" by Kreuzer, Schönberger's position could hardly have been more different from Rauh's. This is very clear from his conclusion: "The Empire was further from parliamentarization at its end than it had been in its early years."[72] The increasing influence of the Reichstag and its committees, Schönberger argued, was not synonymous with parliamentarization. On the contrary, it made the transition to parliamentary government more difficult, since it was based on the kind of bargaining between legislature and executive that is in fact typical of constitutional dualism (it occurs, for instance, between Congress and the President in the US), and, therefore, ultimately had the effect of strengthening rather than weakening the existing system. A second important point made by Schönberger was that the Empire's high degree of democratization – defined in terms of mass participation in political life – also worked against the prospects for parliamentary government. Although it is commonly assumed that parliamentarization and democratization march side-by-side, this is rarely the case. In Britain parliamentarization long pre-dated

---

formalized under the Reichstag's Standing Order reform of 1912, worked "by permitting motions to be attached to legislative interpellations that expressively stated no-confidence in a minister." See Kreuzer, ibid, p. 339.
68 Ibid., p. 343.
69 J. Sperber, "Comments on Marcus Kreuzer's article," *Central European History*, 36 (2003), p. 359.
70 M. Kreuzer, "Response to Ledford and Sperber," *Central European History*, 36 (2003), p. 379.
71 C. Schönberger, "Die überholte Parlamentarisierung. Einflußgewinn und fehlende Herrschaftsfähigkeit des Reichstags im sich demokratisierenden Kaiserreich," *Historische Zeitschrift*, 272 (2001), pp. 623–66.
72 Ibid., p. 655.

democratization, while in Germany "parliamentarization was overtaken by democratization."[73] The Empire's highly segmented and pluralistic society – a legacy of federalism; of confessional, ethnic, and social division; and of the early introduction of a democratic franchise – produced a party political landscape dominated by "structural minority" parties, with understandably little enthusiasm for a system based on majority rule. Countries characterized by this kind of "segmented pluralism" (V. R. Lorwin) – Switzerland, the Netherlands, and Belgium are other examples – rarely adopt Westminster-style parliamentarism, but instead develop a form of "consociational democracy" (*Konkordanzdemokratie*), with checks and balances to guarantee compromise and the representation of interests on a proportional basis. In Schönberger's view the late Wilhelmine Empire was an "unstable consensual structure" (*labiles Konsensgefüge*) which had little prospect of ever evolving into a parliamentary system, but may indeed have followed a similar route to democracy as its continental neighbors.

In fact, as Schönberger notes, the burning issue for political parties in the late Wilhelmine era was not parliamentary government at all, but rather the reform of the three-class franchise used for Prussian state elections.[74] The clamor for further democratization made parliamentarization seem a rather esoteric issue, of interest only to constitutional lawyers, historians, and newspaper columnists. This view is endorsed by Mark Hewitson (born 1967), who in another essay from 2001 argued that a broad cross-party consensus existed in pre-1914 Germany in favor of "the comparatively successful dualism of the *Kaiserreich*," not least because of the perceived failure of parliamentary regimes elsewhere in Europe.[75] Hewitson's description of a relatively stable *Kaiserreich*, in which "many Wilhelmine Germans refused to accept that the regime was a flawed compromise, and many more who did have misgivings about the political system nevertheless continued to make that compromise work, in the absence of a better alternative," echoes Gustav Schmidt's earlier notion of a "stable crisis" and provides a useful counterweight to the pervasive images of chaos and paralysis in Germany on the eve of World War One.[76] Paradoxically, Hewitson observes, "the era before the First

---

73   Ibid., p. 624.
74   See T. Kühne, *Dreiklassenwahlrecht und Wahlkultur in Preußen 1867–1914. Landtagswahlen zwischen korporativer Tradition und politischem Massenmarkt* (Düsseldorf, 1994).
75   M. Hewitson, "The *Kaiserreich* in question: Constitutional crisis in Germany before the First World War," *Journal of Modern History*, 73 (2001), p. 727.
76   Ibid., p. 727; also G. Schmidt, "Parlamentarisierung oder 'Präventive Konterrevolution?,'" in G. A. Ritter, ed., *Gesellschaft, Parlament und Regierung* (Düsseldorf, 1974), p. 260.

World War witnessed both a constitutional crisis and widespread acceptance of the existing political system in Germany." As a result, he suggests, the counter-intuitive idea that constitutional monarchy was actually stabilized in the later Wilhelmine years seems "more tenable than either Manfred Rauh's notion of a 'parliamentarization of the German Empire' or Hans-Ulrich Wehler's idea of a stalemate within a semi-authoritarian, sham democracy."[77]

This conclusion, which places Hewitson squarely in Kreuzer's "skeptical" camp, is very much in line with current thinking, but it is important to acknowledge that many historians – and not only diehard "pessimists" – continue to uphold the notion of a critical stalemate or blockade in German politics in the immediate pre-war years. Certainly, it is not hard to perceive a polarization of domestic political forces into reformist and conservative blocks, with the former too divided to press home its notional numerical advantage, and the latter increasingly estranged from its natural allies in government, particularly after the formation of the reactionary Cartel of Productive Estates in 1913. This undoubtedly left the government in an unenviable position: "Severed from its accustomed relations with the right, it could not embrace a decisive departure to the left," as Geoff Eley put it.[78] As a result, the hapless Chancellor Bethmann Hollweg had little option but to pursue his ill-fated "zig-zag" course (*Politik der Diagonale*), which as Feuchtwanger wryly remarks, "looked more like squaring the circle."[79] Wilfried Loth agrees, describing Bethmann's strategy as "merely an administering of the crisis," which inevitably "had to be paid for by increasing immobilism."[80] Whether this left Germany "ungovernable" and incapable of evolutionary change, as Mommsen, Röhl, Wehler, Berghahn, and most recently Winfried Halder have argued,[81] or whether the crisis was essentially a "stable" one, in which there was still potential for constructive development, must remain open to debate, since the outbreak of the First World War suddenly confronted all Germans with more pressing concerns than the "death-agony of Bismarck's constitutional structure."[82]

Nevertheless, the events of summer 1914 serve to remind us that while debates about parliamentarization and democratization can often

---

77 M. Hewitson, "The Kaiserreich in question," pp. 779–80.
78 G. Eley, *Reshaping the German Right*, p. 351.
79 E. Feuchtwanger, *Imperial Germany*, p. 152.
80 W. Loth, *Das Kaiserreich*, pp. 132–3.
81 W. Halder, *Innenpolitik im Kaiserreich 1871–1914* (Darmstadt, 2003). Halder describes the First World War as "the catalyst, not the cause, of [the Empire's] implosion" (p. 148).
82 The phrase is from W. Mommsen, "A delaying compromise: the Imperial constitution of 1871," p. 39.

appear rather arcane – Brett Fairbairn describes some of the historiographical exchanges from the 1970s and 1980s as "exciting as leftover porridge"[83] – Imperial Germany's domestic political difficulties do possess a wider significance. Research into the origins of the First World War has, of course, long focused on the internal politics of the *Kaiserreich*, particularly following the paradigm shift to the "primacy of domestic politics" in the 1960s. Many have since argued that the Empire's rulers deliberately sought war in 1914 as a "flight forwards," to break the domestic stalemate or to "turn the clock back" in German politics.[84] We shall return to this issue in Chapter 5, but clearly it is a theory that "depends heavily upon assessments of how real the threat was," as Woodruff Smith and Sharon Turner once put it.[85] As things stand, if we accept Schönberger's important distinction between democratization and parliamentarization, then the evidence would seem to suggest that parliamentarization was not an imminent "threat" in 1914; with regard to democratization, however, it would appear that Germany's rulers had more reason to fear.

From the Politics of Notables to a Political "Mass Market"?

At the zenith of the "new orthodoxy" German historians showed remarkably little interest in researching the Empire's party politics or elections. With real power located elsewhere in the political system, the *Kaiserreich's* "parliamentary trappings" (Mommsen) appeared barely worthy of analysis, unless it was to highlight the manipulative strategies with which the electorate was mobilized. Historians were "less curious about the fig leaf than what they suspected was underneath," as Margaret Anderson puts it.[86] As a result, more monographs were published in Germany during the late 1960s and 1970s on economic pressure groups than on political parties,[87] and Nipperdey's 1961 survey of the party political

---

83   B. Fairbairn, "Political mobilization," p. 304.
84   See W. J. Mommsen's essay "Domestic factors in German foreign policy before 1914," *Central European History*, 6 (1973), pp. 3–43, reprinted in Mommsen, *Imperial Germany 1867–1918*, pp. 163–88.
85   W. Smith and S. A. Turner, "Legislative behavior in the German reichstag, 1898–1906," *Central European History*, 14 (1981), p. 4.
86   M. L. Anderson, *Practicing Democracy: Elections and Political Culture in Imperial Germany* (Princeton, 2000), pp. 10–11.
87   The best know of these are H.-J. Puhle, *Agrarische Interessenpolitik und preußischer Konservatismus im Wilhelminischen Reich 1893–1914* (Hanover, 1967) on the Agrarian League; H. Kaelble, *Industrielle Interessenpolitik in der Wilhelminischen Gesellschaft. Zentralverband deutscher Industrieller 1895–1914* (Berlin, 1967) on the Central Association of German

landscape remained the standard work in its field right up to the mid-1980s.[88] An interest in labor movement politics and the history of German Social Democracy was merely the exception that proved the rule. Of course, no one would deny that pressure groups and other mass organizations – such as the Navy League, the Army League, the Pan-German League, the Imperial League Against Social Democracy, or the war veterans' associations – were a significant and distinctive feature of the Empire's political life from the 1890s onwards, exerting an influence both on the Reichstag and on the executive, but they had no real prospect of replacing political parties and their importance should not be overstated.[89] In the face of German indifference it was left to Anglo-American historians to demonstrate that, far from being irrelevant, "political parties provide the historian ... with an essential link between politics at the centre and the periphery."[90] In the mid-1970s a steady stream of English-language monographs on Imperial Germany's party politics (often with a regional perspective) began to flow, which as yet shows little sign of drying up.[91] German scholars responded to the challenge, producing numerous studies of their own in the late 1980s and 1990s, so that all the Reichstag parties gained at least one, and usually several party histories.

Industrialists; I. Hamel, *Völkischer Verband und nationale Gesellschaft. Der Deutschnationale Handlungsgehilfen-Verband, 1893–1933* (Frankfurt, 1967) on a leading white-collar union; H.-P. Ullmann, *Der Bund der Industriellen* (Göttingen, 1976) on the German Industrialists' League; S. Mielke, *Der Hansa-Bund für Gewerbe, Handel und Industrie 1909–1914* (Göttingen, 1976) on the failed attempt to create a liberal pressure group to rival the conservative Agrarian League. It was also indicative that D. Stegmann's *Die Erben Bismarcks. Parteien und Verbände in der Spätphase des Wilhelminischen Deutschlands* gave more attention to pressure groups than to parties, despite the implication of its title.

88 T. Nipperdey, *Die Organisation der deutschen Parteien vor 1918* (Düsseldorf, 1961) remained largely unchallenged until the publication of G. A. Ritter's *Die deutschen Parteien 1830–1914* (Göttingen, 1985).

89 Wehler, it should be noted, still argues that "power migrated from parliament to those informal decision-making collectives hovering outside, so that often nothing more was left for the elected representatives of the voting public than the ratification of their resolutions." See his *Gesellschaftsgeschichte*, vol. 3, p. 674. For a recent study of Imperial Germany's pressure groups see A. Grießmer, *Massenverbände und Massenparteien im wilhelminischen Reich. Zum Wandel der Wahlkultur 1903–1912* (Düsseldorf, 2000). Individual studies of pressure groups in English include R. Chickering, *We Men Who Feel Most German. A Cultural Study of the Pan-German League 1886–1914* (Boston, 1984); and M. S. Coetzee, *The German Army League. Popular Nationalism in Wilhelmine Germany* (New York and Oxford, 1990).

90 D. Blackbourn, "Introduction," *Populists and Patricians*, p. 19.

91 B. Heckart, *From Bassermann to Bebel. The Grand Bloc's Quest for Reform in the Kaiserreich, 1900–1914* (New Haven, 1974); J. Hunt, *The People's Party in Württemberg and Southern Germany 1890–1914* (Stuttgart, 1975); R. J. Ross, *Beleaguered Tower: The Dilemma of Political Catholicism in Wilhelmine Germany* (South Bend, 1975); D. S. White, *The Splintered Party: National Liberalism in Hessen and the Reich, 1867–1918* (Cambridge, MA, 1976); D. Blackbourn, *Class, Religion and Local Politics in Wilhelmine Germany*, etc.

One area of imperial politics where the Anglo-Saxons have continued to set the agenda, however, is that of electoral politics and, in particular, electoral culture. The work of Stanley Suval (1933–86) in the 1980s, followed by Brett Fairbairn, Jonathan Sperber, and Margaret Anderson in the 1990s and 2000s, has not only reinvigorated study of the *Kaiserreich*'s electoral history, but provided new impulses for German history as a whole.[92] Together with German-language studies by the likes of Thomas Kühne, Jürgen Winkler, Jürgen Schmädeke, and Robert Arsenscheck, they have helped to place the spotlight on the "fig leaf" for the first time.[93] While employing very different methodologies – sophisticated quantitative analysis in the case of Sperber; cultural history and anthropological "thick description" in the case of Anderson – these historians are united in the belief that elections mattered in Imperial Germany. Certainly they were hard to ignore: "a German living in Bavaria experienced a national or statewide election every two years; in Prussia, every twenty-one months; in Saxony, every fifteen months."[94] All the recent accounts subscribe to the view that the imperial electorate, at least in the Wilhelmine era, was more mobile and dynamic than previously believed. They are careful, however, not to overstate their case and conjure up whiggish tales of progress and emancipation. Anderson, for instance, describes in great detail the bullying and intimidation that was a persistent feature of all Reichstag elections – by no means only in agrarian constituencies east of the River Elbe – and which often made a mockery of the supposedly "secret" ballot.

One point of agreement between the new school of electoral historians and more traditional accounts is the changing nature of the Empire's electoral contests, summed up in the well-worn phrase "from the politics of notables to mass politics." It is generally accepted that most elections in the early decades of the Empire were contested by local notables (*Honoratioren*), gentleman-politicians who relied on personal status and informal influence to gain election, rather than the backing

---

92 S. Suval, *Electoral Politics in Wilhelmine Germany* (Chapel Hill and London, 1985); B. Fairbairn, *Democracy in the Undemocratic State*; J. Sperber, *The Kaiser's Voters*, M. L. Anderson, *Practicing Democracy*.
93 T. Kühne, *Dreiklassenwahlrecht und Wahlkultur in Preußen*; J. R. Winkler, *Sozialstruktur, politische Traditionen und Liberalismus. Eine empirische Längsschnittstudie zur Wahlentwicklung in Deutschland 1871–1933* (Opladen, 1995); J. Schmädeke, *Wählerbewegung im Wilhelminischen Deutschland. Eine historisch-statistische Untersuchung zu den Reichstagswahlen von 1890 bis 1912*, 2 vols. (Berlin, 1994–5); R. Arsenscheck, *Der Kampf um die Wahlfreiheit im Kaiserreich. Zur parlamentarischen Wahlprüfung und politischen Realität der Reichstagswahlen 1871–1914* (Düsseldorf, 2003).
94 M. L. Anderson, *Practicing Democracy*, p. 9.

of a party machine. Although party caucuses existed in the Reichstag, they had little permanent presence on the ground and only engaged with voters at election time. As a result, turnouts remained relatively low (about 51 per cent in the first Reichstag elections of 1871), and voters were primarily motivated by traditional patterns of thought based on religion, region, or ethnicity. Precisely when this state of affairs began to change, however, remains open to debate. Some would argue that the masses were already being mobilized in the 1870s and 1880s – evidenced by rising Reichstag turn outs – while others would argue that change only began to set in during the 1890s, when urbanization, improvements in public education, and cheap mass-circulation newspapers led to the entry of "the masses" into political life, producing novel ways of campaigning, institutionalized parties, and a new breed of professional politicians, more likely to rely on populist demagoguery than deference.[95] Like all such generalizations, therefore, the *Honoratiorenpolitik–Massenpolitik* paradigm is not without its problems. Similarly, the claim that the 1890s saw the "politics of ideals" (*Ideenpolitik* or *Weltanschauungspolitik*) supplanted by "interest politics" (*Interessenpolitik*) – meaning that voters were increasingly motivated by social class, economic interest, or the "fairness" of government policy – remains hotly contested too.[96]

What is clear, however, is that the extent to which individual parties adapted to, or embraced, the emergence of mass politics varied considerably. The party which is generally considered to have been most at home with "politics in a new key" (Carl Schorske) was the Social Democratic Party of Germany or SPD, founded in 1875 with the merger of the General German Workers' Party (1863) and the Social Democratic Workers' Party (1869).[97] Banned between 1878 and 1890 under the Anti-Socialist Law – which profoundly alienated at least one generation of party supporters from the Prusso-German state[98] – the SPD quickly became a mass party in every respect, increasing its share of the vote at all but one Reichstag election after 1890, and becoming the parliament's largest faction in 1912. Indeed it is viewed by many as the first modern, mass political

---

95 Reichstag deputies remained unsalaried and did not begin to receive an allowance until 1906, though increasing numbers (particularly in the SPD and Center) were employed by their parties, for instance as journalists on party newspapers. See H. Butzer, *Diäten und Freifahrt im Deutschen Reichstag. Der Weg zum Entschädigungsgesetz von 1906* (Düsseldorf, 1999).
96 See ch. 1 of J. Retallack's *The German Right 1860–1920. Political Limits of the Authoritarian Imagination* (Toronto, 2006) for a more detailed discussion of these issues.
97 It was known as the Socialist Workers' Party of Germany (SAPD) until 1890.
98 See K. Schönhoven and B. Braun, eds., *Generationen in der Arbeiterbewegung* (Munich, 2005).

party in Europe. Even so, as Marcus Kreuzer notes, "mass politics still confronted [the party] with new challenges to which they were reluctant to adapt themselves. At the core of this challenge was the debate over whether liberal democracy, and the mass politics it engendered, facilitated or hindered working-class emancipation."[99] The extensive literature on the SPD – and there has been more written on it "than on all the other political parties in Imperial Germany put together"[100] – has traditionally centered on this issue, and in particular the theoretical struggles between the party's "revolutionary," "revisionist," and "reformist" elements. Two other themes have loomed large in the historiography: the sources of the party's remarkable electoral growth; and its alleged "negative integration" into imperial German society.[101]

The latter thesis was first advanced by the sociologist Günther Roth in the late 1950s and later developed by Dieter Groh, before becoming a cornerstone of the "new orthodox" view of the *Kaiserreich*.[102] It was motivated as much by a desire to understand the SPD's lack of enthusiasm for revolution in 1918–19 and its apparent paralysis in the Weimar Republic, as its role in imperial politics. The thesis suggested that socialists in the Empire existed in a separate sub-cultural ghetto, which "both generated and assured the isolation of their social grouping."[103] Not only did this sub-culture reflect many of the characteristics of the dominant culture, but it also had the unintended effect of reconciling working-class Germans with their existing environment, and weakened the long-term prospects of radical change. Thus while the SPD remained revolutionary in theory, it became reformist in practice. Held together by Karl Kautsky's compromise formula of a "revolutionary but not a revolution-making party," organization became a substitute for political action (Helga Grebing) and the Empire's socialist leaders were content to accrue ever more votes while they awaited capitalism's inevitable collapse, in a strategy sometimes dubbed "revolutionary *attentisme*." Ironically, as

---

99 M. Kreuzer, *Institutions and Innovation. Voters, Parties, and Interest Groups in the Consolidation of Democracy – France and Germany, 1870–1939* (Ann Arbor, 2001), p. 25.
100 J. Sperber, *The Kaiser's Voters*, p. 36.
101 For a good introduction to these issues see S. Berger, *Social Democracy and the Working Class in Nineteenth and Twentieth Century Germany* (London, 2000).
102 G. Roth, *The Social Democrats in Imperial Germany. A Study in Working-Class Isolation and National Integration* (Totowa, 1963); D. Groh, *Negative Integration und revolutionärer Attentismus. Die deutsche Sozialdemokratie am Vorabend des Ersten Weltkrieges* (Frankfurt, 1973).
103 S. Suval, *Electoral Politics in Wilhelmine Germany*, p. 88. For the socialist sub-culture see V. Lidtke, *The Alternative Culture: Socialist Labor in Imperial Germany* (Oxford, 1985); L. Abrams, *Workers' Culture in Imperial Germany* (London, 1992); A. Hall, *Scandal, Sensation and Social Democracy: the SPD Press and Wilhelmine Germany* (Cambridge, 1977); G. A. Ritter, ed., *Arbeiterkultur* (Königstein, 1979).

Edgar Feuchtwanger points out, "it was the unresolved nature of the German political system as a whole that allowed the SPD to live with its own contradictions."[104]

Writing in the 1980s, Stanley Suval attempted to pull together the various strands of what was already a vast body of literature.[105] A vote for the SPD, he suggested, "expressed the isolation of these workers from the other social groupings and the dominant society; it connected everyday oppression with the process of identifying and responding to labeling of political and social deviance." At the same time, "[t]he vote and the successes associated with it became ends in themselves, forestalling revolutionary movement and containing radical elements of the party."[106] It would be wrong to suggest that in the intervening quarter-century all this valuable scholarship has been thrown out of the window, but there have been some significant revisions. It is now widely accepted, for example, that the labor movement's sub-culture was not hermetically sealed, and there was no "simple polarity between an essentially coherent 'dominant culture' on the one side and an excluded Social Democratic 'subculture' on the other."[107] Historians today favor the looser notion of a "socio-cultural milieu" (M. Rainer Lepsius),[108] in which the party was just one of many competing influences. In any case, the ever-growing numbers who voted for the SPD often had only tenuous links to the party's organizations. Moreover, when it came to elections, "Social Democrats were not 'negatively integrated,' but were (even without revolution) challenging the government, the regime, and its allied parties for legitimacy and for hegemony in civil society."[109] The system of "run-off" elections ensured that informal (and in some cases formal) co-operation took place between the SPD and many other parties. Although the image of a typical SPD voter – "Protestant, urban, blue-collar, and … young"[110] – may not have changed drastically, the latest research provides some important new insights in this regard too. Jonathan Sperber has made the striking claim that "social class did not play a major role in

---

104 E. Feuchtwanger, *Imperial Germany*, p. 109.
105 For a helpful overview of the pre-1980 literature see R. J. Evans, "Introduction: The sociological interpretation of German labour history," in *The German Working Class*, pp. 15–53.
106 S. Suval, *Electoral Politics in Wilhelmine Germany*, p. 95.
107 Vernon Lidtke, *The Alternative Culture*, p. 10.
108 M. R. Lepsius, "Parteiensystem und Sozialstruktur: Zum Problem der Demokratisierung der deutschen Gesellschaft," in G. A. Ritter, ed., *Deutsche Parteien vor 1918* (Cologne,1973), pp. 56–80.
109 B. Fairbairn, *Democracy in the Undemocratic State*, p. 214.
110 S. Suval, *Electoral Politics in Wilhelmine Germany*, p. 84. As Sperber notes, this view was "one of the few points of agreement" between West and East German scholars of the imperial era. *The Kaiser's Voters*, p. 36.

the SPD vote ... after 1900, the middle class voted for the labor party to almost as great an extent as did the working class."[111] In other words, while the SPD has traditionally been viewed as a workers' party (*Arbeiterpartei*), Sperber's statistical analysis indicates it was already becoming a broad "people's party" (*Volkspartei*), albeit one largely confined to urban areas, in the years before World War One. Even if Sperber's methodology exaggerates the "substantial proportion of Protestant businessmen, professionals, civil servants, and salaried employees" who voted for the SPD, they certainly existed, as evidenced by local studies from Hamburg, Frankfurt, and Ludwigshafen, and from Jürgen Winkler's national-level analysis.[112]

In terms of social class, however, the SPD electorate remained less heterogeneous than that of the Center, another section of the population to be labeled by Bismarck as "enemies of the Empire" (*Reichsfeinde*). Founded in the winter of 1870–1 to defend the religious rights and values of both Christian confessions, the Center Party quickly became a bastion for the one-third of Germans who owed their allegiance to the Catholic faith.[113] It advanced from 58 Reichstag seats in 1871, to 91 in 1874, winning over 80 per cent of the Catholic vote at the height of the *Kulturkampf*. More impressive still, however, was the way in which it succeeded in maintaining this constituency long after the most blatant persecution was over, achieving a remarkably consistent share of Reichstag votes and seats throughout the lifetime of the Empire and beyond. David Blackbourn, whose work on the party and the wider Catholic community has been influential, believes that the Center should be viewed as a "normal" political party, acting as a vehicle for particular economic interests, but nevertheless concedes it was something of an "oddity." It was "an awkward party, as difficult for historians to fit into the normal political spectrum as it was for contemporaries to accept it as a normal political party."[114] In the 1970s John Zeender (1917–2002) tried to place it on a conventional left-right scale by classifying it as "a moderate conservative social party on a Catholic foundation";[115] more recently,

---

111 This broad social mix did not apply to the party's membership, however, which remained dominated by skilled blue-collar workers and tradesmen. See ibid, p. 72.
112 Ibid., p. 68; also J. R. Winkler, *Sozialstruktur, politische Traditionen und Liberalismus*.
113 A Catholic faction of the same name had sat in the Prussian Landtag until 1866. The Center's leaders were divided over whether to pursue an inter-confessional approach. As it was, the Center never achieved more than 1 per cent of the Protestant vote, and between 1887 and 1914 only one member of the Center's Reichstag faction was a Protestant.
114 D. Blackbourn, "Catholics and politics in Imperial Germany: the Centre Party and its constituency," in *Populists and Patricians*, p. 191.
115 J. K. Zeender, *The German Center Party, 1890–1906* (Philadelphia, 1976), p. 4.

Brett Fairbairn has suggested a "better formulation would be that the Center was right-wing on most economic questions, but rather more left-wing on constitutional ones."[116] In fact it was precisely because of this ability to form Reichstag coalitions with either right or left, that the party became "the pivotal party in German politics," at least from the 1890s onwards.[117]

Despite its undoubted importance the Center was long neglected by historians, perhaps because it seemed a "strange interloper" (Blackbourn) in the supposedly "rational" world of modern mass politics, or maybe as a consequence of lingering anti-Catholic sentiments in an overwhelmingly secular profession. Either way, the historiographical attention paid to it over the past three decades has offered belated acknowledgment of its significance.[118] Much of the literature focuses on the party's complex relationship with its apparently loyal electorate, but the Center's connections with the Catholic Church have also come under scrutiny. While Blackbourn argues that the Center was not a clerical party, Anderson reminds us that "no fewer than 91 of the Centrum's 483 deputies during the course of the empire were clergymen." For many Catholics, she suggests, "[v]oting was not just a civic, or even a moral, but a religious act."[119] Certainly, the Center's consistent electoral performance was not a reward for developing an effective party machine. Unlike the SPD, it "never developed a party organization with a dues-paying membership, a party leadership elected by it, or a full-time, paid party staff."[120] It was, Suval argued, "social cohesion, not strong Church organization, that moved the German Catholic voter to the polls."[121] Even so, it is clear that ancillary organizations such as the People's Association for Catholic Germany (1890), which had over 800,000 members by 1914, played a key role in attempting to protect the Center's electoral constituency from the lure of socialism.[122] It is also apparent, however, that despite the People's Association's best efforts, it proved increasingly difficult to hold together a Catholic electorate divided on all the key social and economic

---

116 B. Fairbairn, *Democracy in the Undemocratic State*, pp. 181–2.
117 J. Retallack, *Germany in the Age of Kaiser Wilhelm II*, p. 45.
118 See R. J. Ross, *Beleaguered Tower*; D. Blackbourn, *Class, Religion and Local Politics*; J. K. Zeender, *The German Center Party*; also E. E. Evans, *The Center Party 1870–1933: A Study in Political Catholicism* (Carbondale, IL., 1981); W. Loth, *Katholiken im Kaiserreich. Der politische Katholizismus in der Krise des wilhelminischen Deutschlands* (Düsseldorf, 1984); J. Sperber, *Popular Catholicism in Nineteenth Century Germany* (Princeton, 1984).
119 M. L. Anderson, *Practicing Democracy*, pp. 108, 133.
120 J. Sperber, *The Kaiser's Voters*, p. 98.
121 S. Suval, *Electoral Politics in Wilhelmine Germany*, p. 69.
122 See T. Nipperdey, *Deutsche Geschichte 1866–1918*, vol. 1, p. 440; H. Heitzer, *Der Volksverein für das katholische Deutschland im Kaiserreich 1890–1918* (Mainz, 1979).

issues. Thus while the Center benefited from the failure to reform constituency boundaries and from the geographical concentration of Catholic voters on the peripheries of the Empire, this only helped to disguise a gradual drift of supporters away to other parties.

The Empire's liberal and conservative parties, sometimes not altogether helpfully grouped together as "national" parties, were a testament to Bismarck's dramatic impact on the political landscape. Not only did the *Kulturkampf* kill off any prospect of an inter-denominational bourgeois party emerging in the *Kaiserreich*, but as we saw in Chapter 2 the events of the 1860s created deep divisions among both liberals and conservatives. Prussia's liberals, organized in the German Progressive Party since 1861, fell out in 1866 over the German "civil war" and the Indemnity Bill. It is often said that pro-Bismarckians put their nationalism above their liberalism when they broke away to form the National Liberal Party, but this is something of a false opposition: mid-nineteenth century European liberals generally regarded these as two sides of the same coin. Those who remained as left-liberal Progressives may have upheld their liberal principles, but they also proved particularly susceptible to splits and secessions in the decades that followed, with the result that some Reichstag elections were contested by as many as four liberal parties. In practice, however, electoral politics was not quite as complicated as this might suggest, since most constituencies were fought by only two liberal candidates, and many by only one.[123]

Even so, as classic "parties of notables" all the liberal factions found the transition to mass politics traumatic. Nineteenth-century liberals, for whom the individual was paramount, distrusted the irrationality and unpredictability of the "mob," and the partisan trappings of modern party politics were viewed with suspicion: the National Liberal Party did not hold its first party conference until 1892, and did not adopt a party statute until 1905. It was little wonder then that the liberal parties failed to develop the kind of ancillary organizations which were so important in integrating the SPD and Center party memberships, even if nationalist groups such as the Navy League could perform some of these functions. As a political creed that had always aspired to represent the common good, liberalism was fatally weakened by the growth of sectoral and interest politics. Unlike the SPD or Center, the liberal parties did not possess a broadly homogenous social or geographic constituency – their supporters

---

123 In fact, despite the dozen or so parties represented in the Reichstag at any one time, constituency contests in the Wilhelmine era were on average no more than three-way affairs, with parties reluctant to put up candidates in seats where there was no chance of winning (unless vote maximization was important, as it was for the SPD).

came from town and country, industry and handicraft, the professions and farming – and the conflicting economic interests they represented could only be held together by fragile compromises, and by the frequent resort to nationalist or anti-socialist rhetoric. Thus while the combined liberal parties won more than half the seats in the first Reichstag elections, their share declined steadily in subsequent polls: to less than one-third of the seats in 1890; and less than one-quarter in 1912. This electoral decline – which was more pronounced for the National Liberal Party than for the left liberals, who benefited from being "everyone's second choice" in run-off elections[124] – coupled with a loss of influence on the executive after Bismarck's shift to the right in the late 1870s, and an inability, or unwillingness, to secure parliamentary government, are familiar motifs in the frequently-painted picture of German liberalism's "failure."

In recent years, however, historians have become more sensitive to the particular problems faced by the Empire's liberals – not least the unusually wide franchise, which led to the rise of mass parties earlier than elsewhere in Europe – and their "failure" has to some extent been relativized.[125] It has been argued, for instance, that their Reichstag election performance resembled a series of peaks and troughs rather than a steady decline; and even in the pronounced trough of 1898–1903, liberal parties still won almost a quarter of the votes, making them "one of the four strong groupings in Wilhelmine politics."[126] Sperber's statistical analysis has shown that while the liberals lost large numbers of voters, they also gained some new ones too, and not only from the middle classes: "Just as the SPD had a large middle-class vote and a small middle-class party membership, the liberal parties had a substantial working-class vote and small working-class membership," he argues.[127] It is important to acknowledge too that the strength of liberal Germany was not necessarily reflected in the performance of liberal parties in Reichstag elections. Liberals continued to play a leading role in local and state government and, more broadly, their political values set the tone of German public life. Finally, it is also possible to argue that the liberal parties were victims of

---

124 B. Fairbairn, *Democracy in the Undemocratic State*, p. 152.
125 See J. J. Sheehan, *German Liberalism in the Nineteenth Century* (Chicago and London, 1978); K. Jarausch and L. E. Jones, eds., *In Search of a Liberal Germany: Studies in the History of German Liberalism from 1789 to the Present* (New York, 1990); D. Langewiesche, *Liberalism in Germany* (Basingstoke, 2000); A. Thompson, *Left Liberals, the State, and Popular Politics in Wilhelmine Germany* (Oxford, 2000). The historiography is significantly more extensive for the left-liberal parties than for the National Liberals.
126 B. Fairbairn, *Democracy in the Undemocratic State*, p. 145.
127 J. Sperber, *The Kaiser's Voters*, pp. 149–50.

their own success. Dieter Langewiesche (born 1943) has put this case with particular eloquence: "It may be one of the great ironies of German history that the liberal parties had to pay for the surprisingly rapid consolidation of the national state with the loss of their own political hegemony." Their success as a national movement, he argues, "was reflected in their weakness as political parties."[128]

The Empire's two conservative parties – the enthusiastically pro-Bismarck Free Conservatives (1866), and the more belatedly Bismarckian German Conservative Party (re-founded in 1876) – were both "throne and altar" parties, which generally supported the executive and received significant government assistance in return. The German Conservative Party was a predominantly Prussian faction with its stronghold in the agricultural lands east of the Elbe.[129] It was a more ideological party than its smaller sister, also known as the Imperial Party, which regarded itself as the party of compromise, representing commercial and industrial, as well as agrarian, interests.[130] Both parties were, initially at least, classic examples of the politics of notables. Anderson, for example, describes the German Conservatives as "less a party than an affinity," "a skeletal clearinghouse through which the Conservative parliamentary delegation tried to coordinate its re-election campaigns."[131] Similarly, Fairbairn sees the Free Conservatives as not "a free-standing party" at all, but rather an "a flag of convenience for governmental candidates."[132] In the 1890s, however, the pressures of mass politics and growing rural radicalism forced both parties into change. The German Conservative Party, in particular, underwent a "pseudo-democratization" (Hans Rosenberg), adopting a populist program with elements of anti-Semitism, and a more demagogic political style. The influence of the Agrarian League, which provided financial and organizational assistance to both conservative parties (as well as to some National Liberals), became increasingly apparent as the conservatives' long-term decline was slowed, if not halted.[133]

---

128   D. Langewiesche, "German liberalism in the Second Empire," in K. Jarausch and L. E. Jones, eds., *In Search of a Liberal Germany*, p. 219.
129   See J. Retallack, *Notables of the Right*; J. Retallack, *The German Right 1860–1920*; also L. E. Jones and J. Retallack, eds., *Between Reform, Reaction and Resistance. Essays on German Conservatism* (Providence, RI, 1983).
130   See the recent studies by V.Stalmann, *Die Partei Bismarcks. Die Deutsche Reichs- und Freikonservative Partei 1866–1890* (Düsseldorf, 2000); and M. Alexander, *Die Freikonservative Partei 1890–1918. Gemäßigter Konservatismus in der konstitutionellen Monarchie* (Düsseldorf, 2000).
131   M. L. Anderson, *Practicing Democracy*, pp .175–6.
132   B. Fairbairn, *Democracy in the Undemocratic State*, pp. 116–17.
133   For the Agrarian League see G. Eley, *Reshaping the German Right*; H.-J. Puhle, *Agrarische Interessenpolitik und preußischer Konservatismus*.

As recently as the mid-1980s, Gerhard A. Ritter spoke of the conservative parties as "still hardly researched."[134] Things have improved since then, but they remain the least studied of the Empire's parties; partly because of the difficulty of obtaining source material, but also through inclination. Historians' attention, moreover, has tended to focus on a few selected themes: the relationship between "old" and "new" forms of right-wing politics; the extent to which the latter can be characterized as "pre-fascist"; and the degree of coercion required to mobilize the conservative vote. Although more research is needed, the evidence gathered by Kühne and Anderson, among others, would seem to suggest that while landlords' "effortless dictatorship" (Bethmann Hollweg) over the rural population had begun to crumble by the 1890s and 1900s, it remained a formidable obstacle to truly free Empire-wide elections.

Certainly, while the emergence of mass politics in late nineteenth-century Germany is generally accepted, the notion of a political "mass market" in the later *Kaiserreich* remains contentious. Hans Rosenberg's term often appears in studies of the Wilhelmine era, yet although the idea of voters as consumers, choosing their party like a brand, may well apply to electoral politics in the late twentieth century, is it appropriate for the *Kaiserreich?*[135] Blackbourn criticized Rosenberg's phrase for its implications of passivity, since in his view the German electoral "consumer" was a potent and active agent of change.[136] Anderson also considers the phrase inappropriate, although for a different reason: the imperial German voter, she suggests, "rarely acted as a consumer acts, expressing his taste as an individual. It was not in the exercise of individual freedom, but in competition between groups, that democratic politics took hold in Germany."[137] This was certainly the dominant view in the literature of the 1970s and 1980s, which emphasized the division of the German electorate into more or less rigid blocks, usually characterized as "milieus" or "camps." As we have seen, the former term was coined by the sociologist M. Rainer Lepsius (born 1928) in the 1960s and proved hugely influential.[138] Lepsius argued there were four main "socio-moral milieus" in nineteenth- and early twentieth-century Germany: the Catholic milieu; the Protestant urban middle class milieu; the Protestant rural milieu; and

---

134 G. A. Ritter, *Die deutschen Parteien 1830–1914*, p. 11.
135 It appears, for example, in H.-P. Ullmann, *Das Deutsche Kaiserreich 1871–1918*, p. 126; P. Steinbach, "Reichstag elections in the Kaiserreich," p. 138; and in many other places.
136 D. Blackbourn, "The politics of demagogy," p. 222.
137 M. L. Anderson, *Practicing Democracy*, p. 417.
138 M. R. Lepsius, "Parteisystem und Sozialstruktur: zum Problem der Demokratisierung der deutschen Gesellschaft," reprinted in G. A. Ritter, ed., *Die deutschen Parteien vor 1918* (Cologne, 1973).

the Protestant urban working class milieu. Voting for a political party was a means of affirming one's membership of such a milieu, rather than an expression of personal aspiration or self-interest. Lepsius's first three milieus, formed by a combination of religious, cultural, social, and economic factors, predated the *Reichsgründung*, while the Protestant urban working-class began to develop shortly thereafter. This development, and with it the rise of the SPD (largely through the conversion of previous non-voters), proved the only innovative element in an otherwise remarkably settled picture, with voters rarely straying beyond the friendly confines of their own milieu.

The milieu theory was both simple and persuasive – the total votes cast for parties within each milieu did indeed appear to remain stable for the best part of half a century, breaking down only in the late 1920s – but while it may have conveyed an accurate picture of elections in the Bismarckian era, it did not do justice to the more complex patterns of voting after 1890, which could not all be put down to internal movements within the milieus. This led the political scientist Karl Rohe (1934–2005) to develop an alternative model of camps (*Lager*), which were larger and more heterogeneous than milieus.[139] Based on his research into the Ruhr industrial region, Rohe identified three such camps in imperial politics – the Catholic, the Socialist, and the National – which were characterized by their mutual hostility and exclusivity. While correcting some of the weaknesses of Lepsius's model, Rohe's approach raised issues of its own. It denied, for instance, the possibility of voters moving between the left-liberal parties and the SPD – parties that were next to each other on a conventional left-right scale – yet allowed for the transference of votes "from the Conservatives to the south German Democrats, taking in National Liberals and anti-Semites on the way."[140]

One way in which historians have sought to acknowledge a more complex and fractured electorate than either the "milieu" or "camp" model allows, is to incorporate the psephological concept of "cleavage."[141] Writing in the 1980s, Stanley Suval argued that such cleavages – which could run through, as well as between, milieus or camps – explained why "Germans were unlikely to vote for Poles, whatever the class interest of the Polish candidate" or why "German working class Catholics were unlikely to join the Socialist party despite the possible economic advantages

---

139 K. Rohe, *Wähler und Wählertraditionen in Deutschland. Kulturelle Grundlagen deutscher Parteien und Parteiensysteme im 19. und 20. Jahrhundert* (Frankfurt, 1992).
140 J. Sperber, *The Kaiser's Voters*, p. 286.
141 A concept first developed by the Norwegian Stein Rokkan (1921–79), and introduced into the German historiography of the *Kaiserreich* by Peter Steinbach.

that might accrue from this act."[142] More broadly, Suval accepted the notion of a "pillarized" electorate – two-thirds of the Wilhelmine electorate could be characterized as "affirming voters," he suggested, with identifiable and habitual voting patters based upon their commitments to social groupings – but drew rather different conclusions than his German colleagues.[143] Where Lepsius had seen milieus as an unfortunate historical legacy which handicapped the long-term prospects of democracy, the American was more optimistic: "Politicization through affirming social groupings does not necessarily lead to democratization. Yet it did produce demands for reform of the system in order to extend, strengthen, and regularize the process and increase the prestige of the electoral system and of voting in general," he wrote.[144] In historiographical terms Suval's book was therefore an important part of the Anglo-Saxon challenge to the "new orthodoxy." Fairbairn, for instance, described its impact as "a welcome antidote to generations of functionalism, reductionism, and sweeping generalizations that diminished the significance of elections."[145]

More recently, Sperber's statistical analysis of Reichstag election results, based on a technique known as "ecological inference," has challenged both the "milieu" and "camp" theories. Although both sophisticated and controversial, his approach is founded on a piece of simple common sense: "it is entirely possible for a party to receive a similar percentage of votes at different elections but to have very different individuals cast these votes."[146] The results of his research suggest there were more significant electoral movements between the blocks than previously believed: This conclusion is also supported by Fairbairn, who notes: "Measured statistically, the 'volatility' of voting in Imperial Germany – the changes between parties in percentage vote – was second only to France and the Netherlands among ten European countries surveyed by Bartolini and Mair ... The unchangingness of Imperial German parties is a myth."[147] Recent research, therefore, offers important statistical support to Blackbourn and Eley's long-held conviction that the Wilhelmine electorate was essentially dynamic rather than static.

---

142 S. Suval, *Electoral Politics in Wilhelmine Germany*, pp. 5–6.
143 Suval's "affirming voters" were German Catholics, the Protestant working class, the German rural population east of the River Elbe, and the Empire's Polish population. He suggested, moreover, that the absence of such "affirming solidarities" within the Protestant middle classes explained the fluctuating fortunes of Imperial Germany's various liberal parties. See Suval, ibid, pp. 6–7.
144 Ibid., p. 244.
145 B. Fairbairn, *Democracy in the Undemocratic State*, p. 6.
146 J. Sperber, *The Kaiser's Voters*, p. 9.
147 B. Fairbairn, *Democracy in the Undemocratic State*, pp. 241–2.

Sperber also addresses the vexed issue of periodization with the Empire, and concludes that the traditional high-political caesura of 1890 remains valid for the Empire's electoral history. Contests up to 1887 ("the central election in the history of the empire") were fought predominantly on issues of nation-building, he argues, while from 1890 onwards economic issues dominated.[148] He differentiates between the periods in another way too: "the era of non-voters" before 1890 gave way to "the era of party politics" thereafter.[149] In fact, as Langewiesche noted as far back as 1979, "there is no shortage of suggestions for periods, epochs, and caesuras in the recent literature" on the *Kaiserreich*.[150] Although the majority of historians continue to identify the 1890s as the "crucial decade of political mobilization in Germany,"[151] this thesis can be challenged (not least because turnout actually declined at each Reichstag election during those turbulent years!)[152] Today a growing body of opinion highlights the years sandwiched between the Reichstag elections of 1898 and 1903 as the more significant turning point. As Fairbairn puts it: "[w]hat was emerging in these elections was a new kind of politics, perhaps a new political nation, that was not driven by the government."[153] Perhaps surprisingly, Hans-Peter Ullmann agrees: "around the turn of the century, the conditions under which politics were made in the Empire changed."[154] The most impressive spokesman for this school of thought, however, is Thomas Kühne (born 1958), who argues that it was in these years that the old Bismarckian dichotomy of *Reichsfreunde* and *Reichsfeinde* (friends and enemies of the Empire) finally broke down, to be replaced by a new demarcation between economic "producers" and "consumers." As a result, he suggests, a search for more integrative and consensual modes of politics was set in motion, and the politics of "and" came to replace the politics of "either/or."[155] Kühne is quick to point out that this did not mean the *Kaiserreich* became a fully pluralist, democratic society. Even so, "in the half-decade between 1898 and 1903 the process of "fundamental democratization," which was to transform German society in the long-term, reached a new level," albeit more swiftly in the south than in the

---

148 J. Sperber, *The Kaiser's Voters*, pp. 269–71.
149 Ibid., pp. 266–7.
150 D. Langewiesche, "Das Deutsche Kaiserreich – Bemerkungen zur Diskussion," p. 632.
151 See, for instance, R. J. Evans, "From Hitler to Bismarck," in *Rethinking German History*, p. 75; D. Blackbourn, "The politics of demagogy," pp. 222–3.
152 J. Sperber, *The Kaiser's Voters*, p. 287.
153 B. Fairbairn, *Democracy in the Undemocratic State*, p. 34.
154 H.-P. Ullmann, *Das Deutsche Kaiserreich 1871–1918*, p. 126.
155 T. Kühne, "Die Jahrhundertwende, die 'lange' Bismarckzeit und die Demokratisierung der politischen Kultur," in L. Gall, ed., *Otto von Bismarck und Wilhelm II. Repräsentanten eines Epochenwechsels?* (Paderborn, 2000), p. 90.

north of the Empire, and more obviously at the imperial level than in state or municipal government.[156]

An important aspect of the 1898 and 1903 Reichstag elections, emphasized by both Kühne and Fairbairn, is that the parties which "won" in popular support were not the ones favored by the imperial government. It was one of the idiosyncrasies of the Empire's dualistic system that while the government was not democratically responsible to the electorate, it did campaign in elections – as the rallying call of *Sammlungspolitik* in 1898 showed – and, whether it liked it or not, "general elections were about government policies."[157] At the same time, however, all attempts by government to influence the outcome of Reichstag elections ran the risk of undermining the necessary fiction of being "above the parties." Not only could this damage the government's credibility – and hence that of the crown as well – but it also had a legitimizing effect on the parliamentary opposition. Where the government did succeed in mobilizing voters (particularly first-time voters) by playing the nationalist card in "plebiscitary" elections, as happened in 1878, 1887, 1893, and 1907, it rebounded on them at the next election, when the same voters moved to the left, as occurred in 1881, 1890, 1898, and 1912.[158] It seems clear, moreover, that efforts to influence the outcome of elections became steadily less effective during the lifetime of the Empire, as mass electoral politics slithered out of government control.

Concluding his study of democracy in the undemocratic state, Fairbairn argued that the "flaw in German society lay less at the bottom than at the top." In other words, the cause of Imperial Germany's incomplete democracy – which, it is important to remember, was far from unusual in early twentieth-century Europe – "was not the fragmentation of the electorate, the parties, the ideologies, or the social groups. The problem was the ineffectiveness or unwillingness of specific elites to pursue the accommodations necessary for democracy."[159] This conclusion would provoke little dissent, but it also begs a question: why study the Empire's "parliamentary trappings" if there was little prospect of the "blockage" at the top from being removed? One answer is provided by Margaret Anderson. Democracy, she argues, is a "learning process"; a process that was well underway in the *Kaiserreich*, despite the handicaps and obstructions placed on it from above. The extent to which democratic values had taken root in German soil was apparent, she contends, in the

---

156 T. Kühne, "Die Jahrhundertwende," pp. 116–17.
157 B. Fairbairn, "Political mobilization," p. 314.
158 J. Sperber, *The Kaiser's Voters*, p. 269.
159 B. Fairbairn, *Democracy in the Undemocratic State*, p. 259.

events of 1918–19, when the overwhelming majority of the population "turned to elections rather than to other modes of effecting the changes they desired."[160] This may be an optimistic view – precious little was learnt about parliamentary government before 1918, and the history of the Weimar Republic suggests that democracy's "roots" were all too shallow – yet it is a defensible one. Historians, as Kenneth Ledford recently observed, have by and large come to accept that "Imperial Germany and its institutions, whatever their peculiarities, simply ranked somewhere on a spectrum, and need not be measured against some hypostacized, normative measuring rod, simply because of the *Sonderend* of 1933–45."[161]

---

160 M. L. Anderson, *Practicing Democracy*, p. 426.
161 K. Ledford, "Comparing comparisons: Disciplines and the Sonderweg," *Central European History*, 36 (2003), p. 372.

4

"Familiar Features in an Unfamiliar Light"? Social and Cultural Perspectives

Assessing the state of Germany's electoral and parliamentary history in 1998, Thomas Kühne identified three avenues which he believed merited further exploration: the everyday experience of voters at a local or regional level; the cultural history of elections (*Wahlkultur*); and the fresh perspectives offered by gender history.[1] Kühne's desideratum, in other words, was for political history to engage with approaches that had already become well established elsewhere in the discipline and which form the main focus of this chapter. Although the history of everyday life, gender history, and cultural history are all closely related, they retain their own distinctive research methods and agendas. What they share is a desire to move beyond the top-down and generalizing approach of historical social science, with its emphasis on "big structures, large processes, huge comparisons,"[2] yet without returning to the event- and state-orientated narratives that have been so central to the writing of history for the past two hundred years. This chapter explores the impact of these so-called "poststructuralist" approaches on the study of the German Empire. Where have the new approaches come from and what kind of questions do they ask? To what extent have they succeeded in casting the Empire's "familiar features in an unfamiliar light" (Richard Evans)? In order to understand the poststructuralist challenge, however, it will

---

1 T. Kühne, "Parlamentarismusgeschichte in Deutschland," p. 335.
2 The title of a book by Charles Tilly (New York, 1984).

first be necessary to consider some of the historical social science literature that preceded it.

Social History or the History of Society?

In the English-speaking world the term "social history" has long been identified with "history from below" or "grassroots" history, and one can certainly find examples of this in Germany too. In the mid-1970s, for instance, a group of academics based in the industrial Ruhr, including Lutz Niethammer (born 1939), Jürgen Reulecke (born 1940), and Franz-Josef Brüggemeier (born 1951), began highlighting the importance of individual agency in history. One collection edited by Niethammer even adapted Marx's famous quote as its programmatic title: "men make their own history; not in circumstances of their own choosing, but they make it themselves."[3] At around the same time, the small Peter Hammer publishing house in Wuppertal published two essay collections – *Factory, Family, Finishing Time* and *A Social History of Leisure* – which demonstrated a growing interest in British-style social history among younger historians in the Federal Republic.[4] This, however, was by no means the only strand within German social history. Some sought to follow the anthropological approach of the Swiss Rudolf Braun (born 1930), who was based in Berlin during the early 1970s;[5] while a more conservative variant was practiced in Tübingen by Karl Erich Born (1922–2000). Born's principal achievement was a huge multi-volume collection of documents on German social policy between 1867 and 1914: a fitting legacy for a historian who viewed Bismarck's social legislation with admiration.[6] For the most part, however, the version of social history that held the upper hand in late twentieth-century Germany was that developed by the school of historical

---

3   Lutz Niethammer et al., eds, *Die Menschen machen ihre Geschichte nicht aus freien Stücken, aber sie machen sie selbst. Einladung zu einer Geschichte des Volkes in NRW* (Berlin and Bonn, 1984).
4   J. Reulecke and W. Weber, eds, *Fabrik, Familie, Feierabend. Beiträge zur Geschichte des Alltags im Industriezeitalter* (Wuppertal, 1978); G. Huck, ed., *Sozialgeschichte der Freizeit. Untersuchungen zum Wandel der Alltagskultur in Deutschland* (Wuppertal, 1980).
5   Braun's best-known work, *Industrialisierung und Volksleben* first appeared in 1960. An English translation, *Industrialisation and Everyday Life* (Cambridge, 1990) was published 30 years later.
6   *Quellensammlung zur Geschichte der deutschen Sozialpolitik 1867–1914*, conceived by Karl Erich Born and Peter Rassow on behalf of the Historical Commission of the Academy of Sciences and Literature, Mainz. The first introductory volume appeared in 1966 and around one-half of the planned 27 volumes have since followed, mostly edited by Born, Hansjoachim Henning, and Florian Tennstedt. See also Born's *Wirtschafts- und Sozialgeschichte des Deutschen Kaiserreichs 1867/71–1914* (Wiesbaden, 1985).

social science, with its close links to sociology and economics. In his introduction to an important set of essays on *Modern German Social History* (1966), Hans-Ulrich Wehler defined it as the "history of social classes and groups, structures, and institutions."[7] Consequently, the later 1960s and 1970s saw the publication of numerous studies of industrialization, urbanization, migration, and class formation in nineteenth-century Germany, often with a strongly quantitative dimension.

The emergence of historical social science, with its new analytical methods and sharply defined concepts, marked a significant break with German historiographical traditions. As Jürgen Kocka recalled in a retrospective essay published in 2003, "social-scientific history was a field of experiment, excitement, and innovation in which many new insights were generated, old legends criticized and challenging hypotheses brought forward for further research."[8] One such hypothesis, of course, was built around the apparent disjuncture between Germany's rapid social and economic development on the one hand, and political stasis on the other. Works like Helmut Böhme's short *Introduction to the Social and Economic History of Germany* suggested that the particular way in which industrialization had occurred in Germany – on the basis of a political compromise between modern industrial and "feudal" agrarian interests – had contributed significantly to the crises of the twentieth century.[9] While it was a hypothesis predicated on modernization theory and the now unfashionable *Sonderweg* paradigm, the combination of economic success and political failure nevertheless remains central to many general accounts of German history, and not only those written in the spirit of the "new orthodoxy." At first sight there would appear to be a consensus that industrialization occurred later in Germany than in other parts of Europe, and that it was unusually dynamic and traumatic as a result. As Berghahn puts it in the opening sentences of his *Modern Germany*:

> The development of modern Germany is best understood against the background of the Industrial Revolution, which affected Central Europe with full force in the final decades of the nineteenth century. Britain had experienced the blessings and traumas of industrialization earlier and more slowly, but nowhere else in Europe did the transition from an economy based on agriculture to one dominated by industry occur with the same rapidity as in Germany.

---

7 H.-U. Wehler, ed., *Moderne deutsche Sozialgeschichte* (Cologne and Berlin, 1966), p. 9. See also J. Kocka, *Sozialgeschichte: Begriff, Entwicklung, Probleme* (Göttingen, 1977).

8 J. Kocka, "Losses, gains and opportunities: Social history today," *Journal of Social History*, 37 (2003), p. 22.

9 H. Böhme, *An Introduction to the Social and Economic History of Germany* (Oxford, 1978 – first published in Germany in 1968).

Later in the same volume he suggests there is "little doubt" that Germany's "extraordinarily violent course" in the twentieth century was directly linked to this rapid industrialization.[10]

In fact, the rapid and dislocating nature of German industrialization is referred to so often in the history books that it has become something of a truism. It is certainly not difficult to point to figures comparing the growth of coal or pig iron production in late nineteenth-century Germany, France, and Britain, which seem to indicate that the *Kaiserreich* was industrializing at a startling rate. As with all historical orthodoxies, however, it is a view that can be challenged. In 1983, for instance, Hartmut Kaelble used the house journal of historical social science, *Geschichte und Gesellschaft*, to argue that Germany's rapid industrialization was a "myth."[11] Kaelble's short but provocative essay highlighted the limited and problematic statistical evidence on which it is based. Many of the statistics used by historians, particularly for the earlier years of the Empire, are "estimates" taken from a 1965 book by Walther Hoffmann, whose accuracy has often been questioned.[12] That aside, while it is clear that the economy did grow quickly, all the relevant indices – per capita production, per capita incomes, industrial employment, female employment, demographic growth, internal migration, and urbanization – suggest that developments in Germany were not significantly out of line with those in other European countries. By the late nineteenth century, Kaelble argued, the exceptional cases were actually Britain (where the great spurt of growth had long since passed) and Sweden, where annual growth rates were nearly double those of the *Kaiserreich* between 1890 and 1910.

A different take on these issues is offered by Oliver Grant's recent study of *Migration and Inequality in Germany 1870–1913*. While he accepts the "unprecedented" scale and intensity of German industrialization – it was the first "developing economy," he suggests, and "no other European country had such a rapid transition to an urban industrial society"[13] – the problems it faced were far from unusual. By comparing Imperial Germany to today's industrializing nations, and by using concepts and tools taken from the contemporary field of development economics, Grant arrives at very different conclusions from those of Böhme or Berghahn. Where they see the *Kaiserreich* as an era of "missed opportunities" and

---

10   V. R. Berghahn, *Modern Germany. Society, Economy and Politics in the Twentieth Century* (Cambridge, 1989 – first published 1982), pp. 1, 267.
11   H. Kaelble, "Der Mythos von der rapiden Industrialisierung in Deutschland," *Geschichte und Gesellschaft*, 9 (1983), pp. 108–18.
12   W. G. Hoffmann, *Das Wachstum der deutschen Wirtschaft seit der Mitte des 19. Jahrhunderts* (Berlin, 1965).
13   O. Grant, *Migration and Inequality in Germany 1870–1913* (Oxford, 2005), pp. 293, 353.

"skirted decisions," Grant argues that "few if any" countries have made political progress during a period of rapid industrialization. "Imperial Germany was not moving towards an internally generated catastrophe, but was a society with as good a chance of achieving full economic maturity, social modernization, and political democratization as any other. The decisive factor in the equation, which shifted German history onto a different course, was the outbreak of war in 1914," he claims. Whether one accepts this "optimistic" view or not, most would nowadays agree with Grant's observation that economic and political advance seldom go hand in hand. Contrary to the linear perspective of modernization theory, asynchronic or "'incomplete modernization' is the normal state for an industrializing society."[14]

With regard to the timing of Germany's industrial revolution, a surprisingly wide variety of dates have been cited.[15] The fact that the first mechanized factory on German soil – Johann Brügelmann's Cromford cotton mill at Ratingen near Düsseldorf – was erected in 1784 is something of a red herring, but the genesis of Germany's industrial take-off has been located as early as 1800 (with the onset of factory production in Saxony), 1815 (in the territorial changes instituted by the Congress of Vienna), or 1834 (with the expansion of the Customs Union). In fact, the 1830s, 1840s, and 1850s all have their adherents, with many pointing to the discovery of large deposits of deep-lying bituminous coal in the Ruhr valley around 1850 as the decisive stimulus. Arguably, however, it was not until the so-called "second industrial revolution" – the rapid expansion of the electrical engineering and chemical industries in the 1890s – that the Empire really made its transition from an agrarian state (*Agrarstaat*) to an industrial state (*Industriestaat*).[16] Many historians cite the 1895 census – when the numbers employed in industry and mining overtook those in agriculture for the first time – as a decisive turning point, though the primary sector remained a significant factor in German economic and political life until well into the twentieth century. Part of the problem with this debate, as the economic historian Frank Tipton has pointed out, is that "[m]odern economies grow, change,

---

14 Ibid., p. 5.
15 See W. G. Hoffmann, "The take-off in Germany," in W. W. Rostow, ed., *The Economics of Take-Off into Sustained Growth* (London, 1963), pp. 95–118; K. Borchardt, *The Industrial Revolution in Germany, 1700–1914* (London, 1972); W. O. Henderson, *The Rise of German Industrial Power, 1834–1914* (London, 1975); R. H. Tilly, *Vom Zollverein zum Industriestaat: Die wirtschaftlich-soziale Entwicklung Deutschlands 1834 bis 1914* (Munich, 1990); G. Hardach, "Aspekte der Industriellen Revolution," *Geschichte und Gesellschaft*, 17 (1991), pp. 102–13.
16 This milestone prompted much debate in Germany at the time. See K. Barkin, *The Controversy over German Industrialization, 1890–1902* (Chicago, 1970).

and fluctuate, but they do not experience the sort of sudden qualitative change implied in many historians' accounts. Failure to appreciate this," he suggests, "has led to much of the confusion in the interpretation of the economic dimension of German history."[17] It is perhaps little wonder then that most social and economic historians now prefer to describe industrialization in evolutionary rather than revolutionary terms.

Another problem is the regional dimension. As Tipton, Gary Herrigel, and Hubert Kiesewetter (born 1939) have all documented, Germany's industrial development was highly uneven.[18] While Saxony, Upper Silesia, and the Ruhr were already industrialized in 1871, Mecklenburg, Pomerania, and East Prussia were most definitely not. This helps to explain why national – or in this case imperial – statistics only tell part of the story. For people living in Berlin or the Ruhr during the late nineteenth- and early twentieth-centuries, there was certainly nothing "mythical" about the speed of industrialization or urbanization. As Tipton rightly observes, "the patterns are only obvious in retrospect, after several generations of observation and research. The experience of those who lived through these decades was not of a gradually unfolding process of growth and progress, but of instability and fluctuation."[19] This was particularly the case of the period between 1873 and 1895, which contemporaries and some later historians (see Chapter 1) characterized as a "great depression," but which now appears to have been an "optical illusion" (David Landes).

The leading sector of German industrialization was initially textiles; by the Wilhelmine era it was the electrical and chemical industries; but for the middle decades of the nineteenth century historians are divided as to whether railway construction, iron, or coal was the driving force. If this is something of a "chicken or egg" debate, a more fruitful discussion has centered on the role of big banks in the industrialization process. The famous hypothesis of the economic historian Alexander Gerschenkron (1904–78) was that as a "latecomer of the first generation" Germany could not rely on private accumulation or the stock market to provide the capital required to "catch up" with its western neighbors.[20] Thus it fell

---

17 F. B. Tipton, "The economic dimension in German history," in G. Martel, ed., *Modern Germany Reconsidered*, p. 212.
18 F. B. Tipton in *Regional Variations in the Economic Development of Germany during the 19th Century* (Middletown, 1976); G. Herrigel, *Industrial Constructions. The Sources of German Industrial Power* (Cambridge, 1996); H. Kiesewetter, *Industrielle Revolution in Deutschland 1815–1914* (Frankfurt, 1989); H. Kiesewetter, *Region und Industrie in Europa 1815–1995* (Stuttgart, 2000).
19 F. B. Tipton, "Technology and industrial growth," in R. Chickering, ed., *Imperial Germany*, p. 67.
20 A. Gerschenkron, *Economic Backwardness in Historical Perspective* (Cambridge, MA, 1962).

to the banks – and in particular the Empire's "universal" banks – to supply the investment necessary to acquire the best available technology in manufacturing, transport, and communication. In return for this investment they were rewarded with seats on the supervisory boards of industrial joint-stock companies. One consequence of this was that German businesses seem to have had more time to develop their products than their stock-market dependent British or American rivals: the Mannesmann seamless steel tube is a good example.[21] It also meant, however, that industry in the *Kaiserreich* became more highly concentrated than elsewhere in Europe, with the banks encouraging processes of vertical and horizontal integration, cartelization, and monopoly formation. Gerschenkron was by no means the only observer to see in Germany a particular kind of state-approved "organized capitalism" or "co-operative managerial capitalism,"[22] but his theses have demonstrated unusual staying power, continuing to generate discussion more than 40 years after their first formulation.[23]

Industrialization brought with it far-reaching changes in the structure and nature of German society, creating vast inequalities in health, wealth, education, and housing. Indeed, for most social historians it is the effects of industrialization, rather than the process itself, which are of primary interest.[24] Changing patterns of work, family life, and leisure – itself a product of the industrial age – accordingly feature prominently in the historiography of Imperial Germany, as do "instruments of socialization," such as schools, the army, and the church. Traditional privileges and status counted for less, money and merit for more, as Germany evolved from a corporate or estates-based society to one based on relations of class. While most historians are careful to emphasize the limits of social mobility, which was much more apparent around the middle of the social scale than at its top or bottom, they nevertheless accept that Germany was a society in "restless movement" by the end of the nineteenth century.[25] The growing complexity of the industrial economy required a

---

21 H. Pogge von Strandmann, *Unternehmenspolitik und Unternehmensführung. Der Dialog zwischen Aufsichtsrat und Vorstand bei Mannesmann, 1900–19* (Düsseldorf, 1978).
22 The latter term is from A. D. Chandler, *Scale and Scope: the Dynamics of Industrial Capitalism* (Cambridge, MA, 1990). On the former see H. A. Winkler, ed., *Organisierter Kapitalismus: Voraussetzungen und Anfänge* (Göttingen, 1974).
23 See C. Fohlin, *Finance Capitalism and Germany's Rise to Industrial Power* (Cambridge, 2007); also J. Edwards and S. Ogilvie, "Universal banks and German industrialization: A reappraisal," *Economic History Review*, 49 (1996), pp. 427–46.
24 A good introduction is the collection edited by D. Langewiesche and K. Schönhoven, *Arbeiter in Deutschland. Studien zur Lebensweise der Arbeiterschaft im Zeitalter der Industrialisierung* (Paderborn, 1981).
25 V. Berghahn, *Imperial Germany*, p. 123.

better-educated and more flexible population, but also reinforced class distinctions such as those between blue- and white-collar work, or trades and professions. As a substantial body of literature since the 1960s has documented, it was a process which produced both "winners" and "losers."

A seminal work in this field was Kocka's 1969 study of the management and administration of the giant Siemens electrical concern between 1847 and 1914.[26] With its rigorous conceptual framework and fascination for structures and processes, the book epitomized the historical social science approach for which its author quickly became a standard-bearer.[27] Strongly influenced by Marx and Weber, but also utilizing the tools of organizational sociology, Kocka examined how the firm evolved from a family business with a personal and paternal regard for its workers, to a modern bureaucracy run by salaried managers. The book was published by the Working Group for Modern Social History, established by Werner Conze and Otto Brunner in 1957. The group had been at the forefront of social history research in Germany since the early 1960s, but its output increased prodigiously in the 1970s, with more than 60 monographs and essay collections published under the banner of the "Industrial World." While it attempted to represent all strands within social history, the prominent presence of Kocka and Wehler in the Working Group ensured that practitioners of historical social science were seldom short of outlets for their work.

A clear majority of titles in the "Industrial World" series focused on aspects of working-class history. The formation of an industrial proletariat and the development of working-class organizations did not, of course, overlap neatly with the lifetime of the *Kaiserreich*: "social history has its own distinct rhythm" as Jean Quataert puts it.[28] Even so, many studies of the German working class have chosen to adopt the 1871–1918 timeframe as their own. Arguably the most important of these is *Workers in the German Empire*, a 900-page tour-de-force by Gerhard A. Ritter and Klaus Tenfelde (born 1944), published in 1992 as part of another key series,

---

26 J. Kocka, *Unternehmensverwaltung und Angestelltenschaft am Beispiel Siemens 1847–1914* (Stuttgart, 1969). In English see J. Kocka, *Industrial Culture and Bourgeois Society: Business, Labor, and Bureaucracy in Modern Germany* (New York and Oxford, 1999).
27 Kocka's subsequent publications included a comparative study of American white-collar employees between 1890 and 1940, and an analysis of German society during the First World War. See J. Kocka, *White Collar Workers in America 1890–1940* (London and Beverley Hills, 1980 – first published in German in 1977); J. Kocka, *Facing Total War: German Society 1914–1918* (Leamington Spa, 1984 – first published in German in 1973).
28 J. Quataert, "Demographic and social change," in R. Chickering, ed., *Imperial Germany*, p. 123.

Workers and the Labor Movement in Germany since the end of the 18th Century.[29] The 12-volume series is not yet complete, but it will eventually include four titles on the imperial era alone. The series involves contributions from many of historical social science's most prominent figures, and therefore offers a useful illustration of the strengths and weaknesses of the approach in general. The books are undoubtedly impressive pieces of scholarship, rich in tables and statistics, and with lengthy bibliographies. Great care is taken to place the social in its proper economic and political context, and to include not only industrial workers, but rural laborers, artisans, and domestic employees too. Yet this has not stopped critics from finding a variety of faults. It has been suggested, for instance, that the series perpetuates the misconception that working-class history and labor-movement history are one and the same. In fact, of course, even in the heyday of Wilhelmine Social Democracy, three-quarters of the German working class remained outside the labor movement and its sub-culture. The series has also been criticized for regarding class formation as a process caused by anonymous, abstract forces, rather than by the initiatives and experiences of real people; and for privileging class over other forms of social inequality, such as gender, ethnicity, or confession. Finally, it has been argued that the practitioners of historical social science have failed to recognize that their favored Weberian tools of analysis are better suited to the study of formal structures and organizations than to informal or symbolic systems. As one critic recently put it: "There remains a particularly entrenched way of thinking about history in Germany, a not very subtle disciplinary culture that persists in its conviction that there has to be one correct way to explore the past."[30]

Such criticisms are nothing new. Indeed, when in the 1980s, some of Germany's most prominent social historians, including Wehler, began to adopt the alternative term of *Gesellschaftsgeschichte* (the history of society or "societal history") to characterize their approach, it was partly in response to comments of this kind. The semantic shift from social history to the history of society – with the latter aspiring to embrace the four "axes" of economy, society, politics, and culture – did little, however, to placate the critics. As we saw in Chapter 1, the attacks on the "new orthodoxy" came from both the "right" and the "left": from historist

---

29 G. A. Ritter and K. Tenfelde, *Arbeiter im Deutschen Kaiserreich: 1871 bis 1914* (Bonn, 1992), volume 5 in the series *Geschichte der Arbeiter und der Arbeiterbewegung in Deutschland seit dem Ende des 18. Jahrhunderts*. The series is published with the support of the Friedrich-Ebert-Foundation: a body established in 1925 and re-founded in 1947 with close links to the SPD.
30 E. D. Weitz, "Still two trains passing in the night? Labor and gender in German historiography," *International Labor and Working-Class History*, 63 (2003), p. 34.

traditionalists and from social history radicals. The latter consisted primarily of British proponents of "history from below" and German supporters of *Alltagsgeschichte*, the history of everyday life. As a result, the broad church of social history experienced a great schism from which it has never fully recovered.[31] In seeking to place these historiographical trends in a wider intellectual context, Richard Evans found a useful analogy. Historical social science had offered a "modernist version of history," but like the modernist architecture of the 1960s, a history based on social-scientific concepts "neglected the human dimension and reduced the people of the past to anonymous categories."[32] Thus when many of the assumptions underpinning this modernist version of history began to break down – not least the idea of progress itself – it became "more important to reinstate subjective experience at the centre of history than to continue the futile search for a conclusively scientific explanation of the objective factors thought to have determined people's behaviour in the past." Of course, as a central figure in these developments, Evans's view was not that of a disinterested spectator, but few would dispute his observation that "[g]ender, ethnicity, generational identity, sexual orientation, all of which had been neglected by modernist historians, began to attract historical research as they became more important in the present."[33]

The View from Below: Does it Really Matter?

History from below and the history of everyday life both start from the same premise: that ordinary people are historical actors in their own right. Yet while the idea of looking at history from the perspective of the "little man" (or woman) can hardly be considered a novelty, the German concept of *Alltagsgeschichte* – with its focus on "housing and homelessness, clothing and nakedness, eating habits and hunger, people's loves and hates, their quarrels and cooperation, memories, anxieties, [and] hopes for the future"[34] – is still a comparatively recent phenomenon. It developed in the years around 1980, at a time of crisis for the German left,

---

31 Even in 2003 a downbeat Kocka suggested it "may not have reached its rock-bottom yet." J. Kocka, "Losses, gains and opportunities: Social history today," p. 21.
32 R. J. Evans, "German history – past, present and future," in G. Martel, ed., *Modern Germany Reconsidered*, pp. 244–5.
33 Ibid., p. 244.
34 A. Lüdtke, "Introduction. What is the history of everyday Life and who are its practitioners," in A. Lüdtke, ed., *The History of Everyday Life: Reconstituting Historical Experiences and Ways of Life* (Princeton, 1995), p. 3.

symbolized by the decline and fall of Helmut Schmidt's social-liberal coalition, the conservative "turn" under Helmut Kohl, and the new challenge of the Green movement. These developments had serious implications for Germany's social historians, and not only because they had benefited considerably from the years of SPD rule. With trade union membership falling, and social democratic parties seemingly in decline across Europe, it appeared as if some of the fundamental assumptions behind the trajectory of social history had been wrong. As Geoff Eley observed in 1989, *Alltagsgeschichte* was "driven less by the motivating purpose of older labor history – the belief in the forward march of the working class – than by the realization of its opposite, that by the late 1970s the march had stopped."[35]

Much of the initial impetus for "the new history movement," as the German media first dubbed it, came from so-called "barefoot" historians. These were amateur or semi-professional enthusiasts active in local history projects, alternative tourism, and citizens' action groups. The inspiration for such grassroots initiatives came from a variety of sources: the British "history workshops" of the late 1960s,[36] oral history, and the "dig where you stand" movement pioneered by Sven Lindquist in Sweden; all of which sought to capture the authentic historical experience of hitherto neglected social groups.[37] Many of these initiatives adopted the rather vague term of *Alltag*, or everyday life, as a means of distinguishing themselves from the "big" history offered by both the old and the new orthodoxies, even though the term's elastic meaning was always likely to provoke debate. The sociologist Norbert Elias was one of the first to recognize its problematic nature, and in a 1984 essay entitled "Difficulties with the Everyday," Klaus Tenfelde urged historians to resist its usage, since even Bismarck had an everyday life.[38] By then, however, it was

---

35 G. Eley, "Labour history, social history, Alltagsgeschichte: Experience, culture, and the politics of the everyday – a new direction for German social history?," *Journal of Modern History*, 61 (1989), p. 341.

36 Significantly, a history workshop was not held in Germany until 1982 and a national History Workshop Association not founded until April 1983. In the following year, a History Workshop Festival took place in Berlin. See A. McElligott, "The German history workshop festival in Berlin," *German History*, 2 (1985), pp. 21–9; also V. Böge, ed., *Geschichtswerkstätten gestern – heute – morgen. Bewegung! Stillstand. Aufbruch?* (Munich and Hamburg, 2004). A journal entitled *Geschichtswerkstatt* was launched in 1983, becoming *Werkstatt-Geschichte* in 1992.

37 R. Fletcher, "History from below comes to Germany: The New History Movement in the Federal Republic of Germany," *Journal of Modern History*, 60 (1988), pp. 557–68. For a contemporary German account see "Ein kräftiger Schub für die Vergangenheit," *Der Spiegel*, 37 (June 6, 1983), pp. 36–42.

38 K. Tenfelde, "Schwierigkeiten mit dem Alltag," *Geschichte und Gesellschaft*, 10 (1984), p. 388.

already too late: a flood of publications, ranging from photocopied brochures to lavishly-illustrated coffee table books, ensured that "the new history movement" now had a name.[39]

This populist element, together with the fact that its emergence coincided with an alleged "revival of narrative" in historical writing, fuelled the suspicions of Germany's structuralist historians, who feared for a "loss of intellectuality."[40] Initially many in the historians' guild saw the history of everyday life as a kind of "history lite," which would appeal to publishers and general readers, but lacked the scholarly rigor of historical social science. *Alltagshistoriker* were accused of "antiquarianism, conservative neo-historism, neo-romanticism and pseudo-realism,"[41] and many leading German historians found the focus on "values, beliefs, mentalities, and lifestyles," rather than "structures, class antagonisms, or economic fluctuations," a potentially dangerous one. Structuralists such as Wehler and Kocka were quick to point out that the new trends risked losing sight of history's major frameworks and processes, replacing serious analysis with trivial anecdotes and vague assertions.[42] Historians of everyday life responded by accusing historical social science of a naïve faith in progress, and a fixation on socio-economic circumstances to the neglect of actual human beings.[43] The acrimonious tone of these exchanges was perhaps understandable given what was at stake: "In emphasizing the burdens of modernization on the men, women, and children who had to endure it," Roger Chickering (born 1942) observed, "*Alltagsgeschichte* challenged the

---

39 Good overviews of debates surrounding *Alltagsgeschichte* include G. Eley, "Labour history, social history, Alltagsgeschichte"; E. Rosenhaft, "History, anthropology, and the study of everyday life," *Comparative Studies in Society and History*, 29 (1987), pp. 99–105; D. Crew, "Alltagsgeschichte: A new social history from below," *Central European History*, 22 (1989), pp. 394–407; L. Niethammer, "Anmerkungen zur Alltagsgeschichte," in K. Bergmann and R. Schorken, eds., *Geschichte im Alltag – Alltag in der Geschichte* (Düsseldorf, 1982); F.-J. Brüggemeier and J. Kocka, eds., *"Geschichte von unten – Geschichte von innen": Kontroversen um die Alltagsgeschichte* (Hagen, 1985). Some important early essays by the pioneers of Alltagsgeschichte are available in translation in A. Lüdtke, ed., *The History of Everyday Life*. There was also a (very different) East German version of *Alltagsgeschichte*: see J. Kuczynski, *Geschichte des Alltags des deutschen Volkes*, 5 vols, (East Berlin, 1980).
40 J. Kocka, "Zurück zur Erzählung? Plädoyer für historische Argumentation," *Geschichte und Gesellschaft*, 10 (1984), pp. 395–408.
41 S. Berger, *The Search for Normality*, p. 80.
42 H.-U. Wehler, "Alltagsgeschichte: Königsweg zu neuen Ufern oder Irrgarten der Illusionen?," in *Aus der Geschichte lernen?* (Munich, 1988), pp. 130–51; J. Kocka, "Sozialgeschichte zwischen Struktur und Erfahrung. Die Herausforderung der Alltagsgeschichte," in *Geschichte und Aufklärung* (Göttingen, 1989), pp. 29–44.
43 See, for example, H. Medick, "Missionäre im Ruderboot," *Geschichte und Gesellschaft*, 10 (1984), pp. 295–319; available in English in A. Lüdtke, ed., *The History of Everyday Life*, pp. 41–71.

enthusiastic embrace of modernity that seemed to underlie Wehler's diagnosis of the aberrations of German history."[44]

Such criticisms diminished in the course of the 1980s and 1990s as *Alltagsgeschichte* gained an institutional foothold in German academia. Indeed, recent critiques of the approach have tended to take the opposite tack: that its works are overburdened with weighty theory, but utilize their "cryptic conceptual vocabulary to expose some pretty ordinary, unexciting truths."[45] The changed perception of *Alltagsgeschichte* was largely down to two historians from the Max-Planck-Institute for History at Göttingen: Hans Medick (born 1939) and Alf Lüdtke (born 1943). Neither Medick nor Lüdtke was a specialist on the *Kaiserreich* – the former is a historian of the Early Modern period, who made his name with a study of "proto-industrialization" in south-western Germany; while the latter's main interest lies in the working-class under Fascism[46] – but their work has come to exert an important theoretical and methodological influence on studies of the imperial era too. Almost any theoretical approach that offered something different from the then dominant Weberian paradigm has at some time been connected with *Alltagsgeschichte*, which remains "an extremely heterogeneous phenomenon."[47] E. P. Thompson's Anglo-Marxism, and especially his 1963 classic *The Making of the English Working Class* was an obvious inspiration, as was the French *Annales* school, with its focus on mentalities. The critiques of "grand narratives" offered by the likes of Michel Foucault and Jean-François Lyotard, and the social and cultural anthropology of Clifford Geertz also deserve mention. Geertz argued that "the informal logic of actual life" is best revealed through "thick description" – by immersing oneself in the actual life of the people under observation – rather than through the application of external theories, and his influence has lent an anthropological or ethnographical flavor to many of the school's key works.[48] This required casting off the

---

44 R. Chickering, "The quest for a usable German Empire," in R. Chickering, ed., *Imperial Germany*, p. 9.
45 See, for instance, Karl Wegert's review of Lüdtke's *The History of Everyday Life* in the *Canadian Journal of History*, 31 (1996), pp. 157–60.
46 H. Medick, *Weben und Überleben in Laichingen, 1650–1900. Lokalgeschichte als Allgemeine Geschichte* (Göttingen, 2001); A. Lüdtke, *Eigen-Sinn. Fabrikalltag, Arbeitererfahrungen und Politik vom Kaiserreich bis in den Faschismus* (Hamburg, 1993). In 1999 the two men became joint heads of the Max-Planck-Institute's Department for Historical Anthropology at the University of Erfurt.
47 G. Eley, "Labour history, social history, Alltagsgeschichte," p. 319.
48 C. Geertz, "Thick description: Toward an interpretative theory of culture," in *The Interpretation of Cultures* (New York, 1973). It should be noted that *Alltagsgeschichte* was by no means the only area of history to reflect the influence of social anthropology in the late twentieth century: it can be found in women's and gender history, family history and

scientist's "baggage of distain" (David Blackbourn) and embarking on "voyages of discovery into one's own people" (Franz-Josef Brüggemeier). Since history's anonymous victims and losers rarely left written testimonies, new ways had to be found of decoding the "visual or gesture-based 'languages' in which oppressed or marginalized groups" expressed themselves.[49] Leading practitioners of *Alltagsgeschichte* lobbied hard for the introduction of anthropological techniques into mainstream history, and concepts such as habitus, agency, process, and performance began to appear with increasing frequency in German historiography.[50] In return, one of Germany's leading ethnographers, Wolfgang Kaschuba (born 1950), was happy to traverse the disciplinary boundaries in the opposite direction.[51]

A core feature of *Alltagsgeschichte* was, and is, its decentralization of perspective. Whereas historical social science focuses on the macro level – what one might term "history on a grand scale" – *Alltagsgeschichte* pursues a form of microhistory. This approach, pioneered in the late 1970s by Italian historians such as Carlo Ginzburg and Carlo Ponti, has been condemned by its opponents as a "history of details" (*Detailgeschichte*), but is seen by its supporters as a "history of the whole in its details" (*Detailgeschichte des Ganzen*). It can demonstrate, in other words, how big structures (such as the state) and processes (such as modernization or nation-building), were formed and transformed in practice by the actions of ordinary people at a local level. Of course, social history has always used case studies to demonstrate how structures and processes impacted on particular communities – David Crew's study of the city of Bochum is a classic example[52] – but works of *Alltagsgeschichte* have gone further, suggesting that experiences at a local level were driving and shaping the larger processes; that local history was itself general history.[53] Indeed, the insistence that politics has a spatial element – that it "is not

---

Volksgeschichte too. Significantly, a new journal specifically for *History and Anthropology* was founded in the US in 1983. Germany's *Historische Anthropologie* followed ten years later.
49 A. Lüdtke, "Introduction. What is the history of everyday life and who are its practitioners," p. 22.
50 R. Berdahl, A. Lüdtke, and H. Medick, *Klassen und Kultur. Sozialanthropologische Perspektiven in der Geschichtsschreibung* (Bodenheim, 1982); H. Medick, "Wer sind die 'Missionäre im Ruderboot'? Oder: Kulturanthropologie und Alltagsgeschichte," in U. Becher and K. Bergmann, eds., *Geschichte – Nutzen oder Nachteil für das Leben?* (Düsseldorf, 1986), pp. 63–8.
51 See W. Kaschuba, "Popular culture and workers' culture as symbolic orders. Comments on the debate about the history of culture and everyday life," in A. Lüdtke, ed., *The History of Everyday Life*, pp. 169–97.
52 D. Crew, *Town in the Ruhr: A Social History of Bochum 1860–1914* (New York, 1979).
53 H. Medick's *Weben und Überleben in Laichingen, 1650–1900* is actually sub-titled *Lokalgeschichte als Allgemeine Geschichte.*

performed in the abstract, but is physically located somewhere, and this somewhere ... is constitutive of politics itself" – is, as Maureen Healy recently observed, one of the main achievements of the approach.[54] This is amply demonstrated by two recent studies of a single and hitherto obscure event: the gruesome and unsolved murder of an eighteen-year old grammar school boy in the West Prussian town of Konitz in March 1900. The way in which Ernst Winter's body was dissected and drained of blood led many in the local community to believe that his death was a Jewish ritual murder. Consequently, in an atmosphere of panic and rumor, the town's small Jewish population was harried and hounded by vigilantes, egged on by sections of the right-wing press, until the Prussian army was forced to intervene. For both Christoph Nonn (born 1964) and Helmut Walser Smith (born 1962) the case provides an opportunity to explore much larger questions about the relationship between Protestants, Catholics, and Jews in Wilhelmine Germany, and about the ways in which latent anti-Semitism could be instrumentalized for political ends.[55]

The British historian G. M. Trevelyan (1876–1962) once famously quipped that social history was "the history of a people with the politics left out."[56] Some of its detractors have made much the same criticism of *Alltagsgeschichte*, although with little justification. Politics, and the exercise of power, is in fact central to much of the school's best work, even if it is not always readily apparent. This is because *Alltagsgeschichte* operates a broader definition of the political than the school of historical social science. Whereas the latter take a Weberian view of power, historians of everyday life are more influenced by Foucault, invoking a "multilayered social field" (Alf Lüdtke) or a "web of oppression, resistance, agreements, stagings, and rituals" (Dorothee Wierling), in which power relations are infinitely more complex.[57] According to this view, "*Alltag* is the domain in which people exercise a direct influence – via their behavior – on their immediate circumstances."[58] Power in the German Empire was thus wielded not only by rulers and employers, but by anonymous individuals

---

54   M. Healey, "Review of German Studies Association conference 2003. Sessions 3 and 22: Revisiting alltagsgeschichte. Praxis in everyday life and the discipline of history," *H-German, H-Net Reviews*, October 2003. Online at: http://www.h-net.msu.edu/reviews/showrev.cgi?path=545.
55   C. Nonn, *Eine Stadt sucht einen Mörder. Gerücht, Gewalt und Antisemitismus im Kaiserreich* (Göttingen, 2002); H. W. Smith, *The Butcher's Tale: Murder and Anti-Semitism in a German Town* (New York and London, 2002).
56   G. M. Trevelyan, *English Social History. A Survey of Six Centuries: Chaucer to Queen Victoria* (Harmondsworth, 1967 – first published 1942), p. 9.
57   D. Wierling, "A history of everyday life and gender relations: On historical and historiographical relationships," in A. Lüdtke, ed., *The History of Everyday Life*, p. 158.
58   Ibid., p. 151.

such as the working-class patriarchs who "ruled" their wives and families, and by those small-scale exploiters and oppressors who can always be found within the ranks of the exploited and oppressed. Power was even generated by the actions of ordinary men and women in their homes, factories, and neighborhoods. This broader definition of politics brings with it both dangers as well as opportunities, as James Retallack points out: "if social history and political history diverge too far, if the politics of everyday life is not related to events of national significance, we may find ourselves trying to write the history of Germany's working classes 'with the SPD left out.'"[59]

This is a genuine concern, but there seems little risk of it occurring in the near future. Indeed, it is important to recognize that *Alltagsgeschichte* and historical social science have been able to find a measure of common ground in recent years. The Kassel-based research project "Lifeworlds (*Lebenswelten*) and Political Culture in the Years around 1900," with its focus on mentalities and perceptions, is a case in point. Its co-ordinators – Jens Flemming (born 1944), Klaus Saul (born 1939), and Peter-Christian Witt – may be late converts to *Alltagsgeschichte*, but they have already published some impressive work, including a valuable document collection on everyday life between 1871 and 1914.[60] In fact, all but the most doctrinaire proponents of historical social science would nowadays acknowledge that *Alltagsgeschichte* has made a positive impact on at least some aspects of Imperial Germany's history. This is perhaps most apparent in studies of working-class life, such as Brüggemeier's portrait of Ruhr miners, *Life at the Coalface*, or Lüdtke's acclaimed set of "miniatures" documenting the ways in which industrial workers were able to maintain a limited degree of self-will or obstinacy (*Eigen-Sinn*) in the most oppressive of political circumstances.[61] It is also evident in some of the many excellent accounts of life on the home-front during World War One, including studies of Hamburg, Berlin, and Vienna.[62]

Despite this, however, it would be fair to say that *Alltagsgeschichte* has so far promised more than it has delivered, with regard to the *Kaiserreich* at

---

59 J. Retallack, "Wilhelmine Germany," in G. Martel, ed., *Modern Germany Reconsidered*, p. 47.
60 J. Flemming, K. Saul, and P.-C. Witt, eds., *Quellen zur Alltagsgeschichte der Deutschen vom Mittelalter bis Heute*, vol. 7 (Darmstadt, 1997). A further volume for the First World War years is in preparation.
61 A. Lüdtke *Eigen-Sinn*; F.-J. Brüggemeier, *Leben vor Ort. Ruhrbergleute und Ruhrbergbau 1889–1919* (Munich, 1984).
62 V. Ullrich, *Kriegsalltag. Hamburg im ersten Weltkrieg* (Cologne, 1982); B. Davis, *Home Fires Burning. Food, Politics, and Everyday Life in World War One Berlin* (Chapel Hill and London, 2000); M. Healy, *Vienna and the Fall of the Habsburg Empire. Total War and Everyday Life in World War One* (Cambridge, 2004).

least. This is perhaps inevitable, given that history is more than just past experiences (more, even, than the sum total of all past experiences). The key is clearly to strike a balance. History requires both the general and the particular; the view "from above" and "from below." While it has proved a difficult balance to achieve, it is not impossible, as an innovative history of urban working-class housing by Adelheid von Saldern (born 1938) demonstrates.[63] Saldern's book contains two separate chapters for each chronological period, with one offering a conventional "top down" perspective – government policies, market shifts, reform movements – and the other attempting the altogether more challenging task of documenting workers' own perceptions of their homes and neighborhoods. Moreover, by ensuring that women's experiences are not overlooked either, Saldern's book can be considered an important contribution to gender history too.

Gendering the *Kaiserreich*?

Although the early protagonists of *Alltagsgeschichte* paid relatively little attention to women's historical experience, a number of feminist historians – Karin Hausen (born 1938), Regina Schulte (born 1949) and Dorothee Wierling (born 1950) – saw the history of everyday life as an ideal opportunity to establish gender as a central category of historical research.[64] While this did not happen overnight, by the late 1980s it was possible for Eley to state that there was "now a strong convergence" between *Alltagsgeschichte* and gender history.[65] Of course, women's history had been developing independently for some years before the emergence of *Alltagsgeschichte*, and had already done valuable work in recovering women's lost voices and experiences. It had also called into question history's conventional periodization, theories, and methods.[66]

---

63 A. von Saldern, *Häuserleben: Zur Geschichte städtischen Arbeiterwohnens vom Kaiserreich bis heute* (Bonn, 1995).
64 K. Hausen, ed., *Frauen suchen ihre Geschichte. Historische Studien zum 19. und 20. Jahrhundert* (Munich, 1983); D. Wierling, "Vom Mädchen zum Dienstmädchen. Kindliche Sozialisation und Beruf im Kaiserreich," in K. Bergmann and R. Schorken, eds., *Geschichte im Alltag – Alltag in der Geschichte*, pp. 57–87; R. Schulte, "Peasants and farmers' maids: female farm servants in Bavaria at the end of the nineteenth century," in R. J. Evans and W. R. Lee, eds., *The German Peasantry* (London, 1986), pp. 158–73.
65 G. Eley, "Labour history, social history, alltagsgeschichte," p. 320.
66 Most of the pioneers of women's history came from the English-speaking world, and some of the earliest work on German women was written in English too. See, for instance, R. Bridenthal and C. Koonz, eds., *Becoming Visible: Women in European History* (Boston, 1977); J. C. Fout, ed., *German Women in the Nineteenth Century: A Social History* (New York and London, 1984); B. Franzoi, *At The Very Least She Pays The Rent: Women and German*

By and large, however, this had occurred on the margins of the male-dominated historical profession. *Alltagsgeschichte*'s critical focus on the home and the workplace opened up new contexts in which to explore the historical experience of women in regular university seminars, as well as in women's groups and evening classes. Yet if this helped women's history in Germany to move closer to the historical mainstream – itself a problematic concept – it was not a development universally applauded in feminist circles. Its academic respectability was largely predicated on the transformation of women's history into "gender history": a form of history that had been developing in American universities since the mid-1970s, and was vigorously championed in landmark essays by Joan Kelly and Joan Scott.[67] The grammatical term "gender" was appropriated to highlight the socially-constructed nature of masculinity and femininity. These were not, it was suggested, objective descriptions of inherent traits, but fluid and unstable categories, "formed, negotiated and contested over time through discourse, language and social action."[68] The fear of some feminists, therefore, was that women's long-hidden history would again become submerged under a welter of works studying the social construction of masculinity, and "herstory" would be marginalized once more.[69] Such concerns are still aired from time to time, but have not been borne out in practice. Women's history has continued to thrive, both alongside and within gender history.[70] The relationship between gender as a social construct and sex as a physiological fact remains the subject of much

---

Industrialization, 1871–1914 (Westport, 1985). The best overview of the subject, however, was written in German: U. Frevert's *Women in German History: From Bourgeois Emancipation to Sexual Liberation* (Oxford and New York, 1989), which appeared in a German edition in 1988. The first Chairs in Women's History at German universities were established in the mid- to late-1980s, for example at Bonn in 1986. By the mid-1990s there were some 20 in the state of North-Rhine Westphalia alone.

67 J. Kelly, "The social relation of the sexes," in *Women, History and Theory* (London and Chicago, 1984), first published in 1976; J. W. Scott, "Gender: A useful category of historical analysis," *The American Historical Review*, 91 (1986), pp. 1053–75.

68 L. Abrams and E. Harvey, "Introduction," in L. Abrams and E. Harvey, eds., *Gender Relations in German History. Power, Agency and Experience from the Sixteenth to the Twentieth Century* (London, 1996), p. 1.

69 For the relationship between women's history and gender history see K. Hausen and H. Wunder, eds., *Frauengeschichte – Geschlechtergeschichte* (Frankfurt and New York, 1992); or C. Eifert et al, eds., *Was sind Männer, was sind Frauen? Geschlechterkonstruktion im historischen Wandel* (Frankfurt, 1995).

70 Good recent overviews of gender history, its problems and achievements, are offered by H. Medick and A.-C. Trepp, eds., *Geschlechtergeschichte und Allgemeine Geschichte. Herausforderungen und Perspektiven* (Göttingen, 1998); B. G. Smith, *The Gender of History: Men, Women, and Historical Practice* (Cambridge, MA, 2000); M. E. Wiesner-Hanks, *Gender in History* (Oxford, 2001); L. L. Downs, *Writing Gender History* (London, 2004); and K. Canning, *Gender History in Practice. Historical Perspectives on Bodies, Class and Citizenship* (Ithaca, 2006).

debate – not least in the German speaking world, where no linguistic distinction exists between the two[71] – but gender has nevertheless become widely accepted as a category of historical analysis, far beyond the specific niche of feminist historiography. It is now the norm, for instance, for textbook surveys of the Empire to include at least a section on women or gender.[72] To be sure, these can sometimes smack of tokenism, but it is nevertheless clear that in the two decades since Scott's influential essay, historians have made considerable strides in developing a gendered perspective on the *Kaiserreich*.

One obvious starting point was the family – as a microcosm of society – and another was the world of work, in which gender was often a more significant factor than labor history had acknowledged.[73] Mirroring late nineteenth-century attitudes, work and domestic life have often been treated as two distinct and separate spheres, but in the 1990s historians such as Mary Jo Maynes (born 1949) and Kathleen Canning began to conceive them as part of a single experiential continuum. Maynes' comparative study of *French and German Workers' Autobiographies in the Era of Industrialization* and Canning's *Languages of Labor and Gender: Female Factory Work in Germany 1850–1914*, both combined elements of gender history, *Alltagsgeschichte*, and the new cultural history in strikingly innovative ways.[74] If Maynes' study was inevitably constrained by its

---

71   In German the word *Geschlecht* connotes both sex and gender.
72   Berghahn's *Imperial Germany* has a chapter entitled "Women and men" (pp. 65–78), and Retallack's *Germany in the Age of Kaiser Wilhelm II* has a section on "Gender and sexuality" (pp. 61–4), although there is nothing on gender in Feuchtwanger's *Imperial Germany*, or in Seligmann and McLean's *Germany from Reich to Republic*. Interestingly, Chickering's *Historiographical Companion* opts to confront the theme "across the many chapters in which it figures centrally," rather than have a specific chapter on gender.
73   J. Quataert, "The politics of rural industrialization: Class, gender, and collective protest in the Saxon Oberlausitz of the late nineteenth century," *Central European History*, 20 (1987), pp. 91–124; S. Meyer, "The tiresome work of conspicuous leisure: On the domestic duties of the wives of civil servants in the German Empire," in M. Boxer and J. Quataert, eds., *Connecting Spheres* (New York and Oxford, 1987), pp. 156–65; D. Wierling, *Mädchen für alles. Arbeitsalltag und Lebensgeschichte städtischer Dienstmädchen um die Jahrhundertwende* (Berlin, 1987); D. S. Linton, "Between school and marriage: Young working women as a social problem in late imperial Germany," *European History Quarterly*, 18 (1988), pp. 387–408; U. Daniel, *Arbeiterfrauen in der Kriegsgesellschaft: Beruf, Familie und Politik im Ersten Weltkrieg* (Göttingen, 1989); L. Abrams, "Martyrs or matriarchs? Working-class women's experience of marriage in Germany before the First World War, *Women's History Review*, 1 (1992), pp. 81–100; S. Schmitt, *Der Arbeiterinnenschutz im Deutschen Kaiserreich: zur Konstruktion der schutzbedürftigen Arbeiterin* (Stuttgart, 1995); C. E. Adams, *Women Clerks in Wilhelmine Germany* (Cambridge, 1998).
74   M. J. Maynes, *Taking the Hard Road: Life Courses in French and German Workers' Autobiographies in the Era of Industrialization* (Chapel Hill, 1995); K. Canning, *Languages of Labor and Gender: Female Factory Work in Germany, 1850–1914* (Ithaca, 1996).

source material – 90 published autobiographies – Canning's book was able to utilize a much wider range of sources, including company personnel records, factory inspectors' reports, and police files. By focusing on female workers in the Rhenish-Wesphalian textile industry, the Michigan historian sought to address an area of labor history that has been generally neglected by historical social science, despite its "occasional concession to the history of experience or *Alltag*."[75] The aforementioned series on *Workers and the Labor Movement in Germany since the end of the 18th Century* was cited by Canning as an example of the way in which German historians have continued to exclude female workers, "implicitly or explicitly," from their analyses. The reason for this, she suggested, is that women are difficult to accommodate within "the decisive domain of German labor history" – class – and in particular the "levels" model of class formation favored by historical social science. Her response, informed by one of the great scholarly debates of the late twentieth century (the so-called "linguistic turn"), was that concepts such as class should not be regarded as merely reflective of social reality, but constitutive of it too. Consequently, she suggested, the careful use of discourse analysis could "retrieve" the lost voices of female workers.[76] We shall return to the "linguistic turn" later, but Canning's award-winning book certainly highlighted a growing "Atlantic divide" between English- and German-language approaches to social and cultural history.

Just as the dichotomy between the home and the workplace has been shown up as a nineteenth-century social construct, so gender historians have begun to break down the traditional distinction between "private" and "public" spheres, which was in fact "more prescriptive than descriptive" (Nancy Reagin).[77] The particular difficulties involved in assessing women's public role at a time when they were denied the vote, were explored in an important 1990s essay by Eve Rosenhaft (born 1951). The Liverpool-based historian noted that "[t]he tendency of empirical research up to now has been to establish the role of women in politics as a positively charged absence ... in order to find women in politics, historians have had to expand the definition of politics."[78] Although Rosenhaft's conclusion may have appeared somewhat downbeat – "It may well be that the best we can hope for from political history is an

---

75 Ibid., pp. 5–6.
76 Ibid., pp. 8–10.
77 N. Reagin, "The imagined *Hausfrau*: National identity, domesticity, and colonialism in imperial Germany," *Journal of Modern History*, 73 (2001), p. 56.
78 E. Rosenhaft, "Women, gender, and the limits of political history," in L. E. Jones and J. Retallack, eds., *Elections, Mass Politics and Social Change in Modern Germany*, p. 150.

account that regretfully and self-consciously excludes women"[79] – her essay offered substantial evidence that women can be found in nineteenth-century German politics, provided that the different character of women's politics is recognized.

Margaret Anderson's research on Imperial Germany's Catholic community, for example, has highlighted how "[w]omen and girls were active in the resistance to the *Kulturkampf*, thronging cathedral squares in demonstrations, collecting signatures on statements of solidarity, holding sit-down strikes, and at one point requiring the intervention of the army."[80] Anderson argues that "while accepting the premise that ballots were to be cast by men, the Catholic milieu insisted that politics concerned everyone."[81] Political Catholicism might not be the first place one would expect to find women's activism, but it did not appear out of the blue. In the 1840s Catholic and non-conformist women had had their own lively debates on the national question,[82] and a recent study by the American historian Michael Gross (born 1961) has offered a specific explanation for the female mobilization of the 1870s. According to Gross, the *Kulturkampf* was highly gendered from the start: in liberal discourse the Church repeatedly appeared as a meddling old woman, while the state was conceived as a vigorous young man. German liberals were, therefore, happy to support the "War against Catholicism" because the "irrational," "emotional," and "feminine," Church threatened their masculine worldview, with its neat gender-specific division into public and private spheres. "For German liberals," Gross suggests, "the women's question and the 'Catholic problem' were one and the same."[83] Given the growing numbers of female teachers, nurses, and welfare workers – not to mention nuns – within the Catholic milieu at this time, it is a plausible thesis, and one which has been supported by Derek Hastings, Geoff Eley, and others.

Of course, women's activism on behalf of the Catholic Center Party remained constrained within clear limits. In the German Empire women's inferior status was not just a matter of popular prejudice or convention, they were subordinate to men in almost every area of society: education; marriage; property; citizenship rights; and the law. Even so, one must be wary of assuming that because they were denied the vote, German women

---

79 Ibid.
80 M. L. Anderson, *Practicing Democracy*, p. 126.
81 At election time, for instance, it was routine for Catholic newspapers to appeal to female readers to help get out the vote. See ibid, p. 128.
82 S. Paletschek, *Frauen und Dissens: Frauen im Deutschkatholizismus und in den freien Gemeinden, 1841–52* (Göttingen, 1989).
83 M. B. Gross, *The War against Catholicism. Liberalism and the Anti-Catholic Imagination in Nineteenth-Century Germany* (Ann Arbor, 2004), pp. 196–7.

were also denied a voice. While the language of German politics and identity remained strongly gendered throughout the nineteenth (and well into the twentieth) century, this did not mean that women were entirely absent from the public sphere. Gossip on tenement stairs and over garden fences can be seen as one way in which women regularly participated in some kind of public discourse; literature, the arts, and journalism offered opportunities for middle-class women too. It has been estimated, for instance, that around 6,000 female writers were active in Germany during the second half of the nineteenth century, and some were extremely successful.[84]

By the 1890s, moreover, women in Imperial Germany were the focus of several key debates – on the protection of female industrial workers through new social legislation; on prostitution and public health; and on their civil and legal rights – and were much more than silent bystanders. Indeed, in the public discussion of the proposed new Civil Code (*Bürgerliches Gesetzbuch*) of 1896–1900, women's organizations made detailed submissions to the official drafting commission, and whipped up a storm of protests in the so-called *Frauenlandsturm* when it became apparent that women's subordinate legal status was going to be retained.[85] Moreover, though it is often claimed that women were barred by law from all political gatherings until the celebrated Imperial Law of Assembly and Association of 1908, Anderson has shown that the reality was more complex: "Women were never legally excluded from political clubs and assemblies in Württemberg, Baden, Hessen, Saxe-Meiningen, Saxe-Coburg-Gotha, the Hanse city-states, and some of the other smaller polities. After 1898 their presence was permitted in Bavaria as well," she notes, and in 1902 women were even permitted to attend election rallies in conservative Prussia: "provided that some kind of barrier – which might be no more than a line of chalk or a piece of string – segregated the sexes."[86] Although Anderson is probably guilty of exaggerating the level of female participation, the history of women in German politics is certainly no longer just a bleak compendium of patriarchy, discrimination, and subordination. The emphasis is on female agency, strategy, and empowerment: to chart how working-class women in wartime Berlin, for example, were able "as consumers, producers, reproducers,

---

84   H. Scheuer, ed., *Naturalismus. Bürgerliche Dichtung und soziales Engagement* (Stuttgart, 1974), p. 136.
85   See E. Rosenhaft, "Women, gender, and the limits of political history," p. 152. Similar protests occurred over the 1913 Citizenship Law: see E. Nathans, *The Politics of Citizenship in Germany. Ethnicity, Utility and Nationalism* (Oxford, 2004).
86   M. L. Anderson, *Practicing Democracy*, pp. 297–8.

and political agents" to achieve "significant political ends";[87] or to show how female-led consumer protests – including boycotts of individual shops and tradesmen[88] – became one of the SPD's most effective political weapons.[89]

Such studies of women's "spontaneous" political activism have to some extent deflected interest away from Germany's organized women's movement: the largest in the world at the end of the nineteenth century, albeit one divided into bourgeois, socialist, and Jewish factions.[90] Yet even here the historiography continues to grow at an impressive rate, with works not only on the various women's organizations,[91] but also on the misogynistic backlash they provoked, and the pseudo-scientific demonization of women that developed in certain circles of German society at the end of the nineteenth century.[92] The virulent strain of anti-feminine sentiment in Wilhelmine Germany – which was as widespread among liberals as it was conservatives – may partly explain why most German women's organizations famously chose not to follow British suffragism in prioritizing the campaign for full voting rights. However, it was not simply for tactical reasons that the principal umbrella group for Germany's bourgeois women's movement – the League of German Women's Associations (*Bund Deutscher Frauenvereine*, or BDF) – instead sought political recognition on the basis of women's own unique contribution to society, through motherhood and the caring professions. Emancipation, the BDF argued, should not be confused with conformity to male standards: "motherly" policies were required to humanize the family and society at large. Although this has often led to the BDF being portrayed as a "tepid

---

87 B. Davis, *Home Fires Burning*, p. 3.
88 M. L. Anderson, *Practicing Democracy*, p. 324.
89 C. Nonn, *Verbraucherprotest und Parteiensystem im wilhelminischen Deutschland*. (Düsseldorf, 1996).
90 The Jewish Women's Federation was a member of the bourgeois BDF, but generally pursued specifically Jewish aims. See M. A. Kaplan, *The Jewish Feminist Movement in Germany: The Campaigns of the Jüdischer Frauenbund 1904–38* (Westport, 1979).
91 R. J. Evans, *The Feminist Movement in Germany 1894–1933*; J. Quataert, *Reluctant Feminists in German Social Democracy, 1885–1917* (Princeton, 1979); B. Greven-Aschoff, *Die bürgerliche Frauenbewegung in Deutschland 1894–1933* (Göttingen, 1981); C. Sachße, *Mütterlichkeit als Beruf: Sozialarbeit, Sozialreform und Frauenbewegung, 1871–1929* (Frankfurt, 1986); I. Stoehr, *Emanzipation zum Staat? Der Allgemeine Deutsche Frauenverein – Deutsche Staatsbürgerinnenverband, 1893–1933* (Pfaffenweiler, 1990); N. R. Reagin, *A German Women's Movement: Class and Gender in Hanover, 1880–1933* (Chapel Hill, 1995); E. R. Dickinson, "Reflections on feminism and monism in the kaiserreich, 1890–1913," *Central European History*, 34, 2 (2001), pp. 191–230.
92 U. Planert, *Antifeminismus im Kaiserreich: Diskurs, soziale Formation und politische Mentalität* (Göttingen, 1988); M. Stibbe, "Anti-feminism, nationalism, and the German right, 1914–20: A reappraisal," *German History*, 20 (2002), pp. 185–210.

movement ... based on notions of distinct male and female values, contributions, and proper roles,"[93] many early German feminists were undoubtedly sincere in their conviction that women should be treated as equal but different. Thus while this "maternalist" approach has been portrayed as fundamentally conservative by historians such as Richard Evans and Claudia Koonz – with the latter even suggesting a line of continuity between the ideals of early German feminism and National Socialism[94] – a powerful revisionist view of the German women's movement has also developed in recent years.

Ann Taylor Allen, for instance, has highlighted significant ways in which the bourgeois women's movement of Wilhelmine Germany might even be seen as more radical than its Anglo-Saxon counterparts, pointing out that a number of contemporary feminists have also moved away from a narrow "equal rights" agenda to reassert the value of "maternal thinking."[95] Just as in the Empire, many women today "have begun creating their own space of action, places where they set the standards themselves and where they are able to develop feminine individuality, interests and talents unfettered by male competition and dominance," as Ute Frevert puts it.[96] At the same time, Elisabeth Meyer-Renschhausen has argued that women's morality campaigns at the turn of the century were far from a tame alternative to real political engagement, but a "manifestation of a genuinely feminist, woman-centred politics which challenged the social as well as the gender order."[97] Two things are undisputed: the radicalism of at least some early German feminists was undoubtedly down-played by the conservative women who wrote the first histories of the movement in the 1920s; and second, the BDF did adopt a distinctly more cautious line in the years before World War One. Ironically, as Evans has shown, it was an important emancipatory reform – the Imperial Law of Assembly and Association – that was largely responsible for the latter change. Many moderate women who had previously shied away from political campaigning joined women's associations in the aftermath of 1908, and succeeded in outvoting the radicals.[98]

---

93 J. Quataert, "Introduction 2: Writing the history of women and gender in imperial Germany," in G. Eley, ed., *Society, Culture and the State in Germany*, p. 52.
94 C. Koonz, *Mothers in the Fatherland: Women, the Family and Nazi Politics* (London, 1987).
95 A. T. Allen, *Feminism and Motherhood in Germany* (New Brunswick, 1991), p. 244.
96 U. Frevert, *Women in German History*, p. 2.
97 Quoted by E. Rosenhaft, "Women in modern Germany," in G. Martel, ed., *Modern Germany Reconsidered*, p. 152.
98 R. J. Evans, "Liberalism and society: The feminist movement and social change," in *Rethinking German History*, p. 238.

Despite the seemingly international character of the women's movement in the years around 1900 – the International Council of Women was founded in 1888, the International Women's Suffrage Alliance in 1904, the Socialist Women's International in 1907, and International Women's Day in 1910 – a particular focus of recent research has been the role of gender in nationalism. Significantly, Imperial Germany's biggest women's organization was the Patriotic Women's Association, which saw the care of wounded soldiers as its principal priority and had half a million members by 1913.[99] The theme of gender and nationalism has been the focus of a number of broad-based conceptual works and more detailed case studies in the past decade or so, although it is still very much a field in its infancy.[100] The works published so far highlight the way in which the modern nation was conceived metaphorically as a family (*Volksfamilie*), to which the utmost devotion was required. As in "real" families, there was to be a strict separation of male and female roles: this usually began with the king and queen – the "father" and "mother" of the nation – and extended down to their humblest subjects or "children," who were expected to fight and die, or to breed, care, and mourn, depending on their sex.[101] Despite the veneer of equality provided by the notion of separate and specific roles, the fact that women were not expected to serve militarily provided a useful justification for the denial of the female franchise. In the nineteenth century the "body of the nation" (*Volkskörper*) was invariably imagined as male, and explicit connections were made between national strength and masculinity. The language ("mother tongue") and iconography of nation-states were highly gendered too, as the figures of Britannia, Marianne, and Germania clearly testify. The "nationalization of the masses,"[102] which began during the constitutive phase of modern nation-states, therefore involved a nationalization of the gender order as well. Much of this may seem self-evident, but it is easy to forget that

---

99 See J. Quataert, *Staging Philanthropy: Patriotic Women and the National Imagination in Dynastic Germany, 1813–1916* (Ann Arbor, 2001).
100 I. Blom, K. Hagemann, and C. Hall, eds., *Gendered Nations. Nationalisms and Gender Order in the Long Nineteenth Century* (Oxford, 2000); U. Planert, ed., *Nation, Politik, Geschlecht. Frauenbewegungen und Nationalismus in der Moderne* (Frankfurt and New York, 2000); S. Küster: "Inklusion und Exklusion: Nationsbildung und Geschlecht in Deutschland im 19. Jahrhundert," in D. Münkel and J. Schwarzkopf, eds., *Geschichte als Experiment. Studien zu Politik, Kultur und Alltag im 19. und 20. Jahrhundert. Festschrift für Adelheid von Saldern* (Frankfurt and New York, 2004).
101 These ideas are explored by Karen Hagemann in her study of Prussia at the time of the Napoleonic Wars, *"Männlicher Muth und Teutsche Ehre": Nation, Militär und Geschlecht zur Zeit der Antinapoleonischen Kriege Preußens* (Paderborn, 2002).
102 G. L. Mosse, *The Nationalization of the Masses* (New York, 1975); G. L. Mosse, *Nationalism and Sexuality: Respectability and Abnormal Sexuality in Modern Europe* (New York, 1985).

relatively recent and highly-acclaimed studies of modern nationalism, such as John Breuilly's *Nationalism and the State* or Eric Hobsbawm's *Nations and Nationalism since 1780*, ignore the dimension of gender entirely.[103] For many historians of the German Empire it was only in 1990, at a conference held in Philadelphia under the programmatic title "The *Kaiserreich* in the 1990s: New Research, New Directions, New Agendas," that gender became a central focus of debate. A collection of papers from the conference was published under the editorship of Geoff Eley,[104] whose interest in gender issues had first developed in the 1980s, and led to a flurry of publications in the 1990s and 2000s.[105]

Although women were excluded from the gymnastic, shooting, and choral societies that feature so prominently in the history of early German nationalism, they still made a contribution to the "construction" of the nation. Louise Otto's pioneering General German Women's Association of 1865, for instance, was launched in Leipzig on the anniversary of the Battle of Leipzig, the so-called *Völkerschlacht* of 1813.[106] There were also "national" organizations specifically for women, such as the aforementioned Patriotic Women's Association (founded by Prussia's Queen Augusta in 1866), the German Women's Association for the Eastern Marches (1895), the German Women's Navy League (1905), and the Women's League of the German Colonial Society (1907).[107] Attention among gender historians, however, has tended to focus not on the voluntary associations and festivals associated with the male-dominated public sphere, but on a different set of symbolic practices. In a 2001 essay, for example, Nancy Reagin (born 1960) investigated "how national identity was projected into the household." Using housekeeping advice literature to chart "the emergence of collective identity among bourgeois German women" – or, in homage to Benedict Anderson, "the imagined community of German *Hausfrauen*" – she showed how a "nationalized domesticity" was formed after 1871, in "opposition to or contrast with (imagined)

---

103 J. Breuilly, *Nationalism and the State*, 2nd ed. (Manchester, 1993); E. Hobsbawm, *Nations and Nationalism since 1780: Programme, Myth, Reality* (Cambridge, 1990).
104 G. Eley, ed., *Society, Culture and the State in Germany*.
105 Most recently: G. Eley, "Culture, nation, and gender," in I. Blom, K. Hagemann, and C. Hall, eds., *Gendered Nations*, pp. 27–40; G. Eley, "Frauen und der geschlechtsbezogene nationale Staatsbürgerstatus in Deutschland 1860–1914," in D. Münkel and J. Schwarzkopf, eds., *Geschichte als Experiment*, pp. 217–26.
106 S. Berger, *Inventing the Nation: Germany* (London, 2004), p. 58.
107 See R. Chickering, "'Casting their gaze more broadly': Women's patriotic activism in imperial Germany," *Past and Present*, 118 (1988), pp. 156–85; A. Schaser, "Women in a nation of men: The politics of the League of German Women's Associations (BDF) in imperial Germany, 1894–1914," in I. Blom, K. Hagemann, and C. Hall, eds., *Gendered Nations*, pp. 249–68.

foreigners."[108] These foreigners were as likely to be African as British or French, for in the age of imperialism European gender norms were exported around the globe and instrumentalized in the service of colonial ambition. "Nations," in Ruth Pierson's phrase, "came to be perceived as not only gendered but also 'raced.'"[109] Colonialist discourse indulged in a "feminization of the other," and issues such as interracial marriage, miscegenation, and male sexual privilege grew in prominence.[110] Nowhere was this more apparent than in the debates provoked by the horrific actions of Imperial Germany's controversial colonial pioneer Carl Peters, who hanged one of his black African mistresses in an act of apparent sexual jealousy.[111]

From its earliest days, gender history has also shown an understandable interest in sexuality and the body, with numerous studies of contraception, abortion, rape, and prostitution. Under Imperial Germany's Criminal Code, abortion was illegal (even in the case of rape), and those found guilty of performing or assisting in such operations faced up to five years imprisonment. As Evans notes, this was typical of the era's double standard in questions of sexual morality: "according to which women were responsible for the consequences of sexual intercourse but men were not."[112] Similarly, women merely suspected of prostitution were forced to undergo a compulsory medical examination at the hands of the dreaded "Morals Police" (*Sittenpolizei*), whereas their male clients faced no such humiliation. This double standard colored much of the Civil Code; not least the section on divorce, which was only to be granted in very limited circumstances. From the mid-1980s onwards, much of the historiography in this area has been strongly influenced by the work of Foucault, who saw the body itself as a construction of discursive practice, and therefore also subject to historical change.[113] Indeed, in the wake of Foucault, a whole new sub-discipline of "body history" (*Körpergeschichte*) has developed on European and North American university campuses, with a

---

108 N. Reagin, "The imagined hausfrau, pp. 57, 68.
109 R. R. Pierson, "Nations: Gendered, racialized, crossed with empire," in I. Blom, K. Hagemann, and C. Hall, eds., *Gendered Nations*, p. 42.
110 L. Wildenthal, "'She is the victor': Bourgeois women, nationalist identities, and the ideal of the independent woman farmer in German South West Africa," in G. Eley, ed., *Society, Culture and the State in Germany*, pp. 371–96; L. Wildenthal, *German Women for Empire, 1884–1945* (Durham, NC, 2001); S. Zantop, *Colonial Fantasies: Conquest, Family and Nation in Precolonial Germany 1770–1870* (Durham, NC, 1997).
111 A. Perras, *Carl Peters and German Imperialism 1856–1918. A Political Biography* (Oxford, 2004).
112 R. J. Evans, *The Feminist Movement in Germany*, p. 16.
113 M. Foucault, *The History of Sexuality: An Introduction* (Harmondsworth, 1978).

particular stronghold in Germany.[114] Its growing importance was recognized in a special edition of the journal *Geschichte und Gesellschaft* in the year 2000.[115] While some historians may harbor suspicions of what is undoubtedly a fashionable area of research, it is clear that many of Wilhelmine Germany's aspirations and insecurities were projected on to the body. The steely self-discipline displayed by the Empire's gymnasts, body-builders, and early naturists; the fears of physical weakness apparent in turn-of-the-century discourses on "nervousness," "hygiene," and "degeneracy"; together with the social and cultural impact of mutilated soldiers returning from the trenches, have all been the subject of recent studies.[116]

Foucault's influence can also be seen in the first attempts to address the development of normative ideals of masculinity in historical perspective. Joan Scott once observed that "[p]olitical history has ... been enacted on the field of gender,"[117] yet though men have traditionally been the focus of historical research – first in the arenas of war, diplomacy, and high politics; later in trade unions and factories – the gender dimension remained largely unseen. It is only in recent years that historians have begun to look at ways in which society and its institutions gendered men as well as women. For the most part, this work has so far focused on areas of "hegemonial masculinity" – such as the military, the duel, and the national gymnastics movement – rather than on areas in which men and women interacted.[118] It is likely, however, that future studies will place a greater emphasis on the relations *between* constructions of masculinity and femininity. There have also been studies of the nascent homosexual

---

114 Good introductions to "body history" include M. Lorenz, *Leibhaftige Vergangenheit. Einführung in die Körpergeschichte* (Tübingen, 2000); C. Wischermann and S. Haas, eds., *Körper mit Geschichte* (Stuttgart, 2000); P. Sarasin, *Reizbare Maschinen. Eine Geschichte des Körpers 1765–1914* (Frankfurt, 2001).

115 *Geschichte und Gesellschaft*, 26 (2000) 4, edited by U. Frevert. An English-language journal, *Body and Society*, was founded in 1995.

116 M. Krüger, *Körperkultur und Nationsbildung: Geschichte des Turnens in der Reichsgründungsära* (Schorndorf, 1996); S. Goltermann, *Körper der Nation. Habitusformierung und die Politik des Turnens 1860–1890* (Göttingen, 1998); S. Illig, *Zwischen Körperertüchtigung und nationaler Bewegung. Turnvereine in Bayern 1860–1890* (Cologne, 1998); M. Hau, *The Cult of Health and Beauty in Germany. A Social History, 1890–1930* (Chicago, 2003); C. Ross, *Naked Germany. Health, Race and the Nation* (Oxford, 2005).

117 J. W. Scott, "Gender: A useful category of historical analysis," p. 1074.

118 K. McAleer, *Dueling. The Cult of Honor in Fin-de-Siecle Germany* (Princeton, 1994); U. Frevert, *Men of Honour* (Cambridge, 1995); U. Frevert, *A Nation in Barracks: Modern Germany, Military Conscription and Civil Society* (Oxford, 2004); T. Kühne, ed., *Männergeschichte – Geschlechtergeschichte: Männlichkeit im Wandel der Moderne* (Frankfurt, 1996); R. Schilling, *"Kriegshelden": Deutungsmuster heroischer Männlichkeit in Deutschland 1813–1945* (Paderborn, 2002).

rights movement in Wilhelmine Germany and suggestion of an alleged "crisis of masculinity" in the years around 1900, which came to a head in the bitter controversy surrounding the Kaiser's confidante Philipp Eulenburg.[119] Whether one accepts the notion of a Wilhelmine "crisis of masculinity" or not, it seems clear that established notions of a stable gender order were indeed plunged into chaos by the events of 1914–18, as revealed all too graphically in Klaus Theweleit's remarkable and compelling study of *Male Fantasies*.[120]

How Do We "Read" Imperial Germany After the Cultural Turn?

The loss of faith in progress and other "grand narratives," together with the concomitant boom in identity politics during the late 1970s and early 1980s, formed the backdrop not only to the birth of *Alltagsgeschichte* and gender history, but also to the rise of "culture" as a new historical paradigm. Indeed, in a customarily vigorous broadside from 1996, Hans-Ulrich Wehler claimed that "all avant-garde scholars of *Alltagsgeschichte* in Germany have long ago switched to the new 'cultural history.'"[121] While Wehler was correct to point to the close ties between these approaches, which can and do overlap, his attempt to dismiss them as ephemeral fads was disappointingly narrow-minded. A glance at any academic publishers' current catalogue should be sufficient to prove him wrong. The much-discussed "cultural turn" in historical studies has profoundly influenced the historiography of the *Kaiserreich*. Indeed, much of the best work done on the Empire in recent times can be placed under this heading, whose definition has been disputed with almost as much vigor as that of culture itself, but which has nevertheless become indispensable to publishers and historians alike.[122]

---

119 J. C. Fout, "Sexual politics in Wilhelmine Germany: The male gender crisis, moral purity, and homophobia," *Journal of the History of Sexuality*, 2 (1992), pp. 388–421; E. R. Dickinson, "The men's morality movement in Germany, 1880–1914: Some reflections on sex, politics, and sexual politics," *Journal of Modern History*, 75 (2003), pp. 59–110.
120 K. Theweleit, *Male Fantasies*, 2 vols, (Cambridge, 1987–9), first published in German in 1977–8.
121 H.-U. Wehler, "A guide to future research on the Kaiserreich?," *Central European History*, 29 (1996), p. 548.
122 On the definition of cultural history see P. Burke, *Varieties of Cultural History* (Cambridge, 1997); P. Burke, *What is Cultural History?* (Cambridge, 2004); G. Eley, "What is cultural history?," *New German Critique* 65 (1995), pp. 19–36.

For a long time, cultural history was regarded as "a Cinderella among the disciplines, neglected by its more successful sisters."[123] In 1882 the German philosopher Friedrich Nietzsche had lamented: "hitherto all that has given color to existence has lacked a history: where would one find a history of love, of avarice, of envy, of conscience, of piety, of cruelty? ... The customs of the learned, of trades-people, of artists, and of mechanics – have they already found their thinkers?"[124] To its admirers, the new cultural history represented nothing less than an attempt to fill this gap: to create a history of "all that has given color to existence." Its antecedents were many and varied. Among Nietzsche's contemporaries, Jacob Burckhardt and Karl Lamprecht probably came closest to addressing the philosopher's concerns, with their interest in "the recurrent, the constant, and the typical," although both were more concerned with capturing the "spirit of an age" (*Zeitgeist*).[125] Burckhardt, like the early twentieth-century Dutch historian Johan Huizinga, focused principally on the arts and ideas, or in the latter's words: "figures, motifs, themes, symbols, concepts, ideas, styles, and sentiments."[126] Neither, however, paid much attention to the social and economic conditions that spawned them. Mid-twentieth century Marxists, such as Francis Klingender and Arnold Hauser, attempted to address this shortcoming by developing a new form of cultural history – or, more properly, a social history of culture – which considered not only the cultural superstructure, but the economic base as well. By attempting to reduce culture to a simple product of social and economic forces, however, these authors' works went too far in the other direction. After all, culture is not just "formed" by society; it is a social force in its own right. As less orthodox Marxists such as E. P. Thompson, Raymond Williams, and Eric Hobsbawm showed in the 1960s, books, buildings, and other products of material culture do not simply "illustrate" or "reflect" reality, but can constitute an active force in shaping that reality.

Dissatisfied with the rigid Marxist terminology of base and superstructure, a number of historians with an interest in culture began to move away from social history and to turn instead to anthropology. This offered what Peter Burke calls "an alternative way to link culture to society, one that did not reduce it to a reflection of society or a superstructure."[127] Anthropologists, moreover, defined the notoriously "clumpish" "c"-word

---

123 P. Burke, *What is Cultural History?*, p. 1.
124 F. Nietzsche, *The Joyful Wisdom*, translated by T. Common, (New York, 1974), p. 42.
125 Burckhardt quoted by P. Burke, *What is Cultural History?*, p. 8.
126 Huizinga quoted by P. Burke, *Varieties of Cultural History*, p. 184.
127 P. Burke, *What is Cultural History?*, p. 40.

in a broader, more everyday way than historians had traditionally dared. Culture was no longer just concerts and paintings, but "the whole complex of signifying practices and symbolic processes in a particular society."[128] As such it had already been embraced by the pioneers of the new discipline of cultural studies, who wanted to examine popular culture with the same seriousness and scholarly rigor as the products of "high" culture. By the early 1980s the cognoscenti were beginning to talk of a paradigm shift from the social to the cultural or, in Roger Chartier's phrase, "from the social history of culture to the cultural history of society."[129] Since French historians – and English-speaking historians of France – had been at the forefront of moves to "anthropologize" or "culturalize" history, it was no surprise that the book that came to embody the new approach, and belatedly gave it a name, emerged from a 1987 conference on "French History: Texts and Culture" at the University of California. Edited by Lynn Hunt, *The New Cultural History* was a heterogeneous collection of essays, reflecting a wide range of methodological and theoretical influences from anthropology to semiotics and poststructuralist literary theory.[130] Underpinning the whole collection was an awareness of the shortcomings of earlier approaches, a strong interest in theory, and a desire to draw attention to the multiplicity of possible historical perspectives. The goal was, in Patricia O'Brien's words, "a history of culture that can neither be reduced to the product of social and economic transformations nor return to a world of ideas cut free of them."[131] In practice this meant following the example of cultural studies in examining a very wide range of "texts" and by paying as much attention to their transmission and reception as to their creation. It also meant questioning the historian's general assumption that the social context of a particular cultural product is more "real" than the text itself. As the American intellectual historian Dominick LaCapra put it, "the context itself is a text of sorts."[132]

The interdisciplinary spirit and theoretical verve of the new cultural history were widely praised. By encouraging historians to rethink their conceptual frameworks and revise their writing strategies the new approach certainly had an invigorating effect. Yet from the start there were also warning voices. As early as 1982, Kocka cautioned against an

---

128 T. Eagleton quoted by G. Eley, "What is Cultural History?," p. 24.
129 Quoted in Peter Burke, *What is Cultural History?*, p. 74.
130 L. Hunt, ed., *The New Cultural History* (Berkeley, 1989).
131 P. O'Brien, "Foucault's history of culture," in L. Hunt, *The New Cultural History*, p. 26.
132 Quoted by L. S. Kramer, "Literature, criticism, and historical imagination," in L. Hunt, *The New Cultural History*, p. 114.

"impractical inflation" of the concept of culture,[133] which was becoming apparent in the proliferation of terms such as "gun culture," "visual culture," and even "cappuccino culture." Wehler bemoaned the new cultural history's "political abstinence" and accused it of making "the wildest generalizations about love, passion, and identity on the basis of a handful of texts."[134] "For every successful study," he suggested, "there are a dozen works that are only swimming along on the cultural tide; cultivating a modish verbiage of difference and deconstruction, discourse and identity; feeling released from the tight methodological constraints of the discipline of history and turning instead to a refined form of literary journalese."[135] Kocka and Wehler were by no means the only members of the German historians' guild to identify a lack of methodological stringency as the critical weakness of the new cultural history. Indeed, for many the term quickly became a synonym for the impressionistic and the anecdotal. Yet as Peter Jelavich – himself a leading cultural historian of Imperial Germany – pointed out in the mid-1990s, this was hard to avoid. Working in the "no-man's-land" between the humanities and the sciences, historians can often find themselves methodologically exposed, but the problem is particularly acute for cultural historians because the humanities "have traditionally focused on interpretation, on 'pure' textuality, while historians are concerned with change over time, which invariably involves contexts and causality." The only solution for the cultural historian, Jelavich suggested, was "to combine interpretation and causal explanation without collapsing the one into the other."[136]

Nowhere was the new cultural history more provocative than on the issue of language. Indeed, for some the "cultural turn" was overshadowed by an even more significant paradigm shift, which had first reared its head in the late 1960s and had returned with a vengeance in the 1980s: the so-called "linguistic turn."[137] The role of language in constituting social reality was undoubtedly one of the most difficult questions to face historians in the late twentieth century, although some aspects of its agenda were easier to accept than others. Few would nowadays dispute that history's own keywords – "class," "citizen," "nation," "state," – are

---

133 J. Kocka, "Klassen oder Kultur," *Merkur*, 36 (1982), pp. 955–65.
134 H.-U. Wehler, *Historisches Denken am Ende des 20. Jahrhunderts*, pp. 57–8.
135 Ibid., p. 66.
136 P. Jelavich, "Method. What method? Confessions of a failed structuralist," *New German Critique*, 65 (1995), p. 76.
137 P. Burke, *What is Cultural History?*, p. 76; G. Eley, "Is all the world text? From social history to the history of society two decades later," in T. McDonald, ed., *The Historic Turn in the Human Sciences* (Ann Arbor, 1996), pp. 193–243; G. Eley, "Problems with culture: German history after the linguistic turn," *Central European History*, 31 (1998), pp. 197–227.

cultural constructs and, therefore, inherently unstable. Similarly, few historians would deny the use of story-telling techniques, such as emplotment, in the architecture of their works. On the other hand, to dissolve history into an unending multiplicity of equally valid stories, or to argue that the past itself is merely a linguistic construction, would be regarded by most historians as a metaphor too far.[138] Whatever one's view on these thorny issues, however, it was certainly ironic that the new cultural history's engagement with the issue of language was characterized by an unusually dense or even opaque vocabulary. As Russell Jacoby observed wryly, "[t]he concentration on language and texts by the new intellectual historians ignores language and texts – their own."[139]

While an excessive use of terms such as "metaphors" and "discursive fields" may have given the unfortunate impression that history was developing into a branch of linguistics, those who hoped that the new cultural history would be revealed as a case of the emperor's new clothes were to be disappointed. Despite its initially hostile reception, the guild responded to the "challenge" of cultural history with a host of conferences, books, and journal editions; by no means wholly skeptical in tone. Even Wehler eventually acknowledged that the rise of cultural history marked a shift as significant as the turn to historical social science in the late 1960s.[140] The Bielefeld School's acceptance of cultural history may only have been partial – accepting some strands while rejecting others – but it was more than "an exercise in damage control."[141] In fact one could argue that cultural history has today become the dominant trend within the German historians' guild. Certainly, the proportion of young German historians employing its methods is broadly in line with the English-speaking world, where it acts as a welcoming umbrella under which almost any area of historical research can shelter; or, to borrow another metaphor, a black hole into which all areas of history can be sucked. As Eley has noted, "all sorts of diverse subject matters got subsumed under the rubric of social history during the 1970s, just as all sorts are being gathered beneath the banner of cultural history today."[142] These include such disparate topics as the history of travel and tourism,[143]

---

138 H. White, *Metahistory: The Historical Imagination in Nineteenth-Century Europe* (Baltimore, 1973); R. J. Evans, *In Defence of History* (London, 1997).
139 Quoted by R. J. Evans, ibid., p. 69.
140 H.-U. Wehler, "Kommentar," in T. Mergel and T. Welskopp, eds., *Geschichte zwischen Kultur und Gesellschaft: Beiträge zur Theoriedebatte* (Munich, 1997), p. 351.
141 G. Eley, "Problems with culture," p. 217.
142 G. Eley, "Forum," *German History*, 22 (2004), p. 241.
143 R. Koshar, *German Travel Cultures* (Oxford, 2000); A. Schmidt, *Reisen in die Moderne: Der Amerika-Diskurs des deutschen Bürgertums vor dem Ersten Weltkrieg im europäischen Vergleich* (Berlin, 1997).

sport,[144] the media,[145] knowledge and collecting (whether in museums, galleries, or zoos),[146] and of the city as a "text" or "spectacle,"[147] not to mention many other aspects of both high and popular culture.[148] The historicity of identity, taste, emotion, memory, and imagination are underlying themes in many of these works. Imagination, in particular, has provided a fashionable twist to countless book titles over the past two decades, while the current boom in memory studies will be addressed in the final section of this book.[149]

Cultural history's most important contribution to our understanding of the German Empire, however, lies elsewhere. For all its merits, the structural approach of historical social science was poorly suited to making those elusive but vital connections between the sphere of politics and culture, and this is where cultural history can demonstrate its true value. For, contrary to the opinion of dyed-in-the-wool structuralists, cultural history does not have to equate to "soft" history, privileging cultural representations at the expense of social relations. Recent works, for instance, have demonstrated how the study of iconography and symbolic practices can shed new light on "hard" political structures;[150] how the vernacular imagery of *Heimat* could act as a "metaphor" to help Germans imagine the abstract category of the nation, and reconcile their complex local, regional, and national identities;[151] and how analysis

---

144 C. Eisenberg, *'English Sports' und deutsche Bürger. Eine Gesellschaftsgeschichte 1800–1939* (Paderborn, 1999).
145 P. Fritzsche, *Reading Berlin 1900* (Cambridge, MA, 1996).
146 J. J. Sheehan, *Museums in the German Art World: From the End of the Old Regime to the Rise of Modernism* (Oxford, 2000); S. Crane, *Collecting and Historical Consciousness in Early Nineteenth-Century Germany* (Ithaca, 2000); H. G. Penny, *Objects of Culture. Ethnology and Ethnographic Museums in Imperial Germany* (Chapel Hill and London, 2002).
147 B. Ladd, *The Ghosts of Berlin: Confronting German History in the Urban Landscape* (Chicago, 1997); T. Lindenberger, *Straßenpolitik: Zur Sozialgeschichte der öffentlichen Ordnung. Berlin, 1900–1914* (Berlin, 1995); W. Maderthaner and L. Musner, *Die Anarchie der Vorstadt. Das andere Wien um 1900* (Frankfurt, 1999).
148 For "high" culture see M. Jefferies, *Imperial Culture in Germany 1871–1918* (Basingstoke, 2003); for popular culture see W. Kaschuba and K. Maase, eds., *Schund und Schönheit. Populäre Kultur um 1900* (Cologne, 2001).
149 For example, F. Forster-Hahn, *Imagining Modern German Culture 1889–1910* (Hanover, NH, 1996), which was a work of "old" cultural history in all but name. The model for many of these titles was, of course, Benedict Anderson's seminal study of modern nationalism, *Imagined Communities: Reflections on the Origin and Spread of Nationalism* (London, 1983).
150 See J. Paulmann, *Pomp und Politik. Monarchenbegegnungen in Europa zwischen Ancien Regime und Erstem Weltkrieg* (Paderborn, 2000); S. Behrenbeck and A. Nützenadel, eds., *Inszenierungen des Nationalstaats. Politische Feiern in Italien und Deutschland seit 1860–71* (Cologne, 2000).
151 See C. Applegate, *A Nation of Provincials: The German Idea of Heimat* (Berkeley and London, 1990); A. Confino, *The Nation as a Local Metaphor: Württemberg, Imperial Germany*

of Wilhelmine Germany's contradictory "paths to modernity" – whether in architecture and town-planning, public health and hygiene, criminology and social welfare, scientific management or the professions – can illuminate significant long-term processes within German society. Indeed, for younger historians the main attraction for studying the German Empire would currently seem to be located in this general area. If that is the case, then it is not only because of a morbid fascination with the particular way in which the German bourgeoisie "found" modernity, but also because of a recognition that cultural history – broadly defined – can "push forward and accelerate the process of opening up the political history of the *Kaiserreich* for alternative readings." Paramount among these is the recognition that modernity is not synonymous with political liberalism; that "there is no inherent reason why 'modernizing' initiatives in one area should reinforce the interests of 'modernization' in another."[152]

The "cultural turn" has also served to remind historians – if a reminder was needed – that German identities at the time of the *Kaiserreich* were extremely complex and diverse. Two current growth areas in the historiography can be cited by way of illustration. In the historical social science literature of the 1970s and 1980s, with its emphasis on powerful "modernizing" processes such as secularization and nation-building, there was a tendency to downplay the significance of religious confession or regional allegiance in shaping the way Germans thought about themselves. Yet both religion and region have returned with a vengeance in the post-1990 historiography. Indeed, some have even spoken of a "religious turn." While this may be unhelpful, there has certainly been no shortage of younger historians willing to follow Blackbourn, Sperber, and Nipperdey in seeking to re-establish confession as a central determinant of imperial life.[153] If the primary focus remains the interplay of religion and politics, attention no longer dwells solely on the Center Party or the Christian trade unions. Historians have become willing to engage with issues of piety and spirituality, as well as milieus and mentalities. Recent studies, for instance, have analyzed apparitions of the Virgin Mary in a Saarland village; the virulently anti-Catholic discourse of the Empire's Protestant

---

and National Memory 1871–1918 (Chapel Hill and London, 1997); A. Green, *Fatherlands: State-Building and Nationhood in Nineteenth-Century Germany* (Cambridge, 2001); J. Jenkins, *Provincial Modernity: Local Culture and Liberal Politics in Fin-de-Siècle Hamburg* (Ithaca, 2003); M. Umbach and B. Hüppauf, eds., *Vernacular Modernism. Heimat, Globalization, and the Built Environment* (Stanford, 2005).
152 G. Eley and J. Retallack, "Introduction," in *Wilhelminism and its Legacies*, pp. 4–6.
153 D. Blackbourn, *Class, Religion and Local Politics*; J. Sperber, *Popular Catholicism in Nineteenth Century Germany* (Princeton, 1984); T. Nipperdey, *Religion im Umbruch: Deutschland 1870–1918* (Munich, 1988).

League; the populist religiosity of the cult of the Sacred Heart; the ongoing debates surrounding the banning of the Jesuit Order; and the pervasive influence of a quasi-religious "longing for myth" in German culture.[154] Arguably the most important works in this field, however, are those that address confessional interaction, and in particular the three-way relationship between Protestants, Catholics, and Jews. Nowhere were these relations more complex than in areas – such as Silesia and the Ruhr – where a substantial Polish minority was also part of the mix. Here Catholics were often forced to choose between their national identity and their confessional identity. Such dilemmas were particularly fraught for Catholic workers, who could also be torn between their confession and their class.[155] While inter-confessional relations in Germany have been the subject of several extensive essay collections,[156] some of the most revealing insights have come from micro-historical studies of individual cities, such as Till van Rahden's excellent book on *Jews and other Breslauers*, or Anthony Steinhoff's study of imperial Strasbourg.[157]

As Rahden and Steinhoff would testify, a strong sense of place continued to characterize life in Germany well into the twentieth century, whatever homogenizing tendencies were generated at the imperial level. While there are exceptions – Wehler's *Gesellschaftsgeschichte* has predictably little to say on the subject – most historians today acknowledge that the Germans were "a nation of provincials" (Celia Applegate). This does not mean that the old question "Who ruled in Berlin?" has simply been replaced by "Who ruled in Munich?" Instead, as Retallack observes, historians "have begun to address problems of political consciousness and the interrelationship of local, regional, and national identities."[158]

---

154 D. Blackbourn, *The Marpingen Visions. Rationalism, Religion and the Rise of Modern Germany* (London, 1995); H. W. Smith, *German Nationalism and Religious Conflict: Culture, Ideology, Politics 1870–1914* (Princeton, 1995); M. B. Gross, *The War against Catholicism*; N. Busch, *Katholische Frömmigkeit und Moderne. Die Sozial- und Mentalitätsgeschichte des Herz-Jesu-Kultes in Deutschland zwischen Kulturkampf und Erstem Weltkrieg* (Gütersloh, 1997); A. Müller-Dreier, *Konfession in Politik, Gesellschaft und Kultur des Kaiserreichs. Der Evangelischer Bund, 1886–1914* (Paderborn, 1998); R. Healy, *The Jesuit Specter in Imperial Germany* (Boston, 2003); G. S. Williamson, *The Longing for Myth in Germany: Religion and Aesthetic Culture from Romanticism to Nietzsche* (Chicago, 2004).
155 M. Bachem-Rehm, *Die katholischen Arbeitervereine im Ruhrgebiet 1870–1914: Katholisches Arbeitermilieu zwischen Tradition und Emanzipation* (Stuttgart, 2004).
156 H. W. Smith, ed., *Protestants, Catholics, and Jews in Germany, 1800–1914* (Oxford, 2001); O. Blaschke, ed., *Konfessionen im Konflikt: Deutschland zwischen 1800 und 1970* (Göttingen, 2002).
157 T. van Rahden, *Juden und andere Breslauer: Die Beziehungen zwischen Juden, Protestanten und Katholiken in einer deutschen Großstadt von 1860 bis 1925* (Göttingen, 2000); A. J. Steinhoff, "Religion as urban culture: A view from Strasbourg, 1870–1914," *Journal of Urban History*, 30 (2004), pp. 152–88.
158 J. Retallack, *Germany in the Age of Kaiser Wilhelm II*, p. 111.

Indeed, one could add "imperial identities" to this list as well.[159] Historians have generally found that Germans were more successful at tackling problems at local and regional level than in the governance of the Empire. Indeed, as Richard Evans has pointed out, "[t]he national political arena was occupied by demagogy and rhetoric precisely because so many political issues vital to the interests of capital and labour were resolved at the level of the federated states."[160] It would not be an exaggeration, therefore, to claim that the cultural turn, along with other historiographical developments of the past quarter century, has forced historians to rethink the nation-state as their central unit of analysis. Certainly, much of the most important current work on the *Kaiserreich* focuses on larger or smaller contexts than the Empire itself: whether in the form of comparative transnational history, or meticulously detailed micro-history.

In 1995 Michael Geyer and Konrad Jarausch highlighted the long-standing disjunction between the "violent diversity" of German history as it was experienced, and the "utterly homogenous" way in which it was told.[161] It was an important observation, but one which had been overtaken by events: *Alltagsgeschichte*, gender history, and the cultural turn had already fractured the framework within which German history was to be examined. When the American historian Rudy Koshar used the aforementioned 1990 conference in Philadelphia to call for "new emplotments," emancipating the *Kaiserreich* from "its previously determinate or predictable relationship to Weimar, the rise of Nazism, and the Federal Republic," it was clear that much was in flux.[162] However, while the demise of the *Sonderweg* thesis and other grand narratives clearly had a liberating effect, some areas of historiography seemed more resistant to change than others. Nowhere was this more apparent than in the fields of foreign policy and military history. These were traditionally seen as the most prestigious and methodologically conservative branches of the historians' guild, and not only in Germany. How would the new historiographical pluralism impact on studies of the *Kaiserreich*'s external relations? Could the fresh perspectives of postcolonial studies, gender, or

---

159 See P. Ther, "Imperial instead of national history: Positioning modern German history on the map of European empires," in A. Miller and A. J. Rieber, eds., *Imperial Rule* (New York and Budapest, 2004), pp. 47–68.
160 R. J. Evans, "The myth of Germany's missing revolution," in *Rethinking German History*, p. 114.
161 M. Geyer and K. H. Jarausch, "Great men and postmodern ruptures: Overcoming the 'belatedness' of German historiography," *German Studies Review*, 18 (1995), p. 267.
162 R. Koshar, "The *Kaiserreich*'s ruins: Hope, memory, and political culture in imperial Germany," in G. Eley, ed., *Society, Culture and the State in Germany*, pp. 487–512.

cultural history shed new light on the origins of World War One, or would the seminal catastrophe of the twentieth century remain a bastion of history in its most recognizably Rankean form? Above all, what contribution would the growing vogue for transnational history make to our understanding of Imperial Germany's place in the world? Chapter 5 will attempt to find answers to these questions.

5
The *Kaiserreich* Transnational? Foreign Policy, Colonialism, and the First World War

In a recent essay, Alon Confino and Peter Fritzsche (born 1959) observe that "there are no traditional topics, only traditional historians."[1] This may be so, but it is clear that "traditional" historians prefer certain habitats over others. Foreign policy is an obvious example. Most of Germany's leading experts on the *Kaiserreich*'s external relations – Michael Stürmer, Klaus Hildebrand, and Gregor Schöllgen (born 1952) – are unashamedly traditionalist in outlook.[2] That is to say, they base their arguments on the existing corpus of diplomatic documents rather than the use of new methodologies and, by and large, continue to uphold Ranke's nineteenth-century dictum of the "primacy of foreign policy." It follows, therefore, that their main focus is on the European alliance system, with its treaties, ententes, and secret diplomacy, which famously developed to the *Kaiserreich*'s disadvantage in the decades before 1914. With regard to the origins of World War One, these "new" conservative

---

1 A. Confino and P. Fritzsche, "Introduction: Noises of the past," in *The Work of Memory: New Directions in the Study of German Society and Culture* (Urbana and Chicago, 2002), p. 4.
2 See in particular G. Schöllgen, ed., *Escape into War? The Foreign Policy of Imperial Germany* (Oxford, 1990). Also G. Schöllgen, *Die Macht in der Mitte Europas. Stationen deutscher Außenpolitik von Friedrich dem Großen bis zur Gegenwart* (Munich, 1992); M. Stürmer, *Die Grenzen der Macht: Begegnung der Deutschen mit ihrer Geschichte* (Berlin, 1992); M. Stürmer, "A nation-state against history and geography: The German dilemma," in G. Schöllgen, ed., *Escape into War?*, pp. 63–72; K. Hildebrand, *Reich, Nation-State, Great Power. Reflections on German Foreign Policy, 1871–1945* (London, 1995); G. Schöllgen, *Das vergangene Reich. Deutsche Außenpolitik von Bismarck bis Hitler 1871–1945* (Stuttgart, 1995).

historians share much in common with the "old orthodoxy" of the pre-Fischer era, even if there are differences of emphasis and tone. Schöllgen concedes, for instance, that "[i]t is beyond doubt that Fritz Fischer's research ... has had a profound effect on German historical writing. Whether one accepts his main theses or not, the results of his work now form an integral part of any analysis of the foreign policy of Imperial Germany."[3]

However, despite this apparent concession, Schöllgen continues to see Germany's actions in 1914 as essentially defensive in character, and like Stürmer and Hildebrand, places particular emphasis on Germany's "exposed" geopolitical position. The *Kaiserreich*'s infamous "encirclement" (*Einkreisung*) – which first became apparent during the first Morocco Crisis of 1905–6 and was "sealed" by the Anglo-Russian Entente of 1907 – is portrayed as a matter of historical fact rather than of political perception. With Britannia ruling the waves, and with Russia and France regaining strength in Europe, Germany's leaders were trapped in a deteriorating strategic position, offering precious little room for maneuver. If there was continuity in twentieth-century German history, Schöllgen argues, it was also a "continuity of fear."[4] Hildebrand's approach is more nuanced, identifying offensive as well as defensive impulses behind the *Kaiserreich*'s actions in the summer of 1914, and even accepting the German leadership's "initiating responsibility" for the July Crisis. Nevertheless, he too argues that the "flight forwards" into war was primarily a consequence of the desperate situation in which the Empire found itself.[5] A similar position is adopted by a diplomatic historian from the next generation, Sönke Neitzel (born 1968). Neitzel's 2002 handbook *Kriegsausbruch* places the principal blame for the outbreak of war on Germany (and to a lesser extent Austria), but suggests that the "anti-German" stance of the British Foreign Office was a long-term contributory factor. Indeed, he contends that the Triple Entente's failure to accommodate Germany in a new world order made war unavoidable, sooner or later.[6]

As we saw in Chapter 1, the primacy of foreign policy was forcefully challenged in the wake of the Fischer controversy by the revival of Eckart Kehr's counter-notion, the *Primat der Innenpolitik*. Historians such as Wehler and Böhme stressed the role of internal socio-economic and

---

3 G. Schöllgen, ed., "Introduction," in *Escape into War?*, p. 4.
4 Cited in A Mombauer, *The Origins of the First World War. Controversies and Consensus* (London, 2002), p. 178.
5 K. Hildebrand, *Reich, Nation-State, Great Power*.
6 S. Neitzel, *Kriegsausbruch: Deutschlands Weg in die Katastrophe 1900–1914* (Munich, 2002), p. 195.

political interests in shaping the Empire's actions before and during World War One, with the role of rapacious industrialists, frightened bourgeois politicians, radical nationalist pressure-groups, and the machinations of the "agrarian-industrial complex" all coming under suspicion. As a consequence it appeared for a time in the 1970s and 1980s that the influence of diplomatic history – once the dominant mode of historical writing – was in a state of terminal decline. This impression proved misleading, however, as the long and successful careers enjoyed by Schöllgen, Hildebrand, and Stürmer testify. In the final analysis, neither side in the "primacy" debate was ever able to establish a monopoly. Moreover, by the end of the twentieth century, the Kehrite approach was looking every bit as dated as its Rankean counterpart. Less dogmatic historians had long since begun to occupy the middle ground, recognizing "the interdependence of foreign and domestic politics" (Volker Berghahn) in many of the key areas: the building of the naval fleet;[7] the state of the Prussian army;[8] and the expansion of Germany's colonial empire.[9]

This did not mean, however, that self-proclaimed "middle way" historians were any less inclined to grant one set of questions "primacy" over all others. This was readily apparent from Berghahn's own 2002 essay in the journal *Central European History*, which criticized cultural history scholarship on the *Kaiserreich* for losing sight of what he termed "the more immediate task"; namely "to explain how the country got into a 'great war' in 1914."[10] As Jennifer Jenkins (born 1966) noted in an article for the internet forum H-German, "Berghahn's assessment reinscribes the 'primacy' argument, privileges the status of foreign policy and foregrounds the type of questions about the imperial state that were at the core of the 'primacy' debate."[11] The context of Jenkins' article was the emergence, in the late 1990s and early 2000s, of transnational history: a new approach which differs from both comparative history and international history. Unlike the latter, which focuses on the relationship between states and their rulers, the emphasis of transnational history is on the wide variety of links and influences that transcend state

---

7 V. Berghahn, *Germany and the Approach of War in 1914*; H. H. Herwig, *"Luxury" Fleet: The Imperial German Navy, 1888–1918* (London, 1980); M. Epkenhans, *Die wilhelminische Flottenrüstung, 1908–1914* (Munich, 1991).

8 A. Bucholz, *Moltke, Schlieffen and Prussian War Planning* (Oxford, 1991); A. Mombauer, *Helmuth von Moltke and the Origins of the First World War* (Cambridge, 2001).

9 See K. Canis, *Von Bismarck zur Weltpolitik. Deutsche Außenpolitik, 1890 bis 1902* (Berlin, 1997).

10 V Berghahn, "The German Empire, 1871–1914: Reflections," p. 76.

11 J. Jenkins, "Transnationalism and German history," H-NET list on German History, H-GERMAN@H-NET.MSU.EDU (23 January 2006).

boundaries: global trade and business patterns; ethnic diasporas; cultural and technological transfers; religious and political ideologies. By opening up fresh perspectives on the complex networks that linked late nineteenth- and early twentieth-century Germans to the wider world, the new approach offers a chance to move on from the tired and false opposition of the "primacy" debate, revealing "the interwoven reality of politics within states and politics across borders."[12] The first part of this chapter is devoted to assessing its impact so far. The assertion that "there are no traditional topics, only traditional historians" will be further tested by looking at the contribution of other recent historiographical innovations – such as postcolonial studies and the new cultural history – to our understanding of the Empire's foreign and colonial relationships. The chapter then closes with a review of the current state of the debate on the origins of World War One, as the historians' guild prepares to mark the centenary of Fritz Fischer's birth.

"The First Age of Globalization?"

Although world histories tend to locate the beginnings of globalization somewhere between the fourteenth and sixteenth centuries, and identify a quickening of the tempo in the eighteenth and nineteenth centuries, it is in the decades either side of 1900 that the first "grand acceleration" is said to have occurred.[13] The lifetime of the German Empire coincided, therefore, with what is increasingly thought of as "the first age of globalization," when concepts such as the "world market," "world economy," and "world power" became common currency; and when a host of international organizations (both intergovernmental, and non-governmental) were established.[14] Indeed, the level of global integration achieved in the years before 1914 would not be reached again until the second half of the twentieth century. "With its rapid economic expansion and its will to politicize world economic connections," Niels Petersson suggests, the German Empire did not merely coincide with the first surge of globalization,

---

12 R. Granieri, "Crossing borders: Transnationalism, diplomatic history, and the future of German studies," H-NET list on German History, H-GERMAN@H-NET.MSU.EDU (17 January 2006).
13 See, for example, J. Osterhammel and N. Petersson, *Globalization: A Short History* (Princeton, 2005); C. A. Bayly, *The Birth of the Modern World, 1780–1914: Global Connections and Comparisons* (Oxford, 2004).
14 Such as the International Council of Women (1888), the Socialist International (1889), the International Peace Bureau (1891), or the Fédération Internationale de Football Association, (FIFA, 1904).

it was the epoch's "globalization leader" (*Globalisierungsvormacht*).[15] Of course, Wilhelmine Germany has long been associated with *Weltpolitik* – a "nebulous and inchoate" mixture of naval enthusiasm, social Darwinism, colonialism, and straightforward power politics[16] – and is often rightly portrayed as a period of dramatic social, economic, and demographic change, yet the extent to which these upheavals were merely part of a wider global phenomenon has only recently been acknowledged. One contribution transnational history can make to our understanding of the Empire, therefore, is to illuminate the many global networks to which it was connected, and to assess how they operated.[17] Another is to highlight the parallels between the first age of globalization and our own time. These include transcontinental migration on a large scale, with all its associated aspirations and anxieties; a communications revolution, with the accompanying perception of living in a rapidly shrinking world; and a stridently assertive global capitalism. Then as now, globalization had its losers and victims too, with the agrarian lobby's campaign for tariff protection just one expression of the "globalization backlash" in Germany.[18]

Of course, such parallels can be taken too far. As yet, transnational history is still very much in its infancy. Its meanings and methodologies remain open to debate. Some bemoan its undoubted tendency to produce broad-brushstroke generalizations; while others suspect it is merely "flavor of the month." Diplomatic historians – a much maligned community in recent years, albeit rather less so in Germany than in the English-speaking world – argue that they have been doing transnational history for decades, without ever receiving due credit. Certainly, not all historians of foreign policy are crusty conservatives, inherently elitist in their outlook, and not all diplomatic historians restrict themselves to "The High Politics of the European Cabinets." Moreover, as Ron Granieri points out, "[a]t a time when some fields struggle to 'bring the state back in,' diplomatic history has always appreciated the role of the state."[19] Even so, it remains to be seen whether the young guns of transnational history will want old school diplomatic historians on board. When Sebastian Conrad

---

15 N. Petersson, "Das Kaiserreich in Prozessen ökonomischer Globalisierung," in S. Conrad and J. Osterhammel, eds., *Das Kaiserreich transnational. Deutschland in der Welt 1871–1914* (Göttingen, 2004), p. 67.
16 The quote is from M. Seligmann and R. McLean, *Germany from Reich to Republic*, pp. 124–5.
17 Transnational historians' use of the concept of networks owes much to theorists such as John W. Burton (the "cobweb" model) and Manuel Castells (the "network society"). See N. Petersson, "Das Kaiserreich in Prozessen ökonomischer Globalisierung," p. 50.
18 Ibid., p. 64.
19 See R. Granieri, "Crossing Borders: Transnationalism, Diplomatic History, and the Future of German Studies." H-NET list on German History, H-GERMAN@H-NET.MSU.EDU (17 January 2006).

(born 1966) and Jürgen Osterhammel (born 1952) published a collection of 15 essays under the programmatic title *Das Kaiserreich transnational* in 2004, they specifically included "the history of foreign policy and international relations" within the scope of the new approach. However, none of their selected contributors had a foreign policy focus, and one of them actually suggested that "the official relations between states" fell outside transnational history's remit.[20]

Despite such inconsistencies, Conrad and Osterhammel's volume undoubtedly represents the most concerted attempt to apply the transnational paradigm to the *Kaiserreich* to date. The book has aroused sufficient interest, moreover, to suggest that the approach will be around for years to come, even if some of the contributions might be considered old wine in new bottles. The editors' declared aim is to explain Imperial Germany's history from "the outside in," rather than "the inside out." The Empire, they argue, was not an island and never could be one. So why is it that "no other phase of modern German history is as strongly regarded as endogenously driven as the *Kaiserreich*"?[21] In Conrad and Osterhammel's view, it is because proponents of historical social science have proved just as unwilling to depart from the nation-state paradigm as traditional upholders of the "primacy of foreign policy." Consequently, many important aspects of the complex relationship between the internal and the external have been left unexplored. With this in mind, the contributors to *Das Kaiserreich transnational* suggest a number of potentially productive ways in which historians of Imperial Germany can "go beyond the nation."[22]

One possibility is to emphasize the global character of so much that occurred in the *Kaiserreich*: trade; migration; cultural exchange. The economic issues that increasingly dominated the Empire's daily political life, for instance, can only really be understood in a global context: how else can one explain why it cost exactly the same to transport a ton of wheat from New York to Mannheim, as it did from Berlin to Kassel?[23] In 1914 the Royal Institute for Maritime Transport and World Economics was established at Kiel in an attempt to make sense of such conundrums. As David Blackbourn observes, a renewed focus on transnational trade

---

20 D. Blackbourn, "Das Kaiserreich transnational. Eine Skizze," in S. Conrad and J. Osterhammel, eds., *Das Kaiserreich transnational*, p. 305.
21 S. Conrad and J. Osterhammel, "Einleitung," in S. Conrad and J. Osterhammel, eds., *Das Kaiserreich transnational*, p. 11.
22 This is a phrase much beloved of transnational historians. See, for example, P Ther, "Beyond the nation. The relational basis of a comparative history of Germany and Europe," *Central European History*, 36 (2003), pp. 45–75; J. Osterhammel, *Geschichtswissenschaft jenseits des Nationalstaats. Studien zu Beziehungsgeschichte und Zivilisationsvergleich* (Göttingen, 2001).
23 S. Conrad and J. Osterhammel, "Einleitung," p. 24.

patterns and the history of material culture might help to restore economic history to its position of central importance after decades of neglect.[24] By focusing on a single commodity, Sven Beckert's fascinating essay on the "Empire of Cotton" – the "first real mass product," which was as important to the nineteenth century as oil is today – suggests one way in which this might be achieved.[25] Another means of going "beyond the nation" is to privilege the experience of ordinary individuals and families, whose unprecedented mobility in the second half of the nineteenth century made a mockery of nationalist assumptions. Between the 1840s and 1914 four-and-a-half million people left German-speaking Europe for the New World, mostly to the US; while some one-and-a-half million immigrant workers had settled in the *Kaiserreich* by 1914.[26] It has, of course, become fashionable in recent years to think of nations as "imagined communities," but it is also important to consider the impact of mass migration on people's "mental maps."[27]

A rather different approach is outlined in the same volume by Philipp Ther (born 1967). He adopts a Polish perspective to argue that the German Empire should be taken at face value: as a multinational continental empire – analogous to the Habsburg, the Russian, or the Ottoman Empires – rather than a "proper" nation-state.[28] Inspired by Dominic Lieven's work on the Russian Empire,[29] Ther suggests that Prussia's status as an imperial power dates back to the Partition of Poland, or at least to the Congress of Vienna, and, therefore, long pre-dates both its opportunistic acquisition of a small maritime empire in the 1880s, and the build-up of domestic social pressures highlighted by Wehler or Mommsen. For Ther, in other words, German colonial history is by no means just a "historical episode" of three decades duration.[30] After all, the Germans' most enduring colonial fantasies were projected not on the jungles of

---

24 D. Blackbourn, "Das Kaiserreich transnational. Eine Skizze," p. 308.
25 S. Beckert, "Das Reich der Baumwolle. Eine globale Geschichte," in S. Conrad and J. Osterhammel, eds., *Das Kaiserreich transnational*, pp. 280–301.
26 The emigration from Germany to America occurred in three main waves: 1846–57; 1864–73; and 1880–93. Statistics from D. Blackbourn, "Das Kaiserreich transnational. Eine Skizze," pp. 310–13.
27 See F. B. Schenk, "Mental Maps. Die Konstruktion von geographischen Räumen in Europa seit der Aufklärung," *Geschichte und Gesellschaft*, 28 (2002), pp. 493–514.
28 P. Ther, "Deutsche Geschichte als imperiale Geschichte," in S. Conrad and J. Osterhammel, eds., *Das Kaiserreich transnational*, pp. 129–48. For an English version see his essay "Imperial instead of national history," in A. Miller and A. J. Rieber, eds., *Imperial Rule* (Budapest and New York, 2004), pp. 47–68.
29 D. Lieven, *Empire: The Russian Empire and its Rivals* (New Haven and London, 2001).
30 The view of K. Bade, ed., *Imperialismus und Kolonialmission. Kaiserliches Deutschland und koloniales Imperium* (Stuttgart, 1982).

Africa or Asia, but on the Teutonic equivalent of the "wild west": *Mitteleuropa*, with its vast plains stretching eastward to the Russian steppes. These imperial dreams came tantalizing close to reality too, first in the infamous Peace Treaty of Brest-Litovsk imposed on the Russians in March 1918, and later in the National Socialist policy of *Lebensraum*. Indeed, as Blackbourn notes in the volume's closing paragraph, the German equivalent to the end of the British or French Empires came not in 1919 (when it lost all its overseas possessions) but in 1945, with the loss of its East European settlements.[31] Ther's stimulating observations on German history from a Polish perspective – shaped, no doubt, by his affiliation to the European University Viadrina in the border town of Frankfurt an der Oder – can be criticized in a number of ways: they are, for instance, unduly Prussocentric, obscuring both the diverse reality of the *Kaiserreich*'s federal structure, and the degree to which a German *Reichspatriotismus* developed before 1914. Also, as Ther acknowledges, while Poles might have become "second class citizens" in the *Kaiserreich*, they were never colonial subjects and were allowed to assimilate in ways that would have been impossible for black Africans. Nevertheless, his essay highlights an important virtue of the transnational approach: its willingness to examine issues from multiple and often unconventional viewpoints.

This aspect of transnational history is perhaps most apparent when dealing with relationships between Europe and the non-European world. Whatever contemporaries might have thought,[32] globalization was never simply a European project, and transnational history endeavors to reflect the multicentric nature of the process. In this it owes much to the influence of postcolonial studies, which for more than a decade has been challenging the notion that the "domestic" and the "imperial" were separate and discrete domains. By "reversing the telescope" – in other words, inverting the conventional relationship between the metropolitan centre and the colonial periphery [33] – the interdisciplinary postcolonial studies approach has re-invigorated scholarly work on imperialism.[34]

---

31 D. Blackbourn, "Das Kaiserreich transnational. Eine Skizze," p. 324.
32 Many of the Empire's leading thinkers predicted a future in which the world's resources would be divided up between three or four vast European and North American empires. According to this so-called *Weltreichslehre*, if Germany did not control such an empire it would a face bleak struggle for survival. See S. Neitzel, *Weltmacht oder Niedergang. Die Weltreichslehre im Zeitalter des Imperialismus* (Paderborn, 2000).
33 See, for instance, U. van der Heyden and J. Zeller, eds., *"Macht und Anteil an der Weltherrschaft." Berlin und der deutsche Kolonialismus* (Münster, 2000).
34 See R.Young, *Postcolonialism. An Historical Introduction* (Oxford, 2001); L. Gandhi, *Postcolonial Theory: A Critical Introduction* (New York, 1998). The key figures in postcolonial theory are Homi Bhabha (born 1949) and Edward Said (1935–2003). The latter's *Orientalism: Western Conceptions of the Orient* (London, 1978) paved the way for the new approach.

Arguably the most successful contributions to *Das Kaiserreich transnational* are those that look at these interactions and mediations, such as Dieter Gosewinkel's study of colonial and racial influences on the evolution of German citizenship law, or the investigation by Dirk van Laak (born 1961) into whether the German colonies fulfilled the role of "laboratories of the modern age."[35] Even if both authors ultimately conclude that the influence of the periphery on the center was less profound than is sometimes claimed, the exercise is still a valuable one. More generally, it would appear that transnational history is at its most convincing when it takes the nation-state seriously. It was, after all, the most emulated and admired state form in the nineteenth century, and – as the examples of Germany and Japan show – the processes of nationalization and globalization could, and did, run concurrently. While it is highly desirable to explore counternarratives that "go beyond the nation," to lose sight of the national dimension altogether would serve only to undermine the new approach's credibility.

The Empire Strikes Back?

Even without the rise of the transnational paradigm, the impact of postcolonial studies on the history of German imperialism would have been considerable. Until the 1990s, the historiography in this area was relatively sparse and uninviting; "a subsidiary field for a few specialists."[36] One of these, the Manchester historian W. O. Henderson (1904–93), observed not unreasonably that "there are limits as to what can be said about an empire which lasted only thirty-five years."[37] Three aspects of Germany's colonial experience which did arouse more than passing interest in the English-speaking world were the initial motives that lay behind Bismarck's brief and unexpected flirtation with colonialism (see Chapter 2); the role and composition of colonial pressure groups;[38] and

---

35 D. Gosewinkel, "Rückwirkungen des kolonialen Rasserechts? Deutsche Staatsangehörigkeit zwischen Rassestaat und Rechtstaat"; and D. von Laak, "Kolonien als 'Laboratorien der Moderne?,'" in S. Conrad and J. Osterhammel, eds., *Das Kaiserreich transnational*, pp. 236–56 and 257–79 respectively.
36 S. Conrad and J. Osterhammel, "Einleitung," p. 22.
37 W. O. Henderson, *Studies in German Colonial History* (London, 1962), p. x.
38 The German Colonial Association was founded in 1882 and Carl Peters' Society for German Colonization in 1884. The two merged as the German Colonial Society (DKG) in 1887. The Pan-German League (ADV) was established in 1891. The DKG was later challenged by the German Colonial League (1903) and the German National Colonial Association (1904).

the longer-term impact of German rule on its overseas Protectorates.[39] On the last point, two starkly contrasting schools of thought developed during the course of the twentieth century: one that considered German colonial administrators to have been particularly brutal and exploitative; and another which saw them as "strict but fair," with an unusual sensitivity to cultural difference. Prejudice and propaganda colored both views, not least because the issue became subsumed in the acrimonious debates triggered by World War One and the Treaty of Versailles. As Uta Poiger (born 1965) observes, however, the striking thing about both schools of thought from today's perspective is "that these histories of German colonialism rarely talked about race and that they were largely histories of colonialism without the colonized."[40]

The German overseas empire was also touched on by a more general, and rather turgid, debate in the 1960s and 1970s, focusing on the nature of imperialism. Historians from the GDR were particularly to the fore, determined to reveal the pivotal role of monopoly capitalism behind German imperialism.[41] Whatever the merits (or otherwise) of this earlier literature, however, few could have predicted the recent boom in studies of German colonialism.[42] Certainly, it would have come as a surprise to Henderson, who could surely not have foreseen either the cultural studies jargon, or the intense preoccupation with colonialism's metropolitan impact, so evident in current texts. In both respects, however, it is apparent that the historiography has been following wider developments in the field as a whole, rather than a specifically German research agenda.[43] This is perhaps inevitable, given that the lifetime of Germany's colonial empire

---

39 Earlier general histories of the German colonial empire include W. Smith, *The German Colonial Empire* (Chapel Hill and London, 1978); H. Stoecker, ed., *German Imperialism in Africa: From the Beginnings until the Second World War* (London, 1986– first published in the GDR); W. O. Henderson, *The German Colonial Empire: 1884–1919* (London, 1993); G. Schöllgen, *Imperialismus und Gleichgewicht: Deutschland, England und die orientalische Frage 1871–1914* (Munich, 1984); and H. Gründer, *Geschichte der deutschen Kolonien* (Paderborn, 1985).
40 U. Poiger, "Imperialism and empire in twentieth-century Germany," *History and Memory*, 17 (2005), pp. 117–43, here p. 118.
41 For an overview see S. Förster, "Imperialismus, Militarismus und das Deutsche Kaiserreich. Grundtendenzen in der Historiographie der DDR zur Deutschen Geschichte von 1897/98 bis 1914," in A. Fischer and G. Heydemann, eds., *Geschichtswissenschaft in der DDR*, vol. 2, pp. 711–34. Also H.Gründer, "Kolonialismus und Marxismus. Der deutsche Kolonialismus in der Geschichtsschreibung der DDR," in A. Fischer and G. Heydemann, eds., *Geschichtswissenschaft in der DDR*, vol. 2, pp. 671–709.
42 For a concise but well-informed overview of recent trends see D. van Laak, *Über alles in der Welt. Deutscher Imperialismus im 19. und 20. Jahrhundert* (Munich, 2005).
43 See A. L. Stoler and F. Cooper, eds., "Between metropole and colony. Rethinking a research agenda," in *Tensions of Empire: Colonial Cultures in a Bourgeois World* (Berkeley, 1997), pp. 1–56.

coincided almost exactly with the high point of imperialism in Europe, Eric Hobsbawm's famous "Age of Empire."[44]

Although brief, German colonial history is nevertheless often divided into three or four phases. Winfried Baumgart (born 1938) labeled them "annexation euphoria," "anti-climax," and "revolt."[45] The initial expansion (1884–5) consisted of a series of ad hoc initiatives by individual merchants and adventurers, to which Bismarck responded opportunistically. At first the German Protectorates were administered privately, through chartered companies, but when this proved unsatisfactory a small Colonial Department was set up in the Foreign Office in 1890. Further acquisitions followed in the late 1890s, such as the port of Tsingtao on China's Kiao Chow Bay, and a scatter of territories in the South Seas, but German colonial rule was increasingly characterized by embarrassing scandals and aggressive confrontations with the native populations. These included the brutal suppression of uprisings by the Herero and the Nama in South West Africa (1904–7), and some 20 different tribes in East Africa (the so-called Maji Maji Rising of 1905–7). A more subtle and technocratic course, sometimes dubbed "scientific colonialism," was then adopted under the liberal banker Bernhard Dernburg, who was appointed Secretary of State in the newly-created Office for Colonial Affairs in 1907.[46] Dernburg was in office for less than four years, and German colonial policy "remained a haphazard and improvised affair,"[47] but his aim of treating the native population as a valuable commodity rather than an obstacle did appear to work. Certainly, there were no more major risings, and the native populations remained largely loyal to the German Empire throughout World War One.

According to Seligmann and McLean's recent textbook, four recurring arguments were used to justify Germany's colonial expansion throughout this 30-year period: economic benefits (new markets and raw materials); demographic benefits (emigrants settling under the German flag, rather than the Stars and Stripes); ethnic benefits (incorporating territories already settled by "Teutons" – such as the Boers – into the "Germanic" world); and finally, the benefits of cohesion (bringing together existing but scattered overseas possessions into a single unit).[48] Objectively, it is clear that none of these criteria were ever met; the costs of empire always

---

44 E. Hobsbawm, *The Age of Empire, 1875–1914* (London, 1987).
45 W. Baumgart, "Die deutsche Kolonialherrschaft in Afrika: neue Wege der Forschung," *Vierteljahrschrift für Sozial- und Wirtschaftsgeschichte*, 58 (1971), pp. 468–81.
46 D. van Laak, "Kolonien als 'Laboratorien der Moderne?,'" pp. 273–4.
47 W. Baumgart, "German Imperialism in historical perspective," in A. Knoll and L. H. Gann, eds., *Germans in the Tropics: Essays in German Colonial History* (New York, 1987), p. 158.
48 M. Seligmann and R. McLean, *Germany from Reich to Republic*, p. 116.

exceeded the rewards. As Holger Herwig (born 1941) observes, the empire was a "disparate and far-flung collection of largely undesirable real estate in Africa and Asia," which at no time constituted "the cherished El Dorado of colonial enthusiasts."[49] Indeed, in view of the empire's modest lifespan, its unattractiveness to settlers, and its unimpressive economic performance – the colonial share of the *Kaiserreich*'s foreign trade never amounted to more than 0.6 percent, and was declining rather than rising by 1914 – it would be all too easy to dismiss Germany's short and imitative history as a colonial power.

Yet the impact of the colonial experience cannot be measured in economic or political terms alone. It stimulated the imagination of writers and artists, from the popular adventure stories of Karl May,[50] to the vivid Expressionist art of Emil Nolde, Ernst-Ludwig Kirchner, or Walter von Ruckteschell, who in 1914 painted "Germany's highest mountain": Mount Kilimanjaro. It inspired Imperial Germany's scientists to be at the forefront of a host of nascent academic disciplines (ethnology, anthropology, zoology, oceanography, tropical medicine, and more dubiously phrenology, eugenics, and racial science).[51] It helped Berlin to become an acknowledged center for the study of African and Asian languages and cultures. It encouraged new methods of collection, organization, and display in the *Kaiserreich*'s museums and zoos.[52] It provided entertainment for thousands of paying spectators at the era's many colonial shows (*Völkerschauen*), including the "Zanzibar Town" set up at the Berlin Trade Exhibition of 1896, where 103 native subjects of Germany's colonies performed scripted roles in supposedly authentic surroundings.[53]

---

49 H. H. Herwig, "Industry, empire and the First World War," in G. Martel, ed., *Modern Germany Reconsidered*, p. 54.
50 N. Berman, "Orientalism, imperialism, and nationalism: Karl May's *Orientzyklus*," in S. Friedrichsmeyer, S. Lennox, and S. Zantop, eds., *The Imperialist Imagination. German Colonialism and its Legacy* (Ann Arbor, 1998), pp. 51–68.
51 A. Zimmerman, *Anthropology and Antihumanism in Imperial Germany* (Chicago and London, 2001); P. Grosse, *Kolonialismus, Eugenik und bürgerliche Gesellschaft in Deutschland 1850–1918* (Frankfurt, 2000); W. Eckart, *Medizin und Kolonialimperialismus: Deutschland 1884–1945* (Paderborn, 1997); P. Weindling, *Health, Race and German Politics between National Unification and Nazism, 1870–1945* (Cambridge, 1989).
52 H. G. Penny, *Objects of Culture: Ethnology and Ethnographic Museums in Imperial Germany*. A German Colonial Museum opened in 1898, with more than three thousand cultural artifacts from Africa alone. The Hamburg zoo pioneer Carl Hagenbeck, who also staged "human showcases," has been the subject of several studies: H. Thode-Adora, *Für fünfzig Pfennig um die Welt. Die Hagenbeckschen Völkerschauen* (Frankfurt, 1989); L. Dittrich and A. Rieke-Müller, *Carl Hagenbeck (1844–1913). Tierhandel und Schaustellungen im Deutschen Kaiserreich* (Frankfurt, 1998); M. Gretzschel and O. Pelc, eds., *Hagenbeck. Tiere, Menschen, Illusionen* (Hamburg, 1998).
53 See A. Honold, "Ausstellung des Fremden. Menschen- und Völkerschau um 1900," in S. Conrad and J. Osterhammel, eds., *Das Kaiserreich transnational*, pp. 170–90. The Berlin

Above all, it touched millions through its influence on everyday language,[54] popular culture (songs, travelogues, illustrated magazines), and advertising.[55] Colonial imagery in the latter field was not confined to so-called *Kolonialwaren* – "exotic" groceries such as coffee, chocolate, and bananas – but was also employed to sell products and services ostensibly unrelated to the colonial world (the "whitening" power of soap, toothpaste, and washing-powder, for instance). Colonial representations of this kind have been at the forefront of much recent work by Anglo-American scholars in the field of German Studies. It has been convincingly demonstrated – by Susanne Zantop (1945–2001) and Russell Berman (born 1950) among others – that the "imperialist imagination" both predates and postdates Germany's actual colonial empire.[56] In other words, Germans were constructing "colonial fantasies" well before the acquisition of real colonies, while memories of the colonial experience have continued to echo through works of German art, film, and literature long after the territories were lost.[57]

Despite all this, however, a note of caution needs to be struck. Were the Germans really as deeply affected by imperialism as the British or the French? It seems unlikely, given the brevity of Germany's colonial experience, and the relative lack of migration from the empire's periphery to its centre.[58] Africans were a much rarer sight on the streets of Wilhelmine Berlin than Indians in Edwardian London, and as Conrad and Osterhammel concede, the favorite trick of postcolonial studies – to focus on

---

show was by no means unusual. Paul Greenhalgh notes that "Between 1889 and 1914, the [colonial] exhibitions became a human showcase, when people from all over the world were brought to sites in order to be seen by others for their gratification and education." *Ephemeral Vistas. The Expositions universelles, Great Exhibitions, and World's Fairs, 1851–1939* (Manchester, 1988), p. 82.

54   Catholic districts in German towns, for instance, were sometimes referred to by Protestants as "nigger villages" [*Negerdörfer*]. See D. Blackbourn, "Das Kaiserreich transnational. Eine Skizze," p. 304.

55   On advertising see D. Ciarlo, "Rasse konsumieren: von der exotischen zur kolonialen Imagination in der Bildreklame des wilhelminischen Kaiserreichs," in B. Kundrus, ed., *Phantasiereiche: Zur Kulturgeschichte des deutschen Kolonialismus* (Frankfurt and New York, 2003), pp. 135–79.

56   S. Zantop, *Colonial Fantasies: Conquest, Family and Nation in Precolonial Germany* (Durhan, NC and London, 1997); R. A. Berman, *Enlightenment or Empire. Colonial Discourse in German Culture* (Lincoln, NE, 1998).

57   S. Friedrichsmeyer, S. Lennox, and S. Zantop, eds., *The Imperialist Imagination* (Ann Arbor, 1998); A. Honold and O. Simons, eds., *Kolonialismus als Kultur: Literatur, Medien, Wissenschaft in der deutschen Gründerzeit des Fremden* (Tübingen and Basel, 2002); A. Honold and K. P. Scherpe, eds., *Mit Deutschland um die Welt. Eine Kulturgeschichte des Fremden in der Kolonialzeit* (Stuttgart and Weimar, 2004).

58   On black immigrants in Wilhelmine Germany see P. Grosse, "Zwischen Privatheit und Öffentlichkeit: Kolonialmigration in Deutschland, 1900–1940," in B. Kundrus, ed., *Phantasiereiche*, pp. 91–109.

"the voyage in" rather than the "the voyage out" – is harder to pull off for the German empire than for its British or French counterparts.[59] Notwithstanding all the colonial fantasies, Lewis Gann and Peter Duignan are probably correct in their assertion that "[f]or the great majority of Germans, places like Little Popo-Land (with its unfortunate German nursery connotations) were distant, slightly comic regions."[60] Even the so-called "Hottentot Elections" of 1907 had as much to do with domestic hostility to political Catholicism as to the colonial conflict in South West Africa.

Then there is the peculiarly problematic nature of dealing with issues of race in the context of German history. Whether implicit or explicit, the Third Reich forms the backdrop for anyone working in this field. Some choose to confront it head on, addressing directly the famous thesis advanced by Hannah Arendt (1906–75) that twentieth-century totalitarianism had its roots in the colonial experience, where humanitarian taboos were broken and whole populations were dehumanized for the first time.[61] In particular, the mass murder of the Herero and Nama peoples in German South West Africa (1904–7) is often portrayed as the forerunner of all genocides, or more specifically a rehearsal for the Holocaust. Indeed, while the historiography of German colonialism includes monographs on each of the major Protectorates (together with areas of "informal empire" too),[62] the literature on South West Africa threatens to overshadow every other aspect of German colonial history.[63]

---

59 S. Conrad and J., "Einleitung," p. 17.
60 L. H. Gann and P. Duignan, *The Rulers of German Africa, 1884–1914* (Stanford, 1977), pp. 239–40.
61 H. Arendt, *The Origins of Totalitarianism* (London, 1961, first published in 1951), pp. 185–222.
62 J. Noyes, *Colonial Space: Spatiality in the Discourse of German South West Africa, 1884–1915* (Philadelphia, 1992); M. Seligmann, *Rivalry in Southern Africa: The Transformation of German Colonial Policy* (Basingstoke, 1998); D. Walther, *Creating Germans Abroad. Cultural Policies and National Identity in Namibia* (Athens, OH, 2002); B. Kundrus, *Moderne Imperialisten: Das Kaiserreich im Spiegel seiner Kolonien* (Cologne, 2003), which also focuses primarily on South West Africa; E. Wareham, *Race and Realpolitik: The Politics of Colonisation in German Samoa* (Frankfurt, 2002); H. J. Hiery, ed., *Die deutsche Südsee, 1884–1914. Ein Handbuch* (Paderborn, 2001); S. Kuß and B. Martin, eds., *Das Deutsche Reich und der Boxeraufstand* (Munich, 2002); M. Fuhrmann, *Der Traum vom deutschen Orient. Zwei deutsche Kolonien im Osmanischen Reich 1851–1918* (Frankfurt, 2006).
63 See J. Zimmerer, "Krieg, KZ und Völkermord in Südwestafrika. Der erste deutsche Genozid," in J. Zimmerer and J. Zeller, eds., *Völkermord in Südwestafrika. Der Kolonialkrieg (1904–08) in Namibia und seine Folgen* (Berlin, 2003), pp. 45–63; J. Zimmerer, *Deutsche Herrschaft über Afrikaner. Staatlicher Machtanspruch und Wirklichkeit im kolonialen Namibia* (Münster, 2005); also G. Krüger, *Kriegsbewältigung und Geschichtsbewußtsein. Realität, Deutung und Verarbeitung des deutschen Kolonialkriegs in Namibia 1904 bis 1907* (Göttingen, 1999), which has a particularly welcome emphasis on African agency. Two older titles are also

Five factors have contributed to the recent surge in interest: the opening up of Germany's colonial archives after 1989; Namibia's achievement of independence from South Africa (1990) and the subsequent end of apartheid; the centenary of the 1904 tragedy; the growth of "Holocaust Studies"; and the continuing popularity of the cultural history approach, with its emphasis on representations, imagination, and memory.

Most historians remain wary, however, of overly simplistic lines of continuity "from Windhoek to Auschwitz." As Lora Wildenthal (born 1965) observes, "[c]olonialism's connections to Nazism and the Holocaust are both obvious and extremely difficult to specify historically."[64] Andreas Eckl argues that although German generals undoubtedly condemned the majority of the native population in South West Africa to near-certain death, the use of terms like "genocide" is unhelpful and "Eurocentric."[65] While this is a minority view, many more would agree with the conclusion drawn by Birthe Kundrus (born 1963) from a short comparative study of Wilhelmine restrictions on miscegenation and the Nuremberg race laws; namely that the differences outweigh the similarities.[66] As Kundrus' work shows, a particular emphasis of recent literature has been on the gendered, and sometimes sexualized, nature of colonial discourse.[67] Women faced an uphill struggle to be accepted within the *Kaiserreich*'s colonial associations, and later in the colonies themselves, but once they did gain a foothold it is clear they were not afraid to use the colonial realm as a way of expanding the relatively narrow role allowed to them in Germany. Strongly egalitarian views on issues of gender could, and often did, go hand-in-hand with strictly hierarchical positions on questions of race.[68]

---

worth mentioning: H. Bley's *Namibia under German Rule* (Hamburg, 1996, first published in 1971); and the East German historian H. Drechlser's *"Let Us Die Fighting": The Struggle of the Herero and Nama against German Imperialism* (London, 1980).

64   L. Wildenthal, *German Women for Empire*, p. 8. See also I. V. Hull, *Absolute Destruction: Military Culture and the Practices of War in Imperial Germany* (Ithaca, 2005).

65   A. Eckl, "Vorwort," in *"S'ist ein übles Land hier." Zur Historiographie eines umstrittenen Kolonialkriegs. Tagebuchaufzeichnungen aus dem Herero-Krieg in Deutsch-Südwestafrika 1904 von Georg Hillebrecht und Franz Ritter von Epp* (Cologne, 2005).

66   B. Kundrus, ed., "Von Windhoek nach Nürnberg? Koloniale 'Mischehenverbote' und die national-sozialistische Rassengesetzgebung," in *Phantasiereiche*, pp. 110–34.

67   There are frequent references in colonialist discourse to the "penetration" of "virgin" but "fertile" territory, able to generate "daughter" colonies, and so on.

68   L. Wildenthal, *German Women for Empire*; K. Schestokat, *German Women in Cameroon: Travelogues from Colonial Times* (New York and Frankfurt, 2003); F. Eigler, "Engendering German nationalism: Gender and race in Frieda von Bülow's colonial writings," in S. Friedrichsmeyer, S. Lennox, and S. Zantop, eds., *The Imperialist Imagination*, pp. 69–86.

The "Age of Nervousness"?

"Whole libraries have been written on the origins of the First World War, and yet it remains a psychological puzzle why Germany's rulers became involved in this conflict; indeed, conjured it up, even longed for it," suggests the Bielefeld historian Joachim Radkau (born 1943).[69] Certainly, when he came to pen his memoirs, Germany's wartime Chancellor Bethmann Hollweg appeared at a loss to explain the intense domestic pressures that had built up in the *Kaiserreich* by 1914. On the surface, he suggested, everything had seemed fine: "Business was booming, cities were competing with their communal and charitable undertakings, work was readily available, and with the level of general prosperity rising quickly, the living standards of the lower classes were also lifting visibly." The intense strains he had experienced were, therefore, "almost inexplicable."[70] Despite Gregor Schöllgen's exhortations to take the protagonists of 1914 at their word, most historians would nowadays regard Bethmann's comments as somewhat disingenuous.[71] After all, the Prussian statesman had contemplated – in writing, no less – the prospect of armed conflict in every one of his pre-war years in office.[72] Nevertheless, in a weighty tome published in 1998, Radkau did take Bethmann's comments at face value and came up with an explanation which had little to do with the arguments advanced by either side in the "primacy" debate. Neither the internal, structural approach, nor the external, diplomatic approach, he suggested, could offer a fully convincing answer as to why Germany pursued such a singularly reckless and inconsistent course in the weeks and months before the outbreak of war in August 1914. A more convincing explanation, he claimed, lay in the patient files of the *Kaiserreich*'s numerous psychiatric clinics and neurological institutes, where the contemporary discourse on "restlessness" or "nervousness" (*Nervosität*) – the late nineteenth-century equivalent of stress – offered a "hermeneutic key" to unlock many of the period's mysteries, including the Great War itself.

---

69 J. Radkau, *Das Zeitalter der Nervosität. Deutschland zwischen Bismarck und Hitler* (Munich, 1998) p. 13. Radkau had first outlined his thesis in an article for *Geschichte und Gesellschaft*, 20 (1994), pp. 211–41. Interestingly, "The Age of Nervousness" had been used as a book title before: A. Steiner, *"Das nervöse Zeitalter." Der Begriff der Nervosität bei Laien und Ärzten in Deutschland und Österreich um 1900* (Zurich, 1964). V. Ullrich's *Die nervöse Großmacht. Aufstieg und Untergang des deutschen Kaiserreichs, 1871–1918* appeared one year before Radkau's book, but made little direct reference to the nervousness discourse.
70 Quoted by J. Radkau, *Das Zeitalter der Nervosität*, p. 273.
71 G. Schöllgen, "Kriegsgefahr und Krisenmanagement vor 1914," *Historische Zeitschrift*, 267 (1998), pp. 411–12.
72 M. Hewitson, *Germany and the Causes of the First World War* (Oxford, 2004), p. 184.

Radkau's book threw down a challenge, therefore, to his erstwhile Bielefeld colleague Hans-Ulrich Wehler, and to anyone else who believes that the 1914–18 war has a rational explanation.[73]

Radkau describes how, in the period between 1880 and 1914, complaints about nerves and "neurasthenia" – a medical neologism coined by the New York doctor George Beard in 1869, and introduced to Germany by the writer Paul Möbius – reached unprecedented levels. This prompted both an "epidemic" of literature on the subject, and ever more diagnoses of the condition (on the principle that "without the discourse on nervousness, no nervousness").[74] Contemporary observers, including such prominent thinkers as Georg Simmel and Sigmund Freud, diagnosed an anxious excitability, an excess of imagination, and a tendency to succumb to wild fears and longings, as new and defining features of their age. Such symptoms were variously said to be a product of sexual disorder, secularization, increasing acquisitiveness, the revolution in transport, increasing noise levels, or even the growth in competitive sport.[75] As Freud put it in 1908: "All is hurry and agitation; night is used for travel, day for business, even 'holiday trips' have become a strain on the nervous system ... The exhausted nerves seek recuperation in increased stimulation and in highly spiced pleasures, only to become more exhausted than before."[76] While nervousness was a fashionable illness throughout the western world before 1914, its incidence in Germany was particularly striking, affecting all classes and both genders. It is no coincidence, Radkau suggests, that the German word *Angst* has made it into the English dictionary. Moreover, while the metaphoric use of medical terminology in political discourse had a long tradition, the Wilhelmine "medicalization of politics" was in a league of its own.[77] As Chancellor Bülow told the Reichstag in November 1906, "We in Germany have become altogether too nervous, left and right, above and below."[78]

Radkau's eclectic and absorbing thesis undoubtedly offers many useful insights into German culture and society in the late nineteenth- and early twentieth century. Whether it succeeds in its ambitious aim of explaining

---

73 Radkau mentions that when he gave an earlier draft of the manuscript (which once ran to over one thousand pages) to Wehler, his colleague complained it made him nervous. *Das Zeitalter der Nervosität*, p. 470.
74 Ibid., p. 13.
75 See H. Glaser, *Die Kultur der wilhelminischen Zeit: Topographie einer Epoche* (Frankfurt, 1984).
76 Sigmund Freud quoted in H. Glaser, ed., *The German Mind of the 19th Century* (New York, 1981), p. 341.
77 J. Radkau, *Das Zeitalter der Nervosität*, p. 380.
78 Ibid., p. 385.

the origins of the First World War is quite another matter. For this, Radkau would need to establish convincing connections between Germany's leaders and the condition of neurasthenia. He achieves this only in part. As one might imagine, the restless, hypersensitive figure of Wilhelm II looms large in his explication, and Radkau endorses the well-worn view that the Kaiser was a perfect embodiment of the Germans' collective mentality. Interestingly, for all Wilhelm's nervous characteristics, Radkau believes the Kaiser was not "a neurasthenic in the clinical sense."[79] Nevertheless, so many people close to the throne chose to think of Wilhelm in this way – the Prussian Interior Minister von Köller, Eulenburg, and Bülow among them – that only by "holding his nerve" in a wartime crisis could the Kaiser prove he had mastered his condition. Much the same could be said of Bethmann Hollweg, who Radkau characterizes as "one of those weak-willed [men], who – very much in the spirit of contemporary neurological therapy – saw his weakness as a handicap that could be systematically overcome"; namely through the display of "nerves of steel."[80] Radkau's main emphasis, however, is not on individuals, but on the "structural reasons" that lay behind the Empire's inconsistent and contradictory course in the build-up to World War One: "More than anything else, the sense of political crisis which developed in the German Empire was caused by the unmastered multiplicity of possibilities. The fragmentation of foreign policy along contradictory lines led to no single strategy being followed consistently and effectively. The result was a set of overblown, but diffuse and vague desires, accompanied by an increasingly agonizing feeling of not actually achieving anything."[81] In other words, it was the vague and uncoordinated nature of *Weltpolitik* that made it so dangerous.

This may well be true, but whether it can be put down to the nervousness discourse is less certain. Radkau himself concedes that the connections are somewhat tenuous: "The three-way relationship between psychosomatic suffering, technological change, and imperial German policy, gets ever closer as one goes to and fro between works of medical, technological, and political history, but the relationship is never one of simple causalities," he admits.[82] How much credence one gives Radkau's thesis will largely depend on one's attitude to the "mentalities" approach in general,[83] but it is certainly the case that attempts to capture the

---

79 Ibid., p. 278.
80 Ibid., p. 396.
81 Ibid., p. 284.
82 Ibid., p. 271.
83 For a well balanced discussion see P. Burke, "Strengths and weaknesses of the history of mentalities," in *Varieties of Cultural History*, pp. 162–82.

popular "mood" in Germany on the eve of the First World War have multiplied in recent years. These works have emphasized the extent to which the much heralded "war euphoria" of August 1914 was limited to a relatively narrow section of society. The educated middle classes and the military caste may have celebrated, but "depression, frustration, and fear" hung over working-class districts and across great swathes of the German countryside.[84] Case studies of a number of urban centers, including Hamburg, Darmstadt, and Freiburg, have suggested that the excited crowds which thronged city streets in late July and early August were motivated as much by a desire to find out what was happening as by nationalist fervor: special newspaper editions were the only source of up-to-date information in a society without radio or television. The mood of these crowds – whose size owed much to the fine summer weather – was ambivalent and changeable. Although patriotic songs were sung, so were anti-war anthems. In the pubs many people were asking "why is there to be so much suffering for an Austrian archduke?"[85]

In the light of such accounts, one should perhaps be wary of the argument advanced by the Canadian cultural historian Modris Eksteins that the Germans experienced August 1914 as an orgiastic "rite of spring," evoking Stravinsky's iconoclastic 1913 ballet of the same name. "In early August Germans wallow in what appears to them to be the genuine synthesis of past and future, eternity embodied in the moment, and the resolution of all domestic strife ... Life has achieved transcendence. It has become aestheticized," he wrote.[86] Eksteins' innovative approach – his book was structured in three "acts" – was generally well received in the late 1980s, not least for its portrait of Wilhelmine Germany as "the modernist nation par excellence,"[87] but its use of the aesthetics of modern dance as a metaphor for war should not be taken too literally.

---

84 W. Kruse, *Krieg und nationale Integration. Eine Neuinterpretation des sozialdemokratischen Burgfriedensschlusses 1914/15* (Essen, 1993). The first historians to recognize that the popular reaction to the outbreak of war was more nuanced than hitherto believed were K. D. Schwarz, *Weltkrieg und Revolution in Nürnberg. Ein Beitrag zur Geschichte der deutschen Arbeiterbewegung* (Stuttgart, 1971) and V. Ullrich, *Kriegsalltag* (Cologne, 1982). More recent studies include M. Stöcker, *Augusterlebnis 1914 in Darmstadt. Legende und Wirklichkeit* (Darmstadt, 1994); B. Ziemann, *Front und Heimat. Ländliche Kriegserfahrungen im südlichen Bayern 1914–23* (Essen, 1997); C. Geinitz, *Kriegsfurcht und Kampfbereitschaft. Das August-Erlebnis in Freiburg* (Essen, 1998). In English see J. Verhey, *The Spirit of 1914* (Cambridge, 2000).
85 R. J. Evans, *Kneipengespräche im Kaiserreich Stimmungsberichte der Hamburger Politischen Polizei 1892–1914* (Reinbek, 1989), p. 415.
86 M. Eksteins, *Rites of Spring. The Great War and the Birth of the Modern Era* (London, 1989), p. 99.
87 M. Eksteins, "When death was young," in R. Bullen, H. Pogge von Strandmann, and A. Polonsky, eds., *Ideas into Politics: Aspects of European History 1880–1950* (London and Sydney, 1984), p. 30.

Much the same can be said of another widely-read attempt to apply cultural history methodology to the outbreak of the First World War: Stephen Kern's *The Culture of Time and Space*.[88] This book, first published in 1983, highlighted the way in which changing spatial and temporal perceptions impacted on the conduct of diplomacy during the July Crisis. More tenuously, it also developed a metaphor first advanced by the writer Gertrude Stein that the 1914–18 conflict was a "Cubist War," epitomized by the use of camouflage to break up "the conventional visual borders between object and background."[89]

Fritz Fischer's Legacy Today

Although a methodological gulf undoubtedly exists between the work of historians such as Radkau, Eksteins, and Kern, and the more traditional historical scholarship of Fritz Fischer, it is important to note the respect in which the Hamburg historian was held by many of his younger colleagues. Radkau even dedicated *The Age of Nervousness* to him on the occasion of his ninetieth birthday.[90] Such affection was appropriate, for without Fischer's work and the controversy it sparked, much of the literature discussed in this volume would simply not have existed. Moreover, while the temperature of the exchanges has cooled, it is still the case that no aspect of the *Kaiserreich*'s history continues to generate more heat than its role in the outbreak of war in 1914. It may be that "[p]erspective teaches historians to sympathize with all the parties," but where World War One is concerned, "[i]t has still not persuaded them ... that they should abandon the effort to establish who was responsible."[91] Indeed, the historiography in this area is so voluminous that even experts acknowledge the Herculean effort required to master it. In 1929 the famous French historian Pierre Renouvin was already bemoaning the "[t]ens of thousands of diplomatic documents to read, the testimony of hundreds of witnesses to be sought out and criticized, [the] maze of controversy and debate to be traversed in quest of some occasional revelation of importance."[92] Today, nearly eighty years later, the task has become more difficult still. Not only have there been thousands of secondary works analyzing the actions and motives of statesmen in every major European capital, but there has also been a steady flow of "new" primary

---

88 S. Kern, *The Culture of Time and Space, 1880–1918* (London, 1983).
89 Ibid., p. 304.
90 J. Radkau, *Das Zeitalter der Nervosität*, p. 471
91 Sir F. H. Hinsley, "Introduction," in K. Wilson, ed., *Decisions for War, 1914* (London, 1995).
92 Quoted by A. Mombauer, *The Origins of the First World War*, p. 104.

sources, driven by the thirst of historians on all sides for documentary evidence which might prove their case once and for all. Not surprisingly, perhaps, these primary sources – such as the diaries of the Chief of the Kaiser's Naval Cabinet, Admiral Georg von Müller;[93] and Bethmann Hollweg's private secretary Kurt Riezler[94] – have themselves become the focus of historical controversy, as historians question the selectivity of their editing or even their authenticity.

The scholarly literature on World War One has, of course, expanded well beyond the reasons for its outbreak. As Roger Chickering notes, "World War I was an all-embracing experience. No phase of life remained unaffected in Imperial Germany."[95] Thus large specialist historiographies have developed on the wartime economy, with its winners and losers;[96] everyday life on the home front and the politics of food;[97] nationalist propaganda and popular mentalities;[98] the treatment of the wounded

---

93 An edition of von Müller's diaries was published by W. Görlitz in 1965 but crucial references to the Kaiser's controversial "War Council" of 8 December 1912 were omitted. See J. C. G. Röhl, "Admiral von Müller and the approach of war, 1911–1914," *Historical Journal*, 12 (1969), pp. 651–73. Curiously, Röhl himself failed to quote Müller's much-debated final sentence "The result was pretty much nil."

94 After selectively quoting from Riezler's unpublished papers throughout the 1960s, K. D. Erdmann finally published an edition in 1972 under the title *Kurt Riezler: Tagebücher, Aufsätze, Dokumente* (Göttingen, 1972). However, it later became clear that his editing of the diaries left much to be desired. Even the authenticity of some of the entries was questioned. See B. Sösemann, "Die Tagebücher Kurt Riezlers: Untersuchungen zu ihrer Echtheit und Edition," *Historische Zeitschrift*, 236 (1983), pp. 327–70; and Erdmann's reply "Zur Echtheit der Tagebücher Kurt Riezlers. Eine Antikritik," *Historische Zeitschrift*, 236 (1983), pp. 371–402. Also B. F. Schulte, *Die Verfälschung der Riezler Tagebücher: ein Beitrag zur Wissenschaftsgeschichte der 50er und 60er Jahre* (Frankfurt, 1985).

95 R. Chickering, ed., "Imperial Germany at war, 1914–1918," in *Imperial Germany*, p. 489. For an excellent micro-study of the war's impact on a single German town see Chickering's *The Great War and Urban Life in Germany: Freiburg, 1914–1918* (Cambridge, 2007).

96 G. D. Feldman, *Army, Industry and Labor in Germany, 1914–1918* (Princeton, 1966); G. D. Feldman, *The Great Disorder: Politics, Economics, and Society in the German Inflation, 1914–24* (Oxford, 1993); J. Kocka, *Facing Total War: German Society 1914–1918*; F. Coetzee and M. Shevin-Coetzee, eds., *Authority, Identity and the Social History of the Great War* (Providence and Oxford, 1995).

97 V. Ullrich, *Kriegsalltag*; B. Davis, *Home Fires Burning*; U. Daniel, *Arbeiterfrauen in der Kriegsgesellschaft*; R. Wall and J. Winter, eds., *The Upheaval of War: Family, Work and Welfare in Europe 1914–1918* (Cambridge, 1988); G. L. Yaney, *The World of the Manager: Food Administration in Berlin during World War One* (New York, 1994).

98 M. Stibbe, *German Anglophobia and the Great War, 1914–1918* (Cambridge, 2001); S. O. Müller, *Die Nation als Waffe und Vorstellung: Nationalismus in Deutschland und Großbritannien im Ersten Weltkrieg* (Göttingen, 2002); S. Bruendel, *Volksgemeinschaft oder Volksstaat: Die "Ideen von 1914" und die Neuordnung Deutschlands im Ersten Weltkrieg* (Berlin, 2003); A. Lipp, *Meinungslenkung im Krieg. Kriegserfahrungen deutscher Soldaten und ihre Deutung 1914–1918* (Göttingen, 2003); K. Flasch, *Die geistige Mobilmachung. Die deutschen Intellektuellen und der Erste Weltkrieg. Ein Versuch* (Berlin, 2000).

and the mourning of the dead;[99] in addition to the already vast range of military and diplomatic histories of the period, and studies of the "front experience" itself.[100] It is hardly surprising then that some general histories of the Empire choose 1914 rather than 1918 as their cut-off date.[101] Indeed, since neither the war nor the much-vaunted political truce (*Burgfrieden*) was able to silence an increasingly vocal debate on future political models for Germany, it is possible to argue that "the history of the Kaiserreich ended in 1914."[102] The war period was certainly quite different from the four decades that preceded it, and Feuchtwanger is correct to point out that "[m]uch of the poison that vitiated the politics of Weimar and led to the rise of Hitler was incubating in the war years."[103] Although space precludes consideration of such issues here, readers are advised to turn to Chickering's *Imperial Germany and the Great War* for a reliable and accessible synthesis of at least some of the current research.[104]

The obituaries for Fritz Fischer in December 1999 were predominantly warm and respectful, in Germany as in the English-speaking world. Since it has been estimated that even conservative historians in the Federal Republic have come to agree with three-quarters of his claims, this should come as no surprise.[105] It does not mean, however, that Fischer's theses are regarded as sacrosanct or beyond revision. Indeed, his staunchest defenders would now concede that "some of [his] fundamental propositions are untenable."[106] The British historian Mark Hewitson, for example, whose 2004 study of *Germany and the Causes of the First World*

---

99 R. W. Whalen, *Bitter Wounds: German Victims of the Great War, 1914–1939* (Ithaca, 1984); J. Winter, *Sites of Memory, Sites of Mourning: The Great War in European Cultural History* (Cambridge, 1995).
100 See E. Leed, *No Man's Land: Combat and Identity in World War One* (Cambridge, 1979); together with two useful document collections: P. Knoch, ed., *Kriegsalltag* (Stuttgart, 1989); and B. Ulrich and B. Ziemann, eds., *Frontalltag im Ersten Weltkrieg: Wahn und Wirklichkeit* (Frankfurt, 1994).
101 See, for example, V. Berghahn, *Imperial Germany 1871–1914*; E. Frie, *Das Deutsche Kaiserreich*; and most of the contributors to Chickering's *Imperial Germany. A Historiographical Companion*.
102 A. Mombauer, review of Müller and Bruendel, *Journal of Modern History*, 77 (2005), p. 1144.
103 E. Feuchtwanger, *Imperial Germany*, p. 182.
104 R. Chickering, *Imperial Germany and the Great War, 1914–1918* (Cambridge, 1998). See also H. H. Herwig, *The First World War. Germany and Austria-Hungary 1914–1918* (London, 1997); and W. J. Mommsen, *Der erste Weltkrieg. Anfang vom Ende des bürgerlichen Zeitalters* (Frankfurt, 2004).
105 The view of H.-U. Wehler, cited by H. H. Herwig, "Introduction," in H. H. Herwig ed., *The Outbreak of World War I* (Boston, 1997), p. 9.
106 M. Hewitson, *Germany and the Causes of the First World War*, p. 3.

War is fiercely critical of attempts to undermine Fischer's legacy, admits that "his assumption in *War of Illusions* that militarism, social Darwinism and xenophobic nationalism ... became at once more widespread and more extreme ... is, at the very least, open to question."[107] With regard to the continuity of German war aims – so central to *Griff nach der Weltmacht* – he acknowledges that the "claim of Fischer and his followers that an alliance of 'iron and rye' ... pushed the Reich towards war in 1914 no longer stands up to historical scrutiny."[108] Hewitson concedes, moreover, that Fischer's "audacious conjecture that Germany's ruling elites planned a war of aggression, proceeding from the Kaiser's so-called 'War Council' of 8 December 1912 to the orchestration of conflict in July 1914, has subsequently, in the absence of supporting evidence, been abandoned by virtually all historians."[109] Where Fischer saw conspiracy and long-term planning, the London historian instead sees brinkmanship and a policy of the "utmost risk"; a policy which had already been evident in German handling of the two Moroccan Crises of 1905–6 and 1911, and in the Bosnian Crisis of 1908–9.[110]

In view of the differences outlined above, Hewitson's support for Fischer appears more symbolic than specific. Nevertheless, he does consider one aspect of Fischer's thesis inviolable. It is summed up in a single sentence: "German leaders were [so] confident that they could win a continental war, that they pursued an offensive policy – at the risk of such a war – at important junctures during the 1900s and 1910s, and that they chose to enter a world war in July 1914."[111] The optimistic outlook of Germany's leaders in the crucial weeks and months before the outbreak of war is absolutely central to Hewitson's account, and stands in direct contrast to the predominantly pessimistic tones identified by Niall Ferguson (born 1963) in an important review article of the early 1990s.[112] Ultimately, Hewitson argues, World War One only broke out because Germany's

---

107 Ibid., p. 4.
108 Ibid., p. 35.
109 Ibid., p. 4.
110 It should be noted that Hewitson's use of the term "utmost risk" goes significantly further than Kurt Riezler's notion of the "calculated risk," later employed by the likes of Zechlin, Ritter, Hillgruber, and Jarausch to defend the Chancellor from some of Fischer's most serious accusations. See, for instance, A. Hillgruber, "Riezlers Theorie des kalkulierten Risikos und Bethmann Hollwegs politische Konzeption in der Julikrise 1914," in *Deutsche Großmacht- und Weltpolitik im 19. und 20. Jahrhundert* (Düsseldorf, 1977); or K. Jarausch, "The illusion of limited war: Chancellor Bethmann Hollweg's calculated risk," *Central European History*, 2 (1969), pp. 48–76.
111 M. Hewitson, *Germany and the Causes of the First World War*, p. 3.
112 N. Ferguson, "Germany and the origins of the First World War: New perspectives," *Historical Journal*, 35 (1992), pp. 725–52.

leaders were confident they could win it. They were not pushed into war by financial weakness, public opinion, or even the army – Bethmann, along with fellow civilians Jagow, Zimmermann, and Stumm, remained in control of German policy-making until mobilization on 31 July – but through their own strategic decisions.

Hewitson's specific objection to a "defensive" reading of the July Crisis centers on "seven overlapping policy initiatives," of which two in particular stand out: Germany's "blank cheque" to Austria; and its cynical attempts to cast Russia as the principal aggressor.[113] He argues that German leaders had a clear view of the possible consequences of giving Austria-Hungary a free hand. They wanted their ailing ally to act decisively and were prepared to run the very real risk of European war as a result. Bethmann's top priority in the last weeks of the Crisis was to portray Russia as the aggressor. This was more important even than securing British neutrality, for the Chancellor was well aware that the parties of the center and the left – which represented majority opinion in Germany by 1914 – might accept a defensive war against Russia, but they were unlikely to tolerate a war of aggression against France. Judging by Admiral von Müller's much quoted diary entry of 1 August 1914, Bethmann's efforts were not in vain: "Brilliant mood. The government has succeeded very well in making us appear as the attacked," he famously wrote.[114]

Hewitson's account is knowledgeable and persuasive, but it jars in its blanket use of the loaded term "revisionist," which is applied to all those who consider that doubts and fears about the Empire's prospects might have played a part in German decision making. The "revisionists" are said to include not only predictable names like Schöllgen and Ferguson, but also Wolfgang Mommsen for his emphasis on the pressure of German public opinion;[115] David Stevenson and David Herrmann for their focus on the European arms race;[116] and Annika Mombauer (born 1967), Stig Förster (born 1951), and Terence Zuber (born 1948) for their studies of German militarism and military planning.[117] Grouped together these

---

113   M. Hewitson, *Germany and the Causes of the First World War*, p. 203.
114   Quoted in J. C. G. Röhl, "Admiral von Müller and the Approach of War, 1911–1914," p. 670.
115   W. J. Mommsen, "Public opinion and foreign policy in Wilhelmine Germany, 1897–1914," in *Imperial Germany 1867–1918*, pp. 189–204. Mommsen suggests that a radicalized public opinion was pushing for war, acting as a spur on the government, and constraining Bethmann Hollweg's room for maneuver.
116   D. Stevenson, *Armaments and the Coming of War: Europe 1904–1914* (Oxford, 1996); D. Herrmann, *The Arming of Europe and the Making of the First World War* (Princeton, 1996).
117   A. Mombauer, *Helmuth von Moltke and the Origins of the First World War*; S. Förster, *Der doppelte Militarismus: Die deutsche Heeresrüstungspolitik zwischen Status-Quo-Sicherung und Aggression, 1890–1913* (Stuttgart, 1985); S. Förster, "The armed forces and military

historians make for strange bedfellows indeed. To be fair, Hewitson spells out his specific use of the term clearly enough:

> All are referred to as "revisionists" ... because they argue – or strongly imply – that such pessimism constituted a significant motive of leaders' actions on the eve of the First World War, altering in the process the thrust of the argument put forward by Fischer ... In this limited but crucial respect, revisionists concur that policy-makers were acting "defensively," even if only in the sense of averting a putative future defeat."[118]

Yet whether it is useful to group together such disparate voices is highly debatable. To suggest that their collective work has "resulted in a substantial mitigation of Wilhelmine statesmen's moral responsibility for the outbreak of war" is, moreover, an unhelpful exaggeration.[119]

It is true that historians' contrasting perceptions of the mood of Germany's leaders in 1914 – in other words, how "desperate" they were – has become a central issue in the scholarship on the origins of World War One, but "optimism" and "pessimism" are notoriously difficult attributes to measure. They are not mutually exclusive states of mind, and the debate is by no means as clear-cut as a binary division into "Fischerites" and "revisionists" might suggest. In fact, if one compares Hewitson's account with some of those he labels "revisionist," one will find many more points of agreement than disagreement. The fundamental difference between Mombauer and Förster on the one hand; and Hewitson on the other, can be reduced to the issue of "optimism." While the latter sees Germany's civilian and military leaders acting from "a long-established position of strength," both of the former give more credence to their fears, and in particular von Moltke's well-documented conviction that since a war was "inevitable" it was better to have it sooner rather than later. This became, of course, a self-fulfilling prophecy. It must be stressed, however, that both Mombauer and Förster fully accept the current consensus that the *Kaiserreich* "bore the main share, or at least a very large share of the blame" for the First World War.[120] No serious historian, Förster emphasizes, would today attempt to mount an apologist defense for Germany's leaders.[121] This is a long way from what would normally be considered

---

planning," in R. Chickering, ed., *Imperial Germany*, pp. 454–88; T. Zuber, *Inventing the Schlieffen Plan: German War Planning, 1871–1914* (Oxford, 2002).
118 M. Hewitson, *Germany and the Causes of the First World War*, p. 4.
119 Ibid., p. 224.
120 A. Mombauer, *The Origins of the First World War*, p. 224.
121 S. Förster, "Im Reich des Absurden: die Ursachen des Ersten Weltkrieges," in B. Wegner, ed., *Wie Kriege entstehen. Zum historischen Hintegrund von Staatenkonflikten* (Paderborn, 2000), pp. 211–52.

"revisionism," such as Ferguson's clever but unconvincing attempts to shift the burden of blame onto Britain and its Foreign Secretary Sir Edward Grey, for turning Germany's continental war into a world war;[122] or the neo-conservative case advanced by Schöllgen, Stürmer, and Hillgruber, with its emphasis on geopolitics and the mechanisms of the alliance system.

If Hewitson's closely-argued study is one kind of book on World War One; Jay Winter and Antoine Prost's recent historiographical survey, which includes films, television documentaries, and museums as well as books, is quite another.[123] Huge in scope, if not in length, *The Great War in History* takes a generational approach to British, French, and German studies of the war, identifying three distinct historiographical "configurations." The works of the most recent cohort, Winter and Prost suggest, reflect the growing influence of cultural history and micro-history, and contrast sharply with both the "top down," Rankean traditions of the first generation; and the "collective," social history methodologies of the second. Another recent textbook to take a historiographical approach is Annika Mombauer's *The Origins of the First World War*, which traces the history of the "war-guilt" debate from August 1914 to the present day. Mombauer places great emphasis on contextualizing the scholarly literature, highlighting how generations of historians have been influenced by contemporary political concerns. The author's admirable efforts to maintain balance, however, mean that the many of her judgments appear rather anemic alongside Hewitson's full-blooded polemics.

As Mombauer shows, one of the principal arguments used against Fischer in the 1960s was that his approach was one-sided, focusing only on Germany's war aims and ignoring those of the other European powers. On one level, of course, this charge was impossible to refute, but Fischer's opponents seldom had the grace to acknowledge that the Hamburg historian had addressed the issue in the preface to his first book, noting that the relevant files had yet to be released in all the European capitals. In the intervening decades detailed analyses of the war aims have been completed for each of the participating powers.[124] While such works have shown that "Germany's leaders are not the only ones whose motivations we need to understand,"[125] most would agree with Pogge von Strandmann that "[t]he evidence gathered makes the view that Germany fought a

---

122 N. Ferguson, *The Pity of War* (London, 1998).
123 J. Winter and A. Prost, *The Great War in History: Debates and Controversies, 1914 to the Present* (Cambridge, 2005).
124 For a detailed analysis of thirteen major (and minor) participants see R. F. Hamilton and H. H. Herwig, eds., *The Origins of World War One* (Cambridge, 2003).
125 A. Mombauer, *The Origins of the First World War*, p. 187.

defensive war untenable and the interpretation that all nations 'slithered over the brink' ... unconvincing."[126] This does not mean that the *Kaiserreich* bears sole responsibility for the war: many of today's foremost specialists in the field place considerable emphasis, for instance, on the far from innocent role of Austria-Hungary in the July Crisis (an aspect which was often overlooked by Fischer and his supporters).[127] Nor does it make it irrelevant to look at the underlying causes and "unspoken assumptions" of the conflict, which were famously explored in the 1970s and 1980s by James Joll.[128] "Both approaches are necessary to give a comprehensive explanation of why one power pushed for war and the others accepted the challenge, and why influential and vociferous sections of the population were willing to endure the war for so long," Pogge von Strandmann points out.[129]

In such a lively and contested field of scholarly activity any conclusions must be regarded as tentative and provisional. It does appear, however, as if attempts to revive the notion that German policy was essentially defensive have, in Seligmann and McLean's phrase, "failed to undermine the new orthodoxy."[130] Most historians today would still concur with John Röhl that "if Germany had not opted for war in 1914, there would have been no war."[131] Nevertheless, debate is likely to continue on the scope and nature of the war(s) envisaged by the leaders in Berlin and Vienna. In this regard, Philip Bell offers the useful reminder that "in 1914, no government believed that it was embarking on a war which would last for over four years ... The tragedy was that the war of 1914 became the war of 1914–18."[132] One does not have to accept the apologetic notion – much loved by conservative historians in Germany – of a "pre-emptive" or

---

126 H. Pogge von Strandmann, "Germany and the coming of war," in R. J. W. Evans and H. Pogge von Strandmann, *The Coming of the First World War* (Oxford, 1988), p. 98.
127 Such as S. R. Williamson, *Austria-Hungary and the Origins of the First World War* (London, 1991); R. J. W. Evans, "The Habsburg Monarchy and the Coming of War," in R. J. W. Evans and H. Pogge von Strandmann, eds., *The Coming of the First World War*, pp. 33–56; or H. Strachan, *The Outbreak of the First World War* (Oxford, 2004). As A. Mombauer notes, "[w]ithout the initial willingness of Vienna's statesmen for a 'reckoning' with Belgrade, Berlin's decision-makers would not have been able to use this particular crisis as the trigger for war." *The Origins of the First World War*, p. 191.
128 J. Joll, *The Origins of the First World War* (London, 1984); J. Joll, "1914: The unspoken assumptions," in H. W. Koch, ed., *The Origins of the First World War: Great Power Rivalry and German War Aims* (London, 1984), pp. 307–28.
129 H. Pogge von Strandmann, "Germany and the coming of war," p. 96.
130 M. Seligmann and R. McLean, *Germany from Reich to Republic*, p. 140.
131 J. C. G. Röhl, "Introduction," *The Kaiser and his Court*, p. 6.
132 P. Bell, "Origins of the war of 1914," in P. Hayes, ed., *Themes in Modern European History* (London, 1992), pp. 125, 121.

"preventive" war,[133] to acknowledge that fears for the *Kaiserreich*'s military prospects may have played a part in German calculations during the July Crisis. As Ferguson points out, even if one does view the events of 1914 as "a military 'first strike', designed to pre-empt a deterioration in Germany's military position," this is "by no means incompatible with the idea that the outcome of such a strike, if successful, would be German hegemony in Europe."[134]

"Whatever the intentions which underlay it, German policy in the crisis of July 1914 must rank as one of the great disasters of world history," Röhl observes.

> The leaders of arguably the most successful country in Europe, a country bursting with energy, boasting a young and dynamic population and an economy second to none, a country whose army, whose administration, whose scientific and artistic achievements were the envy of the world, took decisions which plunged it and the other powers into a ghastly war in which almost ten million men lost their lives.[135]

In view of the fact that the German Empire was to die "as it had been born, in war,"[136] and that the war was to "[bankrupt] the old regime in every sense: militarily, politically, financially, and morally,"[137] it has been suggested that the attraction of the imperial era to historians lies in its "satirically tragic emplotment." This is not the "tragedy" bathed in pathos traditionally evoked by German historicism. "The tragic element of the *Kaiserreich*," Rudy Koshar observes, "stems from the transitoriness of its anticipated political futures." The Empire and its physical remains continue to fascinate, in other words, because they "leave us with an image of the fleeting nature of power."[138] Of course, we cannot know whether the *Kaiserreich* would have survived without the calamitous impact of the war and, despite the current fashion for counterfactual speculation, we never will.[139] Thus Margaret Anderson's recent assertion that "[p]erhaps the death of the Kaiser at eighty-three would have sped a

---

133 Although Germany's actions in 1914 cannot be described as "preventive" or "pre-emptive" in any normal sense of those terms (i.e. to prevent or pre-empt an attack by a neighbor), the German General Staff had a tradition of planning to pre-empt a situation in which Germany was no longer strong enough to defeat her rivals (particularly France). Thus, in *War of Illusions*, even Fischer refers to 1914 as a "preventive war."
134 N. Ferguson, "Germany and the origins of the First World War," p. 734.
135 J. C. G. Röhl, "Germany," p. 27.
136 R. Chickering, *Imperial Germany and the Great War*, p. 9.
137 R. Bessel, *Germany after the First World War* (Oxford, 1993), p. 48.
138 R. Koshar, "The *Kaiserreich*'s Ruins," pp. 496–7.
139 N. Ferguson, ed. *Virtual History: Alternatives and Counterfactuals* (London, 1997).

regime change – in 1941 – analogous to Spain's at the death of Franco at the same age in 1975," is out of place here.[140] Anderson is on firmer ground, however, with another assertion, which can serve as a fitting coda to this chapter: "Imperial Germany's worst legacy to the next generation was not its political culture," she writes, "but its war."[141]

---

140 M. L. Anderson *Practicing Democracy* (Princeton, 2000), p. 437.
141 Ibid., p. 436.

6
Epilogue: Remembering Imperial Germany

If you should enter a bar or restaurant in Germany with the word "old" in its title – one of the numerous establishments trading under the names "Alt-Berlin" or "Alt-Heidelberg," for instance – you will find that the fixtures and fittings are almost certain to evoke the years between 1890 and 1914. Here, "old" does not connote the age of Luther, or even Goethe, but *Jugendstil* lamps and mirrors; Heinrich Zille cartoons; sepia photographs of trams and tenements; colorful advertisements for Odol mouthwash or Manoli cigarettes; spiked helmets and student fraternity sashes. While the unashamedly apologetic historiography of the pre-Fischer era has long since disappeared, and the *Kaiserreich* no longer bathes in the golden hue of the "good old days," the Wilhelmine Empire continues to find employment as a handy cipher for the German past. This is due partly to the "unusable" nature of much of the country's subsequent history, and partly to the ready availability of material artifacts from an era in which mass production and modern advertising left surprisingly deep traces. The popularity of this "1900-look" may also reflect a form of nostalgia peculiar to the hospitality sector, since bars, hotels, and restaurants represented a notable boom area within the imperial economy, and some – like Berlin's recently rebuilt Hotel Adlon (1907) – remain synonymous with style and luxury to this day.

Whatever the reasons, however, there is something particularly appropriate about contemporary commerce's embrace of the *Kaiserreich*; for it was precisely in these years that what we might call a "heritage industry" began to develop in Germany.[1] In 1899, for instance, the maiden edition of *Monument Preservation* appeared, a journal targeted at a new and still evolving professional group, concerned with the preservation and conservation of historic buildings and townscapes. Prussia's first provincial conservator had been appointed in the Rhineland some eight years previously, and a national congress of conservators and preservationists was staged for the first time in 1900. While *Monument Preservation* focused on the built environment, the botanist and museum director Hugo Conwentz campaigned for a similar level of protection for rare and characteristic features of Germany's natural environment. In 1906 a State Office for the Preservation of Natural Monuments was established within the Prussian Ministry of Education and Ecclesiastical Affairs, with Conwentz at its head, and comparable institutions were set up in Bavaria and Württemberg too.[2] At the same time, Conwentz was also active in a large popular association, the League for Homeland Protection (*Bund Heimatschutz*), founded in 1904 to protect the entire physiognomy of Empire's landscape: from its customs, costumes, and dialects; to its historic buildings and vernacular architectural traditions. Partly in response to *Heimatschutz* agitation, new and stricter planning laws were subsequently introduced in many Germany states, including the Prussian Law against the Disfigurement of Places and Outstanding Landscapes of 1907.[3]

Inventories of historic buildings were issued by each of the German states during the lifetime of the Empire, following the early examples of Bremen and Hessen-Kassel in 1870. The 1900s also saw the initial publication of Georg Dehio's famous series of architectural guides, which was to become a fixture on the bookshelves of middle-class Germans for much of the twentieth century.[4] Just as significant for the circulation and consumption of heritage, however, was the growth in tourism promoted by a host of humbler publications issued by local "beautification" societies, or by illustrated features in the Empire's mass-circulation magazines.[5] Picture postcards of historic buildings or landscapes enjoyed a veritable boom at the turn of the century, with over 60 factories

---

1 See R. Koshar, "The *Kaiserreich*'s ruins"; also S. Muthesius, "The origins of the German conservation movement," in R. Kain, ed., *Planning for Conservation* (London, 1981), pp. 37–48.
2 See T. M. Lekan, *Imagining the Nation in Nature. Landscape Preservation and German Identity 1885–1945* (Cambridge, MA, 2004).
3 M. Jefferies, *Politics and Culture in Wilhelmine Germany: The Case of Industrial Architecture* (Oxford, 1995), ch. 2.
4 G. Dehio, *Handbuch der deutschen Kunstdenkmäler*, 5 vols. (Berlin, 1905–12). See also P. Betthausen, *Georg Dehio: ein deutscher Kunsthistoriker* (Munich, 2004).
5 See K. Belgum, "Displaying the nation. A view of nineteenth-century monuments through a popular magazine," *Central European History*, 26 (1993), pp. 457–74.

producing chromolithographed cards in 1900.[6] Some of the Empire's most successful food and drink manufacturers also contributed by issuing their own small-format collectors' cards of German castles or cathedrals, in an effort to promote brand loyalty.[7] It would be no exaggeration to suggest, therefore, that the commercialization and commodification of the past really began in the Wilhelmine era.

Of course, none of this was unique to Germany, as anyone familiar with William Morris's Society for the Preservation of Ancient Buildings (1877) or the National Trust (1896) in Britain will testify. Nor did it begin with Wilhelm II's accession to the throne. The nineteenth century's preoccupation with history stemmed from a process of historicization or "temporalization" that had started in the eighteenth century and flourished in the "Age of Revolutions." The historical convulsions of the French Revolution, the Napoleonic Wars, the Scientific and Industrial Revolutions had all highlighted the impermanence of political, social, and economic structures. The work of geologists and archaeologists – whose discoveries were effectively elongating the concept of time itself – posed a similarly serious threat to religious authority. The rapid changes ushered in by these and other upheavals showed the extent to which life was historically determined, and prompted an upsurge of interest in the past; not least because "the discovery of one's own historicity is ... the premise for an interest in the past."[8] To see one's self in historical terms was becoming part of the modern condition, as evidenced by "an explosion of autobiographical writing, diary keeping, scrapbook pasting, and portrait taking." Nineteenth-century families also took increasing care "to commemorate personal occasions such as birthdays, holidays, and Christmas."[9] In novels, dramas, and paintings; in architecture, festivals, and processions; the historical was embraced in all its myriad forms.

Central to much of this activity was the state, which continually sought to instrumentalize the past in order to acquire greater legitimacy. The role of history in the creation of identity in nineteenth-century Europe, and particularly the so-called "invention of tradition," has been the subject of

---

6 See M. Moeller, ed., "Postkarte – Kunstkarte – Künstlerpostkarte" in *Expressionistische Grüße* (Stuttgart, 1991), pp. 8–11.
7 As David Crew notes, this "commercial circulation of popular images, combined with the memory-work promoted by *Heimatschutz* organizations, nationalist groups, and city and state governments, always made it difficult for the discourse of official preservation to establish an exclusive claim to national memory." See D. Crew, "Remembering German pasts: Memory in Germany history, 1871–1989," in *Central European History*, 33 (2000), p. 231.
8 A. Wittkau, *Historismus. Zur Geschichte des Begriffs und des Problems* (Göttingen, 1992), p. 27.
9 P. Fritzsche, "The case of modern memory," *Journal of Modern History*, 73 (2001), p. 115.

intense research over the past three decades.[10] However, while much of this literature has focused on the activities of the state or its rulers – such as the building of monuments and museums – it was by no means solely a "top-down" process: the ordinary men, women, and children who belonged to these "imagined communities" played their part as well. Thus, as Peter Fritzsche puts it, the nation "can be usefully thought of as a memory system that enabled individuals to recognize their lives in nonrepeatable, historical time. Because of their boundedness in time and space, national narratives have an unusual ability to organize remembrance and to make the past sensible."[11] It is arguably for this reason that the nation-state continues to provide the framework for most people's memories today – allowing people "to tell and share the history of their lives"[12] – even as it loses much of its power and status to supranational bodies.[13]

As we have seen, it was not until the end of the nineteenth century that the notion of "national heritage" – a product of both individual and collective memory – began to develop more formal structures. In the 1990s these structures became the focus of a series of innovative studies by the Wisconsin-based historian Rudy Koshar, who argued that Wilhelmine preservationist discourse and the "metaphor of the ruin" could shed new light on the Empire's political culture.[14] Koshar suggested that while preservationists claimed to be unpolitical, their work contributed to the creation of a German national identity, and to the maintenance of existing hierarchies of class and gender. Nevertheless, he concluded, historic preservation in Wilhelmine Germany was ultimately a victim of its own success: "The successful conservation of historic sites led to their instrumentalization by the market and the state. The insistence on tradition exposed the vulnerability of nationalist rhetoric and aroused fears of the transitoriness of the national culture ... The desire for memory, invented or spontaneous, suggested the overwhelming power of forgetting."[15]

---

10 Beginning with an essay collection edited by E. Hobsbawm and T. Ranger, *The Invention of Tradition* (Cambridge, 1983). On Germany see A. Green, *Fatherlands*, and S. Weichlein, *Nation und Region. Integrationsprozesse im Bismarckreich* (Düsseldorf, 2004).
11 P. Fritzsche, "The case of modern memory," p. 108.
12 Ibid., p. 101.
13 It remains to be seen whether the rise of transnational history will one day lead to a "Europeanization" of memory culture too. See U. Frevert, "Europeanizing Germany's twentieth century," in a special edition of the journal *History and Memory* on the theme of "Histories and memories of twentieth-century Germany," edited by A. Confino: *History and Memory*, 17 (2005), pp. 87–116.
14 R. Koshar, "The *Kaiserreich*'s ruins"; R. Koshar, "Against the 'frightful leveler': Historic preservation and German cities, 1890–1914," *Journal of Urban History*, 19 (1993), pp. 7–29. Koshar also supervised a number of doctoral dissertations on preservation and conservation issues, including one by the aforementioned T. Lekan.
15 R. Koshar, "Against the 'frightful leveler,'" pp. 25–6.

There are two reasons why Koshar's work is worthy of mention here. First, he was one of the earliest specialists on Imperial Germany to advance the now-fashionable view that "historians should think of the *Kaiserreich*, or any historical period, as a field of objects – written texts, documents, photographs, works of art, buildings, consumer goods – that they use to imagine pasts."[16] To argue, in other words, that modern historians should be prepared to emulate their colleagues in ancient and pre-history by utilizing sources beyond the written word. In Koshar's case it was the built environment that took centre stage: "Although much of the nineteenth-century German city has been destroyed or rebuilt," he suggested, "enough of it remains, and enough of it has been 'preserved' in photographs and drawings, to offer a rich field of material evidence."[17] Second, by seeing the city as a "memoryscape" – a physical expression of memory that offers "an image of the fleeting nature of contending political pasts and futures"[18] – Koshar helped to introduce the approach of "memory studies" to the history of the *Kaiserreich*.[19]

"Memory studies" is one of the key growth areas across the humanities and social sciences today, and represents an important interdisciplinary research area in its own right, with an appeal that stretches well beyond the university campus.[20] Indeed, according to the editors of a recent volume on *The Work of Memory*, it "has become almost an obsession."[21] While its relevance to historians is obvious – history is "not only a science, but equally a form of remembrance" (Walter Benjamin)[22] – many still regard it as something of a mixed blessing. Paul Betts (born 1963), for instance, who has written on aspects of memory and material culture in both German states after 1945, gives the new approach credit for opening up "fresh avenues for rethinking the power and place of the past beyond the groves of academe," yet bemoans the fact that "a good amount of this new historiography still remains conceptually limited and

---

16   R. Koshar, "The *Kaiserreich*'s ruins," p. 494.
17   Ibid., p. 499.
18   Ibid., p. 501.
19   See R. Koshar, *Germany's Transient Pasts: Preservation and National Memory in the Twentieth Century* (Chapel Hill, 1998); R. Koshar, *From Monuments to Traces: Artifacts of German Memory, 1870–1990* (Berkeley, 2001).
20   The remarkable popularity of memory studies among the wider public is not easily explained. The loss of identity experienced by many in an era of rapid globalization and technological change is likely to be one contributory factor. In Germany, the onset of a new chapter in the country's history following the collapse of the GDR, and the lively public debates surrounding the conception and construction of the Holocaust Memorial in Berlin, have also helped to put memory issues at the forefront of popular debate.
21   A. Confino and P. Fritzsche, "Introduction: Noises of the past," in *The Work of Memory*, p. 1.
22   Quoted by S. Ostovich, "Epilogue: Dangerous memories," in A. Confino and P. Fritzsche, eds., *The Work of Memory*, p. 243.

oddly predictable, framed as it so often is by the question of to what extent the past ... has been properly 'mastered' after the event."[23] It is certainly true that until now the main emphasis of memory studies has been on the Holocaust and its remembrance. No nation, we are told, is better suited to exploring the workings of modern memory than one whose division "into two countries with very different versions of the twentieth-century past, confront[s] scholars with fundamental problems of recollection, silence, and denial."[24] Even so, the Third Reich is not the only German past that matters, and at a time when the last personal memories of the *Kaiserreich* are being taken to the grave, it is important we give some consideration to the contribution memory studies can make to our understanding of the German Empire too.[25]

The school's founder is generally acknowledged to have been Maurice Halbwachs (1877–1945), a Durkheimian sociologist who pioneered the concept of "collective memory" in the 1920s.[26] In recent years the lead has been provided by the German husband-and-wife team Jan (born 1938) and Aleida (born 1947) Assmann,[27] along with the French scholar-publisher Pierre Nora (born 1931). The latter's *Realms of Memory: Rethinking the French Past* was a mammoth undertaking, detailing 121 memory sites or "realms of memory" that feature prominently in his nation's history and culture.[28] It provided a model that has since been emulated in a number of countries, including Germany, where Etienne François and Hagen Schulze's *Deutsche Erinnerungsorte*, amassed an inventory of 130 "sites" – people, songs, and phrases, as well as places – in three volumes, covering some 2,226 pages in total.[29] Of course, the idea of

---

23 P. Betts, book review, *German History*, 24 (2006), p. 149.
24 A. Confino and P. Fritzsche, "Introduction: Noises of the past," p. 2.
25 That the approach can be effective beyond the memory of Nazism or Communism is shown by S. Crane, *Collecting and Historical Consciousness: New Forms for Collective Memory in Early Nineteenth-Century Germany* (Ithaca, 2000). Also C. Clark, "The wars of liberation in Prussian memory: Reflections on the memorialization of war in early nineteenth-century Germany," *Journal of Modern History*, 68 (1996), pp. 550–76; and a number of contributors to Confino and Fritzsche's *The Work of Memory*.
26 In his 1925 book *Das Gedächtnis und seine sozialen Bedingungen* (reprinted Frankfurt, 1985). The difference between collective and personal memory remains a central conceptual issue in the field of memory studies.
27 The Assmanns differentiate between two forms of collective memory: the communicative and the cultural. See, for instance, A. Assmann, *Erinnerungsräume: Formen und Wandlungen des kulturellen Gedächtnisses* (Munich, 1999).
28 P. Nora, *Realms of Memory: Rethinking the French Past*, 3 vols. (New York, 1996–8), originally published in 7 vols. as *Lieux de mémoire* (Paris 1984–92).
29 E. Françoise and H. Schulze, eds., *Deutsche Erinnerungsorte*, 3 vols. (Munich, 2001). See also J. Le Rider, M.Csáky, and M. Sommer, eds., *Transnationale Gedächtnisorte in Zentraleuropa* (Innsbruck and Vienna, 2002).

locating *Lieux de mémoire* or *Erinnerungsorte* is only one way of pinning down the elusive concept of memory. Koshar's "memoryscape" is another. For Alon Confino and Peter Fritzsche, however, memory should not be seen as a "location, or a group of people, or a thing, but as a set of practices and interventions, a symbolic representation of the past embedded in social action."[30]

Whether one agrees with this definition or not, Confino and Fritzsche are surely right to caution that "we should not assume a production of an absolute coherent, univocal voice, but rather the presence of multiple voices, often contradictory and opposed to each other but in dialogue," for "[p]olyphony seems to be the sound that best characterizes German memory."[31] It is important to remember, moreover, that not all these voices are filtered and edited by professional historians. In fact, historians have never held a monopoly on the transmission of history. Our contemporary view of the German Empire – and the way it is remembered – is just as likely to be shaped by television programs or film-makers as professional historians. Arguably, for instance, Peter Schamoni's entertaining but flawed documentary film *His Majesty Needs Sunshine* – a surprise hit in German cinemas in 1999 – has done more to shape popular perceptions of Wilhelm II than the collected works of John Röhl. Similarly, Bismarck's strong showing in ZDF Television's 2003 poll of the Greatest Germans of All Time – he came ninth, ahead of such luminaries as Einstein, Beethoven, and Kant – suggests that the "Bismarck Myth" still retains considerable popular appeal, despite decades of historical deconstruction.[32]

So how might the memory studies approach usefully contribute to our understanding of the *Kaiserreich*? Two potentially fruitful lines of enquiry – the "memoryscape" of the built-environment, and the barely-explored world of travel-guide literature (a genre in which Germans led the world in the nineteenth century) – have been opened up by Koshar in quick succession,[33] and both fields have much to offer. Arguably, however, even more stands to be gained from a renewed and refocused engagement with the countless private archives documenting the lives of ordinary German families. Not the carefully filed papers of politicians or industrialists, but the boxes of unsorted letters, scribbled postcards, and proud family photographs which await their historian in dusty attics and damp cellars.

---

30   A. Confino and P. Fritzsche, "Introduction: Noises of the past," p. 5.
31   Ibid. pp. 12, 15.
32   On the Bismarck Myth see R. Gerwarth, *Bismarck in Weimar*, and R. E. Frankel, *Bismarck's Shadow. The Cult of Leadership and the Transformation of the German Right, 1898–1945* (Oxford and New York, 2005).
33   R. Koshar's *German Travel Cultures*, which appeared in 2000, was sandwiched (in 1998 and 2001) by his two studies of the built environment.

Beneath the cobwebs and mildew is a rich and largely untapped seam of source material, which can often shed new light on the intricacies of class, gender, and national identity. Photographs are particularly important, because as Fritzsche observes, they elaborate "a commemorative culture that permitted the family to think of itself in historical terms."[34] It may well be that "[n]o social group relied more on the strategic deployment of memory in shaping its identity than the nobility,"[35] but by the end of the nineteenth century even working-class families had a sense of their place in history. Moreover, while many documents of individual memory will lend weight to the great collective narratives of the nation, others will run counter to them too, for "[t]he very 'exuberance of civil society' ... generated a plurality of memories."[36]

As historians become more adept at dealing with visual sources, the value of private archives is likely to rise. The same can be said to apply to another field highlighted by the prolific Koshar in a special 2001 edition of the journal *German History*, which he co-edited with Alon Confino: Germany's emergent consumer culture.[37] While pre-1918 Germany did not yet boast "a society-wide structure of meaning and feeling organized primarily around acts of purchase" (Victoria de Grazia's definition of a consumer culture),[38] it was clearly on the way. It was already apparent, for instance, in the remarkably lively theoretical debates on fashion, consumerism, and commodity culture that took place in Germany before 1914. The art historian Frederic Schwartz has described these debates – featuring early sociologists such as Georg Simmel and Werner Sombart – as "an important part of the first sustained and often sophisticated discussions of the nature of culture in a consumer-oriented capitalist economy."[39] Indeed, they laid the intellectual foundations for later and more celebrated theorists of mass culture like Benjamin, Lukács and Adorno. A recognition that commodity fetishization was a central cultural feature of modernity was also apparent in institutions like the German Werkbund (1907), the German Museum for Art in Trade and Industry

---

34 P. Fritzsche, "The case of modern memory," *Journal of Modern History*, 73 (2001), p. 110.
35 M. Funck and S. Malinowski, "Masters of memory: The strategic use of autobiographical memory by the German nobility," in A. Confino and P. Fritzsche, eds, *The Work of Memory*, p. 87.
36 P. Fritzsche, "The Case of Modern Memory," p. 115 (quoting Jay Winter).
37 A. Confino and R. Koshar, "Regimes of consumer cultures: New narratives in twentieth-century German history," *German History*, 19 (2001). See also A. Confino, "Consumer culture is in need of attention," in S. Denham, I. Kacandes, and J. Petropoulos, eds., *A User's Guide to German Cultural Studies* (Ann Arbor, 1997), pp. 181–8.
38 Quoted by A. Confino and R. Koshar, "Regimes of consumer cultures: New narratives in twentieth-century German history," *German History*, 19 (2001), p. 136.
39 F. Schwartz, *The Werkbund. Design Theory and Mass Culture before the First World War* (New Haven and London, 1996), p. 216.

(1909), and the *Deutsches Warenbuch* (1913); a consumer Bible offering "exemplary mass-produced goods for household use," issued jointly by the Werkbund, Dürerbund, and four German retail associations.[40] As Confino and Koshar put it: "From cars to cigarettes, from tourist guidebooks to furniture, the issue of what to consume and why and how to consume it garnered enduring and often contentious interest."[41]

At present the literature on consumption in Imperial Germany is far from extensive, but it is likely to expand rapidly in the coming years.[42] Connecting memory and materiality, it is a field that clearly offers considerable scope for inter- and multidisciplinary collaboration. It also offers ample opportunity to weave small stories of micro-history into the big picture of macro-history. More important still, perhaps, is the way in which it can integrate the many disparate strands within history itself, including the material dimension which is all too often absent from works of cultural history. Indeed, from *Alltagsgeschichte* to *Unternehmensgeschichte* (business history), one would be hard pressed to find a branch of the discipline that would not be able to contribute to a history of consumption in Imperial Germany. At a time when history appears more diverse and diffuse than ever, this is surely to be welcomed, even if there is (quite rightly) no going back to the "monotheistic" history of Ranke's age.

It is a truism that history reflects the time in which it is written: each generation asks its own questions, which often reveal more about contemporary concerns than the period under investigation. Today's boom in global and environmental history would certainly seem to bear this out.[43] It is clear, however, that as with other current enthusiasms mentioned here – cultural history, memory studies, and the history of consumption – these are not approaches best served by a strict adherence to the conventional markers of German history: 1871, 1918, 1933, and 1945. Long-term processes, like individual human lives, do not stop and

---

40 See M. Jefferies, *Politics and Culture in Wilhelmine Germany*, ch. 3. In the event, the first edition of the *Deutsches Warenbuch* did not appear until 1915.
41 A. Confino and R. Koshar, "Regimes of consumer cultures: New narratives in twentieth-century German history," *German History*, 19 (2001), p. 135.
42 W. G. Breckman, "Disciplining consumption: The debate on luxury in Wilhelmine Germany, 1890–1914," *Journal of Social History*, 24 (1991), pp. 485–505; K. Tenfelde, "Klassenspezifische Konsummuster im Deutschen Kaiserreich," in H. Siegrist, H. Kaelble, and J. Kocka, eds., *Europäische Konsumgeschichte* (Frankfurt and New York, 1997), pp. 245–66.
43 Works of environmental history that deal with the German Empire include F.-J. Brüggemeier and T. Rommelspacher, *Besiegte Natur. Geschichte der Umwelt im 19. und 20. Jahrhundert* (Munich, 1989); C. Mauch, ed., *Nature in German History* (Oxford and New York, 2004); F. Schmoll, *Erinnerung an die Natur. Die Geschichte des Naturschutzes im deutschen Kaiserreich* (Frankfurt and New York, 2004); and D. Blackbourn, *The Conquest of Nature: Water, Landscape and the Making of Modern Germany* (London, 2006).

start with the neat regularity of chapters in a history textbook. Nor indeed do they respect the artificial framework of the nation-state which historians have so often sought to impose upon them. So where does this leave the history of the German Empire in the twenty-first century? To repeat a pertinent question first posed by Geoff Eley in the 1990s: "Is there a history of the *Kaiserreich?*"[44]

The answer has to be a resounding yes. After all, this book is predicated on the belief that the German Empire can, and should, be studied. Nevertheless, it is clear that a history of the Empire in 2010 will look very different from one written in the 1960s or 1970s. There are a number of reasons for this. For a start, poststructuralist critiques of master narratives have made historians reluctant to employ the paradigms that once provided the framework for most studies of the *Kaiserreich*: liberal modernization; Karl Marx's "stages"; even the nation itself. Some have greeted this with a sense of liberation – Marcus Kreuzer, for instance, talks of "casting off the stifling liberal triumphalism, which for too long defined, and hence confined, the discussion of Germany's political development"[45] – but others express concern at the dissolution of "a single history into an unending multiplicity of stories"[46] One thing is certain: the task for those who synthesize and summarize historical knowledge has become more difficult than ever before. Not only has the breaking down of disciplinary boundaries made historians less insular than they once were, but the global expansion of higher education has dramatically increased the size of the profession.[47] The result has been a similarly dramatic proliferation of research methodologies, and it is this – rather than geographical location or national allegiance – that nowadays most divides historians of Imperial Germany. Of course, methodological diversity is not without its dangers too, but history is sufficiently robust and flexible to allow for more than one approach. Indeed, if diversity has become the new orthodoxy, then it should be taken as a cause for celebration rather than alarm.

---

44 The title of the introduction in G. Eley, ed., *Society, Culture and the State in Germany, 1870–1930*, pp. 1–42.
45 M. Kreuzer, "Response to Ledford and Sperber," *Central European History*, 36 (2003), p. 378.
46 S. Berger, *The Search for Normality*, p. 81.
47 There are, for example, more than 1,500 professors of history in Germany today, compared to just 170 in 1960. See H.-U. Wehler, "A guide to future research on the Kaiserreich?," *Central European History*, 29 (1996), p. 556, n. 27.

Bibliography

Abrams, L., "Martyrs or matriarchs? Working-class women's experience of marriage in Germany before the First World War," *Women's History Review*, 1 (1992).
Abrams, L., *Workers Culture in Imperial Germany. Leisure and Recreation in the Rhineland and Westphalia* (London: Routledge, 1992).
Abrams, L., *Bismarck and the German Empire, 1871–1918* (London: Routledge, 1995).
Abrams, L. and Harvey, E., eds., *Gender Relations in German History* (London: UCL Press, 1996).
Adams, C. E., *Women Clerks in Wilhelmine Germany* (Cambridge: Cambridge University Press, 1998).
Afflerbach, H., ed., *Wilhelm II. als Oberster Kriegsherr im Ersten Weltkrieg. Quellen aus der militärischen Umgebung des Kaisers 1914–1918* (Munich: Oldenbourg, 2004).
Alexander, M., *Die Freikonservative Partei 1890–1918. Gemäßigter Konservatismus in der konstitutionellen Monarchie* (Düsseldorf: Droste, 2000).
Allen, A. T., *Feminism and Motherhood in Germany* (New Brunswick: Rutgers University Press, 1991).
Aly, G., *Macht-Geist-Wahn. Kontinuitäten deutschen Denkens* (Berlin: Argon, 1997).
Anderson, B., *Imagined Communities: Reflections on the Origin and Spread of Nationalism* (London: Verso, 1983).
Anderson, M. L., *Windthorst. A Political Biography* (Oxford: Clarendon, 1981).
Anderson, M. L., "The Kulturkampf and the course of German history," *Central European History*, 19 (1986).
Anderson, M. L., *Practicing Democracy: Elections and Political Culture in Imperial Germany* (Princeton: Princeton University Press, 2000).
Anderson, M. L. and Barkin, K., "The myth of the Puttkamer purge and the reality of the Kulturkampf: Some reflections on the historiography of imperial Germany," *Journal of Modern History*, 54 (1982).

Applegate, C., *A Nation of Provincials. The German Idea of Heimat* (Berkeley and London: University of California Press, 1990).

Arendt, H., *The Origins of Totalitarianism* (London: Allen and Unwin, 1961, first published 1951).

Arsenschek, R., *Der Kampf um die Wahlfreiheit im Kaiserreich. Zur parlamentarischen Wahlprüfung und politischen Realität der Reichstagswahlen 1871–1914* (Düsseldorf, Droste, 2003).

Augustine, D. L., *Patricians and Parvenus: Wealth and High Society in Wilhelmine Germany* (Oxford: Berg, 1994).

Bachem-Rehm, M., *Die katholischen Arbeitervereine im Ruhrgebiet 1870–1914: Katholisches Arbeitermilieu zwischen Tradition und Emanzipation* (Stuttgart: Kohlhammer, 2004).

Bade, K., ed., *Imperialismus und Kolonialmission. Kaiserliches Deutschland und koloniales Imperium* (Stuttgart: Steiner, 1982).

Balfour, M., *The Kaiser and His Times* (London: Cresset, 1975, first published 1964).

Barkin, K., *The Controversy over German Industrialization, 1890–1902* (Chicago: University of Chicago Press, 1970).

Barkin, K., "1878–1879: The second founding of the Reich," *German Studies Review*, 10 (1987).

Barkin, K., "Bismarck in a postmodern world," *German Studies Review*, 18 (1995).

Barraclough, G., *From Agadir to Armageddon* (London: Weidenfeld and Nicholson, 1982).

Bauerkämper, A., Sabrow, M., and Stöver, B., eds., *Doppelte Zeitgeschichte. Deutschdeutsche Beziehungen 1945–90* (Berlin and Bonn: Dietz, 1998).

Baumgart, W., "Die deutsche Kolonialherrschaft in Afrika: neue Wege der Forschung," *Vierteljahrschrift für Sozial- und Wirtschaftsgeschichte*, 58 (1971).

Baumgart, W., *Deutschland im Zeitalter des Imperialismus 1890–1914* (Stuttgart: Kohlhammer, 1982).

Bayly, C. A., *The Birth of the Modern World, 1780–1914: Global Connections and Comparisons* (Oxford: Blackwell, 2004).

Bechhaus-Gerst, M. and Klein-Arendt, R., eds., *Die (koloniale) Begegnung. AfrikanerInnen in Deutschland 1880–1945, Deutsche in Afrika 1880–1918* (Frankfurt: Lang, 2003).

Behrenbeck, S. and Nützenadel, A., eds., *Inszenierungen des Nationalstaats. Politische Feiern in Italien und Deutschland seit 1860/71* (Cologne: SH Verlag, 2000).

Benner, T. H., *Die Strahlen der Krone. Die religiöse Dimension des Kaisertums unter Wilhelm II. vor dem Hintergrund der Orientreise 1898* (Marburg: Tectum, 2001).

Berdahl, R. M., "New thoughts on German nationalism," *American Historical Review*, 77 (1972).

Berdahl, R. M., Lüdtke, A., and Medick, H., *Klassen und Kultur. Sozialanthropologische Perspektiven in der Geschichtsschreibung* (Bodenheim: Athenaeum, 1982).

Berger, S., "Historians and nation-building in Germany after reunification," *Past and Present*, 148 (1995).

Berger, S., *The Search for Normality. National Identity and Historical Consciousness in Germany since 1800* (Leamington Spa: Berg, 1997).

Berger, S., *Social Democracy and the Working Class in Nineteenth and Twentieth Century Germany* (London: Longman, 2000).
Berger, S., "National paradigm and legitimacy: Uses of academic history writing in the 1960s," in P. Major and J. Osmond, eds., *The Workers' and Peasants' State. Communism and Society in East Germany under Ulbricht 1945–71* (Manchester: Manchester University Press, 2002).
Berger, S., *Inventing the Nation: Germany* (London: Arnold, 2004).
Berger, S., Donovan, M., and Passmore, K., eds., *Writing National Histories. Western Europe since 1800* (London: Routledge, 1998).
Berghahn, V. R., "Die Fischer-kontroverse – 15 Jahre danach," *Geschichte und Gesellschaft*, 6 (1980).
Berghahn, V. R., *Modern Germany. Society, Economy and Politics in the Twentieth Century* (Cambridge: Cambridge University Press, 1987, first published 1982).
Berghahn, V. R., *Germany and the Approach of War in 1914*, 2nd edn. (London: Macmillan, 1993, first published 1973).
Berghahn, V. R., *Imperial Germany 1871–1914: Economy, Society, Culture and Politics* (Providence and Oxford: Berghahn, 1994).
Berghahn, V. R., "The German Empire, 1871–1914: Reflections on the direction of recent research," *Central European History*, 35 (2002).
Bergmann, K., and Schorken, R. eds., *Geschichte im Alltag – Alltag in der Geschichte* (Düsseldorf: Patmos, 1982).
Berman, R. A., *Enlightenment or Empire: Colonial Discourse in German Culture* (Lincoln: University of Nebraska Press, 1998).
Berman, S. E., "Modernization in historical perspective. The case of imperial Germany," *World Politics*, 53 (2000).
Biefang, A., *"Der Reichsgründer?" Bismarck, die nationale Verfassungsbewegung und die Entstehung des Deutschen Kaiserreichs* (Friedrichsruh: Otto von Bismarck-Stiftung, 1999).
Blackbourn, D., *Class, Religion and Local Politics in Wilhelmine Germany. The Centre Party in Württemberg before 1914* (New Haven: Yale University Press, 1980).
Blackbourn, D., *Populists and Patricians. Essays in Modern German History* (London: Allen and Unwin, 1987).
Blackbourn, D., *The Marpingen Visions. Rationalism, Religion and the Rise of Modern Germany* (London: Fontana, 1995).
Blackbourn, D., *The Fontana History of Germany, 1780–1918. The Long Nineteenth Century* (London: Fontana, 1997).
Blackbourn, D., "How wicked and horrid," *London Review of Books*, 15 July 1999.
Blackbourn, D., *The Conquest of Nature: Water, Landscape and the Making of Modern Germany* (London: Cape, 2006).
Blackbourn, D. and Eley, G., *The Peculiarities of German History* (Oxford: Oxford University Press, 1984).
Blackbourn, D. and Evans, R. J., eds., *The German Bourgeoisie* (London: Routledge, 1991).
Blänsdorf, A., "Die deutsche Geschichte in der Sicht der DDR," *Geschichte in Wissenschaft und Unterricht*, 39 (1988).

Blaschke, O., ed., *Konfessionen im Konflikt: Deutschland zwischen 1800 und 1970* (Göttingen: Vandenhoeck und Ruprecht, 2002).
Bley, H., *Namibia under German Rule* (Hamburg: LIT, 1996, first published 1971).
Blom, I., Hagemann, K., and Hall, C., eds., *Gendered Nations: Nationalisms and Gender Order in the Long Nineteenth Century* (Oxford and New York: Berg, 2000).
Böckenförde, E.-W., "Der deutsche Typ der konstitutionellen Monarchie im 19. Jahrhundert," in W. Conze, ed., *Beiträge zur deutschen und belgischen Verfassungsgeschichte im 19. Jahrhundert* (Stuttgart: Klett, 1967).
Böge, V., ed., *Geschichtswerkstätten gestern – heute – morgen. Bewegung! Stillstand. Aufbruch?* (Munich and Hamburg: Dölling und Galitz, 2004).
Böhme, H., *Deutschlands Weg zur Großmacht. Studien zum Verhältnis von Wirtschaft und Staat während der Reichsgründungszeit 1848–1881* (Cologne and Berlin: Kiepenheuer und Witsch, 1966).
Böhme, H., ed., *Die Reichsgründung* (Munich: DTV, 1967).
Böhme, H., *An Introduction to the Social and Economic History of Germany* (Oxford: Blackwell, 1978, first published in German in 1968).
Böhme, H., "Primat und Paradigmata. Zur Entwicklung einer bundesdeutschen Geschichtsschreibung am Beispiel des Ersten Weltkrieges," in H. Lehmann, ed., *Historikerkontroversen* (Göttingen: Wallstein, 2000).
Bonnell, A., *The People's Stage in Imperial Germany. Social Democracy and Culture 1890–1914* (London and New York: Tauris, 2005).
Borchardt, K., *The Industrial Revolution in Germany, 1700–1914* (London: Collins, 1972).
Boxer, M. and Quataert, J., eds., *Connecting Spheres* (New York and Oxford: Oxford University Press, 1987).
Brandt, P., "War das deutsche Kaiserreich reformierbar? Parteien, politisches System und Gesellschaftsordnung vor 1914," in K. Rudolph and C. Wickert, eds., *Geschichte als Möglichkeit. Über die Chancen von Demokratie. Festschrift für Helga Grebing* (Essen: Klartext, 1995).
Breckman, W. G., "Disciplining consumption: The debate on luxury in Wilhelmine Germany, 1890–1914," *Journal of Social History*, 24 (1991).
Bridenthal, R. and Koonz, C., eds., *Becoming Visible: Women in European History* (Boston: Houghton Mifflin, 1977).
Breuilly, J., *Nationalism and the State* (Manchester: Manchester University Press, 1993).
Breuilly, J., *The Formation of the First German Nation-State 1800–71* (Basingstoke: Macmillan, 1996).
Breuilly, J., ed., *The State of Germany: The National Idea in the Making, Unmaking and Remaking of a Modern Nation State* (London: Longman, 1992).
Breuilly, J., "Auf dem Weg zur deutschen Gesellschaft? Der dritte Band von Wehlers 'Gesellschaftsgeschichte,'" *Geschichte und Gesellschaft*, 23 (1998).
Breuilly, J., "The Elusive class: Some critical remarks on the historiography of the 'bourgeoisie,'" *Archiv für Sozialgeschichte*, 38 (1998).
Breuilly, J., ed., *Nineteenth Century Germany* (London: Arnold, 2001).
Breuilly, J., *Austria, Prussia and Germany 1806–1871* (London: Longman, 2002).

Bruch, R. vom, *Wissenschaft, Politik und öffentliche Meinung. Gelehrtenpolitik im wilhelminischen Deutschland* (Husum: Matthiesen, 1980).

Bruendel, S., *Volksgemeinschaft oder Volksstaat. Die "Ideen von 1914" und die Neuordnung Deutschlands im Ersten Weltkrieg* (Berlin: Akademie, 2003).

Brüggemeier, F.-J., *Leben vor Ort. Ruhrbergleute und Ruhrbergbau, 1889–1919* (Munich: Beck, 1983).

Brüggemeier, F.-J. and Kocka, J., *"Geschichte von unten – Geschichte von innen": Kontroversen um die Alltagsgeschichte* (Hagen: Fernuniversität, 1985).

Brüggemeier, F.-J. and Rommelspacher, T., *Besiegte Natur. Geschichte der Umwelt im 19. und 20. Jahrhundert* (Munich: Beck, 1989).

Bucholz, A., *Moltke, Schlieffen and Prussian War Planning* (Oxford: Berg, 1991).

Burke, P., *Varieties of Cultural History* (Cambridge: Polity, 1997).

Burke, P., *What is Cultural History?* (Cambridge: Polity, 2004).

Busch, N., *Katholische Frömmigkeit und Moderne. Die Sozial- und Mentalitätsgeschichte des Herz-Jesu-Kultes in Deutschland zwischen Kulturkampf und Erstem Weltkrieg* (Gütersloh: Gütersloher Verlagshaus, 1997).

Butzer, H., *Diäten und Freifahrt im Deutschen Reichstag. Der Weg zum Entschädigungsgesetz von 1906* (Düsseldorf: Droste, 1999).

Canis, K., *Von Bismarck zur Weltpolitik. Deutsche Außenpolitik, 1890 bis 1902* (Berlin: Akademie, 1997).

Canis, K., *Bismarcks Außenpolitik 1870–1890. Aufstieg und Gefährdung* (Paderborn: Schöningh, 2003).

Canning, K., *Languages of Labor and Gender: Female Factory Work in Germany, 1850–1914* (Ithaca: Cornell University Press, 1996).

Canning, K., "Social Policy, Body Politics: Recasting the Social Question in Germany, 1875–1900," in L. Frader and S. Rose, eds., *Gender and Class in Modern Europe* (Ithaca: Cornell University Press, 1996).

Canning, K., *Gender History in Practice. Historical Perspectives on Bodies, Class and Citizenship* (Ithaca: Cornell University Press, 2006).

Carr, W., *A History of Germany, 1815–1985* (London: Arnold, 1987).

Carr, W., *The Origins of the Wars of German Unification* (London: Longman, 1991).

Cecil, L., *The German Diplomatic Service 1871–1918* (Princeton: Princeton University Press, 1976).

Cecil, L., *Wilhelm II.*, vol. 1, *Prince and Emperor, 1859–1900* (Chapel Hill and London: University of North Carolina Press, 1989).

Cecil, L., *Wilhelm II.*, vol. 2, *Emperor and Exile, 1900–1941* (Chapel Hill and London: University of North Carolina Press, 1996).

Chickering, R., *Karl Lamprecht. A German Academic Life, 1856–1915* (Atlantic Highlands, NJ: Humanities, 1983).

Chickering, R., *We Men Who Feel Most German. A Cultural Study of the Pan-German League 1886–1914* (Boston: Allen and Unwin, 1984).

Chickering, R., "'Casting their gaze more broadly': Women's patriotic activism in imperial Germany," *Past and Present*, 118 (1988).

Chickering, R., ed., *Imperial Germany. A Historiographical Companion* (Westport and London: Greenwood, 1996).

Chickering, R., *Imperial Germany and the Great War, 1914–1918* (Cambridge: Cambridge University Press, 1998).
Chickering, R., "The Lamprecht controversy," in H. Lehmann, ed., *Historikerkontroversen* (Göttingen: Wallstein, 2000).
Chickering, R., *The Great War and Urban Life in Germany: Freiburg, 1914–1918* (Cambridge: Cambridge University Press, 2007).
Clark, C., "The wars of liberation in Prussian memory: Reflections on the memorialization of war in early nineteenth-century Germany," *Journal of Modern History*, 68 (1996).
Clark, C., *Kaiser Wilhelm II* (London: Longman, 2000).
Clavin, P., "Defining transnationalism," *Contemporary European History*, 14 (2005).
Coetzee, F. and Coetzee, M. S., eds., *Authority, Identity and the Social History of the Great War* (Providence and Oxford: Berghahn, 1995).
Coetzee, M. S., *The German Army League. Popular Nationalism in Wilhelmine Germany* (Oxford: Oxford University Press, 1990).
Confino, A., *The Nation as a Local Metaphor: Württemberg, Imperial Germany and National Memory, 1871–1918* (Chapel Hill and London: University of North Carolina Press, 1997).
Confino, A. and Fritzsche, P., eds., *The Work of Memory: New Directions in the Study of German Society and Culture* (Urbana and Chicago: University of Illinois Press, 2002).
Craig, G., *Germany 1866–1945* (Oxford: Clarendon, 1978).
Crane, S., *Collecting and Historical Consciousness: New Forms for Collective Memory in Early Nineteenth-Century Germany* (Ithaca: University of North Carolina Press, 2000).
Crankshaw, E., *Bismarck* (New York and London: Macmillan, 1981).
Crew, D., *Town in the Ruhr: A Social History of Bochum 1860–1914* (New York: Columbia University Press, 1979).
Crew, D., "Alltagsgeschichte: A new social history from below," *Central European History*, 22 (1989).
Crew, D., "Remembering German pasts: Memory in German history, 1871–1989," *Central European History*, 33 (2000).
Davis, B., *Home Fires Burning. Food, Politics, and Everyday Life in World War One Berlin* (Chapel Hill and London: University of North Carolina Press, 2000).
Dahrendorf, R., *Society and Politics in Germany* (New York: Anchor, 1967).
Daniel, U., *Arbeiterfrauen in der Kriegsgesellschaft: Beruf, Familie und Politik im Ersten Weltkrieg* (Göttingen: Vandenhoeck und Ruprecht, 1989).
Dehio, L., *Gleichgewicht oder Hegemonie. Betrachtungen über ein Grundproblem der neueren Staatengeschichte* (Krefeld: Scherpe, 1948).
Dehio, L., *Germany and World Politics in the Twentieth Century* (London: Chatto and Windus, 1960).
Denham, S., Kacandes, I., and Petropoulos, J., eds., *A User's Guide to German Cultural Studies* (Ann Arbor: University of Michigan Press, 1997).
Dickinson, E. R., "Reflections on feminism and monism in the Kaiserreich, 1890–1913," *Central European History*, 34 (2001).

Dickinson, E. R., "The Men's Morality Movement in Germany, 1880–1914: Some reflections on sex, politics, and sexual politics," *Journal of Modern History*, 75 (2003).

Doerry, M., *Übergangsmenschen. Die Mentalität der Wilhelminer und die Krise des Kaiserreichs* (Weinheim: Juventa, 1986).

Dorpalen, A., "The German historians and Bismarck," *Review of Politics*, 15 (1953).

Dorpalen, A., *German History in Marxist Perspective. The East German Approach* (London: Tauris, 1985).

Drechlser, H., *"Let us die fighting": The Struggle of the Herero and Nama against German Imperialism* (London: Zed, 1980).

Dukes, J. and Remak, J., eds., *Another Germany: A Reconsideration of the Imperial Era* (Boulder and London: Westview, 1988).

Dülffer, J., ed., *Otto von Bismarck: Person, Politik, Mythos* (Berlin: Akademie, 1993).

Dülffer, J. and Holl, K., eds., *Bereit zum Krieg. Kriegsmentalität im wilhelminischen Deutschland 1890–1914* (Göttingen: Vandenhoeck und Ruprecht, 1986).

Dumke, R., "Der deutsche Zollverein als Modell ökonomischer Integration," in H. Berding, ed., *Wirtschaftliche und politische Integration in Europa im 19. und 20. Jahrhundert* (Göttingen: Vandenhoeck und Ruprecht, 1984).

Eckart, W., "'Die wachsende Nervösität unserer Zeit'. Medizin und Kultur um 1900 am Beispiel einer Modekrankheit," in G. Hübinger, R. vom Bruch, and F. W. Graf, eds., *Kultur und Kulturwissenschaften um 1900*, vol. 2 (Stuttgart: Steiner, 1997).

Eckart, W., *Medizin und Kolonialimperialismus: Deutschland 1884–1945* (Paderborn: Schöningh, 1997).

Eifert, C., et al., eds., *Was sind Männer, was sind Frauen? Geschlechterkonstruktion im historischen Wandel* (Frankfurt: Suhrkamp, 1995).

Eisenberg, C., *"English Sports" und deutsche Bürger. Eine Gesellschaftsgeschichte 1800–1939* (Paderborn: Schöningh, 1999).

Eksteins, M., "When death was young," in R. Bullen, H. Pogge von Strandmann, and A. Polonsky, eds., *Ideas into Politics: Aspects of European History 1880–1950* (London and Sydney: Croom Helm, 1984).

Eksteins, M., *Rites of Spring. The Great War and the Birth of the Modern Age* (London: Bantam, 1989).

Elias, N., "Zum Begriff des Alltags," in K. Hammerich and M. Klein, eds., *Materialien zur Soziologie des Alltags* (Opladen: Westdeutscher, 1978).

Eley, G., *Reshaping the German Right. Radical Nationalism and Political Change after Bismarck* (New Haven and London: Yale University Press, 1980).

Eley, G., "The view from the throne: The personal rule of Kaiser Wilhelm II," *Historical Journal*, 28 (1985).

Eley, G., *From Unification to Nazism. Reinterpreting the German Past* (Boston and London: Allen and Unwin, 1986).

Eley, G., "Labour history, social history, Alltagsgeschichte: Experience, culture, and the politics of the everyday – a new direction for German social history?," *Journal of Modern History*, 61 (1989).

Eley, G., "What is cultural history?," *New German Critique* 65 (1995).

Eley, G., "Is all the world text? From social history to the history of society two decades later," in T. J. McDonald, ed., *The Historic Turn in the Human Sciences* (Ann Arbor: University of Michigan Press, 1996).

Eley, G., ed., *Society, Culture and the State in Germany 1870–1930* (Ann Arbor: University of Michigan Press, 1996).

Eley, G., "Problems with culture: German history after the linguistic turn," *Central European History*, 31 (1998).

Eley, G., "Culture, nation, and gender," in I. Blom, K. Hagemann, and C. Hall, eds., *Gendered Nations: Nationalisms and Gender Order in the Long Nineteenth Century* (Oxford: Berg, 2000).

Eley, G., "Frauen und der geschlechtsbezogene nationale Staatsbürgerstatus in Deutschland 1860–1914," in D. Münkel and J. Schwarzkopf, eds., *Geschichte als Experiment. Studien zu Politik, Kultur und Alltag im 19. und 20. Jahrhundert. Festschrift für Adelheid von Saldern* (Frankfurt and New York: Campus, 2004).

Eley, G. and Retallack, J., eds., *Wilhelminism and its Legacies. German Modernities, Imperialism, and the Meanings of Reform, 1890–1930* (New York and Oxford: Berghahn, 2003).

Engelberg, E., *Bismarck*. vol. 1 *Urpreuße und Reichsgründer* (Berlin: Siedler, 1985).

Engelberg, E., *Bismarck*. vol. 2 *Das Reich in der Mitte Europas* (Berlin: Siedler, 1990).

Engelberg, E., *Bismarck und die Revolution von oben* (Brunswick: Eckert, 1987).

Engelberg, W., *Das private Leben der Bismarcks* (Berlin: Siedler, 1998).

Epkenhans, M., *Die wilhelminische Flottenrüstung, 1908–1914* (Munich: Oldenbourg, 1991).

Erdmann, K. D., *Kurt Riezler: Tagebücher, Aufsätze, Dokumente* (Göttingen: Vandenhoeck und Ruprecht, 1972).

Evans, E. E., *The Center Party 1870–1933: A Study in Political Catholicism* (Carbondale, IL: Southern Illinois University Press, 1981).

Evans, R. J., *The Feminist Movement in Germany, 1894–1933* (London: Sage, 1976).

Evans, R. J., ed., *Society and Politics in Wilhelmine Germany* (London: Croom Helm, 1978).

Evans, R. J., ed., *The German Family: Essays on the Social History of the Family in Nineteenth and Twentieth Century Germany* (London: Croom Helm, 1981).

Evans, R. J., ed., *The German Working Class, 1888–1933. The Politics of Everyday Life* (London: Croom Helm, 1982).

Evans, R. J., "From Hitler to Bismarck: The Reich and Kaiserreich in recent historiography," *Historical Journal*, 26 (1983).

Evans, R. J., *Death in Hamburg. Society and Politics in the Cholera Years 1830–1910* (Oxford: Clarendon, 1987).

Evans, R. J., *Rethinking German History. Nineteenth-Century Germany and the Origins of the Third Reich* (London: Allen and Unwin, 1987).

Evans, R. J., ed., *The German Underworld. Deviants and Outcasts in German History* (London: Routledge, 1988).

Evans, R. J., ed., *Kneipengespräche im Kaiserreich. Stimmungsberichte der Hamburger Politischen Polizei 1892–1914* (Reinbek: Rowohlt, 1989).

Evans, R. J., "Nipperdeys Neunzehntes Jahrhundert. Eine kritische Auseinandersetzung," *Geschichte und Gesellschaft*, 20 (1994).
Evans, R. J., "Whatever became of the Sonderweg?" in *Rereading German History* (London: Routledge, 1997).
Evans, R. J., *In Defence of History* (London: Granta, 1997).
Evans, R. J. and Lee, W. R., eds., *The German Peasantry. Conflict and Community in Rural Society from the 18th to the 20th Centuries* (London: Croom Helm, 1986).
Evans, R. J. W. and Pogge von Strandmann, H., eds., *The Coming of the First World War* (Oxford: Clarendon, 1988).
Eyck, E., *Das persönliche Regiment Wilhelms II. Politische Geschichte des Deutschen Kaiserreiches von 1890 bis 1914* (Zurich: Rentsch, 1948).
Eyck, E., *Bismarck and the German Empire* (London: Allen and Unwin, 1950).
Fairbairn, B., *Democracy in the Undemocratic State. The Reichstag Elections of 1898 and 1903* (Toronto: University of Toronto Press, 1997).
Faulenbach, B., *Ideologie des deutschen Weges. Die deutsche Geschichte in der Historiographie zwischen Kaiserreich und Nationalsozialismus* (Munich: Beck, 1980).
Fehrenbach, E., *Wandlungen des deutschen Kaisergedankens 1871–1918* (Munich: Oldenbourg, 1969).
Feldman, G. D., *Army, Industry and Labor in Germany, 1914–1918* (Princeton: Princeton University Press, 1966).
Feldman, G. D., *The Great Disorder: Politics, Economics, and Society in the German Inflation, 1914–1924* (Oxford: Oxford University Press, 1993).
Ferguson, N., "Germany and the Origins of the First World War: New Perspectives," *Historical Journal*, 35 (1992).
Ferguson, N., ed., *Virtual History: Alternatives and Counterfactuals* (London: Picador, 1997).
Ferguson, N., *The Pity of War* (London: Allen Lane, 1998).
Feuchtwanger, E., *Imperial Germany 1850–1918* (London: Routledge, 2001).
Feuchtwanger, E., *Bismarck* (London: Routledge, 2002).
Fischer, A. and Heydemann, G., eds., *Geschichtswissenschaft in der DDR*, 2 vols. (Berlin: Duncker und Humblot, 1988–90).
Fischer, F., "Deutsche Kriegsziele, Revolutionierung und Separatfrieden im Osten, 1914–18," *Historische Zeitschrift*, 188 (1959).
Fischer, F., *Germany's Aims in the First World War* (London: Chatto and Windus, 1967).
Fischer, F., *War of Illusions: German Politics from 1911 to 1914* (London: Chatto and Windus, 1973).
Fischer, F., *World Power or Decline: The Controversy over Germany's Aims in the First World War* (New York and London: Norton, 1974).
Fischer, F., *Juli 1914: Wir sind nicht hineingeschlittert. Das Staatsgeheimnis um die Riezler-Tagebücher* (Reinbek: Rowohlt, 1983).
Flasch, K., *Die geistige Mobilmachung. Die deutschen Intellektuellen und der Erste Weltkrieg. Ein Versuch* (Berlin: Fest, 2000).
Fletcher, R., "Recent developments in West German historiography: The Bielefeld School and its critics," *German Studies Review*, 3 (1984).

Fletcher, R., ed., *Bernstein to Brandt: A Short History of German Democracy* (London: Arnold, 1987).

Fletcher, R., "History from below comes to Germany: The new history movement in the Federal Republic of Germany," *Journal of Modern History*, 60 (1988).

Forster-Hahn, F., *Imagining Modern German Culture 1889–1910* (Hanover, NH: University Press of New England, 1996).

Förster, S., *Der doppelte Militarismus: die deutsche Heeresrüstungspolitik zwischen Status-Quo-Sicherung und Aggression 1890–1913* (Stuttgart: Steiner, 1985).

Förster, S., "Im Reich des Absurden: Die Ursachen des Ersten Weltkrieges," in B. Wegner, ed., *Wie Kriege entstehen: zum historischen Hintergrund von Staatenkonflikten* (Paderborn: Schöningh, 2000).

Foucault, M., *The History of Sexuality: An Introduction* (Harmondsworth: Penguin, 1978).

Fout, J. C., ed., *German Women in the Nineteenth Century: A Social History* (New York and London: Holmes and Meier, 1984).

Fout, J. C., "Sexual politics in Wilhelmine Germany: The male gender crisis, moral purity, and homophobia," *Journal of the History of Sexuality*, 2 (1992).

François, E. and Schulze, H., eds., *Deutsche Erinnerungsorte*, 3 vols. (Munich: Beck, 2001).

Frankel, R. E., *Bismarck's Shadow. The Cult of Leadership and the Transformation of the German Right, 1898–1945* (Oxford: Berg, 2005).

Franzoi, B., *At the Very Least She Pays the Rent: Women and German Industrialization, 1871–1914* (Westport and London: Greenwood, 1985).

Frauendienst, W., "Demokratisierung des deutschen Konstitutionalismus in der Zeit Wilhelms II," *Zeitschrift für die gesamte Staatswissenschaft*, 113 (1957).

Frevert, U., *Women in German History: From Bourgeois Emancipation to Sexual Liberation* (Oxford: Berg, 1988).

Frevert, U., *Men of Honour: A Social and Cultural History of the Duel* (Cambridge: Polity, 1995).

Frevert, U., *A Nation in Barracks: Modern Germany, Military Conscription and Civil Society* (Oxford: Berg, 2004).

Frevert, U., "Europeanizing Germany's twentieth century," *History and Memory*, 17 (2005).

Frie, E., *Das Deutsche Kaiserreich* (Darmstadt: Wissenschaftliche Buchgesellschaft, 2004).

Friedrichsmeyer, S., Lennox, S., and Zantop, S., *The Imperialist Imagination: German Colonialism and its Legacy* (Ann Arbor: University of Michigan Press, 1998).

Fritzsche, P., *Reading Berlin 1900* (Cambridge, MA and London: Harvard University Press, 1996).

Fuhrmann, M., *Der Traum vom deutschen Orient. Zwei deutsche Kolonien im Osmanischen Reich 1851–1918* (Frankfurt: Campus, 2006).

Gall, L., ed., *Das Bismarck-Problem in der Geschichtsschreibung nach 1945* (Cologne and Berlin: Kiepenheuer und Witsch, 1971).

Gall, L., "Liberalismus und 'bürgerliche Gesellschaft.' Zu Charakter und Entwicklung der liberalen Bewegung in Deutschland," *Historische Zeitschrift*, 220 (1975).

Gall, L., "Bismarck und der Bonapartismus," *Historische Zeitschrift*, 223 (1976).
Gall, L., *Bismarck. The White Revolutionary*, 2 vols. (London: Allen and Unwin, 1986).
Gall, L., ed., *Otto von Bismarck und Wilhelm II: Repräsentanten eines Epochenwechsels?* (Paderborn: Schöningh, 2000).
Gann, L. H and Duignan, P., *The Rulers of German Africa, 1884–1914* (Stanford: Stanford University Press, 1977).
Geertz, C., *The Interpretation of Cultures* (New York: Basic, 1973).
Geinitz, C., *Kriegsfurcht und Kampfbereitschaft. Das August-Erlebnis in Freiburg* (Essen: Klartext, 1998).
Geiss, I., *July 1914: The Outbreak of the First World War* (London: Batsford, 1965).
Geiss, I., *Studien über Geschichte und Geschichtswissenschaft* (Frankfurt: Suhrkamp, 1972).
Geiss, I., *German Foreign Policy 1871–1914* (London: Routledge and Kegan Paul, 1976).
Geiss, I., *Der lange Weg in die Katastrophe. Die Vorgeschichte des Ersten Weltkrieges 1815–1914* (Munich: Piper, 1990).
Geiss, I. and Pogge von Strandmann, H., eds., *Die Erforderlichkeit des Unmöglichen* (Frankfurt: EVA., 1965).
Gerwarth, R., *Bismarck in Weimar. Germany's First Democracy and the Civil War of Memories* (Oxford: Oxford University Press, 2005).
Geyer, M. and Jarausch, K. H., "Great men and postmodern ruptures: Overcoming the 'belatedness' of German historiography," *German Studies Review*, 18 (1995).
Glaser, H., *Die Kultur der wilhelminischen Zeit: Topographie einer Epoche* (Frankfurt: Fischer, 1984).
Gollwitzer, H., "Der Cäsarismus Napoleons III im Widerhall der öffentlichen Meinung Deutschlands," *Historische Zeitschrift*, 173 (1952).
Goltermann, S., *Körper der Nation. Habitusformierung und die Politik des Turnens 1860–1890* (Göttingen: Vandenhoeck und Ruprecht, 1998).
Gooch, G. P., "The study of Bismarck," in *Studies in German History* (London: Longman, 1948).
Grebing, H., *The History of the German Labour Movement* (London: Woolf, 1969).
Grebing, H., et al. *Der deutsche Sonderweg in Europa 1806–1945. Eine Kritik* (Stuttgart: Kohlhammer, 1986).
Green, A., *Fatherlands. State-building and Nationhood in Nineteenth Century Germany* (Cambridge: Cambridge University Press, 2001).
Greven-Aschoff, B., *Die bürgerliche Frauenbewegung in Deutschland 1894–1933* (Göttingen: Vandenhoeck und Ruprecht, 1981).
Grießmer, A., *Massenverbände und Massenparteien im wilhelminischen Reich. Zum Wandel der Wahlkultur 1903–12* (Düsseldorf: Droste, 2000).
Groh, D., *Negative Integration und revolutionärer Attentismus. Die deutsche Sozialdemokratie am Vorabend des Ersten Weltkrieges* (Frankfurt: Propyläen, 1973).
Gross, M. B., *The War against Catholicism. Liberalism and the Anti-Catholic Imagination in Nineteenth-Century Germany* (Ann Arbor: University of Michigan Press, 2004).

Grosse, P., *Kolonialismus, Eugenik und bürgerliche Gesellschaft in Deutschland, 1850–1918* (Frankfurt and New York: Campus: 2000).

Grosser, D., *Vom monarchischen Konstitutionalismus zur parlamentarischen Demokratie. Die Verfassungspolitik der deutschen Parteien im letzten Jahrzehnt des Kaiserreichs* (The Hague: Nijhoff, 1970).

Gründer, H., *Geschichte der deutschen Kolonien* (Paderborn: Schöningh, 1985).

Günter, R. and Rutzen, R. J., *Kultur tagtäglich* (Reinbek: Rowohlt, 1982).

Gutsche, W., *Wilhelm II. Der letzte Kaiser des Deutschen Reiches. Eine Biographie* (Berlin: Verlag der Wissenschaften, 1991).

Guttsman, W. L., *The German Social Democratic Party 1875–1933. From Ghetto to Government* (London: Allen and Unwin, 1981).

Haar, I., *Historiker im Nationalsozialismus. Die deutsche Geschichte und der "Volkstumskampf" im Osten* (Göttingen: Vandenhoeck und Ruprecht, 2000).

Hagemann, K., *"Männlicher Muth und Teutsche Ehre": Nation, Militär und Geschlecht zur Zeit der Antinapoleonischen Kriege Preußens* (Paderborn: Schöningh, 2002).

Halder, W., *Innenpolitik im Kaiserreich 1871–1914* (Darmstadt: Wissenschaftliche Buchgesellschaft, 2003).

Hall, A., *Scandal, Sensation and Social Democracy: The SPD Press and Wilhelmine Germany* (Cambridge: Cambridge University Press, 1977).

Hallmann, H., ed., *Revision des Bismarckbildes. Die Diskussion der deutschen Fachhistoriker* (Darmstadt: Wissenschaftliche Buchgesellschaft, 1972).

Hamerow, T. S., ed., *Otto von Bismarck and Imperial Germany, A Historical Assessment* (Lexington, MA and London: Heath, 1994 – first published 1971).

Hamerow, T. S., ed., *The Age of Bismarck, Documents and Interpretations* (New York: Harper and Row, 1973).

Hammerich, K. and Klein, M., eds., *Materialien zur Soziologie des Alltags* (Opladen: Westdeutscher, 1978).

Hamilton, R. and Herwig, H., eds., *The Origins of World War One* (Cambridge: Cambridge University Press, 2003).

Hank, M., *Kanzler ohne Amt: Fürst Bismarck nach seiner Entlassung 1890–98* (Munich: Tuduv, 1980).

Hargreaves, D., ed., *Documents and Debates: Bismarck and German Unification* (Basingstoke: Macmillan, 1991).

Hartung, F., "Das persönliche Regiment Kaiser Wilhelms II," *Sitzungsberichte der deutschen Akademie der Wissenschaften zu Berlin* (Berlin: Akademie, 1952).

Hau, M., *The Cult of Health and Beauty in Germany. A Social History, 1890–1930* (Chicago: University of Chicago Press, 2003).

Hausen, K., ed., *Frauen suchen ihre Geschichte. Historische Studien zum 19. und 20. Jahrhundert* (Munich: Beck, 1983).

Hausen, K. and Wunder, H., eds., *Frauengeschichte – Geschlechtergeschichte* (Frankfurt and New York: Campus, 1992).

Hayes, P., ed., *Themes in Modern European History* (London: Routledge, 1992).

Healy, M., *Vienna and the Fall of the Habsburg Empire. Total War and Everyday Life in World War One* (Cambridge: Cambridge University Press, 2004).

Healy, R., *The Jesuit Specter in Imperial Germany* (Boston: Brill, 2003).

Heckart, B., *From Bassermann to Bebel. The Grand Bloc's Quest for Reform in the Kaiserreich, 1900–1914* (New Haven and London: Yale University Press, 1974).

Heinemann, U., *Die verdrängte Niederlage. Politische Öffentlichkeit und Kriegsschuldfrage in der Weimarer Republik* (Göttingen: Vandenhoeck und Ruprecht, 1983).

Heitzer, H., *Der Volksverein für das katholische Deutschland im Kaiserreich 1890–1918* (Mainz: Grünewald, 1979).

Henderson, W. O., *The Rise of German Industrial Power, 1834–1914* (London: Temple Smith, 1975).

Henderson, W. O., *Studies in German Colonial History* (London: Cass, 1976, first published 1962).

Henderson, W. O., *The Zollverein* (London: Cass, 1984, first published 1939).

Henderson, W. O., *The German Colonial Empire: 1884–1919* (London: Cass, 1993).

Henig, R., *The Origins of the First World War* (London: Routledge, 1989).

Herrigel, G., *Industrial Constructions. The Sources of German Industrial Power* (Cambridge: Cambridge University Press, 1996).

Herrmann, D., *The Arming of Europe and the Making of the First World War* (Princeton: Princeton University Press, 1996).

Hertz-Eichenrode, D., *Deutsche Geschichte 1871–1890. Das Kaiserreich in der Ära Bismarck* (Stuttgart: Kohlhammer, 1992).

Hertz-Eichenrode, D., *Deutsche Geschichte 1890–1918. Das Kaiserreich in der Wilhelminischen Zeit* (Stuttgart: Kohlhammer, 1996).

Herwig, H., *"Luxury" Fleet: The Imperial German Navy, 1888–1918* (London: Allen and Unwin, 1980).

Herwig, H., "Industry, empire and the First World War," in G. Martel, ed., *Modern Germany Reconsidered* (London: Routledge, 1992).

Herwig, H., "Clio deceived: Patriotic self-censorship in Germany after the war," in K. Wilson, ed., *Forging the Collective Memory: Government and International Historians through Two World Wars* (Providence and Oxford: Berghahn, 1996).

Herwig, H., *The First World War. Germany and Austria-Hungary, 1914–1918* (London: Arnold, 1997).

Herwig, H., ed., *The Outbreak of World War One: Causes and Responsibilities*, 6th edn. (Boston: Houghton Mifflin, 1997).

Hewitson, M., "The Kaiserreich in question: Constitutional crisis in Germany before the First World War," *Journal of Modern History*, 73 (2001).

Hewitson, M., *Germany and the Causes of the First World War* (Oxford: Berg, 2004).

Hildebrand, K., "Geschichte oder 'Gesellschaftsgeschichte'? Die Notwendigkeit einer politischen Geschichtsschreibung von den internationalen Beziehungen, *Historische Zeitschrift*, 223 (1976).

Hildebrand, K., *Das vergangene Reich. Deutsche Außenpolitik von Bismark bis Hitler 1871–1945* (Stuttgart: DVA, 1995).

Hildebrand, K., *Reich, Nation-State, Great Power. Reflections on German Foreign Policy, 1871–1945* (London: German Historical Institute, 1995).

Hillgruber, A., *Deutsche Großmacht- und Weltpolitik im 19. und 20. Jahrhundert* (Düsseldorf: Droste, 1977).

Hillgruber, A., *Otto von Bismarck, Gründer der europäischen Großmacht Deutsches Reich* (Göttingen: Musterschmidt, 1978).
Hillgruber, A., *Die gescheiterte Großmacht. Eine Skizze des Deutschen Reiches 1871–1945* (Düsseldorf: Droste, 1984).
Hobsbawm, E., *The Age of Empire, 1875–1914* (London: Weidenfeld and Nicholson, 1987).
Hobsbawm, E., *Nations and Nationalism since 1780: Programme, Myth, Reality* (Cambridge: Cambridge University Press, 1990).
Hobsbawm, E. and Ranger, T., eds, *The Invention of Tradition* (Cambridge: Cambridge University Press, 1983).
Hohls, R. and Jarausch, K., eds., *Versäumte Fragen. Deutsche Historiker im Schatten des Nationalsozialismus* (Munich: DVA, 2000).
Holborn, H., "Bismarck's Realpolitik," *Journal of the History of Ideas*, 21 (1960).
Honold, A. and Simons, O., eds., *Kolonialismus als Kultur: Literatur, Medien, Wissenschaft in der deutschen Gründerzeit des Fremden* (Tübingen and Basel: Francke, 2002).
Huber, E. R., "Das persönliche Regiment Wilhelms II," *Zeitschrift für Religion und Geistesgeschichte*, 3 (1951).
Huber, E. R., *Deutsche Verfassungsgeschichte seit 1789*, vol. 3 *Bismarck und das Reich*; vol. 4 *Struktur und Krisen des Kaiserreichs* (Stuttgart and Berlin: Kohlhammer, 1963–69, 2nd edn. 1982).
Huck, G., ed., *Sozialgeschichte der Freizeit. Untersuchungen zum Wandel der Alltagskultur in Deutschland* (Wuppertal: Hammer, 1980).
Hucko, E. M., ed., *The Democratic Tradition. Four German Constitutions* (Leamington Spa: Berg, 1980).
Hughes, M., *Nationalism and Society. Germany 1800–1945* (London: Arnold, 1988).
Hull, I. V., *The Entourage of Kaiser Wilhelm II, 1888–1918* (Cambridge: Cambridge University Press, 1982).
Hull, I. V., *Absolute Destruction: Military Culture and the Practices of War in Imperial Germany* (Ithaca: Cornell University Press, 2005).
Hunt, J., *The People's Party in Württemberg and Southern Germany 1890–1914. The Possibilities of Democratic Politics* (Stuttgart: Klett, 1975).
Hunt, L., ed., *The New Cultural History* (Berkeley: University of California Press, 1989).
Iggers, G. G., *The German Conception of History: The National Tradition of Historical Thought from Herder to the Present* (Middletown, CT: Wesleyan University Press, 1968).
Iggers, G. G., ed., *The Social History of Politics: Critical Perspectives in West German Historical Writing Since 1945* (Leamington Spa: Berg, 1985).
Illig, S., *Zwischen Körperertüchtigung und nationaler Bewegung. Turnvereine in Bayern 1860–1890* (Cologne: SH Verlag, 1998).
Institut für Zeitgeschichte, *Deutscher Sonderweg. Mythos oder Realität?* (Munich: Oldenbourg, 1982).
Jäger, W., *Historische Forschung und politische Kultur in Deutschland. Die Debatte 1914–1980 über den Ausbruch des ersten Weltkrieges* (Göttingen: Vandenhoeck und Ruprecht, 1984).

Jarausch, K., *The Enigmatic Chancellor: Bethmann Hollweg and the Hubris of Imperial Germany* (Princeton: Princeton University Press, 1973).
Jarausch, K., "Der nationale Tabubruch. Wissenschaft, Öffentlichkeit und Politik in der Fischer-Kontroverse," in M. Sabrow, R. Jessen, and K. G. Kracht, eds., *Zeitgeschichte als Streitgeschichte. Große Kontroversen seit 1945* (Munich: Beck, 2003).
Jarausch, K. and Geyer, M., *Shattered Past. Reconstructing German Histories* (Princeton: Princeton University Press, 2002).
Jarausch, K. and Jones, L. E., eds., *In Search of a Liberal Germany: Studies in the History of German Liberalism from 1789 to the Present* (Oxford: Berg, 1990).
Jefferies, M., *Politics and Culture in Wilhelmine Germany: The Case of Industrial Architecture* (Oxford: Berg, 1995).
Jefferies, M., *Imperial Culture in Germany 1871–1918* (Basingstoke: Palgrave Macmillan, 2003).
Jelavich, P., "Method. What method? Confessions of a failed structuralist," *New German Critique*, 65 (1995).
Jenkins, J., *Provincial Modernity: Local Culture and Liberal Politics in Fin-de-Siècle Hamburg* (Ithaca: Cornell University Press, 2003).
Joll, J., "1914: The unspoken assumptions," in H. W. Koch, ed., *The Origins of the First World War: Great Power Rivalry and German War Aims* (London: Macmillan, 1984).
Joll, J., *The Origins of the First World War* (London: Longman, 1984).
Jones, L. E. and Retallack, J., eds., *Elections, Mass Politics and Social Change in Modern Germany: New Perspectives* (Cambridge: Cambridge University Press, 1992).
Jones, L. E. and Retallack, J., eds., *Between Reform, Reaction and Resistance. Essays on German Conservatism* (Oxford: Berg, 1993).
Kaelble, H., *Industrielle Interessenpolitik in der Wilhelminischen Gesellschaft. Zentralverband deutscher Industrieller 1895–1914* (Berlin: de Gruyter, 1967).
Kaplan, M. A., *The Jewish Feminist Movement in Germany: The Campaigns of the Jüdischer Frauenbund 1904–38* (Westport and London: Greenwood, 1979).
Kaschuba, W., *Lebenswelt und Kultur der unterbürgerlichen Schichten im 19. und 20. Jahrhundert* (Munich: Oldenbourg, 1990).
Kaschuba, W. and Maase, K., eds., *Schund und Schönheit. Populäre Kultur um 1900* (Cologne: Böhlau, 2001).
Kehr, E., *Battleship Building and Party Politics in Germany 1894–1901* (Chicago: University of Chicago Press, 1973).
Kennan, G. F., *The Decline of Bismarck's European Order: Franco-Russian Relations, 1875–1890* (Princeton: Princeton University Press, 1979).
Kennedy, P., *The Rise of the Anglo-German Antagonism* (London: Allen and Unwin, 1980).
Kern, S., *The Culture of Time and Space, 1880–1918* (London: Weidenfeld and Nicolson, 1983).
Kershaw, I., *Hitler 1889–1936: Hubris* (London: Allen Lane, 1998).
Kershaw, I., *Hitler 1936–1945: Nemesis* (London: Allen Lane, 2000).

Kiesewetter, H., *Industrielle Revolution in Deutschland 1815–1914* (Frankfurt: Suhrkamp, 1989).

Kiesewetter, H., *Region und Industrie in Europa 1815–1995* (Stuttgart: Steiner, 2000).

Kift, D., ed., *Kirmes – Kneipe – Kino. Arbeiterkultur im Ruhrgebiet zwischen Kommerz und Kontrolle, 1850–1914* (Paderborn: Schöningh, 1992).

Knoch, P., ed., *Kriegsalltag: Die Rekonstruktion des Kriegsalltags als Aufgabe der historischen Forschung und der Friedenserziehung* (Stuttgart: Metzler, 1989).

Knoll, A. and Gann, L. H., eds., *Germans in the Tropics: Essays in German Colonial History* (New York: Greenwood, 1987).

Koch, H. W., ed., *The Origins of the First World War. Great Power Rivalry and German War Aims* (London: Macmillan, 1972).

Koch, H. W., *A Constitutional History of Germany in the Nineteenth and Twentieth Centuries* (London: Longman, 1984).

Kocka, J., *Unternehmensverwaltung und Angestelltenschaft am Beispiel Siemens 1847–1914* (Stuttgart: Klett, 1969).

Kocka, J., *Sozialgeschichte: Begriff, Entwicklung, Probleme* (Göttingen: Vandenhoeck und Ruprecht, 1977).

Kocka, J., "Der 'deutsche Sonderweg' in der Diskussion," *German Studies Review*, 5 (1982).

Kocka, J., "Klassen oder Kultur," *Merkur*, 36 (1982).

Kocka, J., *Facing Total War: German Society 1914–1918* (Leamington Spa: Berg, 1984).

Kocka, J., "Zurück zur Erzählung? Plädoyer für historische Argumentation," *Geschichte und Gesellschaft*, 10 (1984).

Kocka, J., ed., *Bürger und Bürgerlichkeit im 19. Jahrhundert* (Göttingen: Vandenhoeck und Ruprecht, 1987).

Kocka, J., "German History before Hitler: The Debate about the German Sonderweg," *Journal of Contemporary History*, 23 (1988).

Kocka, J., *Geschichte und Aufklärung* (Göttingen: Vandenhoeck und Ruprecht, 1989).

Kocka, J., "Nach dem Ende des Sonderwegs: Zur Tragfähigkeit eines Konzeptes," in A. Bauernkämper et al., eds, *Doppelte Zeitgeschichte* (Berlin and Bonn: Dietz, 1998).

Kocka, J., *Industrial Culture and Bourgeois Society: Business, Labor, and Bureaucracy in Modern Germany* (New York and Oxford: Berghahn, 1999).

Kohlrausch, M., *Der Monarch im Skandal: Die Logik der Massenmedien und die Transformation der wilhelminischen Monarchie* (Berlin: Akademie, 2005).

Kohn, H., *The Mind of Germany* (New York: Scribners, 1960).

Kohut, T., *Wilhelm II and the Germans: A Study in Leadership* (Oxford and New York: Oxford University Press, 1991).

Koshar, R., "Against the 'frightful leveler': Historic preservation and German cities, 1890–1914," *Journal of Urban History*, 19 (1993).

Koshar, R., "The *Kaiserreich*'s ruins: Hope, memory, and political culture in imperial Germany," in G. Eley, ed., *Society, Culture and the State in Germany* (Ann Arbor: University of Michigan Press, 1996).

Koshar, R., *Germany's Transient Pasts: Preservation and National Memory in the Twentieth Century* (Chapel Hill and London: University of North Carolina Press, 1998).
Koshar, R., *German Travel Cultures* (Oxford: Berg, 2000).
Koshar, R., *From Monuments to Traces: Artifacts of German Memory, 1870–1990* (Berkeley: University of California Press, 2001).
Koshar, R., "Where does German memory lie?," *Central European History*, 36 (2003).
Kracht, K. G., "Fritz Fischer und der deutsche Protestantismus," *Zeitschrift für neuere Theologiegeschichte*, 10 (2003).
Kreuzer, M., *Institutions and Innovation: Voters, Parties, and Interest Groups in the Consolidation of Democracy – France and Germany, 1870–1939* (Ann Arbor: University of Michigan Press, 2001).
Kreuzer, M., "Parliamentarization and the question of German exceptionalism: 1867–1918," *Central European History*, 36 (2003).
Krieger, L., *The German Idea of Freedom: History of a Political Tradition* (Chicago: University of Chicago Press, 1957).
Krill, H.-H., *Die Ranke-Renaissance. Max Lenz und Erich Marcks* (Berlin: de Gruyter, 1962).
Krüger, G., *Kriegsbewältigung und Geschichtsbewusstsein. Realität, Deutung und Verarbeitung des deutschen Kolonialkriegs in Namibia 1904–07* (Göttingen: Vandenhoeck und Ruprecht, 1999).
Krüger, M., *Körperkultur und Nationsbildung: Geschichte des Turnens in der Reichsgründungsära* (Schorndorf: Hofmann, 1996).
Kruse, W., *Krieg und nationale Integration. Eine Neuinterpretation des sozialdemokratischen Burgfriedensschlusses 1914/15* (Essen: Klartext, 1993).
Kuczynski, J., *Geschichte des Alltags des deutschen Volkes*, 5 vols. (East Berlin: Akademie, 1980).
Kühne, T., "Wahlrecht – Wahlverhalten – Wahlkultur. Tradition und Innovation in der historischen Wahlforschung," *Archiv für Sozialgeschichte*, 33 (1993).
Kühne, T., *Dreiklassenwahlrecht und Wahlkultur in Preußen 1867–1914. Landtagswahlen zwischen korporativer Tradition und politischem Massenmarkt* (Düsseldorf: Droste, 1994).
Kühne, T., ed., *Männergeschichte – Geschlechtergeschichte: Männlichkeit im Wandel der Moderne* (Frankfurt and New York: Campus, 1996).
Kühne, T., "Das Deutsche Kaiserreich 1871–1918 und seine politische Kultur. Demokratisierung, Segmentierung, Militarisierung," *Neue Politische Literatur*, 43 (1998).
Kühne, T., "Parlamentarismusgeschichte in Deutschland: Probleme, Erträge und Perspektiven einer Gesamtdarstellung," *Geschichte und Gesellschaft*, 24 (1998).
Kühnl, R., *Deutschland seit der Französischen Revolution. Untersuchungen zum deutschen Sonderweg* (Heilbronn: Distel, 1996).
Kundrus, B., *Moderne Imperialisten: Das Kaiserreich im Spiegel seiner Kolonien* (Cologne: Böhlau, 2003).
Kundrus, B., ed., *Phantasiereiche: Zur Kulturgeschichte des deutschen Kolonialismus* (Frankfurt and New York: Campus, 2003).

Laak, D. van, *Über alles in der Welt. Deutscher Imperialismus im 19. und 20. Jahrhundert* (Munich: Beck, 2005).

Ladd, B., *Urban Planning and Civic Order in Germany, 1860–1914* (Cambridge, MA and London: Harvard University Press, 1990).

Ladd, B., *The Ghosts of Berlin: Confronting German History in the Urban Landscape* (Chicago: University of Chicago Press, 1997).

Langdon, J., *July 1914. The Long Debate, 1918–1990* (Oxford: Berg, 1991).

Langewiesche, D., "Das Deutsche Kaiserreich – Bemerkungen zur Diskussion über Parlamentarisierung und Demokratisierung Deutschlands," *Archiv für Sozialgeschichte*, 19 (1979–80).

Langewiesche, D., ed., *Das deutsche Kaiserreich 1867/71 bis 1918. Bilanz einer Epoche* (Freiburg: Ploetz, 1984).

Langewiesche, D., *Liberalism in Germany* (London: Macmillan, 2000).

Langewiesche, D. and Schönhoven, K., *Arbeiter in Deutschland. Studien zur Lebensweise der Arbeiterschaft im Zeitalter der Industrialisierung* (Paderborn: Schöningh, 1981).

Ledford, K., "Comparing comparisons: Disciplines and the *Sonderweg*," *Central European History*, 36 (2003).

Lees, A., *Cities, Sin, and Social Reform in Imperial Germany* (Ann Arbor: University of Michigan Press, 2002).

Lehmann, H., ed., *Historikerkontroversen* (Göttingen: Wallstein, 2000).

Lekan, T., *Imagining the Nation in Nature. Landscape Preservation and German Identity 1885–1945* (Cambridge, MA and London: Harvard University Press, 2004).

Lenger, F., *Werner Sombart, 1863–1941: Eine Biographie* (Munich: Beck, 1994).

Lenz, M., *Geschichte Bismarcks* (Leipzig: Duncker und Humblot, 1902).

Lepsius, M. Rainer, "Parteiensystem und Sozialstruktur. Zum Problem der Demokratisierung der deutschen Gesellschaft," reprinted in G. A. Ritter, ed., *Die deutschen Parteien vor 1918* (Cologne: NWB, 1973).

Lerman, K. A., *The Chancellor as Courtier: Bernhard von Bülow and the Governance of Germany, 1900–09* (Cambridge: Cambridge University Press, 1990).

Lerman, K. A., *Bismarck* (London: Longman, 2004).

Lewy, R. S., *The Downfall of the Anti-Semitic Political Parties in Imperial Germany* (New Haven and London: Yale University Press, 1975).

Lidtke, V., *The Alternative Culture: Socialist Labor in Imperial Germany* (New York and Oxford: Oxford University Press, 1985).

Lidtke, V., *The Outlawed Party: Social Democracy 1878–1890* (Princeton: Princeton University Press, 1966).

Lindenberger, T., *Straßenpolitik: Zur Sozialgeschichte der öffentlichen Ordnung. Berlin, 1900–1914* (Berlin and Bonn: Dietz, 1995).

Linton, D. S., "Between school and marriage: Young working women as a social problem in late imperial Germany," *European History Quarterly*, 18 (1988).

Lorenz, C., "Beyond good and evil? The German empire of 1871 and modern German historiography," *Journal of Contemporary History*, 30 (1995).

Lorenz, M., *Leibhaftige Vergangenheit. Einführung in die Körpergeschichte* (Tübingen: edition diskord, 2000).

Loth, W., *Katholiken im Kaiserreich. Der politische Katholizismus in der Krise des wilhelminischen Deutschlands* (Düsseldorf: Droste, 1984).
Loth, W., *Das Kaiserreich. Obrigkeitsstaat und politische Mobilisierung* (Munich: DTV, 1996).
Lowe, J., The *Great Powers, Imperialism and the German Problem, 1860–1925* (London and New York: Routledge, 1994).
Lüdtke, A., " 'Coming to terms with the past': Illusions of remembering, ways of forgetting Nazism in West Germany," *Journal of Modern History*, 65 (1993).
Lüdtke, A., *Eigen-Sinn. Fabrikalltag, Arbeitererfahrungen und Politik vom Kaiserreich bis in den Faschismus* (Hamburg: Ergebnisse, 1993).
Lüdtke, A., ed., *The History of Everyday Life* (Princeton: Princeton University Press, 1995).
Ludwig, E., *Wilhelm der Zweite* (Berlin: Rowohlt, 1925).
MacDonogh, G., *The Last Kaiser. William the Impetuous* (London: Weidenfeld, 2000).
McAleer, K., *Dueling. The Cult of Honor in Fin-de-Siècle Germany* (Princeton: Princeton University Press, 1994).
McElligott, A., "The German history workshop festival in Berlin," *German History*, 2 (1985).
Mann, G., *Deutsche Geschichte des 19. und 20. Jahrhunderts* (Frankfurt: Fischer, 1966).
Marcks, E., *Bismarck* (Stuttgart and Berlin: Cotta, 1909).
Marcks, E., *Otto von Bismarck. Ein Lebensbild* (Stuttgart and Berlin: Cotta, 1915).
Martel, G., ed., *The Origins of the First World War* (London: Longman, 1987).
Martel, G., ed., *Modern Germany Reconsidered 1870–1945* (London: Routledge, 1992).
Mauch, C., ed., *Nature in German History* (Oxford and New York: Berghahn, 2004).
Maynes, M. J., *Taking the Hard Road: Life Courses in French and German Workers' Autobiographies in the Era of Industrialization* (Chapel Hill and London: University of North Carolina Press, 1995).
Medick, H., "Missionäre im Ruderboot," *Geschichte und Gesellschaft*, 10 (1984).
Medick, H., "Wer sind die 'Missionäre im Ruderboot'? Oder: Kulturanthropologie und Alltagsgeschichte," in U. Becher and K. Bergmann, eds., *Geschichte – Nutzen oder Nachteil für das Leben?* (Düsseldorf: Patmos, 1986).
Medick, H., *Weben und Überleben in Laichingen, 1650–1900. Lokalgeschichte als Allgemeine Geschichte* (Göttingen: Vandenhoeck und Ruprecht, 2001).
Medick, H. and Trepp, A.-C., eds., *Geschlechtergeschichte und Allgemeine Geschichte. Herausforderungen und Perspektiven* (Göttingen: Wallstein, 1998).
Meinecke, F., *The German Catastrophe. Reflections and Recollections* (Cambridge, MA and London: Harvard University Press, 1950).
Meinecke, F., *Cosmopolitanism and the National State* (Princeton: Princeton University Press, 1970).
Mergel, T. and Welskopp, T., eds., *Geschichte zwischen Kultur und Gesellschaft: Beiträge zur Theoriedebatte* (Munich: Beck, 1997).
Meyer, A. O., *Bismarck: Der Mensch und der Staatsmann* (Stuttgart: Koehler, 1949).

Meyer-Renschhausen, E., *Weibliche Kultur und soziale Arbeit. Eine Geschichte der Frauenbewegung am Beispiel Bremens 1810–1927* (Cologne: Böhlau, 1989).

Mielke, S., *Der Hansa-Bund für Gewerbe, Handel und Industrie 1909–1914* (Göttingen: Vandenhoeck und Ruprecht, 1976).

Miller, S. and Potthoff, H., *A History of German Social Democracy: From 1848 to the Present* (Leamington Spa: Berg, 1986).

Mitchell, A., "Bonapartism as a model for Bismarckian politics," *Journal of Modern History*, 49 (1977).

Moeller, R., "The Kaiserreich recast? Continuity and change in modern German historiography," *Journal of Social History*, 17 (1984).

Mombauer, A., *Helmuth von Moltke and the Origins of the First World War* (Cambridge: Cambridge University Press, 2001).

Mombauer, A., *The Origins of the First World War: Controversies and Consensus* (London: Longman, 2002).

Mombauer, A. and Deist, W., eds., *The Kaiser. New Research on Wilhelm II's Role in Imperial Germany* (Cambridge: Cambridge University Press, 2003).

Mommsen, W. J., "Domestic factors in German foreign policy before 1914," in J. J. Sheehan, ed., *Imperial Germany* (New York and London: New Viewpoints, 1976).

Mommsen, W. J., "Kaiser Wilhelm II and German politics," *Journal of Contemporary History*, 25 (1990).

Mommsen, W. J., *Das Ringen um den nationalen Staat: Die Gründung und der innere Ausbau des Deutschen Reiches unter Otto von Bismarck 1850 bis 1890* (Berlin: Propyläen, 1993).

Mommsen, W. J., *Bürgerstolz und Weltmachtstreben: Deutschland unter Wilhelm II 1890–1918* (Berlin: Propyläen, 1995).

Mommsen, W. J., *Imperial Germany 1867–1918: Politics, Culture and Society in an Authoritarian State* (London: Arnold, 1995).

Mommsen, W. J., ed., *Kultur und Krieg: Die Rolle der Intellektuellen, Künstler und Schriftsteller im Ersten Weltkrieg* (Munich: Oldenbourg, 1996).

Mommsen, W. J., *War der Kaiser an allem schuld? Wilhelm II. und die preußisch-deutschen Machteliten* (Berlin: Propyläen, 2002).

Mommsen, W. J., *Der erste Weltkrieg. Anfang vom Ende des bürgerlichen Zeitalters* (Frankfurt: Fischer, 2004).

Moses, J. A., *The Politics of Illusion. The Fischer Controversy in German Historiography* (London: Harper and Row, 1975).

Mosse, G. L., *The Crisis of German Ideology. Intellectual Origins of the Third Reich* (New York: Grosset and Dunlap, 1964).

Mosse, G. L., *The Nationalization of the Masses* (New York: Fertig, 1975).

Mosse, G. L., *Nationalism and Sexuality: Respectability and Abnormal Sexuality in Modern Europe* (New York: Fertig, 1985).

Mosse, W. E., *The European Powers and the German Question 1848–1871* (Cambridge: Cambridge University Press, 1958).

Müller, S. O., *Die Nation als Waffe und Vorstellung: Nationalismus in Deutschland und Großbritannien im Ersten Weltkrieg* (Göttingen: Vandenhoeck und Ruprecht, 2002).

Müller-Dreier, A., *Konfession in Politik, Gesellschaft und Kultur des Kaiserreichs. Der Evangelischer Bund, 1886–1914* (Paderborn: Schöningh, 1998).

Münkel, D. and Schwarzkopf, J., eds., *Geschichte als Experiment. Studien zu Politik, Kultur und Alltag im 19. und 20. Jahrhundert. Festschrift für Adelheid von Saldern* (Frankfurt and New York: Campus, 2004).

Muthesius, S., "The origins of the German conservation movement," in R. Kain, ed., *Planning for Conservation* (London: Mansell, 1981).

Na'aman, S., *Der deutsche Nationalverein. Die politische Konstituierung des deutschen Bürgertums 1859–1867* (Düsseldorf: Droste, 1987).

Nathans, E., *The Politics of Citizenship in Germany. Ethnicity, Utility and Nationalism* (Oxford: Berg, 2004).

Neitzel, S., *Weltmacht oder Niedergang. Die Weltreichslehre im Zeitalter des Imperialismus* (Paderborn: Schöningh, 2000).

Neitzel, S., *Kriegsausbruch. Deutschlands Weg in die Katastrophe 1900–14* (Munich: Pendo, 2002).

Neitzel, S., *Blut und Eisen. Deutschland im Ersten Weltkrieg* (Munich: Pendo, 2003).

Niethammer, L., et al., eds, *Die Menschen machen ihre Geschichte nicht aus freien Stücken, aber sie machen sie selbst. Einladung zu einer Geschichte des Volkes in NRW* (Berlin and Bonn: Dietz, 1984).

Nietzsche, F., *The Joyful Wisdom*, (New York: Gordon, 1974).

Nipperdey, T., *Die Organisation der deutschen Parteien vor 1918* (Düsseldorf: Droste, 1961).

Nipperdey, T., "Wehlers 'Kaiserreich.' Eine kritische Auseinandersetzung," in *Gesellschaft, Kultur, Theorie* (Göttingen: Vandenhoeck und Ruprecht, 1976).

Nipperdey, T., "1933 und die Kontinuität der deutschen Geschichte," *Historische Zeitschrift*, 227 (1978).

Nipperdey, T., *Religion im Umbruch: Deutschland 1870–1918* (Munich: Beck, 1988).

Nipperdey, T. *Deutsche Geschichte, 1866–1918*, vol. 1 *Arbeitswelt und Bürgergeist* (Munich: Beck, 1990).

Nipperdey, T. *Deutsche Geschichte, 1866–1918*, vol. 2 *Machtstaat vor der Demokratie* (Munich: Beck, 1992).

Nolan, M., *Social Democracy and Society: Working-Class Radicalism in Düsseldorf, 1890–1920* (Cambridge: Cambridge University Press, 1981).

Nonn, C., *Verbraucherprotest und Parteiensystem im wilhelminischen Deutschland* (Düsseldorf: Droste, 1996).

Nonn, C., *Eine Stadt sucht einen Mörder. Gerücht, Gewalt und Antisemitismus im Kaiserreich* (Göttingen: Vandenhoeck und Ruprecht, 2002).

Nordalm, J., *Historismus und moderne Welt. Erich Marcks (1861–1938) in der deutschen Geschichtswissenschaft* (Berlin: Duncker und Humblot, 2003).

Noyes, J., *Colonial Space: Spatiality in the Discourse of German South West Africa, 1884–1915* (Philadelphia: Harwood, 1992).

Oberkrome, W., *Volksgeschichte. Methodische Innovation und völkische Ideologisierung in der deutschen Geschichtswissenschaft 1918–1945* (Göttingen: Vandenhoeck und Ruprecht, 1993).

Osterhammel, J., "Transkulturell vergleichende Geschichtswisssenschaft," in H.-G. Haupt and J. Kocka, eds., *Geschichte und Vergleich* (Frankfurt and New York: Campus, 1996).

Osterhammel, J., *Geschichtswissenschaft jenseits des Nationalstaats. Studien zu Beziehungsgeschichte und Zivilisationsvergleich* (Göttingen: Vandenhoeck und Ruprecht, 2001).

Osterhammel, J. and Petersson, N., *Globalizaton: A Short History* (Princeton: Princeton University Press, 2005).

Paletschek, S., *Frauen und Dissens: Frauen im Deutschkatholizismus und in den freien Gemeinden, 1841–52* (Göttingen: Vandenhoeck und Ruprecht, 1989).

Palmer, A., *Bismarck* (London: Weidenfeld and Nicholson, 1976).

Palmer, A., *The Kaiser. Warlord of the Second Reich* (London: Weidenfeld and Nicholson, 1978).

Paulmann, J., *Pomp und Politik. Monarchenbegegnungen in Europa zwischen Ancien Regime und Erstem Weltkrieg* (Paderborn: Schoeningh, 2000).

Penny, H. G., *Objects of Culture: Ethnology and Ethnographic Museums in Imperial Germany* (Chapel Hill and London: University of North Carolina Press, 2001).

Perras, A., *Carl Peters and German Imperialism 1856–1918. A Political Biography* (Oxford: Clarendon, 2004).

Pflanze, O., "Bismarck and German nationalism," *American Historical Review*, 60 (1955).

Pflanze, O., "Bismarck's Realpolitik," *Review of Politics*, 20 (1958).

Pflanze, O., *Bismarck and the Development of Germany*. vols. 1–3 (Princeton, NJ: Princeton University Press, 1963, 2nd edn. 1990) vol. 1 *The Period of Unification, 1815–71*; vol. 2 *The Period of Consolidation, 1871–1880*; vol. 3 *The Period of Fortification, 1880–1890*.

Pflanze, O., "'Sammlungspolitik' 1875–1886. Kritische Bemerkungen zu einem Modell," in *Innenpolitische Probleme des Bismarck-Reiches* (Munich: Oldenbourg, 1983).

Planert, U., *Antifeminismus im Kaiserreich: Diskurs, soziale Formation und politische Mentalität* (Göttingen: Vandenhoeck und Ruprecht, 1988).

Planert, U., ed., *Nation, Politik, Geschlecht. Frauenbewegungen und Nationalismus in der Moderne* (Frankfurt and New York: Campus, 2000).

Plessner, H., *Die verspätete Nation. Über die politische Verführbarkeit bürgerlichen Geistes* (Stuttgart: Kohlhammer, 1959).

Pogge von Strandmann, H., "Staatsstreichpläne, Alldeutsche und Bethmann Hollweg," in I. Geiss and H. Pogge von Strandmann, eds., *Die Erforderlichkeit des Unmöglichen* (Frankfurt: EVA, 1965).

Pogge von Strandmann, H., "Domestic origins of Germany's colonial expansion under Bismarck," *Past and Present*, 42 (1969).

Pohl, K. H., ed., *Historiker in der DDR* (Göttingen: Vandenhoeck und Ruprecht, 1997).

Poiger, U., "Imperialism and empire in twentieth-century Germany," *History and Memory*, 17 (2005).

Porter, I. and Armour, I. D., *Imperial Germany 1890–1918* (Harlow: Pearson Education, 1991).

Puhle, H.-J., *Agrarische Interessenpolitik und preußischer Konservatismus im Wilhelminischen Reich* (Hanover: Verlag für Literatur und Zeitgeschehen, 1967).

Puhle, H.-J., "Zur Legende von der 'Kehrschen Schule,'" *Geschichte und Gesellschaft*, 4 (1978).

Puhle, H.-J., "Deutscher Sonderweg. Kontroverse um eine vermeintliche Legende," *Journal für Geschichte*, 3 (1981).

Quataert, J., *Reluctant Feminists in German Social Democracy, 1885–1917* (Princeton: Princeton University Press, 1979).

Quataert, J., "The politics of rural industrialization: Class, gender, and collective protest in the Saxon Oberlausitz of the late nineteenth century," *Central European History*, 20 (1987).

Quataert, J., *Staging Philanthropy: Patriotic Women and the National Imagination in Dynastic Germany, 1813–1916* (Ann Arbor: University of Michigan Press, 2001).

Radkau, J., *Das Zeitalter der Nervosität. Deutschland zwischen Bismarck und Hitler* (Munich: Hanser, 1998).

Radkau, J., *Max Weber* (Munich: Hanser, 2005).

Rahden, T. van, *Juden und andere Breslauer: Die Beziehungen zwischen Juden, Protestanten und Katholiken in einer deutschen Großstadt von 1860 bis 1925* (Göttingen: Vandenhoeck und Ruprecht, 2000).

Rauh, M., *Föderalismus und Parlamentarismus im Wilhelminischen Reich* (Düsseldorf: Droste, 1973).

Rauh, M., *Die Parlamentarisierung des Deutschen Reiches* (Düsseldorf: Droste, 1977).

Reagin, N. R., *A German Women's Movement: Class and Gender in Hanover, 1880–1933* (Chapel Hill and London: University of North Carolina Press, 1995).

Reagin, N. R., "The imagined Hausfrau: National identity, domesticity, and colonialism in imperial Germany," *Journal of Modern History*, 73 (2001).

Rebentisch, J., *Die vielen Gesichter des Kaisers. Wilhelm II in der deutschen und britischen Karikatur, 1888–1918* (Berlin: Duncker und Humblot, 2000).

Reddy, W., *Money and Liberty in Modern Europe: A Critique of Historical Understanding* (Cambridge: Cambridge University Press, 1987).

Reinermann, L., *Der Kaiser in England. Wilhelm II. und sein Bild in der britischen Öffentlichkeit* (Paderborn: Schöningh, 2001).

Retallack, J., "Social history with a vengeance? Some reactions to H.-U. Wehler's 'Das Deutsche Kaiserreich,'" *German Studies Review*, 7 (1984).

Retallack, J., *Notables of the Right: The Conservative Party and Political Mobilization in Germany, 1876–1918* (Boston and London: Routledge, 1988).

Retallack, J., "'What is to be done?' The red specter, franchise questions, and the crisis of German hegemony in Saxony, 1896–1909," *Central European History*, 23 (1990).

Retallack, J., "Wilhelmine Germany," in G. Martel, ed., *Modern Germany Reconsidered* (London: Routledge, 1992).

Retallack, J., *Germany in the Age of Kaiser Wilhelm II* (Basingstoke: Macmillan, 1996).

Retallack, J., *The German Right 1860–1920. Political Limits of the Authoritarian Imagination* (Toronto: University of Toronto Press, 2006).

Reulecke, J. and Weber, W., eds, *Fabrik, Familie, Feierabend. Beiträge zur Geschichte des Alltags im Industriezeitalter* (Wuppertal: Hammer, 1978).

Ritter, G., "Eine neue Kriegsschuldthese? Zu Fritz Fischers Buch 'Griff nach der Weltmacht,'" *Historische Zeitschrift*, 194 (1962).

Ritter, G., *The Sword and the Sceptre. The Problem of Militarism in Germany*, 4 volumes, (Miami: University of Miami Press, 1969–73).

Ritter, G. A., ed., *Gesellschaft, Parlament und Regierung: Zur Geschiche des Parlamentarismus in Deutschland* (Düsseldorf: Droste, 1974).

Ritter, G. A., "Workers' culture in imperial Germany: Problems and points of departure for research," *Journal of Contemporary History*, 13 (1978).

Ritter, G. A., *Die deutschen Parteien 1830–1914. Parteien und Gesellschaft im konstitutionellen Regierungssystem* (Göttingen: Vandenhoeck und Ruprecht, 1985).

Ritter, G. A., *The New Social History in the Federal Republic of Germany* (London: German Historical Institute, 1991).

Ritter, G. A. and Tenfelde, K., *Arbeiter im Deutschen Kaiserreich: 1871 bis 1914* (Bonn: Dietz, 1992).

Rohe, K., *Vom Revier zum Ruhrgebiet. Wahlen, Parteien, Politische Kultur* (Essen: Hobbing, 1986).

Rohe, K., *Wähler und Wählertraditionen in Deutschland. Kulturelle Grundlagen deutscher Parteien und Parteien Systeme im 19. und 20. Jahrhundert* (Frankfurt: Suhrkamp, 1992).

Röhl, J. C. G., *Germany without Bismarck: The Crisis of Government in the Second Reich* (Cambridge: Cambridge University Press, 1967).

Röhl, J. C. G., "Admiral von Müller and the approach of war, 1911–1914," *Historical Journal*, 12 (1969).

Röhl, J. C. G., ed., *Der Ort Kaiser Wilhelms II. in der deutschen Geschichte* (Munich: Oldenbourg, 1991).

Röhl, J. C. G., *The Kaiser and his Court. Wilhelm II and the Government of Germany* (Cambridge: Cambridge University Press, 1994).

Röhl, J. C. G., "Germany," in K. Wilson, ed., *Decisions for War, 1914* (London: UCL Press, 1995).

Röhl, J. C. G., *Young Wilhelm. The Kaiser's Early Life 1859–1888* (Cambridge: Cambridge University Press, 1998).

Röhl, J. C. G., *Wilhelm II. The Kaiser's Personal Monarchy 1888–1900* (Cambridge: Cambridge University Press, 2004).

Röhl, J. C. G. and Sombart, N., eds., *Kaiser Wilhelm II – New Interpretations* (Cambridge: Cambridge University Press, 1982).

Rosenberg, H., *Bureaucracy, Aristocracy and Autocracy: The Prussian Experience 1660–1815* (Cambridge, MA: Harvard University Press, 1958).

Rosenberg, H., *Große Depression und Bismarckzeit. Wirtschaftsablauf, Politik und Gesellschaft in Mitteleuropa* (Berlin: de Gruyter, 1967).

Rosenhaft, E., "History, anthropology, and the study of everyday life," *Comparative Studies in Society and History*, 29 (1987).

Rosenhaft, E., "Women, gender, and the limits of political history," in L. E. Jones and J. Retallack, eds., *Elections, Mass Politics and Social Change in Modern Germany* (Cambridge: Cambridge University Press, 1992).

Ross, C., *Naked Germany: Health, Race and the Nation* (Oxford: Berg, 2005).
Ross, R. J., *Beleaguered Tower: The Dilemma of Political Catholicism in Wilhelmine Germany* (South Bend: University of Notre Dame Press, 1975).
Ross, R. J., *The Failure of Bismarck's Kulturkampf* (Washington, DC: Catholic University of America Press, 1998).
Roth, G., *The Social Democrats in Imperial Germany. A Study in Working-Class Isolation and National Integration* (Totowa, NJ: Badminster, 1963).
Rowe, D., *Representing Berlin: Sexuality and the City in Imperial and Weimar Germany* (Aldershot: Ashgate, 2003).
Sabrow, M., Jessen, R., and Grosse Kracht, K., eds., *Zeitgeschichte als Streitgeschichte. Große Kontroversen seit 1945* (Munich: Beck, 2003).
Sachße, C., *Mütterlichkeit als Beruf: Sozialarbeit, Sozialreform und Frauenbewegung, 1871–1929* (Frankfurt: Suhrkamp, 1986).
Saldern, A. von, *Auf dem Wege zum Arbeiter-Reformismus. Parteialltag im sozialdemokratischer Göttingen, 1870–1920* (Frankfurt: Materialis, 1984).
Saldern, A. von, *Häuserleben: Zur Geschichte städtischen Arbeiterwohnens vom Kaiserreich bis heute* (Bonn: Dietz, 1995).
Saldern, A. von, *The Challenge of Modernity: German Social and Cultural Studies, 1890–1960* (Ann Arbor: University of Michigan Press, 2002).
Samerski, S., ed., *Wilhelm II. und die Religion. Facetten einer Persönlichkeit und ihres Umfelds* (Berlin: Duncker und Humblot, 2001).
Schenk, F. B., "Mental maps. Die Konstruktion von geographischen Räumen in Europa seit der Aufklärung," *Geschichte und Gesellschaft*, 28 (2002).
Schestokat, K., *German Women in Cameroon: Travelogues from Colonial Times* (New York and Frankfurt: Lang, 2003).
Schieder, T., *Das Deutsche Kaiserreich von 1871 als Nationalstaat* (Cologne and Opladen: Westdeutscher, 1961; 2nd edn. Göttingen: Vandenhoeck und Ruprecht, 1992).
Schilling, R.,*"Kriegshelden": Deutungsmuster heroischer Männlichkeit in Deutschland 1813–1945* (Paderborn: Schöningh, 2002).
Schmädeke, J., *Wählerbewegung im Wilhelminischen Deutschland. Eine historisch-statistische Untersuchung zu den Reichstagswahlen von 1890 bis 1912*, 2 volumes, (Berlin: Akademie, 1994–5).
Schmidt, A., *Reisen in die Moderne: Der Amerika-Diskurs des deutschen Bürgertums vor dem Ersten Weltkrieg im europäischen Vergleich* (Berlin: Akademie, 1997).
Schmidt, G., "Parlamentarisierung oder 'Präventive Konterrevolution?,'" in G. A. Ritter, ed., *Gesellschaft, Parlament und Regierung. Zur Geschichte des Parlamentarismus in Deutschland* (Düsseldorf: Droste, 1974).
Schmitt, H. A., "Bismarck as seen from the nearest church steeple: A comment on Michael Stürmer," *Central European History*, 11 (1973).
Schmitt, S., *Der Arbeiterinnenschutz im Deutschen Kaiserreich: zur Konstruktion der schutzbedürftigen Arbeiterin* (Stuttgart: Metzler, 1995).
Schmoll, F., *Erinnerung an die Natur. Die Geschichte des Naturschutzes im deutschen Kaiserreich* (Frankfurt and New York: Campus, 2004).
Schoenbaum, D., *Zabern 1913: Consensus Politics in Imperial Germany* (London: Allen and Unwin, 1982).

Schöllgen, G., *Imperialismus und Gleichgewicht: Deutschland, England und die orientalische Frage 1871–1914* (Munich: Oldenbourg, 1984).

Schöllgen, G., "Griff nach der Weltmacht? 25 Jahre Fischer-Kontroverse," *Historisches Jahrbuch* 106 (1986).

Schöllgen, G., ed., *Escape into War? The Foreign Policy of Imperial Germany* (Oxford: Berg, 1990).

Schöllgen, G., *Die Macht in der Mitte Europas. Stationen deutscher Außenpolitik von Friedrich dem Großen bis zur Gegenwart* (Munich: Beck, 1992).

Schöllgen, G., "Kriegsgefahr und Krisenmanagement vor 1914: Zur Außenpolitik des kaiserlichen Deutschlands," *Historische Zeitschrift*, 267 (1998).

Schönberger, C., "Die überholte Parlamentarisierung. Einflußgewinn und fehlende Herrschaftsfähigkeit des Reichstags im sich demokratisierenden Kaiserreich," *Historische Zeitschrift*, 272 (2001).

Schöttler, P., ed., *Geschichtsschreibung als Legitimationswissenschaft 1918–45* (Frankfurt: Suhrkamp, 1997).

Schridde, R., *Zum Bismarckbild im Geschichtsunterricht* (Ratingen: Henn, 1974).

Schulte, B. F., *Weltmacht durch die Hintertür. Deutsche Nationalgeschichte in der Dikussion*, 2 vols. (Hamburg: BoD, 2003).

Schulze, H., ed., *Nation-Building in Central Europe* (Leamington Spa: Berg, 1987).

Schulze, W., *Deutsche Geschichtswissenschaft nach 1945* (Munich: DTV, 1993).

Schulze, W., ed., *Sozialgeschichte, Alltagsgeschichte, Mikro-Historie* (Göttingen: Vandenhoeck und Ruprecht, 1994).

Schwartz, F., *The Werkbund. Design Theory and Mass Culture before the First World War* (New Haven and London: Yale University Press, 1996).

Scott, J. W., "Gender: A useful category of historical analysis," *The American Historical Review*, 91 (1986).

Seligmann, M. S., *Rivalry in Southern Africa: The Transformation of German Colonial Policy* (Basingstoke: Palgrave Macmillan, 1998).

Seligmann, M. S. and McLean, R., *Germany from Reich to Republic 1871–1918* (Basingstoke: Palgrave Macmillan, 2000).

Sheehan, J. J., ed., *Imperial Germany* (New York and London: New Viewpoints, 1976).

Sheehan, J. J., *German Liberalism in the Nineteenth Century* (Chicago: University of Chicago Press, 1978).

Sheehan, J. J., "What is German history? Reflections on the role of the nation in German history and historiography," *Journal of Modern History*, 53 (1981).

Sheehan, J. J., *German History 1770–1866* (Oxford: Oxford University Press, 1989).

Sheehan, J. J., *Museums in the German Art World. From the End of the Old Regime to the Rise of Modernism* (Oxford: Oxford University Press, 2000).

Showalter, D., *Railroads and Rifles: Soldiers, Technology and the Unification of Germany* (Hamden, CT: Shoe String, 1986).

Siegrist, H., Kaelble, H., and Kocka, J., eds., *Europäische Konsumgeschichte: Zur Gesellschafts- und Kulturgeschichte des Konsums* (Frankfurt and New York: Campus, 1997).

Smith, H. W., *German Nationalism and Religious Conflict: Culture, Ideology and Politics, 1870–1914* (Princeton: Princeton University Press, 1995).
Smith, H. W. ed., *Protestants, Catholics, and Jews in Germany, 1800–1914* (Oxford: Berg, 2001).
Smith, H. W., *The Butcher's Tale: Murder and Anti-Semitism in a German Town* (New York and London: Norton, 2002).
Smith, W., *The German Colonial Empire* (Chapel Hill and London: University of North Carolina Press, 1978).
Smith, W. and Turner, S., "Legislative behavior in the German Reichstag, 1898–1906," *Central European History*, 14 (1981).
Snyder, L. L., *The Blood and Iron Chancellor. A Documentary Biography of Otto von Bismarck* (Princeton: Van Nostrand, 1967).
Sombart, N., *Wilhelm II. Sündenbock und Herr der Mitte* (Berlin: Volk und Welt, 1996).
Southard, R., *Droysen and the Prussian School of History* (Lexington: University of Kentucky Press, 1995).
Spencer, E. G., *Management and Labor in Imperial Germany: Ruhr Industrialists as Employers 1896–1914* (New Brunswick: Rutgers University Press, 1984).
Spencer, E. G., *Police and the Social Order in German Cities. The Düsseldorf District, 1848–1914* (De Kalb: Northern Illinois University Press, 1992).
Spenkuch, H., *Das Preußische Herrenhaus. Adel und Bürgertum in der Ersten Kammer des Landtages 1854–1918* (Düsseldorf: Droste, 1998).
Spenkuch, H., "Vergleichsweise besonders? Politisches System und Strukturen Preußens als Kern des 'deutschen Sonderwegs,'" *Geschichte und Gesellschaft*, 29 (2003).
Sperber, J., *Popular Catholicism in Nineteenth Century Germany* (Princeton: Princeton University Press, 1984).
Sperber, J., "Master narratives of nineteenth-century German history," *Central European History*, 24 (1991).
Sperber, J., *The Kaiser's Voters: Electors and Elections in Imperial Germany* (New York and Cambridge: Cambridge University Press, 1997).
Sperber, J., "Comments on Marcus Kreuzer's article," *Central European History*, 36 (2003).
Stalmann, V., *Die Partei Bismarcks. Die Deutsche Reichs- und Freikonservative Partei 1866–1890* (Düsseldorf: Droste, 2000).
Steefel, L. D., *Bismarck, the Hohenzollern Candidacy and the Origins of the Franco-Prussian War of 1870* (Cambridge, MA: Harvard University Press, 1962).
Stegmann, D., *Die Erben Bismarcks. Parteien und Verbände in der Spätphase des Wilhelminischen Deutschlands* (Cologne: Kiepenheuer und Witsch, 1970).
Steinhoff, A. J., "Religion as urban culture: A view from Strasbourg, 1870–1914," *Journal of Urban History*, 30 (2004).
Steinle, J., "Hitler als 'Betriebsunfall in der Geschichte.' Eine historische Metapher und ihre Hintergründe," *Geschichte in Wissenschaft und Unterricht*, 45 (1994).
Stern, F., *The Politics of Cultural Despair. A Study in the Rise of the German Ideology* (Berkeley: University of California Press, 1961).

Stern, F., *Gold and Iron: Bismarck, Bleichröder and the Building of the German Empire* (New York: Knopf, 1977).
Stevenson, D., *Armaments and the Coming of War: Europe 1904–1914* (Oxford: Clarendon, 1996).
Stibbe, M., *German Anglophobia and the Great War, 1914–1918* (Cambridge: Cambridge University Press, 2001).
Stibbe, M., "Anti-feminism, nationalism, and the German right, 1914–20: A reappraisal," *German History*, 20 (2002).
Stibbe, M., "The Fischer controversy over German war aims in the First World War and its reception by East German historians, 1961–89," *Historical Journal*, 46 (2003).
Stoecker, H., ed., *German Imperialism in Africa: From the Beginnings until the Second World War* (London: Hurst, 1986).
Stöcker, M., *Augusterlebnis 1914 in Darmstadt. Legende und Wirklichkeit* (Darmstadt: Roether, 1994).
Stoehr, I., *Emanzipation zum Staat? Der Allgemeine Deutsche Frauenverein – Deutsche Staatsbürgerinnenverband, 1893–1933* (Pfaffenweiler: Centaurus, 1990).
Strachan, H., *The Outbreak of the First World War* (Oxford: Oxford University Press, 2004).
Stürmer, M., "Staatsstreichgedanken im Bismarckreich," *Historische Zeitschrift*, 209 (1969).
Stürmer, M., ed., *Das kaiserliche Deutschland. Politik und Gesellschaft 1871–1914* (Düsseldorf: Droste, 1970).
Stürmer, M., "Bismarck in Perspective," *Central European History*, 4 (1971).
Stürmer, M., *Regierung und Reichstag im Bismarckstaat, 1871–1880: Cäsarismus oder Parlamentarismus* (Düsseldorf: Droste, 1974).
Stürmer, M., *Die Grenzen der Macht: Begegnung der Deutschen mit ihrer Geschichte* (Berlin: Siedler, 1992).
Stürmer, M., *The German Empire 1871–1918* (London: Phoenix, 2000).
Suval, S., *Electoral Politics in Wilhelmine Germany* (Chapel Hill and London: University of North Carolina Press, 1985).
Sywottek, A., "Die Fischer-Kontroverse. Ein Beitrag zur Entwicklung historisch-politischen Bewußtseins in der Bundesrepublik," in I. Geiss and B. J. Wendt, eds, *Deutschland in der Weltpolitik des 19. und 20. Jahrhunderts. Fritz Fischer zum 65. Geburtstag* (Düsseldorf: Bertelsmann Universitätsverlag, 1973).
Taylor, A. J. P., *The Course of German History* (London: Methuen, 1961, first published 1945).
Taylor, A. J. P., *Bismarck. The Man and the Statesman* (Harmondsworth: Penguin, 1995, first published 1955).
Tenfelde, K., "Schwierigkeiten mit dem Alltag," *Geschichte und Gesellschaft*, 10 (1984).
Ther, P., "Beyond the nation. The relational basis of a comparative history of Germany and Europe," *Central European History*, 36 (2003).
Ther, P., "Imperial instead of national history: Positioning modern German history on the map of European empires," in A. Miller and A. J. Rieber, eds., *Imperial Rule* (New York and Budapest: Central European University Press, 2004).

Theweleit, K., *Male Fantasies*, 2 volumes, (Cambridge: Polity, 1987–9).
Thompson, A., *Left Liberals, the State, and Popular Politics in Wilhelmine Germany* (Oxford: Oxford University Press, 2000).
Tipton, F. B., *Regional Variations in the Economic Development of Germany during the 19th Century* (Middletown: Wesleyan University Press, 1976).
Tipton, F. B., *A History of Modern Germany since 1815* (Berkeley: University of California Press, 2003).
Ullmann, H.-P., *Der Bund der Industriellen* (Göttingen: Vandenhoeck und Ruprecht, 1976).
Ullmann, H.-P., *Das deutsche Kaiserreich 1871–1918* (Frankfurt: Suhrkamp, 1995).
Ullrich, V., *Kriegsalltag. Hamburg im ersten Weltkrieg* (Cologne: Prometh, 1982).
Ullrich, V., *Die nervöse Großmacht. Aufstieg und Untergang des deutschen Kaiserreichs, 1871–1918* (Frankfurt: Fischer, 1997).
Ullrich, V., *Bismarck* (Reinbek: Rowohlt, 1998).
Ulrich, B. and Ziemann, B., eds., *Frontalltag im Ersten Weltkrieg: Wahn und Wirklichkeit* (Frankfurt: Fischer, 1994).
Umbach, M. and Hüppauf, B., eds., *Vernacular Modernism. Heimat, Globalization, and the Built Environment* (Stanford: Stanford University Press, 2005).
Urbach, K., "Between savour and villain. 100 Years of Bismarck biographies," *Historical Journal*, 41 (1998).
Verhey, J., *The Spirit of 1914: Militarism, Myth and Mobilization in Germany* (Cambridge: Cambridge University Press, 2000).
Vogel, J., *Nationen im Gleichschritt. Der Kult der "Nation in Waffen" in Deutschland und Frankreich, 1871–1914* (Göttingen: Vandenhoeck und Ruprecht, 1997).
Vogel, R., Nohlen, D., and Schultze, R.-O., *Wahlen in Deutschland* (Berlin: de Gruyter, 1971).
Wall, R. and Winter, J., eds., *The Upheaval of War: Family, Work and Welfare in Europe 1914–1918* (Cambridge: Cambridge University Press, 1988).
Waller, B., *Bismarck* (Oxford: Blackwell, 1985).
Walther, D., *Creating Germans Abroad. Cultural Policies and National Identity in Namibia* (Athens, OH: Ohio University Press, 2002).
Wareham, E., *Race and Realpolitik: The Politics of Colonisation in German Samoa* (Frankfurt: Lang, 2002).
Wawro, J., *The Franco-Prussian War: The German Conquest of France in 1870–1871* (Cambridge: Cambridge University Press, 2003).
Wehler, H.-U., ed., *Moderne deutsche Sozialgeschichte* (Cologne and Berlin: Kiepenheuer und Witsch, 1966).
Wehler, H.-U., *Bismarck und der Imperialismus* (Cologne: Kiepenheuer und Witsch, 1969).
Wehler, H.-U., "Deutscher Sonderweg oder allgemeine Probleme des westlichen Kapitalismus?," *Merkur*, 35 (1981).
Wehler, H.-U., *The German Empire 1871–1918* (Leamington Spa: Berg, 1985).
Wehler, H.-U., "Wie bürgerlich war das Deutsche Kaiserreich?," in J. Kocka, ed., *Bürger und Bürgerlichkeit im 19. Jahrhundert* (Göttingen: Vandenhoeck und Ruprecht, 1987).

Wehler, H.-U., *Aus der Geschichte lernen?* (Munich: Beck, 1988).
Wehler, H.-U., *Deutsche Gesellschaftsgeschichte*, vol. 3, *Von der "Deutschen Doppelrevolution" bis zum Beginn des Ersten Weltkriegs, 1849–1914* (Munich: Beck, 1995).
Wehler, H.-U., "A guide to future research on the Kaiserreich?" in *Central European History*, 29 (1996).
Wehler, H.-U., *Historisches Denken am Ende des 20. Jahrhunderts* (Göttingen: Wallstein, 2001).
Weichlein, S., *Nation und Region. Integrationsprozesse im Bismarckreich* (Düsseldorf: Droste, 2004).
Weindling, P., *Health, Race and German Politics between National Unification and Nazism, 1870–1945* (Cambridge: Cambridge University Press, 1989).
Westphal, O., *Das Reich*, vol. 1 *Germanentum und Kaisertum*; vol. 2 *Aufgang und Vollendung* (Stuttgart: Kohlhammer, 1941–3).
Wetzel, D., *A Duel of Giants. Bismarck, Napoleon III, and the Origins of the Franco-Prussian War* (Madison: University of Wisconsin Press, 2001).
Whalen, R. W., *Bitter Wounds: German Victims of the Great War* (Ithaca: Cornell University Press, 1984).
White, D. S., *The Splintered Party: National Liberalism in Hessen and the Reich, 1867–1918* (Cambridge, MA: Harvard University Press, 1976).
Whittle, T., *The Last Kaiser. A Biography of Wilhelm II, German Emperor and King of Prussia* (London: Heinemann, 1977).
Wierling, D., *Mädchen für alles. Arbeitsalltag und Lebensgeschichte städtischer Dienstmädchen um die Jahrhundertwende* (Berlin and Bonn: Dietz, 1987).
Wildenthal, L., *German Women for Empire, 1885–1945* (Durham, NC and London: Duke University Press, 2001).
Wilke, E.-T. P. W., *Political Decadence in Imperial Germany. Personnel-Political Aspects of the German Government Crisis 1894–1897* (Urbana and London: University of Illinois Press, 1976).
Williamson, D. G., "The Bismarck debate," *History Today*, 34 (1984).
Williamson, D. G., *Bismarck and Germany, 1862–90* (London and New York: Longman, 1986).
Williamson, G. S., *The Longing for Myth in Germany: Religion and Aesthetic Culture from Romanticism to Nietzsche* (Chicago: University of Chicago Press, 2004).
Williamson, S. R., *Austria-Hungary and the Origins of the First World War* (London: Macmillan, 1991).
Willms, J., *Bismarck – Dämon der Deutschen. Anmerkungen zu einer Legende* (Munich: Kindler, 1997).
Windell, G. G., "Bismarckian empire: Chronicle of failure, 1866–1880," *Central European History*, 2 (1969).
Winkler, H. A., "1866 und 1878: Der Machtverzicht des Bürgertums," in C. Stern and H. A. Winkler, eds., *Wendepunkte deutscher Geschichte, 1848–1975* (Frankfurt: Fischer, 1979).
Winkler, H. A., "Der Deutsche Sonderweg. Eine Nachlese," *Merkur* 35 (1981).
Winkler, H. A., *Der lange Weg nach Westen* vol. 1. *1806–1933* and vol. II. *1933–1990* (Munich: Beck, 2000).

Winkler, H. A., ed., *Griff nach der Deutungsmacht. Zur Geschichte der Geschichtspolitik in Deutschland* (Göttingen: Wallstein, 2004).

Winkler, J., *Sozialstruktur, politische Traditionen und Liberalismus. Eine empirische Längsschnittstudie zur Wahlentwicklung in Deutschland 1871–1933* (Opladen: Westdeutscher, 1995).

Winter, J., *Sites of Memory, Sites of Mourning: The Great War in European Cultural History* (Cambridge: Cambridge University Press, 1995).

Winter, J. and Prost, A., *The Great War in History: Debates and Controversies, 1914 to the Present* (Cambridge: Cambridge University Press, 2005).

Winzen, P., *Das Kaiserreich am Abgrund: Die Daily-Telegraph-Affäre und das Hale-Interview von 1908* (Stuttgart: Steiner, 2002).

Witt, P.-C., "Fritz Fischer," *Kasseler Universitätsreden*, 5 (Kassel: Universität, 1988).

Wittkau, A., *Historismus. Zur Geschichte des Begriffs und des Problems* (Göttingen: Vandenhoeck und Ruprecht, 1992).

Wolf, U., *Litteris et Patriae. Das Janusgesicht der Historie* (Stuttgart: Steiner, 1996).

Wölk, M., *Der preußische Volksschulabsolvent als Reichstagswähler 1871–1912* (Berlin: Colloquium, 1980).

Wolter, H., *Bismarcks Außenpolitik 1871–81. Außenpolitische Grundlinien von der Reichsgründung bis zum Dreikaiserbündnis* (East Berlin: Akademie, 1983).

Yaney, G. L., *The World of the Manager: Food Administration in Berlin during World War One* (New York and Frankfurt: Lang, 1994).

Zantop, S., *Colonial Fantasies: Conquest, Family, and Nation in Precolonial Germany, 1770–1870* (Durham, NC, and London: Duke University Press, 1997).

Zeender, J. K., *The German Center Party, 1890–1906* (Philadelphia: American Philosophical Society, 1976).

Ziekursch, J., *Politische Geschichte des neuen deutschen Kaiserreiches*, 3 vols. (Frankfurt: Societäts-Druckerei, 1925–30).

Ziemann, B., *Front und Heimat. Ländliche Kriegserfahrungen im südlichen Bayern 1914–23* (Essen: Klartext, 1997).

Zimmerer, J., *Deutsche Herrschaft über Afrikaner. Staatlicher Machtanspruch und Wirklichkeit im kolonialen Namibia* (Münster: LIT, 2005).

Zimmerer, J. and Zeller, J., eds., *Völkermord in Deutsch-Südwestafrika. Der Kolonialkrieg (1904–08) in Namibia und seine Folgen* (Berlin: Links, 2003).

Zimmerman, A., *Anthropology and Antihumanism in Imperial Germany* (Chicago: University of Chicago Press, 2001).

Zmarzlik, H.-G., *Das Bismarckbild der Deutschen – gestern und heute* (Freiburg: Beckmann, 1967).

Zmarzlik, H.-G., "Das Kaiserreich in neuer Sicht?," *Historische Zeitschrift*, 222 (1976).

Zuber, T., *Inventing the Schlieffen Plan: German War Planning 1871–1914* (Oxford and New York: Oxford University Press, 2002).

Zwahr, H., *Zur Konstituierung des Proletariats als Klasse. Strukturuntersuchung über das Leipziger Proletariat während der industriellen Revolution* (East Berlin: Akademie, 1978).

Index

Abusch, Alexander 38n
Afflerbach, Holger 88
Africa 76–7, 152, 171, 174–8
Agrarian League 119
agriculture 128, 130
Albertini, Luigi 20
Allen, Ann Taylor 149
Alltagsgeschichte 3, 30, 135–44, 154, 162, 201
Alsace-Lorraine 56n, 76
Anderson, Benedict 151
Anderson, Margaret 68, 109–11, 116, 119, 121, 124, 146–7, 191–2
Anrich, Ernst 15
anti-Semitism 64, 119, 140
Anti-Socialist Law 65, 112
Arendt, Hannah 177
Army League 110
Arsenscheck, Robert 111
Asia 171, 175
Assmann, Jan and Aleida 198
Austria (-Hungary) 7, 54–61, 68, 72, 101, 165, 182, 187, 190

Bad Kissingen 71
Baden 55n, 99n, 147
  Grand Duke of 62

Balkans 71
Bamberger, Ludwig 52n, 77n
Barkin, Kenneth 16, 66, 68
Baumgart, Winfried 174
Bavaria 10, 55n, 61, 64, 99n, 111, 147, 194
Beard, George 180
Beckert, Sven 170
Belgium 106–7
Bell, Philip 190
Benjamin, Walter 197
Berdahl, Robert 55
Berger, Stefan 8, 30, 42, 44, 60
Berghahn, Volker 3–4, 25, 35, 93, 103, 108, 128–9, 166
Berlin 24, 63, 87–8, 95, 101, 103, 127, 131, 141, 147, 161, 169, 175–6, 190, 193
  Congress of 72
  University (East Berlin) 39, 41
Berman, Russell 176
Bethmann Hollweg, T. von 21, 23, 95, 101, 108, 120, 179, 181, 184, 187
Betts, Paul 197–8
Beust, Friedrich F. Von 59
Bhabha, Homi 171n
Biefang, Andreas 66

Bielefeld University 25, 29–30, 34–7, 44, 85, 87, 104, 158, 179–80
Bismarck, Otto von 27, 40, 83
  biographies 9, 17, 41, 47–51, 54, 59, 69
  and colonialism 26, 76, 172–4
  domestic policies 61–70, 90–1, 93–101, 115, 117–19, 123, 127
  foreign policies 70–5
  and founding of Reich 49–61, 91–3, 95, 97
  memoirs 53
  posthumous reputation 12–13, 49, 54, 66, 70–9, 199
  resignation 63, 78–9, 82
Blackbourn, David 31–6, 43, 49, 70, 75, 83, 92, 97, 100, 103, 105, 115–16, 120, 122, 139, 160, 169, 171
Bochum 139
  University 25
Böckenförde, Ernst-Wolfgang 93, 103–4
Böhme, Helmut 21, 55, 62, 128
Bonapartism 74–6
Bonn 143n
Born, Karl Erich 127
bourgeoisie 27, 33, 35, 37, 43–4, 74, 160
Bracher, Karl Dietrich 44
Brandt, Peter 102
Braun, Rudolf 127
Bremen 56n, 194
Brest-Litovsk 171
Breuilly, John 54, 59–60, 151
Broszat, Martin 16
Brügelmann, Johann 130
Brüggemeier, Franz-Josef 127, 139
Brunner, Otto 133
Brunswick 56n
Bülow, Bernhard von 84, 87–8, 95–6, 101, 180–1
Bundesrat 65, 94–6, 101, 104–6
Burckhardt, Jacob 155
Burke, Peter 155

Caesarism 77
Canis, Konrad 72
Canning, Kathleen 144–5
Caprivi, Leo von 101
Carlyle, Thomas 48
Carsten, Francis 21
Cartel of Productive Estates 108
Catholic Church 64–5, 116
Catholics 61, 64–5, 96, 115–17, 121–2, 140, 146, 160–1, 177
Cecil, Lamar 36
Center Party 64, 112n, 115–17, 146, 160
Chartier, Roger 156
Chickering, Roger 2, 137, 184–5
China 174
Civil Code 147, 152
Clark, Christopher 80, 84, 87, 97–8
Cologne University 16, 26
Confino, Alon 164, 199–201
Conrad, Sebastian 168–9, 176
Conservatives 27–8, 61–9, 91, 99, 117, 119–21, 148
  Free Conservatives 61, 65, 119
  German Conservative Party 65, 119
continuity question 5, 13, 18, 24–5, 28–9, 31, 66, 149, 165, 178, 186
Conwentz, Hugo 194
Conze, Werner 14, 16, 35n, 133
Craig, Gordon 49
Crew, David 139, 195n
Crimean War 58
Criminal Code 152

Dahrendorf, Ralf 22, 26
Daily Telegraph Affair 86, 97
Darmstadt 182
Dehio, Georg 194
Dehio, Ludwig 15, 23, 58
Delbrück, Hans 85
Delbrück, Rudolf 61, 63
Denmark 54, 60n
Dernburg, Bernhard 174
Die Welt 19

Die Zeit 19–20
Disraeli, Benjamin 53
Dorpalen, Andreas 70
Droysen, Johann Gustav 8
Duignan, Peter 177
Dukes, Jack 36
Duncker, Max 8

East Anglia, University of 25
Eckl, Andreas 178
Eksteins, Modris 182–3
Eley, Geoff 1, 4, 31–6, 43, 45, 51, 57, 66, 87, 105, 108, 122, 136, 142, 146, 151, 158, 202
Elias, Norbert 85, 136
Emerson, Ralph Waldo 47
Engelberg, Ernst 41, 50, 68–9, 74
Engels, Friedrich 18, 38–9, 74
Epstein, Klaus 29
Erdmann, Karl Dietrich 14, 29–30
Eulenburg, Philipp 85–8, 97, 154, 181
European Union 5
Evans, Richard 5, 21–2, 31–7, 47–8, 80, 87, 126, 135, 149, 152, 162
Eyck, Erich 17, 59, 84–5

Fairbairn, Brett 90, 99, 109, 111, 116, 119, 122–4
Falk, Adalbert 65
Fehrenbach, Elisabeth 82
Ferguson, Niall 186–7, 189, 191
Feuchtwanger, Edgar 51, 55, 68, 72–3, 76, 88, 108, 114, 185
Fischer, Fritz 14, 27, 29–30, 32, 36, 46, 85, 165, 167, 183–92
  Fischer controversy 18–26, 28, 31, 165
Fischer, Wolfram 30
Flemming, Jens 141
Förster, Stig 187–8
Foucault, Michel 3, 138, 140, 152–3
France 11, 20, 53–4, 58, 60n, 68, 71–6, 98, 122, 129, 138, 156, 165, 176–7, 187, 195, 198

François, Etienne 198
Frank, Walter 19
Frankfurt (am Main) 14, 29–30, 35n, 55n, 73, 115
Frankfurt an der Oder 171
Frankfurter Allgemeine Ztg. 19
Frantz, Constantin 60
Franz, Günter 15
Frauendienst, Werner 103–4
Frederick the Great 9, 40, 48, 73, 83
Freiburg 182
Freud, Sigmund 180
Frevert, Ute 149
Fricke, Dieter 40
Friedrich III 63, 77, 97
Fritzsche, Peter 164, 196, 199–200

Gall, Lothar 16, 35n, 52–3, 67–8, 71, 75, 77, 93
Gann, Lewis 177
Geertz, Clifford 138
Geiss, Imanuel 21, 23, 29–30, 59
Gerlach, Ludwig von 74
German Confederation 53–4, 57, 59–61
German Empire
  colonies 76–7, 166–78
  constitution 27, 61–5, 68–9, 74, 76, 84–5, 91–109
  economy 27–9, 38, 40–1, 55–7, 64–8, 76, 123, 128–33, 167–70, 184, 191
  elections 63, 65, 74–6, 90, 98–100, 105, 107, 109–26, 147, 177
  founding 7–9, 49–61, 91
  geopolitical position 24, 58–60, 70–4, 164–92
  modernity 4, 27, 36, 44, 55, 159–60, 201
  "second founding" 28, 61–9
Germany
  belated nation 17
  East (GDR) 21, 37–42, 60, 69, 74–5, 173, 197n
  universities 10–11, 21, 25, 143n

West (FRG) 14, 17–25, 28, 32, 36–7, 42–4, 127, 162, 185
Gerschenkron, Alexander 131–2
Geschichte in Wissenschaft und Unterricht 29–30
Geschichte und Gesellschaft 29, 31, 129, 153
Gesellschaftsgeschichte 44, 134
Geyer, Michael 162
Ginzburg, Carlo 139
Gleichschaltung 14
Gosewinkel, Dieter 172
Göttingen University 17n, 138
Granieri, Ron 168
Grant, Oliver 129–30
Grazia, Victoria de 200
Great Britain 11, 17, 23–4, 31, 58, 68, 76–7, 105–6, 128–9, 189, 195
Grebing, Helga 44, 113
Grey, Edward 189
Groh, Dieter 113
Gross, Michael 146
Grossdeutschland 10, 56–7
Grosser, Dieter 104

Habsburg 60, 170
Hagenbeck, Carl 175n
Hager, Kurt 39
Halbwachs, Maurice 198
Halder, Winfried 108
Halle University 39
Hamburg 56n, 115, 141, 175n, 182
 University 16, 19, 21
Hanover 56n
Hard Labor Bill 100
Harden, Maximilian 84
Hastings, Derek 146
Hausen, Karin 142
Hauser, Arnold 155
Healy, Maureen 140
Heidelberg University 16, 25
Heimat 159, 194
Henderson, W. O. 172–3
Herbert, Ulrich 47–8

Herrigel, Gary 131
Herrmann, David 187
Herwig, Holger 175
Herzfeld, Hans 21n, 23
Hessen 147, 194
Hewitson, Mark 105, 107–8, 185–9
Hildebrand, Klaus 50, 164–6
Hillgruber, Andreas 24, 67, 70–1, 76, 186n, 189
Hintze, Otto 10, 93
historians
 Borussian 7–8, 10, 38, 42, 60
 Catholic 10–11, 60
 conservative 13, 20, 185, 190
 Marxist 33, 37–42, 50, 55, 68, 75, 155
 as nation builders 8–9, 37–42
 Neo-Rankean 8–13, 16, 21, 24, 166, 189
historical profession or guild 8–17, 20–36, 42, 49, 69n, 83, 85, 137, 157–8, 162
historical social science 25, 28–31, 35, 37, 55, 66, 92, 126–9, 133–41, 145, 158–60, 169
Historismus 8–9, 26, 31, 137
Historische Zeitschrift 10, 15, 21, 29
history
 body history 152–3
 church history 40
 cultural history 3, 111, 126, 144–5, 154–63, 166–7, 178, 183, 189, 201
 from below 33–4, 127, 135–42
 gender history 3, 45, 126, 142–54
 microhistory 139, 162
 psychohistory 69, 79–83
 social history 16, 21, 25, 28–9, 36, 39, 66, 127–36, 139–41, 155–6, 158, 189
 transnational history 5, 162–72, 196n
 workshops 136
Hitler, Adolf 5, 13–15, 18, 20, 26–7, 31, 47–8, 73, 78, 83, 185

Hobsbawm, Eric 151, 155, 174
Hoffmann, Walther 129
Hohenlohe, Chlodwig zu 101
Hohenzollern 7, 93
Holstein, Friedrich von 72
Holy Roman Empire 60
Hölzle, Erwin 15
Honecker, Erich 40–1
Honoratiorenpolitik 111–12
Hubatsch, Walther 15
Huber, Ernst Rudolf 93
Hughes, Michael 52, 54, 57n
Huizinga, Johan 155
Hull, Isabel 80, 89
Hunt, Lynn 156

Iggers, Georg 15, 28, 35, 39–40
Imperial Law of Assembly and Association 147, 149
Imperial League against Social Democracy 110
Indemnity Bill 57, 117
industrialization 40, 76, 128–32, 138, 144
industry 13, 28, 64, 118, 128, 130, 132, 145
Italy 10, 58, 68, 139

Jacoby, Russell 158
Japan 172
Jarausch, Konrad 162, 186n
Jelavich, Peter 157
Jenkins, Jennifer 166
Jews 11, 14, 16, 66, 96, 140, 148, 161
John, Michael 92, 95, 98
Joll, James 190
Jugendstil 193
July Crisis 165, 183, 187, 190–1
Junkers 27, 34, 62, 66, 69, 77

Kaelble, Hartmut 29, 129
Kantorowicz, Hermann 12
Kaschuba, Wolfgang 139
Kassel University 25, 141

Kautsky, Karl 113
Kehr, Eckart 13, 24–5, 28, 29, 165
Kelly, Joan 143
Kern, Stephen 183
Kershaw, Ian 47–8, 78
Keynes, John Maynard 55
Kiesewetter, Hubert 131
Kirchner, Ernst-Ludwig 175
Kissinger, Henry 52n, 74
Kleindeutschland 10, 53, 56–7, 60–1
Klingender, Francis 155
Koch, H. W. 93
Kocka, Jürgen 25–6, 29, 35, 44, 128, 133, 135n, 137, 156–7
Kohl, Helmut 136
Kohn, Hans 17–18
Kohut, Thomas 36, 80–2
Königgrätz 54–5
Konitz 140
Koonz, Claudia 149
Koshar, Rudy 162, 191, 196–201
Kracht, Klaus Grosse 19–20
Kreuzer, Marcus 103, 105–6, 108, 113, 202
Krieger, Leonard 17–18
Kuczynski, Jürgen 40
Kuhn, Thomas 25n
Kühne, Thomas 97, 105, 111, 120, 123–4, 126
Kühnl, Reinhard 44n
Kulturkampf 64–5, 68, 115, 117, 146
Kundrus, Birthe 178

Laak, Dirk van 172
Laband, Paul 92
LaCapra, Dominick 156
Lamprecht, Karl 10, 155
Landes, David 131
Langewiesche, Dieter 58, 119, 123
Lasker, Eduard 63, 67
League of German Women's Associations 148–9
League for Homeland Protection 194
Lebensraum 14, 171
Ledford, Kenneth 45, 125

Leipzig 151
 University 39, 41
Lenz, Max 8–13, 16, 48–9
Lepsius, M. Rainer 114, 120–2
Lerman, Katharine 51, 63, 67, 72, 87, 101
Liberals 10, 15, 57–8, 148
 Left liberals/Progressives 12, 17, 61, 63, 96, 117–18, 121
 Liberalism 12, 160
 National Liberal Party 61, 65–8, 117–19, 121
Liebenberg Circle 80
Liebknecht, Karl 100
Lieven, Dominic 170
Lindquist, Sven 136
linguistic turn 145, 157
Lloyd George, David 20
local government 99, 118, 162
London 176, 186
Lorwin, V. R. 107
Loth, Wilfried 49, 72, 104n, 108
Lübeck 56n
Lüdtke, Alf 138, 140–1
Ludwig, Emil 79
Ludwigshafen 115
Lukács, Georg 38n
Luther, Martin 9, 18, 40, 193
Lyotard, Jean-François 138

Mann, Golo 17, 23
Mannesmann 132
Marcks, Erich 8–13, 16, 48–9
Marx, Karl 29, 38–9, 48, 55, 74, 77, 127, 133, 202
May, Karl 175
Mayer, Theodor 15
Maynes, Mary Jo 144
McLean, Roderick 72, 76, 84, 104n, 144n, 174, 190
Mecklenburg 56n, 131
Medick, Hans 138
Meinecke, Friedrich 11–13, 15
memory 3, 6, 159, 178, 196–201
Meyer, Arnold Oskar 49

Meyer-Renschhausen, Elisabeth 149
Miquel, Johannes von 27, 87
Mitchell, Allan 75
Mitteleuropa 171
Mitter, Arnim 42
Möbius, Paul 180
Moltke, Helmuth von 188
Mombauer, Annika 187–90
Mommsen, Wolfgang 16, 24–5, 42, 62, 84, 88–90, 92, 94, 96, 104n, 108–9, 170, 187
Morris, William 195
Moses, John 25
Mosse, George 17–18
Mount Kilimanjaro 175
Müller, Georg von 184

Namibia 178
Napoleon I 9, 50n
Napoleon III 58, 74–7, 99
Nassau 55n
National Association 56
National Socialism 5, 13, 17, 19, 48, 149, 162, 178
Nationalism 34, 55–7, 60, 73, 90, 117, 150–1, 186
Naumann, Friedrich 81
Navy League 9, 34, 110, 117, 151
Neitzel, Sönke 165
Netherlands 60n, 106–7, 122
neurasthenia 179–82
Niethammer, Lutz 127
Nietzsche, Friedrich 155
Nipperdey, Thomas 31, 33–4, 42, 45, 49–51, 103–4, 109, 160
Nolde, Emil 175
Nonn, Christoph 140
Nora, Pierre 198
North German Confederation 54, 57, 61, 91, 98

O'Brien, Patricia 156
Oldenburg 56n
Oncken, Hermann 13, 16
Osterhammel, Jürgen 169, 176

Ostforschung 14
Otto, Louise 151
Ottoman Empire 170
Oxford University 25

Pan-German League 9, 15, 110, 172n
parliamentarization 91, 103–9
Patriotic Women's Association 150–1
Peasants' Revolt 38–9
People's Association for Catholic Germany 116
Peters, Carl 152, 172n
Petersson, Niels 167
Pflanze, Otto 53, 59, 63, 74, 93
Philadelphia 151, 162
Pierson, Ruth 152
Plessner, Helmuth 17
Poiger, Uta 173
Poland 16, 170
Poles 64, 121, 171
Pomerania 131
Ponti, Carlo 139
Pope Leo XIII 65
Pope Pius IX 65
Popper, Karl 9n
Posadowsky, Arthur von 87
Potsdam 19, 21
Prost, Antoine 189
protectionism 65, 68
Protestants 140, 161, 176n
Prussia 7, 9–10, 38, 40–1, 44, 53–63, 74–5, 84, 91–9, 170, 194
  army 62–3, 92, 140, 166
  constitutional conflict 61, 63, 99, 117
  East 131
  Landtag 99, 107, 111, 115n, 147
  ministers 21, 27, 51–2, 65, 70n, 96, 102, 181, 194
  monarchs 13, 63, 74, 84–6, 96–7, 151
  West 140
Puhle, Hans-Jürgen 29
Puttkamer, Robert von 65, 68

Quataert, Jean 133

Radkau, Joachim 4, 179–83
Rahden, Till van 161
Ranke, Leopold von 8–9, 15, 24, 164, 201
Rathenau, Walther 81
Ratingen 130
Rauh, Manfred 103–6, 108
Reagan, Nancy 145, 151
Reddy, William 27
Reformation 9, 39
Reichsfeinde 115, 123
Reichstag 12, 61, 63–4, 67, 75–6, 91–106, 110–12, 115–18, 122–4
Rein, Gustav Adolf 73
Remak, Joachim 36
Renan, Ernst 56
Renouvin, Pierre 183
Retallack, James 1–2, 87, 102, 104n, 141, 161
Reulecke, Jürgen 127
Revolutions of 1848–9 27, 39, 57
Revolutions of 1918–19 113, 125
Rhineland 194
Riezler, Kurt 184
Ritter, Gerhard A. 13, 15–16, 20–1, 23, 60, 73, 103, 105, 120, 133, 186n
Rochau, August Ludwig von 52
Rohe, Karl 121
Röhl, John 23, 36–7, 79–89, 93, 108, 184n, 190–1, 199
Rokkan, Stein 121n
Rosenberg, Hans 17–18, 21–2, 24, 28, 62, 68, 119–20
Rosenhaft, Eve 145–6
Roth, Günther 113
Rothfels, Hans 14, 23, 73
Ruckteschell, Walter von 175
Ruhr 121, 127, 130–1, 141, 161
Russia 58, 60n, 62, 68, 70, 72, 165, 170–1, 187

Sabrow, Martin 41
Said, Edward 171n
Saldern, Adelheid von 142
Sammlungspolitik 27–8, 34, 62, 67, 124
Sauer, Wolfgang 93
Saul, Klaus 141
Saxe-Coburg-Gotha 147
Saxe-Meiningen 147
Saxony 10, 54–5, 99, 111, 130–1
Scandinavia 106
Schäfer, Dietrich 9
Schamoni, Peter 199
Schieder, Theodor 14, 16, 30, 91
Schiller, Friedrich 57
Schleswig-Holstein 56n
Schmädeke, Jürgen 111
Schmidt, Gustav 104, 107
Schmidt, Helmut 136
Schmitt, Bernadotte 20
Schmitt, Carl 93–4
Schmoller, Gustav 10
Schnabel, Franz 11, 14, 60, 73
Schoenbaum, David 103
Schöllgen, Gregor 164–6, 179, 187, 189
Schönberger, Christoph 103, 105–7, 109
Schorske, Carl 22, 112
Schröder, Gerhard 19n
Schulte, Bernd 23
Schulte, Regina 142
Schulze, Hagen 198
Schüssler, Wilhelm 49
Schwartz, Frederic 200
Scott, Joan 143–4, 153
Sedition Bill 100
Seibt, Gustav 29
Seligmann, Matthew 72, 76, 84, 104n, 144n, 174, 190
Sheehan, James 29
Siemens 133
Silesia 131, 161
Simmel, Georg 180
Smith, Helmut Walser 140

Smith, Woodruff 109
Social Democratic Party 11, 65, 99, 110, 112–18, 121, 134n, 136, 141, 148
Sombart, Nicolaus 78, 82–3
Sombart, Werner 11, 200
Sonderweg 10, 12, 17–18, 26–7, 29–34, 38, 42–5, 62, 104, 128, 162
Sontheimer, Kurt 44
Southard, Robert 7
Spain 192
Spenkuch, Hartwin 44
Sperber, Jonathan 99, 111, 114–15, 118, 122–3, 160
Srbik, Heinrich von 60
Stegmann, Dirk 23, 28–9, 34
Stein, Gertrude 183
Steinbach, Peter 99, 103, 121n
Steinberg, Jonathan 83
Steinhoff, Anthony 161
Stern, Fritz 1, 17–18, 23, 93
Stevenson, David 187
Strandmann, H. Pogge von 23, 189–90
Strasbourg 161
Stürmer, Michael 20, 52, 77–8, 93, 164–6, 189
Stuttgart University 17
Sussex University 25, 82
Suval, Stanley 111, 114–16, 121–2
Sweden 60n, 129, 136
Switzerland 106–7
Sybel, Heinrich von 8

Taylor, A. J. P. 18, 51, 53, 62, 72, 92–3, 101–2
Tenfelde, Klaus 133, 136
Ther, Philipp 170–1
Theweleit, Klaus 154
Third Reich 5, 13–15, 19, 22, 24, 31–2, 36, 66, 94, 177, 198
Thompson, E. P. 138, 155
Tipton, Frank 130–1
Treitschke, Heinrich von 8, 30, 48, 77n

Trevelyan, G. M. 140
Triple Entente 16, 165
Troeltsch, Ernst 11
Tübingen University 25, 127
Tuchman, Barbara 36n
Turner, Sharon 109

Ulbricht, Walter 40
Ullmann, Hans-Peter 29, 42, 56, 98, 104n, 123
Ullrich, Volker 19, 50, 58, 104n
United States of America 22n, 68, 170n, 171n
University of East Anglia 25

Versailles 61
  Treaty of 11, 20, 32, 173
Vienna 141, 190
  Congress of 130, 170
Volksgeist 8
Volksgeschichte 14, 16, 139n

Wahl, Adalbert 13
Waller, Bruce 75
Weber, Max 9, 18, 29, 78, 93, 133–4, 138, 140
Wehler, Hans-Ulrich 14, 16, 26–36, 42–6, 50, 52, 54, 58–9, 66–8, 75–8, 85–6, 92–3, 102–4, 108, 110n, 128, 133–4, 137–8, 154, 157–8, 161, 165, 170, 180
Weimar Republic 11–14, 24, 31, 62, 66, 113, 125, 162, 185
Weissmann, Karlheinz 29
Weltpolitik 28, 168, 181
Wendt, Bernd Jürgen 23
Westphal, Otto 13

Wierling, Dorothee 140, 142
Wildenthal, Lora 178
Wilhelm I 9–10, 63, 65
Wilhelm II 36–7, 47, 51, 78–89, 96–7, 103, 181, 199
Wilke, Ekkehard-Teja 88
Williams, Raymond 155
Willms, Johannes 73
Windell, George 61
Windthorst, Ludwig 64
Winkler, Heinrich August 26, 42–3, 56, 62, 67, 103, 104n
Winkler, Jürgen 111, 115
Winter, Jay 189
Witt, Peter-Christian 23n, 29, 141
Wolle, Stefan 42
women 3, 30, 33, 137, 138n, 141–53, 167n, 178, 196
working class 38–9, 41, 56n, 113, 115, 118, 121, 122n, 133–4, 136, 138, 141–2, 147, 182, 200
World War One 5, 11, 14–15, 20, 22, 24, 26, 72, 107–9, 141, 163–4, 166, 173–4, 179, 181–92
World War Two 17, 20, 22, 31
Wuppertal 127
Württemberg 55n, 147, 194

Zabern Affair 98
Zantop, Susanne 176
Zechlin, Egmont 16, 19, 23, 186n
Zeender, John 115
Ziekursch, Johannes 13, 62
Zille, Heinrich 193
Zollverein 55–6, 64, 130
Zuber, Terence 187
Zwahr, Hartmut 41